fashion at the edge

caroline evans

fashion at the edge

spectacle, modernity and deathliness

yale university press   new haven and london

Designed by Gillian Malpass

Printed in China

Library of Congress Cataloging-in-Publication Data

Evans, Caroline.
  Fashion at the edge : spectacle, modernity & deathliness / Caroline
Evans.
      p. cm.
Includes bibliographical references and index.
  ISBN 978-0-300-12467-5 (alk. paper)
  1. Fashion–History. 2. Costume design–History. 3. Fashion–Social
aspects. 4. Costume design--Social aspects. I. Title.
  TT504.E33 2003
  391–dc21
                                                    2003005825

A catalogue record for this book is available from
The British Library

frontispiece   John Galliano, Autumn–Winter 1998–9.
Photograph Patrice Stable, courtesy John Galliano

Contents

Acknowledgements

Many colleagues became friends in the period during which I wrote this book. They read drafts for me and generously shared their insights and their time. Rebecca Arnold's trenchant criticism and grasp of over-arching historiographic questions, combined with her acute knowledge of fashion, saved me from some very bad gaffes. She never missed a detail and always got what I was doing, even when I didn't get it. Christopher Breward's friendship and historian's-eye-view also helped me on many occasions. Judith Clark was immensely generous and encouraging, and initiated a dialogue between this book and her own creative curating, taking my ideas in a direction I never knew they could go. Lorraine Gamman showed an inspired grasp of the macro-issues when the project was in its early stages, generously lent me books and read an entire draft of the manuscript while on holiday, balancing critical scrutiny with enthusiasm. Alistair O'Neill, too, read an entire draft and responded generously with inspiring suggestions to improve it; he lent me books and videos and coined many resonant phrases that have now entered the text as if they were my own. Marketa Uhlirova did all the picture research and some research to the text; her intelligence, originality and critical input made a huge difference. She also read my proofs while on holiday, and found errors that everyone else missed, thus demonstrating that the best Englishman is indeed a foreigner (and a woman). Elizabeth Wilson read the penultimate draft; she eloquently summed up my own arguments for me, and made invaluable editorial suggestions prior to publication.

I am very grateful to them all. I should also like to thank Annie Cooper, Barry Curtis, Joan Farrer, Suzanne Lee, Alison Matthews David, Emma Reeves, Syd Shelton, Andrew Stephenson and Valerie Steele.

I should like to thank the Arts and Humanities Board of Great Britain (AHRB) for funding stages 1 and 2 of the Fashion & Modernity Research Project (1999-2000 and 2001-4) at Central Saint Martins College of Art and Design and at the London Institute. It supported both the first and the final periods of research and writing for this book, and provided invaluable assistance in procuring illustrations. I am grateful also to the AHRB for a one-term sabbatical in 1999 and to Central Saint Martins for a matching one; these allowed me to do much of the preliminary reading. In this period the members of the first Fashion and Modernity research seminars, including Rebecca Arnold, Jamie Brassett, Andrea Stuart and Carol Tulloch, made many valuable suggestions.

Among the many colleagues at Central Saint Martins who have helped me, I should like in particular to thank Jane Rapley, Dean of Fashion & Textiles, for her support for the project, Peter Close, for administering it so seamlessly, Steve Hill for being so helpful and patient with my IT picture problems, Karen Fletcher for her help and good humour over so many years in the slide library, Caroline Dakers for introducing me to Yale University Press, and all the college librarians, especially Alison Church, to whom I owe a particular debt of gratitude, and without whose erudition and energy this would have been a very different book.

At Yale, I should like to thank my editor, Gillian Malpass, for her involvement, dedication and enthusiasm at every stage.

A few sections of my text were first published elsewhere, and I am grateful to the following publishers and authors for permission to reprint. A substantial part of Chapter 6 on Alexander McQueen first appeared in Joanne Entwhistle and Elizabeth Wilson's *Body Dressing* (Berg Publishers, 2001). Parts of Chapter 10 on Shelley Fox first appeared in Christopher Breward, Becky Conekin and Caroline Cox's *The Englishness of English Dress* (Berg Publishers, 2002). Parts of chapter 10 on Martin Margiela first appeared in *Fashion Theory* (1998).

Two conferences helped me to map out my ideas in the early stages, for which I thank their organisers. Djurdja Bartlett organised the First International Discipline of Fashion Conference in Dubrovnik in 2000 at which I gave a paper that later formed the basis of Chapter 1. Julian Stair organised 'The Body Politic' in 1999 at the University of Northumbria, and the paper I gave there forms the basis of Chapter 8.

As everyone who teaches knows, all one's best ideas come from teaching. Most of all I would like to thank all the students I have taught over the years and from whom I have learnt so much, including the fashion students at Central Saint Martins. Particular thanks should go to the Goldsmiths textiles students who came to my 'Fashion at the Edge' seminar series in 2000 during which I first sketched out the ideas for this book.

Finally I thank all the designers, photographers and artists, and their agents, galleries and PRs, for their enthusiasm, for supplying images and facts and, generally, for helping to make the book happen.

And thank you Calum, Caitlin and Ivo, whose company makes everything worthwhile, but who did without mine when I was working on the book.

introduction

Apocalypse

Björk wearing Alexander McQueen's tinkling, red, glass, microscope slide dress on stage, turning it into a percussion object as she danced; a row of dummies in a Dutch museum dressed in Martin Margiela's decayed dress designs grown with moulds and bacteria; Viktor & Rolf's grey-on-grey fashion show of black-clad models with charcoal skin gliding into a darkened room; Hussein Chalayan's moulded resin dress whose flaps opened like an aeroplane coming in to land on the catwalk; Juergen Teller's fashion photographs for a Jigsaw menswear catalogue of a man falling to his death from a high building; John Galliano's *belle époque* vamps and sirens in their aigrettes and maharaja paste jewellery: what sense, if any, can be made of these images from late 1990s fashion? What do they add up to?

The challenge of this book has been to find a way to talk about contemporary and near-contemporary fashion. The existing frameworks did not make it easy. I wanted to find a way to discuss 1990s and turn-of-the-century fashion that offered more than the traditional focus of art and design history on the past, so that I could also accommodate the present meanings and future possibilities of fashion. I did not want to duplicate the role of fashion journalism which, when it is accurate and good, can provide much more up to the minute reports of fashion in magazines, newspapers and websites. A book is a different type of forum that can instead give space to critical and theoretical analyses of contemporary fashion and its context, if need be by reference to its historical precedents.

Rather than describing, I chose to join up disparate histories, designs and ideas in order to cast new light on contemporary practice and its context. The task therefore was to find a language and a methodology to do this that did not eclipse fashion with theory. I love fashion and I am as fascinated by the material conditions of its production and its business protocols as I am by its symbolic and cultural meanings. Too often theoretically oriented academics ignore the infinitely various material facts of fashion and fashion design, while more empirically minded writers have traditionally been resistant to theory (although this is changing now). My own interest has always been in applied, rather than pure, theory as it relates to contemporary visual culture and perhaps this is why I am happiest teaching in an art school, because those are the students' interests too.

I noticed a shift in writings from people as diverse as Peter Ackroyd, Iain Sinclair and W. G. Sebald who, although writers of fiction, had each in their different way tried to find new discourses (including poetic reconstruction) to talk about history, and to understand what T. S. Eliot called 'the place where three dreams cross', those of the past, present and the future:

> Wavering between the profit and the loss
> In this brief transit where the dreams cross
> The dreamcrossed twilight between birth and dying.[1]

Frank Kermode has described the way in which, in the Western tradition, the literature of apocalypse satisfies our need for 'concord fictions' that map endings onto beginnings to

facing page Detail of fig. 114

1 T. S. Eliot, 'Ash Wednesday', *Selected Poems*, Faber and Faber, London, 1954: 92.

make sense of the brief span 'between birth and dying'.[2] If the apocalyptic visions of late twentieth-century fashion can be construed as a kind of concord fiction, in this book I have tried to find a different method from that of design history to talk about contemporary fashion, with its inflections of money, sex and mortality, one that offers a paradigm shift; this new model draws on a metaphysical approach to history to articulate what it means to be modern today.

This is not an attempt to write an account of the present, however, so much as to develop a case study of a method, and this book makes no attempt comprehensively to examine all aspects and all types of contemporary fashion. It focuses on one strand of fashion only, and that one largely in terms of its symbolic and cultural meanings rather than its production, marketing and consumption. Nevertheless, I would argue for a properly materialist analysis of contemporary visual culture, even where such an analysis is concerned primarily with the meanings of texts, images and objects rather than the conditions of their material production. Elizabeth Wilson has written that 'fashion is as much a part of the dream world of capitalism as its economy.'[3] In writing about recent fashion, this has required me to stretch the materialist account and to find some, perhaps metaphysical, connections to explain its uncanny, alienated horrors. To get really underneath the notions of deathliness and haunting that typified 1990s fashion when it presented the real ghosts in the machine of the fashion magazine and catwalk, I turned not so much to psychoanalytic or post-structuralist accounts as to historians and writers such as Walter Benjamin and Karl Marx. But I read Marx, in particular, against the grain, as gothic fiction rather than political economy. And where I used insights from psychoanalysis, it was for the way they give us a glimpse of 'the skull beneath the skin' that was also a concern of the Jacobean literary imagination early in the seventeenth-century.[4]

Fashion at the Edge

From 'heroin chic' to Alexander McQueen, the distressed body of much 1990s fashion exhibited the symptoms of trauma, the fashion show mutated into performance and a new kind of conceptual fashion designer evolved. These are just three examples of fashion 'at the edge', fashion which exists at its own margins. While becoming more vivid in its presentation, many of its themes became correspondingly darker in the 1990s. Often permeated by death, disease and dereliction, its imagery articulated the anxieties as well as the pleasures of identity, alienation and loss against the unstable backdrop of rapid social, economic and technological change at the end of the twentieth century.

Perhaps this new trend marked a paradigm shift in sensibilities but it was also embedded in the tradition of Western consumer capitalism. Rather than examining the experimental fashion of the 1990s merely as a series of rapid style changes, I consider it as part of a broader historical and philosophical trajectory that has a relationship to concepts not always associated with fashion: modernity, technology and globalization. We speak of

2   Frank Kermode, *The Sense of an Ending: Studies in the Theory of Fiction with a New Epilogue*, Oxford University Press, 2000 [1966]. See ch. 1 'The End'.

3   Elizabeth Wilson, *Adorned in Dreams: Fashion and Modernity*, Virago, London, 1985: 14; 2nd ed. I. B. Tauris, 2003 forthcoming.

4   Eliot on Webster in 'Whispers of Immortality', l.2, in *Selected Poems*: 42.

'edgy' fashion to suggest fashion that is sharp, urban, knowing, experimental, unsentimental. We are at the edge of centuries, and on the edge of technological transformation. Such epochal change requires its participants to embrace a knowledge economy, turn their backs on the old age of industrial modernity and begin to make sense of the revolution in communications of the last thirty years. The fashion design discussed here was at the edge commercially, of the big global brands and of mass production. Its themes were on the edge too, at the borders of beauty and horror, where sex and death intersected with commerce. Conceptually as well as stylistically experimental, this strand of fashion design addressed contemporary anxieties and speculations about the body and identity.

These were legitimate concerns for cultural practitioners at the turn of the millenium, set as they were against the backdrop of the dark history of the twentieth century (holocaust and genocide, the rise of totalitarianism, and two world wars), the collapse of older epistemological certainties in the West, the rapid development of information technology since the first satellite was sent into space in 1957, the demise of the old Soviet Union in 1991, the consequent spread of globalisation and the intensification of an ideological divide between Islam and the secular West. Yet, although it is the business of cultural practitioners to speculate about questions of identity and community in a changing world, such concerns have not been the traditional domain of the fashion designer. Despite this, in periods in which ideas about the self seem to be unstable, or rapidly shifting, fashion itself can shift to centre stage and play a leading role in constructing images and meanings, as well as articulating anxieties and ideals. The time and place could be *fin-de-siècle* Vienna, Paris of the 1930s, or 1990s London: each has a relationship to modernity and to technological change and its impact on sensibilities. These sensibilities may be described as the 'decentered subject' of the inter-war years,[5] or the 'emergent identities' of 1990s cyberculture.[6] What is significant in each case is the role which fashion plays in articulating contemporary concerns about the self and the world. Jonathan Dollimore has argued that the decentered self, far from being a singular product of contemporary thought, is simply a reiteration of the idea of the disintegration of human nature after the Fall: the "crisis" of the individual is less a crisis than a recurring instability'.[7] He argues that the individual has always been in crisis in the Western tradition, driven forward by the destabilising forces of mutability and death.[8] But if this 'crisis' has been formally sanctioned in the Western tradition of tragedy, as Dollimore argues, it has also concealed itself, *en travesti*, at the heart of fashion, that discourse of youth, frivolity and lightness. The surface of fashion, like Watteau's *fêtes galantes*, conceals a core of melancholy.[9] The *leitmotif* of mutability, with all its perils and excitements, is threaded through this book, stitching in traces and fragments as it goes, and is ultimately its real, if fugitive, subject.

Many of the features of Western fashion today have their origins in the development of European mercantile capitalism from the fourteenth century, and in what Norbert Elias called 'the civilising process'.[10] For Elias, the evolution of manners since the Middle Ages involved the suppression of aggressive and instinctual behaviour in favour of the development of a reflexive, modelled and nuanced self. It is in this sense that fashion 'speaks', both

5 Carolyn Dean, *The Self and Its Pleasures: Bataille, Lacan and the History of the Decentered Subject*, Cornell University Press, Ithaca and London, 1992.

6 Donna Haraway, *Simians, Cyborgs and Women: The Reinvention of Nature*, Free Association Books, London, 1991. Sadie Plant, *Zeros and Ones: Digital Women and the New Technoculture*, Fourth Estate, London, 1997.

7 Jonathan Dollimore, *Death, Desire and Loss in Western Culture*, Allen Lane, The Penguin Press, London, 1998: xix.

8 Ibid: xviii.

9 For a discussion of melancholy and masquerade in relation to fashion see Caroline Evans, 'Masks, Mirrors and Mannequins: Elsa Schiaparelli and the Decentered Subject', *Fashion Theory*, vol. 2, issue 1, March 1999: 3–31.

10 Norbert Elias, *The Court Society*, Blackwell, Oxford, 1983. See too Christopher Breward, *The Culture of Fashion*, Manchester University Press, Manchester and New York, 1995, and Richard Sennett, *The Fall of Public Man*, W. W. Norton, New York and London, 1992.

as a discourse which articulates what we are, might be or could become, and as a kind of etiquette or style book for the 'care of the self'.[11] The late twentieth-century articulation of the idea of the self as culturally constructed has important implications for fashion. Gilles Lipovetsky has argued that fashion is socially reproductive, training us to be flexible and responsive to change in a fast-changing world: 'fashion socializes human beings to change and prepares them for perpetual recycling.'[12] The kinetic, open personality of fashion is the personality which a society in the process of rapid transformation most needs. No longer derided as superficial, frivolous or deceitful, fashion thus has an important role to play, not merely in adorning the body but also in fashioning a modern, reflexive self.[13]

However, if fashion is part of the 'civilising process', in the form of conventional and mainstream fashion design, it is also and equally, in its experimental and avant-garde manifestations, capable of providing a resistant and opposing voice to that process. On the edge of discourse, of 'civilisation', of speech itself, experimental fashion can act out what is hidden culturally. And, like a neurotic symptom, it can utter a kind of mute resistance to the socially productive process of constructing an identity. As we produce a disciplined and controlled self, via the 'technology' of manners for example,[14] what is repressed comes back as a trace, under the weight of some cultural trauma, of which experimental fashion can function as a tell-tale memory. Seen thus, fashion is hysterical. It can be a symptom of alienation, loss, mourning, fear of contagion and death, instability and change. Like psychoanalysis, it 'investigates the domain and configuration of incoherence, discontinuity, disruption and disintegration.'[15]

In arguing, however, that experimental fashion, like the psychoanalytic model of the unconscious, acts out repressed desires and fears, I do not suggest that these are the desires and fears of the designers themselves. If fashion speaks, it speaks independently of its creators. This book seeks to locate it in the context of historical rather than personal trauma, by relating it to the larger questions of history, rather than to the designers' motives and intentions. Its 'symptoms' are wide-ranging and diffuse: death (or its corollaries mourning, trauma and shock), gender instability and free-floating anxiety. The memory traces invoked here are historical fragments of instability and transience from earlier centuries. These traces come back as fragments under the weight of a cultural trauma which has been expressed by earlier twentieth-century writers on modernity as 'shock' and 'neurasthenia', and by writers about contemporary culture as 'trauma' or 'wound culture'.[16]

Fashion, with its affinity for transformation, can act out instability and loss but it can also, and equally, stake out the terrain of 'becoming' – new social and sexual identities, masquerade and performativity.[17] One of the concerns of this book is to contrast a cynical and knowing decadence on the one hand with a more passionate and hopeful approach on the other. If the imagery of late twentieth-century fashion seemed dark or bleak, it may be because it signalled an attempt to chart new social identities in a period of rapid change, while reflecting contemporary concerns with death and decay. Much fashion from the 1990s appeared, in the glossy closure of its luxurious designs, to shore up and contain anxieties about cultural continuity, the body and mortality. And this was particularly so among the

11 Michel Foucault, *The History of Sexuality, Volume Three: The Care of the Self*, trans. Robert Hurley, Pantheon, New York, 1986 [1984].

12 Gilles Lipovetsky, *The Empire of Fashion: Dressing Modern Democracy*, trans. Catherine Porter, Princeton University Press, 1994 [1987]: 149.

13 Anthony Giddens, *Modernity and Self-Identity: Self and Society in the Late Modern Age*, Polity Press, Cambridge, 1991.

14 Michel Foucault, *The History of Sexuality, Volume Two: The Uses of Pleasure*, trans. Robert Hurley, Pantheon, New York, 1985 [1984].

15 Nicholas Abraham and Maria Torok, *The Shell and the Kernel*, vol. 1, trans. and intro. by Nicolas T. Rand, University of Chicago Press, Chicago and London, 1994: 1.

16 For 'neurasthenia' see Georg Simmel, 'The Metropolis and Mental Life' [1903] in *On Individuality and Social Forms*, ed. and with an intro. by Donald. N. Levine, University of Chicago Press, 1971. For 'shock' see Walter Benjamin, 'On Some Motifs in Baudelaire' [1939] in *Illuminations*, trans. Harry Zohn, Fontana/Collins, London 1973 [1955]. For 'trauma' see, e.g., Hal Foster, *The Return of the Real: The Avant Garde at the End of the Century*, MIT Press, Cambridge, Mass., and London, 1996. For 'wound culture' see Mark Seltzer, *Serial Killers: Death and Life in America's Wound Culture*, Routledge, New York and London, 1998.

17 A range of cultural theorists in the late twentieth century posited anti-essentialist models of gendered identity, which they argued was constituted in and through culture. For example, the psychoanalyst Joan Rivière's 1929 discussion of female identity as a form of masquerade was re-examined in the late 1980s by feminist critics as a model of female agency and power over the image. And in 1990 and 1993 Judith Butler argued that gendered identity was 'performative', that is, not ontologically pre-given but constantly made and re-made through daily acts of repetition. See Joan Rivière, 'Womanliness as a Masquerade' [1929], repr. in V. Burgin, J. Donald, C. Kaplan (eds), *Formations of Fantasy*, Routledge, 1989. Emily Apter, 'Masquerade', in Elizabeth Wright, *Feminism and Psychoanalysis: A Critical Dictionary*, Basil Blackwell, Oxford and Cambridge, Mass., 1992. Judith Butler, *Gender Trouble: Feminism and the Subversion of Identity*, Routledge, New York and London, 1990. Judith Butler, *Bodies that Matter: On the Discursive Limits of "Sex"*, Routledge, London and New York, 1993.

'big players' and global brands of international fashion. But a small proportion of designers, many of them Japanese, Dutch, Belgian or British, rather than French, Italian or American, were among those whose work articulated the experience of cultural discontinuity, transforming 'negative' ideas into critical and questioning designs. In the small and commercially less lucrative hinterland in which they worked, new ideas were able to form, grow and spread. Many of the designers of the 1990s discussed here regarded it as hypocrisy simply to present happy, shiny images, rather than exploring the entire range of human emotion and experience. For them, it went without saying that fashion was an appropriate arena in which to investigate the complexities of modern life. And out of this questioning and experimental tendency in contemporary art and fashion emerged new images, of which some were bleak but others were curiously optimistic.

Segueing between Past and Present

This book looks primarily at the 1990s but also argues that contemporary sensibilities echo earlier moments of modernity, from the growth of mercantile capitalism in seventeenth-century Europe to the accelerated consumption of commodity culture in the industrialised nineteenth-century city. In the course of looking at contemporary fashion, I have made comparisons with other periods of change and instability in European history, and drawn on the imagery of these periods to explain that of the present.

In order to do so, I have relied on the sometimes problematic and perhaps over-used concept of modernity, albeit with some reservations.[18] Definitions of modernity are as many as they are contradictory, particularly between the social sciences and the humanities traditions. A number of historians, for whom the idea of modernity is bound up with an analysis of industrial capitalist society as a form of rupture from the preceding social system, have used the term to designate the enormous social and cultural changes which took place from the mid-sixteenth century onwards in Europe.[19] For the sociologist Max Weber, the origins of capitalism lay in the Protestant ethic; its leitmotifs were modernisation and rationalisation but also, and crucially, ambiguity.[20] This sense of ambiguity underlies an important presumption in this book that there is an intimate connection between opposites – such as despair and optimism, beauty and horror, fashion and mortality – and these couplings are a *leitmotif* of the book, as they are of the type of design and photography it discusses. Rebecca Arnold has argued that it is in the nature of modern fashion to be inherently contradictory. It displays both 'the promise and the threat of the future . . . revealing both our desires and anxieties . . . constructing identities that use stylish dress as a route to self-creation and yet ultimately to self-destruction.'[21]

I have followed Marshall Berman and used the term 'modernity' as one of a triumvirate of terms: modernisation, modernity and modernism.[22] 'Modernisation' refers to the processes of scientific, technological, industrial, economic and political innovation that also become urban, social and artistic in their impact. 'Modernity' refers to the way that mod-

18 Wilson, *Adorned in Dreams*, 63, discusses the problems but also the merits of the term modernity as a way of understanding modern fashion.

19 Bryan S. Turner (ed.), *Theories of Modernity and Postmodernity*, Sage, London, Newbury Park and New Delhi, 1990, discusses the major debates and cites key texts.

20 See Bryan S. Turner, 'Periodization and Politics in the Postmodern', in ibid: 1–13.

21 Rebecca Arnold, *Fashion, Desire and Anxiety: Image and Morality in the Twentieth Century*, I. B. Tauris, London and New York, 2001: xiv.

22 Marshall Berman, *All That is Solid Melts into Air: The Experience of Modernity*, Verso, London, 1983: 16–17. For a critique of Berman's periodisation, see Peter Osborne, 'Modernity is a Qualitative, Not a Chronological Catagory', *New Left Review*, 92, 1992: 67–8.

ernisation infiltrates everyday life and permeates sensibilities; I use it frequently to refer to changes in sensibility and experience in the nineteenth century as a result of late eighteenth-century industrialisation, Berman's 'second stage' of modernisation. And 'modernism' refers to a wave of avant-garde artistic movements that, from early in the twentieth century, in some way responded to or represented these changes in sensibility and experience.[23] In 1863 Baudelaire described the experience of modernity in nineteenth-century Paris as 'the ephemeral, the fugitive, the contingent'.[24] Baudelairean 'modernity' infused many late twentieth-century accounts of the city as a space of flux and unpredictability, and it is this modernity, along with the modernities of Simmel and Benjamin, that figure in the subtitle of this book.

In 1903 Simmel related fashion to the fragmentation of modern life and discussed its neurasthenia, that is, the over-stimulation and nervous excitement that came with the growth of the metropolis.[25] He associated fashion with the middle classes and with the city, as well as with the stylisation of everyday objects (for him the Jugendstil movement in Germany) and he pointed to the close relation of art, fashion and consumer culture, connections which became topical again in the 1990s, for example in the work of Comme des Garçons, Martin Margiela and Viktor & Rolf. In 1939 Walter Benjamin described a change in the structure of experience whereby modern life was characterised by violent jolts and dislocations, a feature equally of many accounts of post-modern experience at the close of the century. Benjamin cites Baudelaire's description of the crowd as 'a reservoir of electric energy'; the man who plunges into it is 'a *kaleidoscope* equipped with consciousness.'[26] Urban encounters with telephones, cameras, traffic and advertising are experienced as 'a series of shocks and collisions' and the fractured and dislocating experience of modernity is made formal in the principle of montage in early modernist cinema.

Ulrich Lehmann has noted that the etymology of the French words for fashion and modernity – *mode* and *modernité* – is the same.[27] Among the many writers on modernity, only Lehmann and Elizabeth Wilson have addressed the role of fashion in modernity by making it central rather than peripheral to their accounts. Both assert the continuing relevance of nineteenth-century modernity to the present, Lehmann in general terms and Wilson in more specific ones.[28] Wilson, writing in 1985, pinpointed the moment of dissonance in the modern city as being key to twentieth-century style; the 'hysteria and exaggeration of fashion' expressed 'the colliding dynamism, the thirst for change and the heightened sensation that characterise the city societies particularly of modern industrial capitalism [that] go to make up this "modernity".'[29] She argued that the late eighteenth- to early nineteenth-century Romantic movement was an early response to the advance of science and the 'dark satanic mills of industrialism.'[30] Unlike other writers on modernity, she traced a connection to today's fashion, comparing Romanticism to the time in which she was writing, the 1980s, arguing that both emphasised individuality in a period of technological development. Wilson described post-modern fashion in 1985 as enacting 'the most hallucinatory aspects of our culture, the confusions between the real and the not-real, the aesthetic obsessions, the vein of morbidity without tragedy, of irony without merriment,

23 The schematic nature of these terms belies the real difficulties of definition and distinction that they raise, particularly in relation to modernity and modernism. Lisa Tickner provides a useful discussion, and gathers many relevant sources, in her 'Afterword: Modernism and Modernity' in *Modern Lives and Modern Subjects*, Yale University Press, New Haven and London, 2000: 184–214. As she points out, the distinction has spawned its own interdisciplinary journal, *Modernism/Modernity*, Johns Hopkins University Press. For another overview, with bibliographic references, also cited by Tickner, see Terry Smith in *The Dictionary of Art*, Macmillan, London, 1996, vol. 21: 775–9. There is also a large body of design history writing on these themes, e.g. Paul Greenhalgh (ed.), *Modernism in Design*, Reaktion Books, London, 1990, and John Thakara (ed.), *Design After Modernism: Beyond the Object*, Thames & Hudson, London, 1988.

24 Charles Baudelaire, 'The Painter of Modern Life', *The Painter of Modern Life and Other Essays*, trans. Jonathan Mayne, Phaidon, London, 1995 [1964]: 12.

25 Simmel, 'Metropolis and Mental Life'.

26 Walter Benjamin, 'On Some Motifs in Baudelaire': 177.

27 Ulrich Lehmann, *Tigersprung: Fashion in Modernity*, MIT Press, Cambridge, Mass., and London, 2000: xv and 5–19. Also xx: 'essentially, *la modernité* equals *la mode* because it was sartorial fashion that made modernity aware of its constant urge and necessity to quote from itself.'

28 Ibid: 401.

29 Wilson, *Adorned*: 10.

30 Ibid: 61.

and the nihilistic critical stance towards authority, empty rebellion almost without political content.'[31] Although from the 1980s many academics differentiated the present from the past by identifying post-modernism as a moment of absolute rupture, Wilson's analysis suggested that she too saw a connection with moments of instability in the past that were reprised in present-day fashion. Perhaps one could make the case for the late twentieth century and early twenty-first as 'neo-Romantic', a rapid response to the changes of the previous few years.

With Wilson and Lehmann, I argue that modern fashion sits on the bedrock of nineteenth-century commercial relations, urbanisation and technological developments, and the impact of these upon sensibilities; further, that modern fashion continues to bear a relationship to them, for all the specific differences of its recent development. While modern modes of fashion production, along with the idea of inbuilt obsolescence, developed largely in the twentieth century, many features of the modern fashion industry and of modern consumption are traceable to the eighteenth and nineteenth centuries, if not earlier. However, it is not my aim to plot a precise and structural genealogy of the connection between Western fashion and modernity by tracking back through European culture. Furthermore, such an enterprise might construct a linear history which, in a sense, runs counter to my project. I have instead drawn on Benjamin's metaphor of fashion as a 'tiger's leap', the metaphor that provides the title to Lehmann's book on fashion and modernity, and on Benjamin's concept of dialectical images, with the aim of juxtaposing the more spectacular manifestations of the consumer explosion of the nineteenth century against those of the late twentieth-century fashion show to illuminate the way that the past can resonate in the present to articulate modern anxieties and experiences. And from Benjamin's references to urban space and time, I have developed the metaphor of history as a labyrinth.

Benjamin described how he once drew a diagram of his life as a labyrinth.[32] The metaphor of history as a labyrinth allows the juxtaposition of historical images with contemporary ones; as the labyrinth doubles back on itself what is most modern is revealed as also having a relation to what is most old. Distant points in time can become proximate at specific moments as their paths run close to each other. Although there is no repetition without difference, nevertheless the conditions of post-industrial modernity are haunted by those of industrial modernity when fashion designers dip into the past for their motifs and themes.[33] These traces of the past surface in the present like the return of the repressed. Fashion designers call up these ghosts of modernity and offer us a paradigm that is different from the historian's paradigm, remixing fragments of the past into something new and contemporary that will continue to resonate into the future. They illuminate how we live in the world today and what it means to be a modern subject.

The effect of developments in communications and information technology of the last thirty years of the twentieth century, and their acceleration in the final ten, as well as their impact on social relations, is still to be quantified. Rapid technological change alters the way we experience the world, from our social relations to the way we inhabit cities and make sense of our lives in them. Consequently, meaning frequently seems to mutate to the

31 Ibid: 63.

32 Walter Benjamin, 'A Berlin Chronicle' in *One Way Street and Other Writings*, trans. Edmund Jephcott and Kingsley Shorter, intro. by Susan Sontag, Verso, London, 1985: 318–19.

33 The reason why I have chosen the term 'post-industrial modernity' as opposed to 'post-modernity' is discussed in Chapter 12.

surface of things; and clothing functions as a metaphor for the instability and contingency of modern life.[34] Many of the fashion designers scrutinised in this book intuitively and inexorably drew on earlier images of disruption and instability from the past to interpret present concerns. In particular, the relevance of Renaissance and Baroque imagery on the one hand and the spectacle of nineteenth-century consumption on the other suggest that we are currently in a stage of capitalist transition as important as those of the sixteenth, seventeenth and nineteenth centuries.[35] Ken Montague has also identified these two periods as having a relation to modernity and dress, arguing that 'Victorian capitalism sought to map out the world of stable, biological, racial and social difference at a time when its own systems of production, observation, and exchange-- were accelerating the "destabilisation and mobility of signs and codes" that began in the Renaissance.[36] This destabilisation of signs and codes appears to have accelerated exponentially throughout the twentieth century, first through print and latterly through electronic media, and Montague's argument too suggests that there is a similarity between the accelerated consumption of the nineteenth century and that of today, and that both have their origins in the fifteenth and sixteenth centuries.[37]

I am not, however, making a claim for any crude historical equivalence between past and present. On the contrary, my historical examples are selective (indeed I have also alighted promiscuously on imagery recycled from the eighteenth century and the 1940s) and are chosen for what they can tell us about fashion today. In comparing, for example, a John Galliano dress with a turn-of-the century vamp, the visual link uncovers interesting things about the present that has echoes in the past. If I have chosen to focus more on contemporary links with specific centuries, it is not because I am making a wider historical claim for similarities between periods but because what designers take from particular periods in the past tells us about our anxieties and concerns in the present. When designers hark back to such periods they are simply providing interesting instances that crystallise the use we make of history in the present. Hence the 'tiger's leap' and the 'dialectical image' are tools to map the modern, rather than to chart the past. For if there are stylistic similarities between the excesses and sleights of hand of late twentieth-century fashion spectacles and those of an earlier century, that does not in itself imply a lineage. Such labyrinthine returns could equally bring two other historical moments into proximity, such as Calvin Klein and Donna Karan's evocations of a modernist aesthetic in the sleek and streamlined elegance of American fashion.[38]

There are risks attached to a form of interpretation that moves apparently irresponsibly across centuries to construct meaning in the present.[39] For example, it might be a mistake to read the late twentieth-century *memento mori* imagery of Chapter 9 as one would interpret that of the seventeenth, for all its stylistic similarities. Perhaps in the 1990s the imagery of death, decay and dereliction came to stand for mutability more than for mortality. Perhaps it sketched a contemporary sense of change, instability and uncertainty that had more to do with rapid technological and social transition than with death itself. The impact of the information revolution of the late twentieth century had particular force and veloc-

34   Mark M. Anderson, *Kafka's Clothes: Ornament and Aestheticism in the Hapsburg Fin de Siècle*, Clarendon Press, Oxford, 1992: 13.

35   Anthony Giddens, *Runaway World: How Globalisation is Reshaping Our Lives*, Profile Books, London, 1999, based on the Reith Lectures Giddens delivered for the BBC in 1999.

36   Ken Montague, 'The Aesthetics of Hygiene: Aesthetic Dress, Modernity and the Body as Sign', *Journal of Design History*, vol. 7, no. 2, 1994: 96.

37   See, e.g., Lisa Jardine, *Worldly Goods*, Macmillan, London, 1996.

38   For an analysis of a specific aspect of the American look see Rebecca Arnold, 'Looking American: Louise Dahl-Wolfe's Fashion Photographs of the 1930s and 1940s', *Fashion Theory*, vol. 6, issue 1, March 2002, 45–60; and for the development of this look in late twentieth-century fashion, see Rebecca Arnold, 'Luxury and Restraint: Minimalism in 1990s' Fashion', in Nicola White and Ian Griffiths (eds), *The Fashion Business: Theory, Practice, Image*, Berg, Oxford and New York, 2000: 167–81.

39   John Tosh, *The Pursuit of History: Aims, Methods and New Directions in the Study of Modern History*, Pearson, London, 3rd ed. 2000: 24–5.

ity from the late 1980s. Perhaps the historical imagery of death was mobilised in the 1990s to articulate a contemporary sense of transience as mutations in technology and culture ushered out old certainties without heralding in new ones, in much the same way that new scientific discoveries in the sixteenth century brought attendant uncertainties. Jonathan Dollimore has argued that cultures which are preoccupied with mutability are cultures of transition in which all fixed points seem to have been removed.[40] He cites a range of causes in the sixteenth century that produced a sensibility attuned to dislocation and disintegration, from the invention of mechanical time, in the form of the clock, to the ideas of Copernicus, Kepler and Galileo, whose scientific speculations infinitely extended the idea of mutability to produce a philosophical, theological and literary conviction that the universe was in a state of decay and decline.[41] As a modern corollary, one could point to the impact of new technology on contemporary sensibilities, even though there are differences of scale as well as meaning between a hierarchical, early modern society and a mass, or popular, late modern society. From the 1980s Sony Walkmans, mobile telephones, closed-circuit television cameras, e-mails, videos, new medical and scientific imaging techniques and other technological novelties altered the experience of space, time and the body, changed the notion of privacy and affected work and leisure practices in varying ways that seemed to some exhilarating and to others profoundly destabilizing.[42]

Ragpicking

If late twentieth-century fashion looped back to earlier moments of modernity in specific formations, it was not because the moments of past and present were the same but because a visual link between them uncovered interesting things about the present that echoed the past. Fashion designers can elucidate these connections visually in a way that historians cannot do without falsifying history. For designers, it is precisely through the liberties they take that contemporary meaning can be constructed. In exploring this phenomenon, I have had recourse to many historical references and examples, but the book itself is not so much a history of either the past or the present, although it does document some aspects of a particular moment, as a case study of what to do with a method. The method in question is a kind of historical scavenging, and like many writers on fashion today, much of my text is inflected with the writing on fashion of Walter Benjamin.[43]

The labyrinthine relay between past, present and imagined future in the work of designers surveyed here is at odds with the idea of linear history, and their design methods approximate more to those of the nineteenth-century ragpicker who figures prominently in Benjamin's Arcades project: 'Method of this project: literary montage. I needn't *say* anything. Merely show. I shall appropriate no ingenious formulations, purloin no valuables. But the rags, the refuse – these I will not describe but put on display.'[44]

Ragpicking, as well as describing fashion designers' methods, is also a useful tool for the cultural historian in thinking about fashion today. Bringing together two moments in the

40 Dollimore, *Death, Desire and Loss*: 68.

41 Ibid: 77.

42 See e.g. Tiziana Terranova, 'Posthuman Unbounded: Artificial Evolution and High-Tech Subcultures', in George Robertson *et al.* (eds), *Future Natural: Nature, Science, Culture*, Routledge, London and New York, 1996: 165–80.

43 Lehmann's *Tigersprung* provides a discussion of the usefulness of Benjamin's historical method to writing about fashion. See also Ulrich Lehmann, '*Tigersprung*: Fashioning History', *Fashion Theory*, vol. 3, issue 3, September 1999: 297–322.

44 Walter Benjamin, The *Arcades Project*, trans. Howard Eiland and Kevin McLaughlin, Belknap Press of Harvard University Press, Cambridge, Mass., and London, 1999: 860.

labyrinth, it gives cultural historians a method of conceiving of the experimental fashion design of the late twentieth century as historically located in the context of, for example, nineteenth-century capitalism. Contemporary fashion has fastened on the themes of instability and alteration, selecting past images of mutability which resonate in the present. Fashion imagery, itself semiotically unstable, thus fixes images of instability and change, but in ways that destabilize conventional history, and run counter to the idea of coherent narrative. It demands, rather, a re-evaluation of the imagery of the past in the light of the present, something that characterises the work of Michel Foucault as well as that of Walter Benjamin.

For Foucault, the breaks, ruptures and discontinuities of history serve to unravel the straightforward relationship of causes and effects over time. All history is written about from the perspective of the present, in the sense that the present throws up the themes to be studied historically. Since the present is always in a state of transformation the past must constantly be re-evaluated; and the past takes on new meanings in the light of new events in the present. This is 'genealogy' – history written in the light of current concerns.[45] It is also closely similar to the actual process of fashion design as it reveals complex historical relays between past and present. In such collections, fragments and traces from the past reverberate in the present. Reversing Foucault's idea of 'genealogy', that is, of history written in the light of current concerns, one might use the idea of the historical fragment to uncover traces from the past and to read the present through them. This book tracks such temporal relays by finding traces of the past in the present that are articulated through visual means. Raphael Samuel's *Theatres of Memory* uses the idea that objects are emotion holders, traces of the past and carriers of discourse from other times into the present.[46] The artist Joseph Beuys proposed that materials, such as the felt and fat which he used as metonyms of survival, carried traces of the past with them.[47] In a similar way contemporary fashion images are bearers of meaning and, as such, stretch simultaneously back to the past and forward into the future. Not just documents or records but fertile primary sources, they can generate new ideas and meanings and themselves carry discourse into the future, so that they take their place in a chain of meaning, or a relay of signifiers, rather than being an end product of linear history.

Benjamin's concept of the trace, from his Arcades project, could be used in a new kind of cultural analysis, more fragmented and less coherent than the historian's, in which the fashion historian and the designer alike are scavengers, moving through cultural history like the figure of the ragpicker sifting rubbish in the nineteenth-century city.[48] The historical fragment, or trace, can illuminate the present. Benjamin uses the term trace to describe the mark left by the fossil (that is, the commodity) on the plush of bourgeois interiors or on the velvet linings of their cases.[49] Here history turns into detective story, with the historical trace as a clue.[50] The figures of the collector, the ragpicker and the detective wander through Benjamin's landscape. Thus the historian's method, like that of the designer, is akin to that of the ragpicker who moves through the city gathering scraps for recycling. Irving Wohlfarth argues that the ragpicker, as a collector of 'the refuse of history',

45   Michel Foucault, *The Order of Things: An Archaeology of the Human Sciences*, trans. A. M. Sheridan-Smith, Vintage, New York, 1973 [1966]; Michel Foucault, *The Archaeology of Knowledge*, trans. A. M. Sheridan-Smith, Tavistock, London, 1974 [1969].

46   Raphael Samuel, *Theatres of Memory: Past and Present in Contemporary Culture*, Verso, London, 1994.

47   Caroline Tisdall, *Joseph Beuys*, Soloman R. Guggenheim Foundation, New York, 1979: 7.

48   For an account of the historian as ragpicker see Irving Wohlfarth, 'Et cetera? The Historian as Chiffonier', *New German Critique*, no. 39, Fall 1986: 142–68.

49   Susan Buck-Morss, *The Dialectics of Seeing: Walter Benjamin and the Arcades Project*, MIT Press, Cambridge, Mass., and London, 1991: 211.

50   Also, on the similarities between psychoanalytic method and the detective story, see Carlo Ginsburg, 'Morelli, Freud and Sherlock Holmes: Clues and Scientific Method', *History Workshop Journal*, vol. 9, Spring 1980: 5–36.

is the *incognito* of the author: 'the historian as *chiffonnier* unceremoniously transports these leftovers of the nineteenth-century across the threshold of the twentieth.'[51] The result is a series of *chiffons*, not fragments but a sort of death mask of its own conception. The rag-and-bone historian is a cousin of the Shakespearean grave digger, 'the grave digger of the bourgeois world'.[52] Indeed the cultural ragpicking of my own method, not less than the bricolage aesthetic of London designers from the 1980s onwards, becomes an emblem of modernity itself.

In the process, the distinction between past and present is almost imploded. In exactly the same way, the fashionable moment that constantly collapses into the outmoded realigns the present as it goes, transforming it into a past that it will one day revive as it trawls through it for new motifs. The modern fashion designer rummages in the historical wardrobe, scavenging images for re-use just as the nineteenth-century ragpicker scavenged materials for recycling. And, in turn, the book does something similar, scavenging images from the past to examine and reinterpret those of the present. I have assumed an equivalence here between the historian and the designer. Perhaps, however, the designer is a better equipped cultural *chiffonnier*. Stephen Greenblatt articulated the notion of a historical method of 'talking to the dead' and the dead themselves leaving textual traces.[53] He has been taken to task for his tendency to 'cultural poetics' rather than 'cultural materialism' by Howard Felperin and Graham Holderness has suggested that Greenblatt's approach tells us more about our own concerns in the present than about the period studied.[54] While such criticisms may legitimately be made of the historian, it is the task of designers to take liberties and poeticise, suborning ghosts to speak to contemporary concerns.[55] My own descriptions of the historical to-ings and fro-ings of contemporary fashion are not properly cultural materialism at all but, rather, examples of how the traces of the past can be woven into the fabric of a new story to illuminate the present. Yet they serve as something more than a mere hermeneutic tool to interpret the work of a few designers. They unlock the way in which the work of these designers – fragmented, episodic and emblematic – helps us to make sense of contemporary culture and its concerns.

Walter Benjamin's historical rummagings in the archive moved among the Middle Ages, the Reformation and the reverberations of the nineteenth century in the twentieth. In them all he saw periods of mourning or decline. The decline of pagan antiquity, the Thirty Years' War, the devastation of the First World War and the threat of the Second World War all caused a heightened sense of transience or, in Benjamin's words, of history as a desolate 'place of skulls'.[56] Perhaps the experience of transience in Benjamin's own historical period, as well as in his personal life, led him to track a comparable sense of transience in earlier periods. And, by the same token, one could argue for a sense of transience, impermanence and anxiety in the modern period which results in fashion images leaping back to comparable ones in the past.

I hope that my own crisscrossings may produce new and unexpected connections by writing about ephemera, images and traces in such a way as to invoke a poetics of history rather than solid historiography. Jacques Derrida described the architecture of the unin-

51 Wolfarth, 'Et cetera?': 146.

52 Ibid: 157.

53 Stephen Greenblatt, *Renaissance Self-Fashioning: From More to Shakespeare*, University of Chicago Press, 1980. See also Ann Rosalind Jones and Peter Stallybrass, *Renaissance Clothing and the Materials of Memory*, Cambridge University Press, 2000.

54 See essays by Howard Felperin and Graham Holderness in Francis Barker, Peter Hulme and Margaret Iverson (eds), *Uses of History*, Manchester University Press, 1991.

55 Leila Zenderland (ed.), *Recycling the Past: Popular Uses of American History*, University of Pennsylvania Press, Philadelphia, 1978: viii.

56 Buck-Morss, *Dialectics of Seeing*: 169–70.

facing page Dai Rees, hat, 1998. Peacock feathers. Photograph Mat Collishaw, courtesy Judith Clark Costume

57 Jacques Derrida, *Writing and Difference*, quoted in Aldo Rossi, *The Architecture of the City*, MIT Press, Cambridge, Mass., and London, 1982: 3.

habited or deserted city, 'reduced to its skeleton by some catastrophe of nature or art', as 'a city haunted by meaning and culture.' This state of being haunted keeps the city from returning to nature.[57] To extend Derrida's analogy of the city as skeleton, late twentieth-century fashion can function, like urban building types that are not neutral but experimental structures, as armatures for ideas, as well as skeletons of history. Looking back at history from the vantage point of contemporary fashion, like Benjamin's angel of history we are blown backwards into the future. As we go, history becomes a kind of haunting, the haunting that keeps nature at bay from the ruined city, so that we may refashion the skeletons of history into armatures for ideas.

part one

one   history

Turns and Returns

On the fiftieth anniversary of the liberation of Auschwitz two young men with shaved heads wearing dressing gowns and striped pyjamas with numbers on them strolled down a Paris catwalk. It was the day of the Comme des Garçons Spring–Summer 1995 menswear collection, disingenuously entitled Sleep. The image was widely criticised, both for its timing and for its resemblance to concentration camp uniform. The dismayed designer, Rei Kawakubo, withdrew her garments from sale, claiming that the similarity was accidental. Five and a half years later, in March 2000, the Belgian designer Martin Margiela showed his Autumn–Winter 2000–1 collection at a French National Railway depot in Paris. Guests with standing tickets only waited on a cold platform; those with seats were ushered onto a stationary train to watch the models parade through the carriages under sparkling disco balls suspended from the roof. But to those seated in the carriages, it was the sight of the standing spectators, glimpsed through grimy windows and doors, rather than the models, that, according to the influential trade journal *Women's Wear Daily*, evoked the image of Hitler's death trains. 'Only the historically impaired would not have had at least a fleeting thought of *Sophie's Choice*', it wrote. It also pointed out that other guests interpreted the show's presentation as a reference to the end of the Soviet state, before moving on to give equal coverage to Margiela's emphatic denial of these interpretations: 'rather than shocking, we fully believed the intimacy would be appreciated by the professional journalists and buyers who would come to the show and often complain of not being able to see the clothes at a show for reasons of either distance or poor lighting.'[1]

The deployment of such themes was to be found not only in the work of more experimental designers like Comme and Margiela who might be expected to produce challenging and controversial presentations, but also in that of more mainstream designers. The academic Joanne Finkelstein opened her book *After a Fashion* (1996) with a description of the French house of Jean-Louis Scherrer's use of Nazi insignia in its 1995 couture collection and the Italian house Dolce e Gabbana's revival of American gangster motifs at a time of Mafia murders in Italy. Finkelstein argued: 'these allusions to fascism, poverty, dislocation and violence in a Europe not only concerned about its undeclared wars in Bosnia and further east but also about its expanding underclass have been regarded by the international media as inexcusably callous.'[2] Steven Meisel's photographs for an underwear spread in Italian *Uomo Vogue* in 1995 were criticised, particularly in the American press, for their connotations of eating disorder and drug abuse, but perhaps to European eyes the imagery was closer to the 1992 news photograph syndicated around the world of severely malnourished Muslim refugees in the Bosnian detention camp at Omarska, an image that at the time was compared to scenes from the Nazi death camps.

In late 1999 the British novelist J. G. Ballard looked back on the twentieth century at the turn of the millennium:

I suspect that within a few years there will be a widespread rejection of the 20th century, its horrors and corruptions. Despite huge advances in science and technology, it will

1 (*facing page*) Olivier Theyskens, *Gloomy Trips*, 1997 (limited edition). Styling Olivier Theyskens. Photograph Les Cyclopes, courtesy Olivier Theyskens

1 'Margiela's Mistake', *Women's Wear Daily*, 6 March 2000.
2 Joanne Finkelstein, *After a Fashion*, Melbourne University Press, 1996: 3.

2 (*facing page*) Walter van Beirendonck, Aesthetic Terrorists, Spring–Summer 1999. Make-up Inge Grognard. Photograph Ronald Stoops, courtesy Walter van Beirendonck

seem a barbarous time. My grandchildren are all under the age of four, the first generation who will have no memories of the present century, and are likely to be appalled when they learn what was allowed to take place. For them, our debased entertainment culture and package-tour hedonism will be inextricably linked to Auschwitz and Hiroshima, though we would never make the connection.[3]

In his comment on the enormity of state-controlled death in the twentieth century Ballard made a connection between its horror and the debased, as he saw it, entertainment culture and hedonism of the century. Without endorsing Ballard's condemnatory tone towards popular culture, in this book I aim to scrutinise just such an attraction of opposites, between fashion and ideas previously considered inimical to fashion. The connection that Ballard argued we ourselves would never make was in fact made, self-consciously and knowingly, in the work of a range of fashion designers at the end of the century that suggested the body as a site simultaneously of perfection and decay, drawing attention to the fascination of beauty and horror entwined. These conjunctions were often articulated through historical design references, particularly in the work of less mainstream commercial designers such as Olivier Theyskens, in whose hands a certain gothicised version of the past was obsessively recycled in 1990s fashion (fig. 1). Despite the fact that fashion is an arena dedicated to novelty, indeed that could be said to fetishise novelty, in the work of such designers the present was constantly invaded by images of the past that seeped in, settled into the cracks and colonised the terrain of 'the new'. Walter van Beirendonck photographed one of his Aesthetic Terrorists collection of rough-cut graffiti-style T-shirts under an eighteenth-century dress. The T-shirt's neon graphics were more vibrant and alive than the model's bleached skin tones that matched the deathly grey of her dress, her scruffily pulled back hair, etiolated arms and depressed expression (fig. 2). In the work of many innovative designers of the period, what was most modern doubled back on itself as the oldest and, to borrow Lynda Nead's phrase from a different context, the past 'returned to disturb and unsettle the confidence of the modern.'[4] Nead develops the idea of modernity as vitally and urgently engaged in a dialogue with its own historical conditions of existence so that 'the modern' can never represent a clean break with the past; instead 'modernity can be understood as a set of historical discourses and processes that are profoundly and necessarily caught up with the construction of the past.'[5] Thus fashion, while ostensibly a paradigm of novelty and innovation, is in fact trammelled by the very historical conditions that produce it; and this is made explicit in the work of some designers. Figures 1 and 2 both suggest this 'dialogue' with the past. Nead uses the metaphor of a crumpled handkerchief to describe the way that historical time folds back on itself in designed objects; in figure 2 the vibrant style of the modern T-shirt is overlaid with the faded, tired fabric of the historical overdress, so that the image is an aggregate of historical moments that, in Michel Serres's words, 'reveal a time that is gathered together, with multiple pleats'. Nead's metaphor of the crumpled handkerchief evokes a topological concept of time as folded, whereby distant points become 'close or even superimposed', and tears in the cloth can

3   J. G. Ballard, 'Diary', *New Statesman*, 20 December 1999 – 3 January 2000: 9.

4   Lynda Nead, *Victorian Babylon: People, Streets and Images in Nineteenth-Century London*, Yale University Press, New Haven and London, 2000: 8.

5   Ibid: 7.

3 (*facing page*)   Olivier Theyskens, corset top, Visionaire 2000. Styling Laetitia Crahay. Photograph Les Cyclopes, courtesy Olivier Theyskens

bring unconnected periods into proximity.[6] She argues that our experience of time resembles the crumpled version of the handkerchief, rather than the flat, ironed one: 'modernity, in this context, can be imagined as pleated or crumpled time, drawing together past, present and future into constant and unexpected relations and the product of a multiplicity of historical eras.'[7] The textural quality of the crumpled evokes the old, just like the tired, greying fabric of the eighteenth-century dress in figure 2; this textile metaphor seems to work particularly well for fashion, not only because of the visceral and material possibilities of both fabric and body, but also because of fashion's particularly promiscuous historical behaviour, its brief life span and its incessant trawling through the old to refabricate the new.

6   Michel Serres cited in ibid: 8.

7   Ibid.

8   Walter Benjamin, 'Theses on the Philosophy of History', *Illuminations*, trans. Harry Zohn, Fontana/Collins, London, 1973 [1955]: 257.

9   Benjamin writes about the labyrinth in urban space in relation to specific cities (New York, Moscow, Berlin and Paris) but he also uses it as a metaphor: the labyrinth spatialises time, memory and autobiography. As well as the Arcades project, see 'Central Park', *New German Critique*, 34, Winter 1985 [1972]: 36; 'Moscow' and 'A Berlin Chronicle' in *One Way Street and Other Writings*, trans. Edmund Jephcott and Kingsley Shorter, intro. by Susan Sontag, Verso, London, 1985 [1970 and 1974]. On the nuances of the metaphor of the labyrinth in Benjamin's writing, and the way it can become a labyrinth of history, see Christine Buci-Glucksmann, *Baroque Reason: The Aesthetics of Modernity*, trans. Patrick Camiller, Sage, London, Thousand Oaks and New Delhi, 1994 [1984]: 84–5 and 93–4.

10   For *jetztzeit* or the 'time of the now' see Benjamin, 'Theses on the Philosophy of History': 263 and 265. For the 'archeology of the modern' see Buci-Glucksman, *Baroque Reason*: 88–9.

11   For the 'complementarity with the past' see Frank Kermode, *The Sense of An Ending: Studies in the Theory of Fiction with a New Epilogue*, Oxford University Press, 2000 [1966]. For the historical constellation, see Benjamin, 'Theses on the Philosophy of History': 265, and Buci-Glucksmann, *Baroque Reason*: 108.

12   On the revival of the corset in late twentieth-century fashion see Valerie Steele, *The Corset: A Cultural History*, Yale University Press, New Haven and London, 2001: 165–76. On revivals in general see Barbara Burman Baines, *Fashion Revivals: From the Elizabethan Age to the Present Day*, B. T. Batsford, London, 1981.

Labyrinth

The recycling of historical motifs that dominated a certain strand of fashion design in the 1990s also punctuates this book as a recurring motif. A consideration of historicism in 1990s fashion enables the articulation of a series of metaphors to think about fashion time and how it operates – crumpled fabric, the labyrinth, the telescope and the tiger's leap. Writing in the 1930s, Walter Benjamin argued that 'every image of the past that is not recognised by the present as one of its own concerns threatens to disappear irretrievably.'[8] As it developed in the 1990s, late twentieth-century fashion had an unerring eye for the topical in its choice of historical imagery that articulated contemporary concerns. The metaphor of historical time as a labyrinth or maze, doubling back on itself, provides a model to understand the historical relay between past and present in 1990s fashion.[9] In particular, Benjamin's concept of the *jetztzeit* or 'now-time' as 'an archaeology of modernity' seems relevant to the historical returns of contemporary fashion.[10] For despite fashion's insistence on innovation and novelty, the historical trace that Frank Kermode has called a 'complementarity with the past' persisted in many designs from the late 1990s, constituting 'a network of historical constellations in which past and present are telescoped together.'[11]

The revival of the corset as outerwear by late twentieth-century designers is a paradigm of this process of historical telescoping.[12] It first appeared in the designs of Vivienne Westwood and Jean-Paul Gaultier in the mid-1980s. In the 1990s the corset became ubiquitous as almost every major European designer incorporated it into her or his collections, ranging from Christian Lacroix's opulent conservatism, through Hussein Chalayan's experimental 'flower press' corset carved from cherry wood and fastened with chrome screws at the side, to Olivier Theyskens' corset with its connotations of the nineteenth-century asylum and madhouse (fig. 3). Alexander McQueen's corsets ranged from the vampish *femme fatale*'s to the orthopaedic neck brace. From the idealised and romantic to the malign and troubling, these reinterpretations of the historical corset evoked a range of ideas about women, spectacle, image and history. Some were benign or nostalgic, others were threatening and darkly disturbing. In itself the corset's range of meanings were a microcosm of

13 'In the final decades of the twentieth century
underwear as outerwear became a panacea for the
fears surrounding sex and the body': Rebecca Arnold,
*Fashion, Desire and Anxiety: Image and Morality in
the Twentieth Century*, I. B. Tauris, London, 2001:
66.

14 Fredric Jameson, 'Postmodernism, or the
Cultural Logic of Late Capitalism', *New Left Review*,
vol. 146, 1984: 53–93. This influential paper was
reprinted without substantial alterations as the first
chapter of Jameson's book *Postmodernism, or the
Cultural Logic of Late Capitalism*, Verso, London and
New York, 1991. But in subsequent chapters Jameson
modified his 1984 analysis of post-modernism as
historically promiscuous, and ultimately meaningless,
to argue for a 'New Historicism' in academic writing
and to analyse examples from American literature
and film that, through representations of either
the past or the future, historicised the present. He
developed his argument to suggest the imbrication
of modernity in post-modernity as a residue or trace
(xvi), and in his penultimate chapter he discussed
the historical novel and the costume film as returns
of the historical repressed, something which I
develop in the next chapter, particularly in relation
to Jean-Michel Rabaté's concept of modernist
'haunting'.

late twentieth-century fashion's ability to draw creatively on its own past to recreate an image for the future, sketching conflicting fears and desires on the one body.[13] These eclectic borrowings together constitute a set of instances that crystallise the use that designers can make of history in the present, retracing convoluted routes through the labyrinth that bring historically separate themes into contact, and returning to the same point via a different route.

In 1984 Fredric Jameson argued that history was being plundered in contemporary visual culture to make a post-modern carnival, and that the incessant return to the past was itself a kind of deathly recycling of history which emptied it of meaning, rendering it bankrupt, good only for costume drama and fantasy.[14] In this analysis, fashion seems to be a quintessentially post-modern form, and on the face of it 1980s fashion bore this out. In 1980s post-punk London, a form of designer-led historicism emerged, initiated first by Vivienne Westwood and then by John Galliano. From the late 1970s onwards, starting with her 1979 Pirates collection, Vivienne Westwood plundered the past, helping herself liberally to seventeenth-century men's shirts and eighteenth-century women's stays. Refashioning the male codpiece as a decorative rosette for women, mixing hunting pink with punk bondage and eighteenth-century stays (fig. 4), her polemical visual games played with images of class and gender in a contemporary way, for all their nostalgic evocations of an aristocratic past. Throughout the 1980s and early 1990s Westwood continued to lead bold and swashbuckling raids on the past, treating history and culture as a dressing-up box from which to recreate the self as a flamboyant and spectacular creature (fig. 5).

At the same time, the gestural mockery of post-punk London clubland produced extreme forms of self-styling that regrouped cultural motifs, such as the club and magazine poses of Leigh Bowery and Trojan from the mid-1980s (fig. 6), creating something from ephemera in their self-representation, as when Trojan cut his ear and then rouged it with lipstick in a parody of Van Gogh. Out of these same groups emerged a form of urban ragpicker, the charity shop stylists whose work figured largely in the magazine *i-D* and whose magpie aesthetic sought items of cultural detritus to recycle into new, cutting-edge, magazine imagery. This bricoleur's aesthetic that characterised British club and sub-cultures in this period also provided a model of the design process for designers like Jean-Paul Gaultier in Paris and Westood and Galliano in London, and goes some way to explaining their own versions of cut-and-mix in the 1980s. For the metropolitan body that was on display in 1980s London was both informed and defined by the street, mediated by the new fashion magazines such as *Blitz, i-D*, with its 'straight-up' street fashion photographs, and *The Face*. In differing degrees these magazines reconfigured the cultural geography of the street through a reportage style of fashion journalism that relied as much on coverage of street- and club-led innovation as on traditional fashion editorial coverage. The power of these magazines' editors was to map fashionable identities onto British cities and then disseminate them across national boundaries through publication.

This scavenging aesthetic underpinned much of the historicism of 1990s design that 'inaccurately' pillaged the past to produce a contemporary aesthetic. Rather than recreating one period, its historical borrowings were multi-layered. Like the 1990s figure of the DJ, fashion designers sampled and mixed from a range of sources to create something new, rummaging through the historical wardrobe to produce clothes with a strictly contemporary resonance. And in the same way that musical history lost its linearity when mixed by the DJ who assumed a relationship with history and tinkered with it in the course of collecting, archiving and mixing tracks,[15] so too did fashion and cultural history lose its linearity when 'remixed' by late twentieth-century designers, folding one historical reference back on another.

6   David Gwinnutt, Leigh Bowery and Trojan, 1984. Photograph courtesy David Gwinnutt

Unhappy Returns

Benjamin traced the metaphor of the labyrinth and made it corporeal through the figures of the *flâneur* and the prostitute, from where Christine Buci-Glucksmann has extended it: 'the image moves from the labyrinth of big cities to the labyrinth of the commodity, and by no means least is the ultimate labyrinth of history.'[16] Many designers in the 1990s exhibited an almost neurotic habit of historical citation, in both experimental and conventional work. One the one hand, several French and Italian designers such as Karl Lagerfeld, Gianni Versace, Christian Lacroix, Krizia, Anna Molinari, Dolce e Gabbana and Hervé Léger, in the early to mid-1990s, produced collections akin to historical fancy dress, drawing on a range of sources from the sixteenth to the nineteenth centuries. On

15   Ulf Poschardt, *DJ Culture*, trans. Shaun Whiteside, Quartet Books, London, 1998: 16.
16   Buci-Glucksmann, *Baroque Reason*: 93.

7 Robert Cary-Williams, Autumn–Winter 1999–2000. Photograph Chris Moore

17 Stephen Gan, *Visionaire's Fashion 2001: Designers of the New Avant-Garde*, ed. Alix Browne, Laurence King, London, 1999 [n.p.].

18 Lou Winwood, 'It's snowtime!', *Guardian*, 3 March 1999: 10–11.

the other hand, some British, Belgian and Dutch designers such as Vivienne Westwood, John Galliano, Viktor & Rolf, Olivier Theyskens, Veronique Branquinho, Robert Cary-Williams, Jessica Ogden and Shelley Fox also reprised historical themes, albeit not such resplendent ones. Theirs, on the contrary, were frequently dark and doom-laden.

To some extent, particularly when fashion historicism evinced romantic nostalgia for a vanished past, this trend could be attributed to the recession of the early 1990s. But the more troubling historical returns of these British, Belgian and Dutch designers was not the quaint and picturesque version of history usually referred to by fashion but a darker, more despairing re-run of the past. Whereas Westwood's tartans (see fig. 5) evoked swaggering eighteenth-century individuality, Alexander McQueen's Highland Rape collection (see fig. 104) reprised a harsher moment, the eighteenth-century Jacobite rebellion and the nineteenth-century Highland clearances that McQueen referred to as genocide. Viktor & Rolf's second collection in 1994 consisted of twenty versions of the same white Victorian dress on which they had carried out various experiments including slamming it in a door, cutting it, burning it and embroidering stains on it. Olivier Theyskens, who first showed in Paris in 1998, designed narrow linen Edwardian dresses made of old sheets, and black ball skirts worn with sinister tight leather jackets that seemed to constrain the model. His compatriot Veronique Branquinho first showed her Bohemian version of Gothic Victoriana in 1997. In London, Robert Cary-Williams's Victorian Car Crash collection (Autumn–Winter 1999–2000) was shown in spring 1999. Smoke poured from under the runway; the air was thick and chalky. In the words of the designer, 'the inspiration for this collection was a woman from the Victorian era who somehow ends up in the present day . . . She's run over by a car. She survives, but the clothes get damaged.'[17] Latex and leather jackets, dresses and full skirts were cut to fall away from the body; other garments were completely sheared away, leaving only an armature of trailing zips and seams. Seams and random pleats were left over from stiffened ecru shift dresses; a flesh-coloured leather coat was shredded into ruched and plaited strands; a pair of shoes that seemed to be morphing into hooves was described by the designer as 'vetinary horse boots'.[18] The full-skirted bride, the final outfit that traditionally ends the catwalk show, was dressed not in white but in black and wore blinkers and a black plume on her head, like a Victorian funeral horse.

Cary-Williams's design and styling (fig. 7) typified the way in which many younger fashion designers, stylists, make-up artists and photographers began to use the visual language of dereliction, death and despair in their work. Fashion, conventionally associated with lightness, frivolity and pleasure, gathered darker meanings, meanings which it seemed could best be articulated by a return to the past. The darkness of this imagery suggested, in the work of designers such as Alexander McQueen and Andrew Groves, that what was being told was a horror story. It is perhaps simplistic to speculate that such designs echoed present-day realities in any straightforward way, but possibly modern life is easier to anatomise and explore at a distance, re-narrativised through a historical lens. Certainly the labyrinthine twists and turns of 1990s fashion made use of historical references from the past to produce a visual economy that seemed to resonate in an entirely new way, even where such designs were nostalgic rather than darkly gloomy. Whereas much fashion shored up and contained anxieties about cultural continuity, the body and mortality, this new type of fashion design, often originating from London or Antwerp, seemed to function like a hysterical symptom that could articulate current concerns. Just as Finkelstein and Ballard's comments cited at the beginning of this chapter drew attention to the particularly bleak history of the twentieth century, so in the 1990s a number of fashion designers' work referred to an equally bleak view of earlier centuries, evoking comparable periods of capitalist excess, instability and change in the past to sketch these features in the present.

In the 1990s the strand of fashion historicism that revisited the past and reconfigured it in the present came mainly from Japanese or European designers, in particular the British, Dutch and Belgians (but not Italians), rather than from American designers. Lynda Nead has differentiated the spatial logic of modernity in nineteenth-century London from that of Paris or New York as being that of the maze rather than the étoile or the grid.[19] Something of this logic is discernible in the historical returns of London- and Antwerp-trained, as opposed to Paris- or New York-trained, designers of the late twentieth century. This might have something to do with their art school training (although Westwood has no formal fashion training). Central Saint Martins College of Art and Design in London emphasises the role of research in the design process; at the Antwerp Academy fashion students devote half their time to historical subjects and materials in some form. The majority of trained fashion designers discussed here graduated from one or other of these schools. However, fashion historicism in the 1990s cannot be explained alone by reference to the training and cultural background of a few individual designers, some of whom worked very much like artists, divorced from the protocols of their industry; it also has to be explored in relation to wider questions of markets and mass culture, themes which are returned to in the final chapter.

Ulrich Lehmann has asserted that a defining characteristic of fashion since the second half of the nineteenth century is that 'in order to become the new, fashion always cites the old – not simply the ancient or classical, but their reflection within its own sartorial past.'[20] Yet what is interesting in such citations is not the similarities but the differences between them; for it is by these that we make sense of them as marking different moments of modernity.[21] The subject matter of this book is not the simple fact of historical returns, which Barbara Burman has effectively shown to have occurred in Western dress at least since the Renaissance,[22] but the nature of specific returns from the late 1990s, and the ways in which these might differ from earlier ones. There is a world of difference, for example, between Vivienne Westwood's late 1980s and 1990s citations and Robert Cary-Williams's late 1990s designs. In his Victorian Car Crash historical images from the past were grafted onto the present in a peculiar temporal hybrid. Other historical images were, so to speak, back-projected onto the present, as where Alexander McQueen photo-printed images of the doomed Russian Romanov children onto a contemporary jacket worn on the catwalk (fig. 8). Sometimes yesterday's history and today's politics came together, for example in Andrew Groves's collection based on the Troubles in Northern Ireland; sometimes

19 Nead, *Victorian Babylon*: 4.

20 Ulrich Lehmann, *Tigersprung: Fashion in Modernity*, MIT Press, Cambridge, Mass., and London, 2000: xx.

21 Kermode, *Sense of an Ending*: 95–6, makes this point about the way that a literature of crisis and apocalypse recurs throughout modernity, not in a generic way but in specific formations that can be correlated to specific moments in and stages of modernism.

22 Burman Baines, *Fashion Revivals*.

 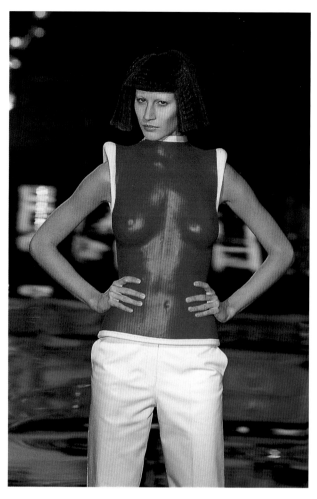

8 (*above left*) Alexander McQueen,
Autumn–Winter 1998–9. Photograph
Chris Moore, courtesy Alexander McQueen

9 (*above right*)   Alexander McQueen for
Givenchy, Autumn–Winter 1999–2000.
Photograph Niall McInerney

23   Herbert Blau, *Nothing In Itself: Complexions of
Fashion*, Indiana University Press, Bloomington and
Indianapolis, 1999: 36.

24   See Jameson, *Postmodernism*: ch. 7, 'Theory':
181–259, and ch. 9, 'Film', subtitled 'Nostalgia for the
Present': 279–96, where Jameson discussed the way
in which America revisited its own recent history
and mythology in films like *Something Wild* and *Blue
Velvet*, as well as in science fiction and historical
novels, to 'historicise the present'.

dystopian images of the future surfaced, as in McQueen's alienated androids for Givenchy (fig. 9). By layering and cross-referencing images from the past and an imagined future, these designers played with time, and historicised the present.

The historical imagery of 1990s fashion that was darkly dystopian and inflected with trauma or, in Herbert Blau's phrase, 'post-modern mourning', signalled a particularly contemporary concern. On the dust jacket of Blau's book on fashion, *Nothing In Itself* (1999) Meaghan Morris asked 'how we might write cultural history for a "post-historical" time in which . . . there's a lot of history about' and Blau himself argued that 'how the past is approached . . . is still the determining problem of post-modern forms'.[23] The effect of rendering the present as history has the effect of making the here and now unfamiliar and alien, estranging the spectator from the present. It makes a cultural space for the representation of estrangement, alienation and reification, as Fredric Jameson has argued in his analysis of the way American film and literature in the 1980s incorporated both historical and futuristic themes to articulate current concerns.[24]

* * *

Dialectical Images

These narratives may therefore either articulate contemporary fears, for example in McQueen's designs, or provide reassurance against them, for example in Galliano's luxurious evocations of Edwardian splendour. In keeping with his celebratory approach to the past, one July day in 1998 an old steam train chuffed into the Gare d'Austerlitz in Paris, drawing up at platform number 21 (fig. 10). Above its front fender was stretched a wall of orange paper, through which a model dressed as the Princess Pocahontas burst as the train steamed into the station. Out of its windows hung more, waving models. The railway platforms were dressed like a set for an oriental souk: the ground was covered in sand on which an audience sat surrounded by huge bronze platters of spices, potted palms, antique Louis Vuitton suitcases and Moroccan lanterns, consuming champagne and turkish delight. Once stationary, the train disgorged its cargo of models onto the platform, dressed in a jumble of native American and sixteenth-century European dress, juxtaposing feather head-dresses and beads with Medici princesses, female page boys and Henry VIII outfits. This Christian Dior Haute Couture Autumn–Winter 1998–9 collection was called A Voyage on the Diorient Express, or the Story of the Princess Pocahontas. Stencilled on the side of the train were the words 'Diorient Express'. They aptly suggested both Galliano's orientalism and the disorienting effects of his showmanship. His collections of this period eclectically combined cultures, continents and centuries, transposing, for example, African beading to Western corsetry which was worn on top of a black evening dress and modelled by a black model with a trilby on her head (fig. 11). The first haute couture collection that Galliano designed for Dior (Spring–Summer 1997) juxtaposed Dinka beading, Edwardian silhouettes and 1950s couture historicism in full-blown evening gowns that required 410 metres of fabric (fig. 12). Subsequent collections collaged together motifs from different cultures, mixing maharaja jewels and an aigrette with Burmese neck jewellery and Afro-Caribbean braids, while styling the model to look uncannily stiff and Parisian. Morphing references and motifs from different periods and cultures into single fusions, his collections eclectically mixed images of empire and Africa, Japonism and the Weimar Republic, early cinema and the *belle époque*.

Galliano's neo-colonial fusions invoked images of empire and otherness from the displays of nineteenth-century world fairs and department stores. Like them, Galliano's fusions reduced non-European cultures to exotic spectacle. Parisian department stores of the second half of the nineteenth century staged oriental scenarios that eclectically mingled goods from different cultures and communities in a fantasy bazaar.[25] Very like Galliano's runway shows at the end of the twentieth century, they often drew on the conventions of theatre and exhibitions to produce either human tableaux set in Turkish harems, Cairo markets and Hindu temples, or dance spectacles with snake charmers and Indian pipes. Similarly, in nineteenth-century world fairs the illusion of exotic locations was created in the form of 'Cairo belly-dancers' and 'Andalusian gypsies' which, in their fantastical hybridity, were comparable to Galliano's catwalk scenarios a hundred years later.[26] His techniques of his-

25   Rosalind H. Williams, *Dream Worlds: Mass Consumption in Late Nineteenth-Century France*, University of California Press, Berkeley, Los Angeles and Oxford, 1982: 66–72. For a review of the literature on the nineteenth-century French department store see Mica Nava, 'Modernity's Disavowal: Women, the City and the Department Store' in Pasi Falk and Colin Campbell (eds), *The Shopping Experience*, Sage, London, Thousand Oaks and New Delhi, 1997: 56–91.

26   At the 1900 exhibition in particular twenty-one out of the thirty-three main attractions involved taking a fantasy journey to 'distant visions'. See Williams, *Dream Worlds*: 73–8.

10   John Galliano for Christian Dior, Haute Couture, Autumn–Winter 1998–9. Photograph Rindoff/Garcia, courtesy Christian Dior

torical pastiche and cultural collage fused disparate cultures and places, much as the World Tour did in the 1900 Paris Universal Exhibition by having standing visitors propelled round the exhibition on a 'travelator' that in a single journey took them promiscuously from culture to culture in a geographical simulacrum that had no regard for spatial distance. Elsewhere the exhibition staged an exotic orient by abutting a Hindu pagoda, a Chinese temple and a Muslim mosque, enlivened by jugglers and geishas.[27] In the modern fashion show the spectator is stationary and the exotic orient parades before her or his eyes, but the overall effect is the same. The effect both of a Galliano show and of the displays in the 1900 exhibition is to normalise, contain and manage non-European cultures through the very process of creating them as spectacle. As the twentieth century developed, early cinema began to replace world fairs and department stores as sources of popular spectacle. In 1907 there were two cinemas in Paris, in 1913 there were 160. Movie houses showed a kind of medley of films, not unlike the medley of fantasy journeys provided by the 1900 Exhibition. One type of film would succeed another: Western, light comedy, travelogue, social documentary. Rosalind Williams has argued that the mixed-up genres had the effect for contemporaries of obliterating reality because all levels of lived experience were reduced to the same level of technical ingenuity, and something of this nature permeates the extravagant catwalk shows of the 1990s.[28]

As Galliano's shows expanded in the late 1990s with the backing of a major couture house, their themes began more and more to revisit the commercial origins of couture in nineteenth-century Paris. Increasingly his collections invoked the themes and images of nineteenth-century Parisian modernity, an important period and city in the development of the modern fashion industry, particularly as regards business, retailing and advertising. His spectacular runway shows were highly innovative, but the link they evoked between spectacle and commodity culture had been made in the second half of the nineteenth century. The 1900 Paris Universal Exhibition had been the first French world fair to feature

27 Philippe Jullian, *The Triumph of Art Nouveau: the Paris Exhibition of 1900*, Phaidon, London, 1974: 169. Williams, *Dream Worlds*: 61–4.

28 Williams, *Dream Worlds*: 79.

11 John Galliano for Christian Dior, Haute Couture, Spring–Summer 1997. Photograph Rindoff/Garcia, courtesy Christian Dior

12 John Galliano for Christian Dior, Haute Couture, Spring–Summer 1997. Photograph Rindoff/Garcia, courtesy Christian Dior

13 (*above left*)   Pavillon de la Mode,
Exposition Universelle, Paris 1990. Photograph
from Philippe Jullian, *The Triumph of Art
Nouveau: The Paris Exhibition*, Phaidon Press,
London, 1974

14 (*above right*)   John Galliano for Christian
Dior, Spring–Summer 1998. Photograph
Rindoff/Garcia, courtesy Christian Dior

29   Emile Zola, *The Ladies' Paradise*, trans. with
an intro. by Brian Nelson, Oxford University Press,
Oxford and New York, 1995: 6.

contemporary fashion, brightly lit by electricity, in glass cases containing couturier-clad wax dummies. In one, the spectacle of a fitting for a wedding dress at Maison Worth brought the luxury and extravagance of haute couture to a wider audience, just as videos of couture shows did a hundred years later (fig. 13). The style of these displays resurfaced, particularly, in the staging of the Dior Spring-Summer ready-to-wear 1998 show, in a series of classical rooms dressed with period furniture around which the models draped themselves like Hollywood starlets from the 1930s (fig. 14).

Galliano's opulent designs also recalled Emile Zola's description in *The Ladies' Paradise*, based on extensive research done in Paris departments stores in the 1860s, of a window display of female dummies dressed in the most sumptuous and elaborate fashion: snow-falls of costly lace, velvet trimmed with fox fur, silk with Siberian squirrel, cashmere and cocks' feathers, quilting, swansdown and chenille.[29] In such shows Galliano created the illusion of a walk through a salon like the earliest couture shows when the mannequins would parade decorously in the salon of the couture house that was decorated to look like a private mansion rather than commercial premises. The more conventional parade down a runway was replaced by a series of rooms dressed like film sets. The audience was scattered through these rooms in small groups so that they were closer to the clothes than in the usual fashion show. The models paraded through, striking attitudes and poses in each room, staging *tableaux vivants* as they went. Each model had only one outfit per show, rather than making a series of rapid costume changes, and was encouraged to feel her way into and act the part of her character. Galliano began to use more theatrical techniques to stage his fashion narratives, for example replacing runway lighting with theatre lighting and minutely choreographing each section of the show three days before, transforming empty venues into fantasy palaces, and creating something evocative from air, like the spectacular displays of the nineteenth-century city.

The juxtaposition of these images, on the one hand of late twentieth-century fashion shows, and on the other of the merchandising and retail extravaganzas of a century earlier, invokes Walter Benjamin's idea of 'dialectical images'. Dialectical images were not based on simple comparisons but, rather, created a more complex historical relay of themes running between past and present. For Benjamin, the relationship between images of the past and the present worked like the montage technique of cinema.[30] The principle of montage is that a third meaning is created by the juxtaposition of two images, rather than any immutable meaning inhering in each image. Benjamin conceived of this relationship as a dialectical one: the motifs of the past and the present functioned as thesis and antithesis. The flash of recognition, between past and present images, was the dialectical image that transformed both. Jolted out of the context of the past, the dialectical image could be read in the present as a 'truth'. But it was not an absolute truth, rather a truth which was fleeting and temporal, existing only at the moment of perception, characterised by 'shock' or vivid recognition. It was not that the past simply illuminated the present, or that the present illuminated the past; rather, the two images came together in a 'critical constellation', tracing a previously concealed connection.[31]

Throughout the 1990s, conjuring something out of nothing, Galliano could be seen as a master of ephemeral ceremonies, whose essence shares the nature of a ghost – transient, restless, evanescent – whose work is haunted by the excessive displays of conspicuous consumption of consumer capitalism. His nostalgic designs conjured up an earlier period of idleness and luxury, yet the historical period he drew on was also, like the present, a time of mutability, instability and rapid change, when all fixed points seemed to be in motion, and in which the image of woman was correspondingly highly charged. For the image of woman as commodity and consumer was as ambivalently coded in the 1990s, in the work of Galliano, as in the 1890s, in the figure of the Parisian woman of fashion. The femme fatale from the late nineteenth to the early twentieth centuries, the cypher of desire and dread simultaneously, finds some contemporary parallels in Galliano's vamps and sirens, and his 1990s luxurious and lingerie-inspired designs recall the image of woman as an *objet de luxe* at the turn of the previous century (figs 15 and 16). By evoking the link between modernity, spectacle and consumption in the late nineteenth- and early twentieth-century city, he simultaneously brought it into the present by picturing the relationship between fashion, women, spectacle and commodification in the present.[32]

Benjamin's concept of dialectical images gives us a way of understanding Galliano's historical and cultural promiscuity in terms of simple stylistic similarities. However, in addition to being an interpretative tool they point more significantly to an underlying structural connection between urban consumer culture then and now. They ground the poetry of the images in a material base. Benjamin's ideas, although formulated in the 1920s and 30s looking back at nineteenth-century Paris, have a new relevance today in understanding the

30 For a discussion of this, see Susan Buck-Morss, *The Dialectics of Seeing: Walter Benjamin and the Arcades Project*, MIT Press, Cambridge, Mass., and London, 1991: 250.

31 Ibid: 185, 221, 250 and 290–1.

32 Caroline Evans, 'Galliano: Spectacle and Modernity', in Nicola White and Ian Griffiths (eds), *The Fashion Business: Theory, Practice, Image*, Berg, Oxford and New York, 2000 discusses the relationship of nineteenth-century consumption, modernity and the 1990s fashion designs of Galliano.

15 (*above left*)   Theda Bara, c. 1900. Private collection

16 (*above right*)   John Galliano for Christian Dior, Haute Couture, Autumn–Winter 1997–8. Photograph Rindoff/Garcia, courtesy Christian Dior

33   Karl Marx, *The Eighteenth Brumaire of Louis Bonaparte*, translated from the German, Progress Publishers, Moscow, 3rd rev. ed. 1954 [2nd revised ed. 1869]: 10–11. Marx described how 'Camille Desmoulins, Danton, Robespierre, Danton, Saint-Just, Napoleon, the heroes as well as the parties and the masses of the old French Revolution, performed the task of their time in Roman costume and with Roman phrases, the task of unchaining and setting up modern *bourgeois* society.'

34   Benjamin, 'Theses on the Philosophy of History': 263.

present. His ideas offer art and design historians a complex and sophisticated model of how visual seduction works, because they are predicated on an understanding of how visual similes function, something on which other historians have not focused. His method allows us to perceive similarities across periods apparently separated by rupture and discontinuity, and to plot historical time not as something that flows smoothly from past to present but as a more complex relay of turns and returns in which the past is activated by injecting the present into it. They enable us to see the relevance of earlier moments of modernity to late twentieth-century fashion.

In the opening passages of *The Eighteeenth Brumaire of Louis Bonaparte* Marx evokes the revolution of 1848 set in a Paris haunted by figures from the revolution of 1789, his 'modern' bourgeois revolution peopled with 'the dead of world history', ghostly revolutionaries from the previous century shrouded in the dress of the past.[33] Writing in 1938, Walter Benjamin described this as typifying the 'tiger's leap' of fashion:

[To the French Revolution] ancient Rome was a past charged with the time of the now . . . blasted out of the continuum of history. The French Revolution . . . evoked ancient Rome the way fashion evokes costumes of the past. Fashion has a flair for the topical, no matter where it stirs in the thickets of long ago; it is a tiger's leap into the past.[34]

The tiger's leap was made and the ghosts of the 1789 revolution were conjured up again over a hundred years later in John Galliano's 1984 debut on a London college catwalk that was influenced by a production of Danton at the National Theatre in London where

Galliano worked as a dresser (fig. 17). Benjamin wrote that 'the true dialectical theatre of fashion' was due to its ability to refabricate the very old as the most up to the minute.[35] At the same time as it looks forward, fashion also looks backwards. Similarly, Galliano's 1990s modern siren is a ghost that reveals a trace of nineteenth-century modernity. In this way, although his designs of the late 1990s were, on the face of it, nostalgic and escapist fantasy, they nevertheless signalled 'a flair for the topical', making a 'tiger's leap into the past'. Ulrich Lehmann has used Benjamin's phrase *tigersprung* to describe the way that fashion can double back on itself. He draws on Proust's and Benjamin's formulation of true memory as 'involuntary' to argue that 'in fashion, quotation is sartorial remembrance' and that fashion activates the past in the present by rewriting its own themes and motifs through historical quotation.[36] In Proust's *mémoire involontaire* chance encounters with objects bring back experiences which would otherwise have remained dormant or forgotten.[37] Lehmann discusses how the early twentieth-century century designs of Jeanne Paquin evoked the French revolutionary period at the end of the eighteenth.[38] In the 1990s Paquin's period furnished the imagery for Galliano's vamps, sirens and seductresses that brought *belle époque* opulence into the present.

17 John Galliano, graduation collection show. Central Saint Martins College of Art and Design, London, 1984. Photograph Niall McInerney, courtesy John Galliano

Suffering from Reminiscences

The designs for Dior by Galliano can be compared with the luxurious displays of the nineteenth-century department store and world fair, but the changes in sensibilities produced as a result of eighteenth- and nineteenth-century industrialisation were not necessarily like those produced in the late twentieth century by the information revolution. Rather, the conditions of post-industrial modernity today are haunted by those of industrial modernity and this is made visible when fashion designers dip into the past for their motifs and themes. If, as Lynda Nead has argued, modernity is 'a set of historical discourses and processes that are profoundly and necessarily caught up with the construction of the past', this is nowhere clearer than in the operations of Western fashion.[39] In particular this can be traced via two of Benjamin's key tropes of nineteenth-century Parisian commodity culture that are evoked in the designs of Galliano and Martin Margiela respectively: the woman of fashion and the ragpicker.

Whereas Galliano produced a range of designs for Dior that remained firmly in the couture house's tradition of exquisite workmanship and luxury fabrics, emphasising techniques such as beading, embroidery and feather work, the equally prestigious Paris-based Belgian designer Martin Margiela, who designed for a very different market, produced, in the same period, a range of designs that were the complete opposite. Instead of fetishising craftwork and luxury, Margiela appeared to deconstruct couture techniques scientifically and to draw instead on debased and abject clothing that he cut up and reassembled in new formations.[40] Old army socks were partially unpicked and resewn to make jumpers, the heel sections ensuring a snug fit over bust and elbows; 'retro' dresses from the 1950s

35 Ibid: 64.

36 Lehmann, *Tigersprung*. Lehmann changes 'fashion has a flair for the topical' to 'fashion has the scent of the modern', and 'the thickets of long ago' becomes 'the thickets of what has been': xvii.

37 See Esther Leslie, 'Souvenirs and Forgetting: Walter Benjamin's Memory-work' in M. Kwint, C. Breward, and J. Aynsley (eds), *Material Memories: Design and Evocation*, Berg, Oxford and New York, 1999: 116–17.

38 Lehmann, *Tigersprung*: 251–6.

39 Nead, *Victorian Babylon*: 7.

40 Caroline Evans, 'Martin Margiela: The Golden Dustman', *Fashion Theory*, vol. 2, issue 1, March 1998: 73–94.

18   Martin Margiela, Autumn–Winter 1997–8.
Photograph Marina Faust, courtesy La Maison
Martin Margiela

19   Martin Margiela, Autumn–Winter 1997–8.
Photograph Marina Faust, courtesy La Maison
Martin Margiela

were cut up and remade into new ones; coarse linen was cut into a bodice that resembled a tailor's dummy (fig. 18); and unrippable industrial paper was made up into a wearable man's jacket cut to resemble a flat paper pattern (fig. 19).

In 1997 Margiela produced an entire exhibition for a museum of art where moulds and bacteria were 'grown' on his clothes (figs 20 and 21). Their tracery of mould and decay recalled the figure of the ragpicker who so fascinated Baudelaire and Benjamin, just as Galliano's designs recall the woman of fashion about whom both Baudelaire and Benjamin were rather more ambivalent. In the nineteenth century the ragpicker scavenged cloth for recycling, recuperating cultural detritus cast aside by capitalist societies. Ingrid Loschek has observed that, when he destroyed his clothes with mould and bacteria, Margiela 'compared the natural cycle of creation and decay to the consumer cycle of buying and discarding.'[41] Although Margiela used the techniques of the avant-garde, his practice was rooted firmly in commerce. His patinated textiles illuminated the parallels which underwrite the free-market economy of fashion, both past and present: between élite fashion and ragpicking, luxury and poverty, excess and deprivation. Contemporary fashion is framed, symbolically, by these two nineteenth-century emblems of the capitalist process to which it obsessively returns: the woman of fashion and the ragpicker, thesis and antithesis, captured eloquently

41   Ingrid Loschek, 'The Deconstructionists', in Gerda Buxbaum (ed.) *Icons of Fashion: The Twentieth Century*, Prestel, Munich, London and New York, 1999: 146.

in the early twentieth-century photographs of Henri Lartigue and Eugène Atget (figs 22 and 23). The status of the woman of fashion was as exalted as that of the ragpicker was debased, but both were equally locked into a dialectical fashion system by nineteenth-century *laissez faire* economic policies, just as Galliano and Margiela were nearly a century later. For Margiela's images of melancholy dereliction are the reverse of capitalist excess, just as the nineteenth-century ragpicker formed an eloquent counterpoint to the woman of fashion: 'Another modernity, dark but not degraded, slipped into view, a modernity that shadowed all that gaiety on the boulevard, picking up its trash; the shadow knew, it looked, it smiled, and then withdrew.'[42] Whereas Galliano's opulent *fin de siècle* evocations evoke the vigour and liveliness of consumer capitalism, Margiela's lifeless mannequins and mouldy clothes signal that there is a dark and deathly side to capitalist modernity as well. These are the twin ghosts of the past that today's designers call up – Galliano in his evocations of *fin-de-siècle* luxury and excess, Margiela in the mouldy tatters of his more experimental practice.

20 Martin Margiela, installation view of the exhibition '9/4/1615', Museum Boijmans Van Beuningen, Rotterdam, 6 June–17 August 1997. Photograph Caroline Evans

Galliano and Margiela both practise a form of 'cultural poetics', evoked through visions of either capitalist excess or melancholy dereliction, the two opposing poles of nineteenth-century *laissez faire* economic policies, both locked equally into the fashion system. This historical relay is an index not merely of sensibilities but also, and equally, of how such sensibilities are anchored in specific moments of capitalist production and consumption, and of technological change. As I have suggested, this is due in part to the sense of instability produced in a period of rapid change that leads it back to comparable images of instability in the past. The historicism of 1990s fashion imagery, which continually revisited the past only to reformulate it in the present, was parallelled by rapid changes in social and economic life at the end of the century. Perhaps the return to the commodity culture of the past helped to make sense of the present when both the commodity form and its appeal to consumer desire were being so rapidly restructured. In this context, the compulsive return to historical imagery by a range of designers in the 1990s, both in the mass market and the designer spectrum, suggests factors beyond merely picturing or reflecting such change; they may equally, and also, be a way of accommodating and understanding its potentially unsettling nature, and as such operate a kind of 'return of the repressed' in which fashion becomes a symptom to articulate cultural trauma.

21 Martin Margiela, installation view of the exhibition '9/4/1615', Museum Boijmans Van Beuningen, Rotterdam, 6 June–17 August 1997. Photograph Caroline Evans

While cultural trauma may be argued to be inherent in modern experience at the end of a century marked by world war, totalitarianism, terrorism and environmental crisis (all invoked in a certain millenarian trend in cultural commentary and historical interpretation[43]), it may equally be attributed to the more banal but no less bruising consequence of rapidly accelerated consumption in the West, where fashion in particular articulates the ambivalent nature of consumer capitalism. The culture is caught up in an oscillation between novelty and decay as cycles of consumption consign everything belonging to 'yesterday' to the scrap heap.[44] This is not in itself new, and the nineteenth-century 'version' is invoked in Galliano's designs at the end of the twentieth; however, increasing affluence and new, infinitely faster communications systems have accelerated the process of con-

42 Molly Nesbitt, *Atget's Seven Albums*, Yale University Press, New Haven and London, 1992: 175.

43 Ranging from e.g. the quotation from J. G. Ballard at the beginning of this chapter to Eric Hobsbawm's history of the twentieth century, *Age of Extremes: The Short Twentieth Century 1914–1991*, Michael Joseph, London, 1994.

44 I am grateful to Elizabeth Wilson for her pithy summaries of my earlier text, some of which have been incorporated here.

22 Jacques-Henri Lartigue, avenue des Acacias, 1911. Photograph, © Ministère de la Culture-France/AAJHL

sumption to such an extent that now, more than ever, everything new and beautiful seems to arrive already haunted by its own demise. Fashion is the paradigm of this process and therefore reveals and comments on a 'crisis' of Western culture at the millennium which is partly a crisis of affluence. In particular, it is the consequence of comfort and security experienced in the West, compared to populations in other parts of the world, to want to feast our eyes in horrified fascination on images of despair, for 'industrial societies turn their citizens into image-junkies', as Susan Sontag argued in her book on photography.[45]

Whereas early twentieth-century 'modernism' thought it could produce a brave new world, the post-modern period was marked, rather, by the sense of an ending;[46] this shift was reflected in the 'cultural poetics' of contemporary designers whose evocations of history and the passage of time suggested a sense of crisis or trauma in the present. The compulsive repetition of their turns and returns to history closely mimicked the structure of trauma itself. After the First World War, in which many soldiers suffered from shell shock, Sigmund Freud described the repetition compulsion of trauma, in which, for example, the subject might vividly relive the traumatic incident in recurring dreams night after night as a way of dominating it.[47] Thus, as Freud wrote, 'hysterics suffer mainly from reminiscences'.[48] Freud's analyses of trauma relate to individual pathologies, rather than to the wider notion of cultural trauma that characterised much cultural production by the end of the century, but his aphorism can be extended from the arena of individual pathology to culture and society. By the end of the twentieth century, like Freud's hysterics at its start, much of the most interesting experimental fashion design seemed to suffer mainly from reminiscences. Its ruminations on the past, and its fragmented and episodic imagery, like a hysterical symptom, seemed able to put a finger on contemporary concerns in ways that more coherent narratives could not achieve. The haunting of contemporary fashion

45 Susan Sontag, *On Photography*, Penguin, Harmondsworth, 1977: 24.

46 E.g., Frank Kermode, *Sense of an Ending*. Jean Baudrillard, *The Illusion of the End*, trans. Chris Turner, Polity Press, Cambridge, 1994.

47 Sigmund Freud, 'Beyond the Pleasure Principle', [1920], in *Works: The Standard Edition of the Complete Psychological Works of Sigmund Freud*, trans. under the general editorship of James Strachey, vol. XVIII, Hogarth Press, London, 1955: 7.

48 Sigmund Freud, with Josef Breuer, *Studies on Hysteria*, SE, vol. II, Hogarth Press, London 1955 [1893–5]: 7.

design by images from the past can thus be understood as a kind of return of the repressed, in which shards of history work their way to the surface in new formations and are put to work as contemporary emblems.

two   haunting

Shadows

In December 1997 German *Vogue* featured a series of photographs by Inez Van Lamsweerde and Vinoodh Matadin of Viktor & Rolf's designs in which the model, 'Missy', her face and hands covered in black make-up, posed in ghostly black on a black ground (figs 25 and 26). Like a shadow that had lost its body, the model's image recalled Marx's description of the revolution of 1848 in Paris: 'if any section of history has been painted grey on grey, it is this. Men and events appear as inverted Schlemihls, as shadows that have lost their bodies.'[1] In the story by Chamisso, Peter Schlemihl sells his shadow to the devil in exchange for a magic purse, with the consequence that, among other things, he can no longer leave the shade for the sunshine.[2] In the *Vogue* photographs Viktor & Rolf's ghostly model appeared as an inverted Schlemihl who had cut herself off from the world of embodied corporeality and who existed solely as a shadow.

In spring 2001 the designers reprised this idea and made their photographic vision real on the catwalk, by sending out the models in their Autumn–Winter 2001–2 ready-to-wear collection dressed entirely in black into a darkened salon on a plain white catwalk, their hands and faces painted as black as their clothes. At the end of the show the two designers took their bow, also silhouetted in black. When, at the finale, all the models paraded back together like an army of disembodied shadows (fig. 24), the effect was to transform the usually vibrant and colourful fashion show into a simulacrum of black and white film, recalling Maxim Gorky's description from 1896 of seeing for the first time two films by the Lumière brothers:

> Last night I was in the Kingdom of Shadows. If only you knew how strange it is to be there. It is a world without sound, without colour. Everything there – the earth, the trees, the people, the water and the air – is dipped in monotonous grey. Grey rays of sun across the grey sky, grey eyes in grey faces, and the leaves of the trees are ashen grey. It is no life but its shadow, it is not motion but its soundless spectre.[3]

Gorky's text ascribed a deathly quality to a medium that we often conceive of as dynamic, lively and modern, just as Viktor & Rolf's early collections pointed to a darker, more mysterious side of fashion than its more familiar upbeat and frenetic aspect. Their third couture collection, Spring–Summer 1999, shown in January of that year, was made entirely in black and white silk gazar (figs 27–9). It was shown first in black light that picked out only the white elements of the clothes, such as a ruff, a frill or a trailing ribbon. Of this collection Rolf Snoeren said 'we had the feeling things were working out. We translated that personal feeling of victory into the black and white show. The first part was shown in black light, the second in white light, as if we had conquered our demons and were in the spotlight'.[4] In the black light the seams and lapels of a trouser suit edged in white appeared as a disembodied fashion sketch; a hugely ruffled white shirt glided above the ground; a skeleton with three-dimensional tubular bones and hips of white bows moved down the catwalk. When the entire line-up appeared again in normal light the collection

24 (*facing page*) Viktor & Rolf, Autumn–Winter 2001–2. Photograph Roberto Tecchio, courtesy Judith Clark Costume

25 and 26 (*following pages*) Inez van Lamsweerde and Vinoodh Matadin, Missy, styling by Viktor & Rolf, *German Vogue* 1997. Photographs courtesy Viktor & Rolf

1 Karl Marx, *The Eighteenth Brumaire of Louis Bonaparte*, trans. from the German, Progress Publishers, Moscow, 3rd rev. ed. 1954 [2nd rev. ed. 1869]: 35.
2 Adalbert von Chamisso, *The Wonderful Story of Peter Schlemihl*, trans. Leopold von Loewenstein-Wertheim, John Calder, London, 1957 [1813].
3 Maxim Gorky quoted in Noël Burch, *Life to Those Shadows*, trans. Ben Brewster, British Film Institite, London, 1990: 23.
4 Rolf Snoeren quoted by Amy Spindler in *Viktor & Rolf Haute Couture Book*, texts by Amy Spindler and Didier Grumbach, Groninger Museum, Gröningen, 2000: 10.

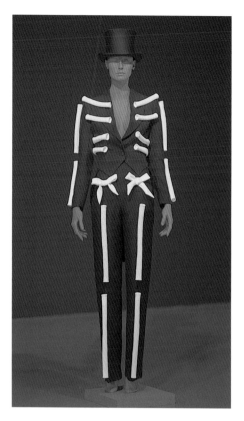
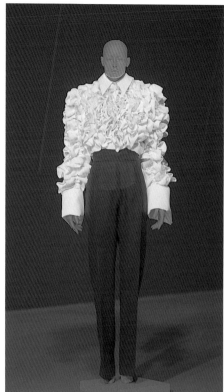

27–9   Viktor & Rolf, Spring–Summer 1999.
Photograph F. Dumoulin/Java, courtesy Viktor &
Rolf

30 (*facing page*)   Hussein Chalayan, Between,
Spring–Summer 1998. Photograph Roberto
Tecchio, courtesy Judith Clark Costume

5   Jacques Derrida, *Specters of Marx: The State
of Debt, the Work of Mourning, and the New
International*, trans. Peggy Kamuf, Routledge, New
York and London, 1994: 119.

6   Ibid: 37, 45 and 104.

7   For a discussion of the way the fashion
commodity mutated in the 1990s see Caroline Evans,
'Yesterday's Emblems and Tomorrow's Commodities:
The Return of the Repressed in Fashion Imagery
Today', in Stella Bruzzi and Pamela Church Gibson
(eds), *Fashion Cultures: Theories, Explorations and
Analysis*, Routlege, London and New York, 2000:
96–7.

was revealed as a series of variations on the theme of the black tuxedo. The ruffled blouse, called 'Nothing', was worn above black trousers; the skeleton 'bones' were stitched onto a black dress-coat called 'Dead'; and a plain white trouser suit called 'No' turned out to be outlined by a large black ruffle projecting from its side seams.

The ghostly presentation was also spectral in terms of manufacturing and selling: the clothes were not intended to go into production but were made as a series of ideas. Literally a vision on the catwalk, they also embodied the designers' vision, and suggested the other meaning of the term vision: a ghost, shade or apparition. This black and white collection was an inventory of the shapes that Viktor & Rolf had been working on since the start of their career, and they intended it to be their last spectral collection before they launched themselves in the real world of embodied fashion and commerce, making clothes to go into production to be sold in the shops.

'Every age has its scenography – we have our ghosts', wrote Derrida, with reference to the 'fantastic panoply' of ghostly metaphors in Marx's writing.[5] On the catwalks of the twenty-first century, and at the end of the twentieth, our ghosts were made vivid and incarnate in the concept of the showpiece. Showpieces function as a marketing tool; they are never intended to go into production and are of no interest to the buyers; but they will get the press and magazine coverage that the designer needs to 'brand' her or his label, perhaps to attract a backer or job offer. They operate as a showcase for the designer's mind, and by differentiating the showing and the selling collections designers can run a business and also have their conceptual pieces included in gallery exhibitions. This is the function of the pieces that do not go into production, such as the wooden 'pods' and translucent glass 'eggs' that covered the models' faces in Hussein Chalayan's Between collection of 1998 (fig. 30).

There are many ways in which fashion can be both spectral and commercial at the same time; indeed, Derrida has argued that the ghost and money are inseparable in capitalist logic, and that 'haunting belongs to the structure of every hegemony'.[6] In 2001 the British-based designer Hamish Morrow took the commercial decision to show only during his first few seasons and not to take orders or manufacture for sale until he had built a reputation for himself. He duly showed meticulously executed and presented pieces such as his all-white collection in which the models walked though a shallow tank of violet ink, tingeing the base of the garments (fig. 33). Viktor & Rolf's black and white collection made up entirely of showpieces was an uncompromising version of the type of marketing strategy whereby every catwalk collection contains one or more highly theatrical and unwearable piece that will make a spectacular photograph or museum piece. After the show, such pieces live on in the images that mark a designer's progress, and may also be lent for museum exhibitions. Alexander McQueen's dress made of two thousand glass microscope slides, each one hand-drilled and hand-painted red to represent the blood that lies beneath the skin, then stitched by hand onto an elongated bodice above a skirt constructed of tiered red ostrich feathers over a crinoline (fig. 31), took six weeks to make and appeared on the catwalk for less than two minutes. The dress was later shown in the Victoria & Albert Museum's 'Radical Fashion' exhibition in London in 2001. Only one version of the dress was ever worn by a woman after the fashion show and she transformed it through its interaction with her own body, making it into a performance piece: the musician Björk wore it on stage in a concert where, as she danced, the tinkling of the glass plates against each other was amplified and incorporated into the music, turning the dress itself into a percussion instrument.

Thus the showpiece exemplifies the way in which much contemporary fashion enters the realm of the commodity and circulates obliquely, not always as an embodied practice but sometimes as an image, an idea or a conceptual piece.[7] It is in this sense too that the showpiece is ghostly, or spectral. Worn once for just a few seconds by the model on the catwalk, after its disappearance the memory of it can fade slowly like a retinal image after the real object has gone. Only the photographs that recorded its brief appearance testify that it was really there. In Antonio Berardi's Autumn–Winter 1997–8 Voodoo collection, shown in London's Roundhouse, models with dishevelled hair and dirty faces danced round a fire to the accompaniment of Techno music and live African drumming (fig. 32). One in particular acted 'spooked' – nervy but trance-like. The show's accessories included celestial candleholders with burning candles shaped into a crown worn on the head, with shells and feathers plaited into long braids. But, as in many fashion shows, the dramatic showpieces which animated the spectacle were never put into production and the collection which appeared in the shops was less spectacular but more wearable.

31 (page 48) Alexander McQueen, Voss,
Spring–Summer 2001. Photograph
Chris Moore, courtesy Alexander McQueen

32 (previous page) Antonio Berardi, Voodoo,
Autumn–Winter 1997–8. Photograph Niall
McInerney

33 Hamish Morrow, Spring–Summer 2002.
Photograph Chris Moore

8 Martin Jay, *Downcast Eyes: The Denigration
of Vision in Twentieth-Century French Thought*,
University of California Press, Berkeley and Los
Angeles, 1993: 425. Guy Debord, *Society of the
Spectacle*, trans. Donald Nicholson-Smith, Zone
Books, London, 1994 [1967]: para. 2.
9 Hal Foster, *The Return of the Real: The
Avant Garde at the End of the Century*, MIT Press,
Cambridge, Mass., and London, 1996: 83.
10 Derrida, *Specters of Marx*: 11.
11 Ibid: 141.
12 Ibid: 148.
13 Jean-Michel Rabaté, *The Ghosts of Modernity*,
University Press of Florida, Gainsville, 1996: xvi.

The word spectacle designates a sight or show; the spectre, a ghost or vision. Etymologically they have the same root, both coming from *specere*, the Latin verb 'to see'. Martin Jay defines the society of the spectacle as 'the deathgrip of desiccated images' for, according to Guy Debord, 'the spectacle in general, as the concrete inversion of life, is the autonomous movement of the non-living'.[8] In Berardi's show, the spectacle of the undead was raised as a purely hollow one, gorgeous images of the undead which, appropriately, did not manifest themselves as 'real' clothes on the rails of the shops. Instead, the spectacle seduces us with 'hyper-reality', that is, with the ravishing and perfect images of the fashion show. Hal Foster argues that 'we become locked in its logic because spectacle both effects the loss of the real and provides us with the fetishistic images necessary to assuage or deny this loss.'[9] Yet 'the real' is not irretrievably lost in such representations, only repressed. As the repressed, it returned in contemporary fashion design when designers intuitively re-interpreted past images of instability in the present. When they peopled their catwalk narratives with ghosts, they evoked the ghosts of modernity – the historical origins of the show in the commodity culture of the late nineteenth century.

Ghosts

'A specter is always a revenant. It begins by coming back', wrote Derrida.[10] It is a spirit that returns from somewhere else, 'a nothing that takes on a body'.[11] But where do these embodied ghosts come from and why are they haunting us? For Derrida, they are the spirit of capitalist striving, the spectre is 'the becoming-fetish of the commodity' described by Marx.[12] And if ghosts and money are inseparable, the world of fashion is a place of ghosts, figures from the past who reconvene in the present through the voracious 'tiger's leap' of fashion. The revenant, in Galliano's collections for Dior, was the commodity culture of an earlier period. From 1997, when Galliano had the backing of a major couture house, he developed a range of historically themed shows, both for his own collections and for Dior, in which more and more he turned back to the image of the past to evoke the vampish women and luxurious consumption of an earlier age. His opulent and theatrical fashion shows of the 1990s sparked against the images of the commodity from the second half of the nineteenth century, whether the seductions of advertising or the fantasy displays, rides and optical illusions of the Parisian department store and world fair. Piling up cultural references like nineteenth-century goods on display, Galliano evoked Paris's reputation as a city of luxury goods in the luxury of his contemporary designs.

The commodity and its history haunt Galliano's shows like a ghost. But the ghost is also a symptom. In *The Ghosts of Modernity* Jean-Michel Rabaté has argued that modernism is haunted by its own ghosts, spectres of history which return to interrogate it: 'what returns is, in a classically Freudian fashion, what has not been processed, accommodated, incorporated into the self by mourning: the shadow of the lost object is still being projected onto the subject.'[13] For Rabaté, the ghosts that haunted the twentieth century were nothing to do with its dark history, as they were for Derrida, who linked ghosts to the trauma and mourning that ensued from the twentieth-century crisis in epistemological certainty, the rise of totalitarianism, two world wars and the collapse of the Soviet Union. In Rabaté's view, the ghosts that haunted modernity came out of modernist ideology and aesthetics; specifically, the ghosts of modernity were the ghosts of history that early modernism, with its utopian belief in progress and the future, denied. Consequently, modernism is haunted by its own past, by spectres of history which come back like a Freudian return of the repressed. He argued that modernity as a philosophical discourse tried to erase history because it wanted to be radically new, but that no movement intent on abolishing the past can avoid the return of a particular historical repressed.

Thus Galliano's historical fusions are a form of historical return of the repressed in which the ghosts of nineteenth-century Parisian consumption return as images, as do other figures of fact and fiction from later twentieth-century culture, for example where his designs looked to Madeleine Vionnet's bias-cutting from the 1920s and 30s, to Hollywood or to late 1980s club culture and the Smiley logo, as well as to native American motifs and to ancient Egypt. Other designers too revealed their own concerns in the cultural references they reprised. Americans such as Donna Karan, Calvin Klein and Ralph Lauren drew on a different set of ghosts of modernity, specifically American mid-twentieth-century ideas and ideals. The influence of sportswear and minimalism in this period was an evocation of the ghosts of streamlined modernist aesthetics.[14]

In this way, the spectacular displays of many different forms of late twentieth-century fashion were haunted by earlier visions. As noted earlier the etymology of the terms spectacle and spectre is the same – a vision. And the spectre returns to haunt the spectacle through the very forms that seek to deny it, the visual displays of consumer culture. Christian Dior's Autumn–Winter 2000–1 haute couture collection spun a fantastical nar-rative based on an imaginary correspondence on fetishism between Freud and Jung, playing out the perverse secrets of an Edwardian family in pictures on the catwalk (fig. 34). Paralleling the psychoanalytic process in which repressed desires, drives and fears come to light as the patient goes back in time to recover lost memories, the show reversed the usual protocol of ending with a bride by starting with a conventional bride and groom before going on to run through a series of sexual fantasies. The opulent, bejewelled, cast list included a number of older women, many of them ex-models, such as Catherine Bailey, Marisa Berenson, Benedetta Barzini and Carmen dell'Orifice. At the beginning the parade of wedding 'guests' looked like extras from the Ascot scene in *My Fair Lady*, the 1964 film with costumes by Cecil Beaton (figs 34c–f), but they became progressively odder and more dysfunctional as the Edwardian silhouettes were interrupted by asymmetrical cuts (fig. 34g) and overtaken by garish and clownish make-up. For all the opulent sexuality on display, hints of the asylum crept in. The wedding guests rapidly gave way to a series of fantasy figures culled as much from childish nightmares as from the sexual fantasies of supposedly straight-laced bourgeois Vienna. They included a marching, female legionnaire, Sophie Dahl as an inexplicably bejewelled French maid (fig. 34h), a nineteenth-century amazon

34 (*following pages*)   John Galliano for Christian Dior, Haute Couture, Autumn–Winter 2000–1. Photographs Rindoff/Garcia, courtesy Christian Dior

14   I am grateful to Rebecca Arnold for pointing this out. See too Rebecca Arnold 'Luxury and Restraint: Minimalism in 1990s' Fashion', in Nicola White and Ian Griffiths, *The Fashion Business: Theory, Practice, Image*, Berg, Oxford and New York, 2000: 167–81.

a

b

c

d

e

f

g

h

i

j

k

l

m

n

o

p

q

r

in ruched grey leather, thigh-high gaiters and skew-whiff lipstick (fig. 34j), and an Edwardian goose-stepping drag king (fig. 34k). Like the contents of the toy cupboard come horribly to life, there were a Roman centurion, a Japanese wizard carrying a cross on her back, an eighteenth-century porcelain doll (fig. 34l) and a figure from the Mexican Day of the Dead in a Posada hat (fig. 34m).

The Edwardian references were inter cut by later twentieth-century figures that moved beyond the world of childhood dreams to adult sexual fantasy: a white leather and rubber-clad dominatrix nurse clutching a huge syringe; a *Night Porter* model in a blue uniform; a model with a noose round her neck; a nun with her wrists tied by her rosary beads (fig. 34q); a manacled model in a black cardinal's hat and a swagger coat whose arms were chained together behind her back; an equestrienne wearing a carriage-horse's bridle, a studded strap covering her mouth; and an Edwardian beauty in a red satin topper led in on a leash by a black and white Leigh Bowery lookalike (fig. 34r). At the end of the Fellini-esque show, the Lesage-embroidered cleric who had opened the show returned for the traditional finale, followed by a procession of the characters who had preceded him. Like the work of psychoanalysis which recalls the ghosts of the past in order to exorcise them in the present, the finale piled up memories out of sequence, bringing the past into the present.

The processes of psychoanalysis, which uncovers repressed materials, resemble those of archaeology, digging up material that has long remained buried, excavating remnants from the past and making sense of them in the light of the present. In the same way, archaeological fragments of previous historical moments work their way to the surface of contemporary fashion. The return of the ghosts of modernity described by Rabaté is paralleled by the archaeology of the psychoanalytic process, in which lost memory is recovered. The Dior show started with an imaginary letter from Freud to Jung, printed in gold on red card for the audience. It read: 'recently I glimpsed an explanation for the case of fetishism. So far it concerns only clothes, but it is probably universal.'[15] In this tongue-in-cheek parody of Freud's many letters to his associates and colleagues, Galliano disguised the way in which the lost memory of commodity fetishism, rather than sexual fetishism, was evoked in the spectacular catwalk shows of the 1990s. Indeed, in these shows commodity fetishism masqueraded as sexual fetishism – but it is the commodity, which seduces, not the person. The reference to clothing fetishism was played out on the Dior catwalk as sexual 'perversion', a fiction that masked the real form of fetishism that was paraded in this collection, that of the commodity.[16]

Future Imperfect

Whereas Galliano's late 1990s fashion shows reified and celebrated spectacular fashion, the British designer Shelley Fox signalled that fashion could have a darker and more melancholic inflection. Galliano produced several collections a year, both in his own

15   Christian Dior show programme, Haute Couture, Autumn–Winter 2000–1.

16   For a discussion of both commodity and sexual fetishism see Lorraine Gamman, and Merja Makinen, *Female Fetishism: A New Look*, Lawrence & Wishart, London, 1994: ch. 1, 'Three types of fetishism, a question of definition', 14–51. Both commodity and sexual fetishism involve the denial or disavowal of human feelings and their displacement onto an inanimate object. In much theoretical writing these types of fetishism are conflated, and this is not simply the fault of writers but due also to the fact that they are not in reality such discrete categories, particularly when they relate to women, as Gamman and Makinen point out. They argue that the image of a sexualised woman is better described as 'consumer fetishism of the erotic': 182.

name and as principal designer for Dior, moving between Paris and London, while Fox
worked in London on an entirely different scale, in a different context and for a different
audience. She was therefore able to play polemically with ideas in the way that artists can;
the small scale and relative poverty of her production limited her but also freed her to
produce ideas-led fashion that appealed to a discrete and limited market.

Fox's collection Number 8 for Spring–Summer 2000 was based on Morse code. Inspired
by its recent abolition, Fox printed and embossed Morse on fabrics as a decorative pattern
(fig. 35). The Morse patterns spelt out a sentence from Nietzsche's 'Human, All Too

Human': 'he who considers more deeply knows that, whatever his acts and judgements may be, he is always wrong'.[17] 'It was the way we were feeling about things', she said, 'that whatever you do, it's wrong.'[18] The sombre theme was also mirrored in the presentation and styling of the show. Opening in darkness, a circle of white light was projected onto the dark wall. In its centre, a pair of hands silhouetted against the light signed Nietzsche's words in deaf and dumb language. The models began to come on and the show started with ambient electronic music that gradually formed itself into the tap tap tap of Morse code that spelt out the same inexorable words. The models wore skirts, dresses and tops patterned with the same despairing message in Morse code.

Very different from Galliano's reification and celebration of fashion itself, Fox's collection suggested a disconsolate sense of alienation and loss, at the heart of the lively and bustling fashion industry. In all fashionable consumption, the new is overlaid on the ruin of the unfashionable. But in the work of a designer like Shelley Fox, where the present can fold back on the past, and decay can be the other of progress, then fashion celebrates nihilism, making it into an aesthetic. Fox achieved this not only literally, as in her use of Morse code for an aphorism by Nietzsche, but also structurally, as when her next collection looped back in time to a vision of hopelessness to come. Her Autumn–Winter 2000–1 show featured burnt sequins and felt frills and was styled with 1940s vintage handbags and shoes, introducing a historical reference into her designs for the first time (fig. 36). It had a soundtrack of children's voices and birdsong mixed with Elvis Presley's 'Are you lonesome tonight?' During this period, she had looked at Roman Vishniac's photographs documenting life in the Warsaw ghetto in the last months before its destruction and the annihilation of its occupants in the Second World War. These pictures of the daily life of its inhabitants are imbued with a tragic foreknowledge that creates what Roland Barthes called a 'vertigo of time defeated.'[19] Fox also listened to stories from her mother and grandmother to remind her that the 1930s and 40s were not as long ago as photographs made them seem. Such imagery brought the instability of the past into the present to demonstrate how fashion too can be 'a vertigo of time defeated'. The labyrinth brings together dizzyingly disconcerting moments of historical loss and trauma to recreate them on a fashion stage in 1990s London, as in Fox's solemn presentation of huge, peat-coloured woollen frills and scorched sequins.

Shelley Fox's work presented yet another form of haunting, a present haunted by the image of ruin in the future. Lynda Nead has argued that the urban modernity of nineteenth-century London was 'not only haunted by the ruins of its past, but also possessed by dystopic visions of its future . . . ruin is the vision of the contradictory impulses of modernity'.[20] Nead describes archaeological remains as a spatial metaphor for ruins, and in Fox's fashion narratives ruination becomes a way of excavating loss in the present through a series of mournful returns to the past. Fox based her earliest collections from 1996 on labour-intensive hand-felting, scarring and scorching her fabrics, either in a heat press or by using a blow torch on them, replicating abject and destroyed textiles to produce an aesthetic of melancholy. The sad patina of her shrunken woollens and wrecked textiles

17 Friedrich Nietzsche, *A Nietzsche Reader*, selected, trans. and with an intro. by R. J. Hollindale, Penguin, Harmondsworth, 1997: 198.

18 Shelley Fox, May 2000.

19 Roland Barthes, *Camera Lucida: Reflections on Photography*, trans. Richard Howard, Vintage, London, 1993 [1980]: 97. Looking at old photographs, Barthes realised that their subjects, so lively in the picture, were going to die, 'they are already dead', and this is the 'vertigo of time defeated' of all photographs.

20 Lynda Nead, *Victorian Babylon: People, Streets and Images in Nineteenth-Century London*, Yale University Press, New Haven and London, 2000: 212 and 214.

evoked a doleful past through which the ghosts of industrial modernity could haunt the present moment of post-industrial modernity. Through her use of craft techniques in a post-industrial age she muddled time in ways that revealed these processes. Fredric Jameson has argued that alienation and reification are a consequence of this process of temporal 'muddling'. He has analysed Philip K. Dick's *The Time is Out of Joint* (a novel that takes its title from Shakespeare's *Hamlet)* as an example of how science fiction permits the layering of fears and fantasies about the present between nostalgic evocations of the past in the present, and an imagined future: the 'trope of the future anterior' is 'the estrangement and renewal as history of our own . . . present . . . by way of the apprehension of that present as the past of a specific future.'[21]

In his Geotropics collection, Hussein Chalayan created a micro-geography of the body in a computer animation that morphed into each other many types of national costumes from various dates and cultures along the Silk Road, plotting changes in distance and time. From the morph Chalayan drew and then designed a series of dresses with white pleats in different stages, as if to make time material in dresses (fig. 37). In his next collection, Echoform, Chalayan, preoccupied with the themes of memory and echo, produced a range of near-identical denim dresses that he imagined as imbued with the memory of other garments (fig. 38). Each had a section omitted, as if only part remembered, like a ghostly dress destroyed by its double, so that each dress bore the traces of an earlier one.

For Medea, Chalayan imagined garments that represented wishes or curses that had become reality via imaginary voodoo dolls. However, unlike the more literal voodoo references in Berardi's show (see fig. 32), Chalayan's designs were more abstract (fig. 39). He imagined the hexes as alterations to the garments caused by layering, twisting and cutting away sections: shearing off a lapel, cutting away the top fabric to leave only the lining, or leaving buttons askew or zips half open. Some areas of the garments were missing completely to suggest the curse affected only that area; in others, the curses cut away at older, or newer, historical layers, peeling one moment of history back to reveal another, just as an unexpected turn of the labyrinth brings two unconnected periods into proximity. Chalayan subsequently said:

> The garment is a ghost of all the multiple lives it may have had. Nothing is shiny and new; everything has a history . . . A '60s dress gets cut away to reveal its past as a medieval dress. A Victorian corset gets cut away to reveal a modern jersey vest. A '30s dress gets cut away to reveal its past as an Edwardian dress. The design is a wish or a curse that casts the garment and its wearer into a time warp through historical periods, like a sudden tumble through the sediment of an archaeological dig.[22]

The resulting shredded and deconstructed garments contained versions of Chalayan's earlier collections that looked as if they had been battered and destroyed by the passage of time. Chalayan raided his own archive to reproduce pieces from past seasons in new combinations, fabrics and colours that were then deconstructed, so a khaki cotton biker dress reworked his fluted black cotton and tulle dress from Autumn–Winter 2000–1. Chalayan

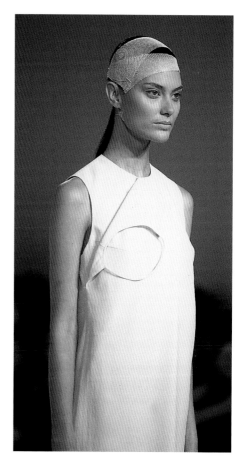

37 Hussein Chalayan, Geotropics, Spring–Summer 1999. Photograph Chris Moore, courtesy Hussein Chalayan

38 (*following pages*) Hussein Chalayan, Echoform, memory dress, Autumn–Winter 1999–2000. Photographs courtesy Marcus Tomlinson

21 Jameson, *Postmodernism, or the Cultural Logic of late Capitalism*, Verso, London and New York, 1991: 285.
22 Hussein Chalayan, lecture at Wexner Center for the Arts, Ohio, 25 April 2002.

39 Hussein Chalayan, Medea,
Spring–Summer 2002. Photograph
Chris Moore, courtesy Hussein
Chalayan

himself identified the design process as archaeological but, rather than simply exhuming items from the past, he wanted to give them a new life in the future.

I wanted it to be like a document and for each garment to have a life of its own. I felt that the way to do that was to create a mini-history with the garments. It was like an archaeological dig in a way, but of our own repertoire as well as of references that are more obviously historical, like the Edwardian top of a 1960s dress. After layering it all up, we cut it away, which, in itself, I think, creates some kind of life.[23]

The connection between the historical trace and trauma in Medea was made explicit by the American curator Jeff Kipnis, who included Chalayan's designs in the exhibition of contemporary design and its impact on everyday life that he curated at the Wexner Centre for the Arts in Ohio where Chalayan held a residency.[24] In a lengthy interview, Melissa Starker described the interaction:

Kipnis explained that the final mood of the exhibition [had] shifted from rage to trauma. 'There's an idea of trauma that [Chalayan] basically finished for us, it's a completely different sensibility, different colours, a whole sense of distressing of material. It was a shock and an incredible bit of luck that he was taking the collection to the limit of the idea.' By cutting dresses from three past eras into fragments and relayering them in a single piece, Chalayan confronted the fashion world with its own history. It was misinterpreted by many in the press as a response to September 11, Kipnis stated. 'When you look at the thing and you don't know any better – and no-one is obligated to know any better – it looks like someone that just came out of an explosion', he said. 'You don't realise that you're looking at fragments of history. But if you pay a little more attention, you'll easily recognise them.'[25]

Backwards into the Future

In *Specters of Marx* Derrida patterns his chapters with riffs on Hamlet's 'the time is out of joint' to speculate on the 'untimeliness and disadjustment of the contemporary' and to conclude that 'the more the new erupts in the revolutionary crisis, the more the period is in crisis, the more it is 'out of joint', then the more one has to convoke the old, 'borrow' from it. Inheritance from the 'spirits of the past' consists, as always, in 'borrowing'.[26] Yet, he argues, 'It is a proper characteristic of the specter, if there is any, that no-one can be sure if by returning it testifies to a living past or a living future'.[27]

Walter Benjamin used a photographic metaphor to describe how some historical images would only develop in the future: 'The past has left images of itself in literary texts, images comparable to those which are imprinted by light on a photosensitive plate. The future alone possesses developers active enough to scan such surfaces perfectly.'[28] The imagery of fashion today can be construed as the 'developer' of earlier moments of capitalist produc-

23 Chalayan quoted in Susannah Frankel, 'Art and Commerce', *Independent on Sunday*, Review, 10 March 2002: 32.

24 'Mood River: An International Exhibition Examining the Impact of Design on Contemporary Life', 2002, Wexner Center for the Arts, Ohio. Kipnis worked closely with Chalayan, the first fashion designer to hold a residency there.

25 Melissa Starker, 'Chalayan UNDRESSED', *Columbus Alive inc*, 25 April 2002.

26 Derrida, *Specters of Marx*: 99.

27 Ibid.

28 André Mongoland, *Le préromanticisme français*, Grenoble, 1930, cited in Walter Benjamin, *The Arcades Project*, trans. Howard Eiland and Kevin Mclaughlin, Belknap Press of Harvard University Press, Cambridge, Mass., and London, 1999: 482.

40   Viktor & Rolf, Autumn–Winter 2000–1. Photograph F. Dumoulin/Java, courtesy Viktor & Rolf

tion and transition, as for example where Galliano's designs are haunted by the ghosts of earlier forms of commodity capitalism. Its fragments can also articulate a sense of cultural loss or trauma in the present, as in Fox's scorched sequins and heavy felted frills. It can even project itself into the future through ghostly traces that announce its presence before it has arrived: Viktor & Rolf's Autumn–Winter 2000–1 couture collection consisted of only twelve outfits, and was shown in a gallery at the Palais de Chaillot in Paris. The audience sat waiting in anticipation as the gallery filled with fog. Gradually the tinkling of tiny bells was heard in the distance, at first so faint as to be imperceptible. Finally the models entered in a series of dresses embellished with a range of bells: soft, tinkling ones lined the edges of a trailing sleeve; bigger ones hung from a fabric belt; the top half of a black organza dress was entirely covered in tiny bells (fig. 40).

Traditionally haute couture has used expensive hand-sewing such as embroidery. Vikor & Rolf used bells as a kind of aural embroidery: 'we saw all these bells almost like pearls, but they made music.' Rolf Snoeren said 'fashion is something you can hear arrive, or it's something you can feel.'[29] But the loving attention to detail and the luxury of haute couture, with the magic of the presentation, were balanced by the dresses' titles. These were taken from the writer Douglas Coupland and fused computer programming language with the official language of the US military. A black wool tuxedo suit embroidered with brass bells was titled 'OPD, PFD, "HAWK", SYSTEM ERROR, PLEASE RESTART, Officially pronounced Dead, PhotoShop File Document, tuxedo'. The black organza evening dress embroidered with graduated clusters of brass bells was called 'CIA DMZ "WASP" YOU'VE GOT MAIL Central Intelligence Agency Demilitarized Zone evening gown'. In this collection, time was out of joint in the jarring fusion of violent militaristic euphemism with genteel and poetical couture presentation.

'What of the future?' asks Derrida. 'The future can only be for ghosts. And the past.'[30] Viktor & Rolf, Shelley Fox and Hussein Chalayan in different ways played on a melancholy aesthetic of temporal instability in which the past can never be laid to rest because it is meshed with images of the present and the future. Fox's mournful nihilism, Chalayan's poetic fragments and Viktor & Rolf's temporal complexity recall Walter Benjamin's image of the angel of history who walks backwards into the future, surveying the ruins behind him, from his description of Paul Klee's picture *Angelus Novus* of 1920:

> A Klee painting named 'Angelus Novus' shows an angel looking as though he is about to move away from something he is fixedly contemplating. His eyes are staring, his mouth is open, his wings are spread. This is how one pictures the angel of history. His face is turned towards the past. Where we perceive a chain of events, he sees one single catastrophe which keeps piling wreckage upon wreckage and hurls it in front of his feet . . . A storm is blowing from Paradise; it has got caught in his wings with such violence that the angel can no longer close them. The storm irresistibly propels him into the future to which his back is turned, while the pile of debris before him grows skyward. This storm is what we call progress.[31]

29   Amy Spindler in *Viktor & Rolf Haute Couture*: 11.

30   Derrida, *Specters of Marx*: 37.

31   Walter Benjamin, 'Theses on the Philosophy of History', *Illuminations*, trans. Harry Zohn, Fontana/Collins, London, 1973 [1955]: 259–60.

This apocalyptic scenario explodes the linear model of history as progress and posits a construction of history that looks backwards rather than forwards, 'at the destruction of material nature as it has actually taken place.'[32] When 1990s fashion imagery played on the idea of a historical relay, images from the past could shift into new constellations, and might again in the future, so that, as Foucault argues, one must constantly re-evaluate history in the light of the present. Just as Walter Benjamin's materialist analysis of consumption in the Arcades project is imbued with the metaphysical melancholy and poetry of the German Baroque mourning plays which were the subject of his first book, so these designers conjured ghostly dresses from the fashion ether, flooding futurist experimentation with traces of loss and poetry.

32 Susan Buck-Morss, *The Dialectics of Seeing: Walter Benjamin and the Arcades Project*, MIT Press, Cambridge, Mass., and London, 1991: 95.

three   spectacle

Capital become an Image

Twenty feet in the air, on top of an over-scaled pile of mattresses, two models in vaguely eighteenth-century dresses and wigs preened and coquetted in a Princess and the Pea scenario (fig. 42). John Galliano's first couture collection after his appointment in July 1995 as principal designer at Givenchy was shown in January 1996. For Givenchy he also did two ready-to-wear collections before being appointed principal designer at Dior in late 1996. In January 1997 Galliano's first couture show for Dior was audaciously staged in a fake *maison de couture*: in the Grand Hotel in Paris Galliano created a scaled-up facsimile of the original Dior showroom, including the famous staircase on which Cocteau and Dietrich had sat in the 1950s to watch Dior's presentations. Subsequent shows were staged in a suburban sports stadium transformed into a forest scene with forty-foot high spruce trees, the Paris Opéra converted into an English garden where the fashion photographers were given straw hats on entry, and the Carousel du Louvre, the official venue for the Paris collections, made over as a Manhattan rooftop scene, complete with battered chimney stacks, designed like most of his shows by the set designer Jean-Luc Ardouin. In every case, Galliano's transformation of the space involved effacing its real characteristics in the interests of imposing his own fantasy vision on the space, weaving instant mythologies and creating something out of nothing (fig. 41).

Rosalind Williams has argued that the seduction of the commodity in the nineteenth-century department store and world fair lay precisely in the way the real, commercial nature of the transaction was veiled in seductive 'dream worlds' in which the consumer lost him or herself in fantasy and reverie.[1] On the face of it, the late twentieth-century spectacle of the fashion show seems to be a precise evocation of this principle, the starriest of star commodities: 'when culture becomes nothing more than a commodity, it must also become the star commodity of the spectacular society'.[2] Guy Debord predicted in 1967 that by the end of the century culture would become the driving force in the development of the economy, as the car was at the beginning of the century, or the railway in the second half of the last. Indeed, the phrase the 'culture industries' suggests that culture is the new motor that drives the economy of our information society, just as coal and iron powered the economy of an earlier, industrial society.

In *The Society of the Spectacle* Debord argued that modern life was dominated by the commodity form and the false desires it engendered. Following Debord's description of the society of the spectacle, the fashion show is a self-absorbed, or narcissistic, 'spectacle unto itself', locked into its own world, self-regarding, sealed in the show space of the runway, with its attendant protocols and hierarchies. Like the spectacle, it spatialises time and destroys memory.[3] It is 'the triumph of contemplation over action'.[4] The fashion show is a form of commercial seduction through novelty and innovation, typically in the form of the showpiece designed to attract press coverage on the catwalk. Appollinaire's ironic phrase from 1916 highlights the seductively fanciful nature of fashion: 'I saw a charming dress

41 (*facing page*) John Galliano for Dior, Haute Couture, Spring–Summer 1998. Photograph Niall McInerney

42 (*below*) John Galliano for Givenchy, Haute Couture, Spring–Summer 1996. Photograph Niall McInerney

1 Rosalind H. Williams, *Dream Worlds: Mass Consumption in Late Nineteenth-Century France*, University of California Press, Berkeley, Los Angeles and Oxford, 1982.

2 Guy Debord, *Society of the Spectacle*, trans. Donald Nicholson-Smith, Zone Books, London, 1994 [1967]: para. 193.

3 Ibid: para 19.

4 Martin Jay, *Downcast Eyes: The Denigration of Vision in Twentieth-Century French Thought*, University of California Press, Berkeley and Los Angeles, 1993: 428.

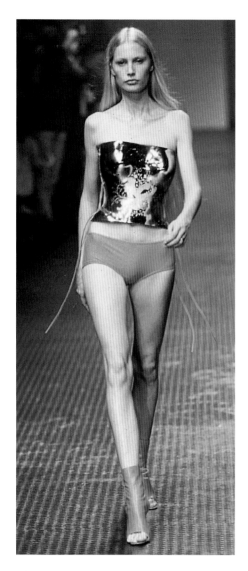

43 Antonio Berardi, Spring–Summer 2000. Photograph Stefano Guindani, courtesy Antonio Berardi/Karla Otto

made of corks . . . they're doing shoes in Venetian glass and hats in Baccarat crystal.'[5] But Apollinaire's poetic conceit was not as fantastical as it sounds. In the late 1990s Antonio Berardi attempted to make Capodimonte porcelain hats for his final London collection, and he succeeded in producing a crystal corset and two brassieres from hand-blown Murano glass for his Spring–Summer 2000 show (fig. 43). The glass bustier is a fairy-tale object, as evocative as Cinderella's glass slipper and in real life just as unwearable; in the realm of the symbolic it parades the dreams and arcane craft skills of elite fashion production, as did Berardi's hand-made lace dress that it took Sicilian lacemakers three months to complete. Yet the glass corset is also about the obvious display of wealth. Its very unwearability suggests the conspicuous waste, consumption and leisure that Thorstein Veblen excoriated in his attack on the ostentation of America's top plutocratic families at the end of the nineteenth century.[6] The realm of consumption is here transposed to the visual, for there is no other way in which we can consume it.

Society as a whole constitutes the spectacle but its visible form is the commodity which occupies everyday life: 'the spectacle is not a collection of images, but a social relation among people, mediated by images'.[7] Photographs of the photographers and journalists at work at fashion shows (figs 44 and 45) can make manifest the commercial reality behind the spectacle, a reality that is glimpsed on the floor and in the audience rather than on the catwalk, whose spectacular displays are calculated to occlude the commercial realities that shadow them. The spectacle, according to Debord, is 'capital become an image';[8] the contrast between the Galliano collections (see figs 41 and 42) and these photographs shows both sides of the way capital is constructed as image, first in the show itself and then in its capture on camera as a literal image and its coverage by the press. This is the background to Berardi's Spring–Summer 2000 show (see fig. 43), where the spectacle is fused with the commodity in the shiny surface of the fragile glass bustier that both deflects the penetrating gaze of the observer and reflects the world back onto itself. In the bustier, capital is both magically invisible and yet at the same time made real. The transparency of glass is rendered opaque, just as the commodity both flaunts and disguises its commercial nature in spectacle. Here is capital turned into an image, at once fragile and precious.

Fashion Desperadoes

In the 1990s the London-trained designers Galliano and McQueen were credited with having recreated the couture show in new terms; the British fashion journalist Sally Brampton described Galliano as 'the greatest image-maker in the world'.[9] She argued that he was partly responsible for the greatly increased attendance at the Paris shows, which she described as 'a media feeding frenzy as newspapers and television stations around the world give increasing prominence to fashion.'[10] On the other hand, Galliano was periodically criticised for over-reaching himself in substituting showmanship and pantomime for

5 Apollinaire, 'Le Poète assassiné', 1916, quoted in Walter Benjamin, *The Arcades Project*, trans. Howard Eiland and Kevin Mclaughlin, Belknap Press of Harvard University Press, Cambridge, Mass. and London, 1999: 19.

6 Thorstein Veblen, *The Theory of the Leisure Classes*, Mentor, New York, 1953 [1899].

7 Debord, *Society of the Spectacle*: para. 4, and Jay, *Downcast Eyes*: 429.

8 Debord, *Society of the Spectacle*: para. 34.

9 Sally Brampton cited in Susannah Frankel, 'Galliano', *The Independent Magazine*, 20 February 1999: 12.

10 *The Guardian*, 14 October 1998.

44 Niall McInerney, chairs in a fashion show, mid-1990s. Photograph Niall McInerney

45 Emanuel Ungaro, Haute Couture, Autumn–Winter 1999. Photograph Niall McInerney

fashion design itself, making clothes that were utterly unwearable.[11] It was far from the first time that a designer had been criticised for excessive theatricality. In the 1980s the French designer Thierry Mugler had staged a series of comparably spectacular shows, including one on which he reputedly spent a million dollars to enact the Virgin Birth on a runway peopled with hooded nuns, cherubs and a madonna and child (fig. 46). For the finale, a model dropped out of the sky from clouds of smoke and a hail of pink confetti. Like Galliano after him, Mugler laid himself open to the charge, from the press that had built him up, that he was substituting theatre for fashion. As one American buyer com-

11   See e.g. Susannah Frankel, 'Galliano Steams Ahead with Any Old Irony', *The Guardian*, 21 July 1998: 10. The show represented the culmination of a series of elaborate and theatrical historical pageants which Galliano had staged in the mid-1990s as the principal designer for Dior.

12 Polly Guerin, *Creative Fashion Presentations*, Fairchild, New York, 1987: 230.

13 Ginger Gregg Duggan (ed.), 'Fashion and Performance', special edition of *Fashion Theory*, vol. 5, issue 3, September 2001: 243–70. The comparison of fashion with performance art, however, fails to acknowledge the commercial reality of fashion shows. Just as Worth and Poiret hid the commercial reality of their business practice behind claims to unique artistry and genius (see Nancy J. Troy, *Couture Culture: A Study in Modern Art and Fashion*, MIT Press, Cambridge, Mass. and London, 2003), so the contemporary fashion show's allegiance with art served, in reality, merely to enhance its status and commercial value in an increasingly sophisticated market.

14 In 1983 the Costume Institute of the Metropolitan Museum of Art in New York showed a 25-year retrospective exhibition of Yves Saint-Laurent, after which other museums gradually also began to mount fashion exhibitions, not always on the topic of single designers. These included 'Fashion and Surrealism' at the FIT Gallery, New York, in 1987 and the Victoria & Albert Museum, London, in 1988; 'Infra-Apparel' at the Costume Institute of the Metropolitan Museum of Art in 1991; 'Street Style' at the Victoria & Albert Museum, London, 1994. In the 1990s, three internationally reviewed exhibitions explicitly linked art and fashion thematically: 'Mode et Art', Brussels and Montreal, 1993; 'Il tempo e le mode (Looking at Fashion)', Florence Biennale, 1996, which was developed as 'Art/Fashion', Guggenheim Museum, Soho, New York, 1997; and 'Addressing the Century: A Hundred Years of Art and Fashion', Hayward Gallery, London, 1998, and Kunstmuseum, Wolfsburg, 1989. In the same period there were also a range of smaller, innovative exhibitions linking art and fashion in Europe and New York. The period also saw a new type of coverage of fashion in art magazines. The March 1982 issue of the New York magazine *Artforum* featured an Issey Miyake collaboration on its cover. Throughout the 1980s and 1990s art magazines such as *Artforum, Art in America, Flash Art* and *Frieze* began to give editorial coverage to more 'avant-garde' designers like Comme des Garçons and Martin Margiela and, subsequently, to feature advertisements from fashion companies like Helmut Lang and Prada. There is a list of some of this editorial coverage, although it is not comprehensive, tabulated in Sung Bok Kim, 'Is Fashion Art?', *Fashion Theory*, vol. 2, issue 1, March 1998: 60–1. See, too, Michael Boodroo, 'Art and Fashion', *Artnews*, September 1990: 120–7, and Robert Radford, 'Dangerous Liaisons: Art, Fashion and Individualism', *Fashion Theory*, vol. 2, issue 2, June 1998: 151–63.

15 Fabio Piras quoted in Hilton Als, 'Gear: Postcard from London', *The New Yorker*, 17 March 1997: 92.

mented, 'the show overshadows the clothes'.[12] Yet in the 1990s that became, more and more, the point of a fashion show, nowhere more so than in Britain.

The role of London as a breeding ground for fashion spectacle was crucial in the 1990s, not least because it could be appropriated by Paris houses when it suited them. In the mid-1990s a range of spectacular fashion shows, first in London and then in Paris, gave rise to the speculation that fashion had become 'the new performance'.[13] Much was made of the convergence of art and fashion in this period.[14] The commercial reality behind these innovative London shows, however, was that the designers had few other options, and nothing to lose, because of the lack of infrastructure in the British fashion industry. Fabio Piras called his generation of designers who graduated from London's Central Saint Martins in the early to mid-1990s 'fashion desperadoes'. Describing how arduous conditions were for newly graduated young designers, Piras said 'you had no money, and a certain synergy grows out of a recession. People said "fuck it, we're going to have a show." And, of course, the first person from my generation to do that was Alexander McQueen.'[15]

McQueen's early shows were styled to make the models look bruised and battered, covered in tyre tracks or smeared with fake dirt and blood (fig. 47). After McQueen had found the backer he needed, his London shows became less violent but more spectacular, as he drenched his models in 'golden showers' or surrounded them with fake snowstorms. Generally, the different shock value of individual designer's shows depended on the context in which their work was situated. If they were at the beginning of their career, had no backer and badly needed press coverage, their shows were likely to be more extreme; nevertheless, it was important to avoid completely alienating the press and a fine line had

47 (*far left*) Alexander McQueen, Nihilism, Spring–Summer 1994. Photograph Niall McInerney

48 (*left*) Alexander McQueen, The Birds, Spring–Summer 1995. Photograph Niall McInerney

46 (*facing page*) Thierry Mugler, Zenith, Autumn–Winter 1984–5. Photograph courtesy Thierry Mugler

to be negotiated. Tristan Webber's Autumn–Winter 1998–9 show had the models staggering through an artificially created wind tunnel. Andrew Groves's collection of the same season was based on the Troubles in Northern Ireland and called Our Selves Alone (translated from the Gaelic *sinn fein*, the name of the principal republican party in Northern Ireland). It featured grey suits, white shirts, orange sashes and charred green taffeta, mixing the colours of the main unionist party with those of Sinn Fein. On the catwalk a model doused herself in lighter fluid and appeared to set fire to herself, while outside there were three thirty-foot burning crucifixes. Staging fashion as transgression, Groves's next show was called Cocaine Nights and featured trails of white powder on the catwalk and a dress composed entirely of razor blades (figs 49 and 50). His shows conveyed a strong sense of disenchantment with the world; so too did those of McQueen, whose staging of models with bloody, post-operative breasts or trussed up in clingfilm and string (fig. 48) was a kind of spoiling of the image akin to the mutant dummies of the London artists Jake and Dinos Chapman.

Young London designers looking for a backer in the 1990s recognised the commercial value of shock and spectacle to attract press, backers and buyers. For these designers, like their Victorian predecessors, the spectacle of the fashion show, far from being art, was simultaneously enticement and advertisement, 'the theatre through which capitalism acts.'[16] Although traditionally Paris had been a centre of both couture and prêt-à-porter, London had the edge in terms of imaginative presentation of fashion shows. Stéphane Wagner, professor and lecturer in communications at the Institut Français de la Mode, said in 1997 that 'if we accept that much of haute couture is about squeezing out maximum media

16 Thomas Richards, *The Commodity Culture of Victorian England: Advertising and Spectacle 1851–1914*, Verso, London and New York, 1991: 251.

coverage – good or bad – then the more spectacular the presentation and collection, the better. And from that point of view the English are the best by far.'[17] His words explain why the French conglomerate LVMH (Louis Vuitton Moët Hennessy, whose many holdings included Givenchy, Dior, Louis Vuitton, Marc Jacobs International, Kenzo, Lacroix and Loëwe) was eager to employ young and relatively inexperienced British designers who had proved themselves on London catwalks. These designers were negligible in terms of global markets. They did not even begin to penetrate the American or Asian markets, or the European mass market. Nevertheless as the large conglomerates successfully disseminated their brands in the late 1990s, there were signs that the big players were beginning to see ways in which to capitalise on the talents of commercially smaller but spectacularly visible named designers.[18] At the time of Galliano's appointment at Dior in 1996, Parisian couture was a loss leader that generated the publicity necessary for the sales of perfume, cosmetics, bags and, sometimes, diffusion ranges of clothes, through which couture houses made their profits. The way in which conglomerates that owned couture houses 'bought in' young British talent to revivify French couture houses in the late 1990s was part of a broader tendency to establish luxury brands such as Givenchy, Dior, Gucci, Fendi, Prada and Chanel in a competitive global market, and one of their principal marketing devices was the fashion show.

A Shop of Images and Signs

In French *spectacle* also means theatrical presentation[19] and the fashion show is undoubtedly a part of Debord's 'society of the spectacle' in the way that it transforms commercial enterprise into dazzling display, aestheticising everyday life on the catwalk. The kitsch excesses of consumer culture were fondly parodied by the American Jeremy Scott. In his Autumn–Winter 2001–2 collection, shown in Paris and called American Excess, the usual runway parade was replaced with a large revolving turntable that staged a *tableau vivant* of twelve models parodying American hostesses. One wore a cocktail dress made from a print of dollar bills that bore the designer's head (fig. 51). Another, dressed in a chain-mail shift of gold coins, pushed a shopping trolley stuffed with bank notes. A third stood beside an open refrigerator full of gold ingots. In the same season the London-based designer Russell Sage's collection featured dresses made of real money, with twenty and fifty-pound notes twisted into rosettes, and a dress made of £6000-worth of notes (fig. 52). Sage's presentation clearly indicated a critical commentary on the industry, as opposed to Scott's gleeful and trashy enjoyment of it. For Debord, the spectacle is deathly because it is capital become an image; it is the other side of money, 'the visible negation of life' and the 'autonomous movement of the non-living': these shows made Debord's imagery all too literal.[20]

The catwalk shows of designers such as Hussein Chalayan, Martin Margiela and Viktor & Rolf, however, issue a challenge to Debord's ideas of spectacle and suggest that it needs

49 and 50 *(facing page left and right)* Andrew Groves, Cocaine Nights, Spring–Summer 1999. Photograph Niall McInerney

51 Jeremy Scott, Autumn–Winter 2001–2 backstage. Photograph Gauliter Gallet, courtesy Jeremy Scott

17 Quoted in Stephen Todd, 'The Importance of Being English', *Blueprint*, March 1997: 42.

18 Terri Agins, *The End of Fashion*, Quill/Harper Collins, New York, 2000.

19 Jay, *Downcast Eyes*: 427.

20 Debord, *Society of the Spectacle*: paras. 10 and 2.

to be modified to accommodate contemporary changes in cultural context and communications technology. While his analysis has proved a fruitful model for understanding a number of other periods, from the Paris of the Impressionists to the commodity culture of nineteenth-century London, and the image of woman as spectacle in relation to modernity,[21] his relevance to late twentieth-century consumer culture is limited by shifts in the nature of commodity and image in the electronic age. Debord's descriptions were rooted in a Marxist critique of the commodity form as economic object; the overarching transformations of the 1990s (globalisation, new technology and new communications) radically altered its form. As electronic media and global markets developed, and service industries replaced older forms of industrial production, information became a valuable commodity in its own right.[22] In the shifting constellations of the culture industries fashion began to signify in a number of different registers. Debord's sour denunciations of the image seem curiously redundant in a culture in which the fashioned garment circulates in a network of signs as both image and object: no longer representation, the image is frequently the commodity itself, be it in a fashion show, magazine, website or even an idea. Indeed, Thomas Richards suggests that the days of spectacle are numbered, and that 'it may turn out that the semiotics of spectacle played a transitional role in capitalist mythology'.[23] By the late twentieth century, in an increasingly visualised global market dominated by new technologies of the image, it became all the more important for designers to produce strong, graphic runway images that could be transmitted round the world via print and electronic media.

Hussein Chalayan, for example, worked mainly independently of the large conglomerates to produce his own collections, apart from a period when he also designed for Tse in New York. In his Autumn–Winter 1998–9 show, Panoramic, models paraded like sleepwalkers along a stark, modernist set involving a mirrored catwalk and white walls with slits for entrances and exits (fig. 53). The visual coup of the show was the way that, as it progressed, the human elements of performance receded. The models wove mesmerically in and out of the set, appearing to disappear into walls and reappear in mirrors, until the difference between illusion and reality was effaced and their bodies became mere patterns in a moving picture. The visual play of models appearing and disappearing in this austere space was mirrored by a slide show on another white wall in which a scene was gradually reduced to a set of abstract elements. Chalayan's starting point was the final sentence of Wittgenstein's *Tractatus logico-philosophicus*: 'what you cannot speak of you must pass over in silence.'[24] He was concerned with the limitations of language, and the way that discourses of technology, religion and science create parameters in which people find themselves trapped. In the final moments of the show he wanted to camouflage the models to show the loss of self through reflections, and reflections of reflections, and thus to represent the dissolution of the self in infinity.

Chalayan's show was poised between the worlds of performance and commerce, where aesthetics and metaphysics vie with spectacle and illusion. The illusory nature of the mirror in the show evoked the words with which Debord opened *The Society of the Spectacle*: 'in

21   T. J. Clark, *The Painting of Modern Life: Paris in the Art of Manet and his Followers*, Princeton University Press and Thames & Hudson, London, 1984. Richards, *Commodity Culture*. Heather McPhearson, 'Sarah Bernhardt: Portrait of the Actress as Spectacle', *Nineteenth-Century Contexts*, vol. 20, no. 4, 1999: 409–54. I thank Carol Tulloch for bringing this invaluable article to my attention.

22   See e.g. Daniel Bell, 'The Third Technological Revolution and its Possible Socio-Economic Consequences', University of Salford, Faculty of Social Sciences Annual Lecture, 1988.

23   Richards, *Commodity Culture*: 258.

24   Ludwig Wittgenstein, *Tractatus logico-philosophicus*, trans. P. David, Routledge, London, 1991: 74.

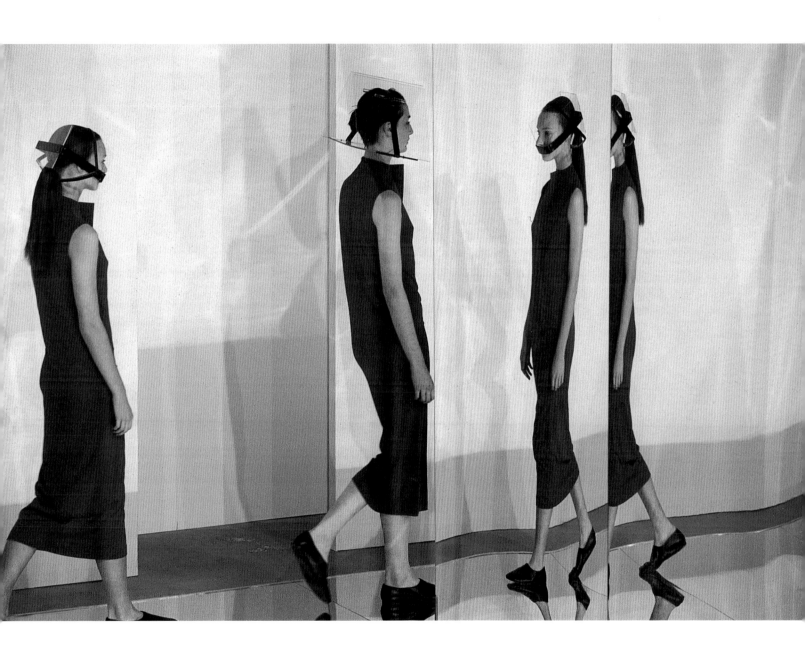

53 (*above*)   Hussein Chalayan, Panoramic,
Autumn–Winter 1998–9. Photograph Niall
McInerney

52 (*facing page*)   Russell Sage,
Autumn–Winter 2001–2. Photograph
Anthea Simms

54 Hussein Chalayan, Between,
Spring–Summer 1998. Photograph
Chris Moore, courtesy Hussein Chalayan

25   Debord, *Society of the Spectacle*: para. 1.
26   Iain Chambers, 'Maps for the Metropolis:
A Possible Guide to the Present', *Cultural Studies*,
vol. 1, no. 1, January 1987: 2.
27   Ibid: 5.
28   Ibid.

societies where modern conditions of production prevail all of life presents itself as an immense accumulation of spectacles. Everything that was directly lived has moved away into a representation.'[25] Debord characterised modern life as a world colonised by false desires and illusions, epitomised by the ubiquity of the commodity form. While Chalayan's show referred to the high art *gravitas* of the installation, the faithlessness of the mirror also testified to the slippery instability of the surface in modern consumer culture with its constantly changing flow of signs, images and information. There the mirror is shimmery rather than reflective; instead of telling the truth it dazzles and confuses, perpetrates an act of deception, like consumerist display.

In Chalayan's shows, however, the mirror could also function as a *mis-en-abîme*, an abyss. For his show Between of Spring–Summer 1998 some of the models' heads were bisected by oblong mirrors which simultaneously framed their faces and reflected the audience's faces back to them (fig. 54). Here Chalayan intended to reverse the relationship between voyeur and subject, and to investigate and challenge the way we define cultural and geographic territory in space in his explorations of the negative space around the body. The audience, looking at the model, does not just gaze at an object, but finds the object interacts with the viewer. The mirror that frames the model's face thereby grants the audience a vision of itself.

In the 1980s Iain Chambers described fashion as a rootless world which we experience as a 'semiotic blur' because its signifiers move too fast for interpretation and are too limitlessly cross-referring.[26] He argued that this was the spectacle of consumerism in a new guise, or disguise, the obscenity of obsessive transparency: 'it . . . encourages the vertiginous experience of the pleasure-in-itself' and the 'brutal purpose' of this pleasure, those signs and sensations, is 'to make money, and reproduce the situations that permit that exercise.'[27] Drawing on Debord's view that the society of the spectacle was the insidious function of capital that seduced through the commodity form, Chambers wrote that 'today we have reached such a level of cultural commodification that the duplicity of the sign, i.e. that the product might actually "mean" something, can be done away with.'[28] Chambers's text prefigures the references to developments in digital technology of the 1990s that a few designers began to use on and off their runways. For the W&LT (Wild and Lethal Trash) Autumn–Winter 1995–6 show Walter van Beirendonck sent masked, robotic figures onto the catwalk, styling them as a brightly coloured community of aliens beamed down from outer space (fig. 55). For the following collection, for Spring–Summer 1996, instead of a catwalk presentation he released an interactive CD ROM, turning the 'catwalk' into a virtual experience where live models with surreal plastic-finish make-up and robotic gestures interacted with a virtual world of computer-generated images. Hussein Chalayan's Spring–Summer 2001 show, Ventriloquy, started with a computer-generated film of wireframe models whose pixellated actions prefigured the narrative that was subsequently staged by the real models in the show's finale (fig. 56).

Both van Beirendonck and Chalayan played on the contrast between computer model and fashion model, between virtual and actual body, between image and object. This tech-

55 Walter van Beirendonck for W&LT,
Autumn–Winter 1995–6. Photograph Pascal
Therme, courtesy Walter van Beirendonck

56 (*below*) Hussein Chalayan, Ventriloquy,
Spring–Summer 2001. Photograph Chris
Moore, courtesy Hussein Chalayan

29 Gilles Lipovetsky, *The Empire of Fashion: Dressing Modern Democracy*, trans. Catherine Porter, Princeton University Press, 1994 [1987]: 10.

30 'An Introduction from Philip Glass', sleeve notes to *Philip on Film: Filmworks by Philip Glass*, 7559-79660-2, Nonesuch Records, 2001.

31 All these textile collaborations are documented in Sarah Braddock and Marie O'Mahony (eds), *Fabric of Fashion*, The British Council, London, 2000.

32 Susan Sontag, *On Photography*, Penguin Books, Harmondsworth, 1977: 153. For more empirically based studies of the impact of new visual technologies on sensibilities see Jonathan Crary, *Techniques of the Observer: On Vision and Modernity in the Nineteenth Century*, MIT Press, Cambridge, Mass., and London, 1990; Scott McQuire, *Visions of Modernity: Representation, Memory, Time and Space in the Age of the Camera*, Sage, London, Thousand Oaks and New Delhi, 1998.

33 Jean-Michel Rabaté, *The Ghosts of Modernity*, University Press of Florida, Gainsville, 1996.

34 Richards, *Commodity Culture*.

35 Cited in Susan Buck-Morss, *The Dialectics of Seeing: Walter Benjamin and the Arcades Project*, MIT Press, Cambridge, Mass., and London, 1991: 177.

57 (*facing page*) Hussein Chalayan, Along South Equator, Autumn–Winter 1995–6. Photograph courtesy Hussein Chalayan

nological play is a feature, Gilles Lipovetsky has argued, of 'a society structured by fashion, where rationality functions by way of evanescence and superficiality, where objectivity is instituted as a spectacle, where the dominion of technology is reconciled with play and the realm of politics is reconciled with seduction.'[29] In Ventriloquy, Chalayan segued between the new technology of digital imagery and the tradition of the catwalk show: after the video projection the audience saw a stark, white, angular set painted with receding black perspectival lines to echo the architectural space of the video. On the premise that in times of catastrophe morals are destroyed, the computer animation showed alter egos that came into being and then, within a short lifespan, interacted ruthlessly before fracturing into thousands of pieces, like Manga images of self-sacrifice in Japanese cartoons. The actual show that followed echoed the alter egos of the computer animation in the figures and actions of the live models, thus creating an interplay between the real and the virtual narratives. And when, in the finale of the show, three models produced a hammer each and smashed the rigid sugar-glass dress of the three models next to them, the real-time narrative looped back to the moment at the end of the video, replaying the past in the present, when one figure 'exploded' the one next to her. The three models with their hammers mirrored the three without; like the three Graces but doubled and fractured, the living models dressed in soft, organic fabric turned on those in dresses like rigid shells and destroyed them. And the show scrambled time, as it repeated the past in the future, all within the twenty-minute ambit of the fashion show. Thus, as in his earlier use of mirrors, Chalayan effaced the difference between graphic representation and human flesh, turning all before him into an image.

Just as many of Chalayan's shows featured computer animations that were matched by the actions of the models on the catwalk (Panoramic, Geotropics and Ventriloquy), so in Philip Glass's music for Cocteau's *La Belle et la Bête* live singers on stage interact with their counterparts on screen. When the stage Beauty looks up at the screen Beauty, or the stage Beast sings his last words as the screen Beast is dying, a powerful counterpoint is created that spans live performance and film, music and image.[30] As music for his Medea show, Chalayan found a Philip Glass specialist in Belgium to perform Glass's *Mishima*, the score for Paul Schrader's 1985 film, that had never before been performed live. Glass has experimented with many forms of composing music for a 'moving image', including in the 1980s the combination of visually cued live music and film, sometimes with performers in front of the screen, sometimes behind it but still visible (as Chalayan did with Bulgarian singers in his After Words collection). For Chalayan to reintegrate the score for *Mishima* with the formal choreography of a 'real time' fashion performance is very much in the spirit of Glass's other work of the 1980s that combined live music performance with image alone (as in *Koyaanisquati*), opera (*La Belle et la Bête*) and melodrama (*Dracula*).

Ostensibly like installation art, Chalayan's conceptual work turned its back on *frou frou* ephemerality. His techniques were those of artful experimentation using avant-garde music in modernist spaces (fig. 57). Unlike other designers whose shows were staged by pop promoters and video makers, Chalayan's were designed for a period in collaboration with the product designer Michael Anastassiades. Chalayan moved outside the limits of his own discipline to collaborate with musicians, jewellers, textile and product designers; he repudiated many of the features of the fashion system, such as its emphasis on seasonal novelty (by repeating shapes and ideas across collections) and on individuality (by hiding the models' heads in wooden pods or mirrors). He designed an airmail envelope that could be sent through the post and that unfolded into a wearable dress in Tyvek, a tough, paper-like fabric made from pulped polymer fibre; he showed clothes in mid-air by suspending them from helium-filled balloons attached to their shoulder straps. His fabrics were printed with the patterns of flight paths (Autumn–Winter 1995–6), with wireframe architectural drawings (Spring–Summer 2000) and pixel patterns designed by Eley Kishimoto in intense colours to mimic the computer screen (Spring–Summer 1996). He collaborated with the textile designer Sophie Roet to develop a double-weave fabric to be worn as an overdress with the underdress glowing underneath.[31]

Despite Chalayan's engagement with ideas from music and philosophy, his repetitive turn to the image, and to the seductions of new technology, also chimes with consumer culture and the society of the spectacle. Susan Sontag argued that in the modern period our perception of reality is shaped by the type and frequency of images we receive. She wrote that from the mid-nineteenth century 'the credence that could no longer be given to realities understood in the form of images was now being given to realities understood to be images, illusions', and went on to cite Feuerbach's observation of 1843, also cited by Debord at the beginning of *The Society of the Spectacle*: 'our era prefers the image to the thing, the copy to the original, the representation to the reality, appearance to being.'[32] Indeed, many fashion historians as well as consumers tend to privilege image over object, a point that is invoked in Chalayan's oscillation between image and object in his shows. In Chalayan's innovative and sophisticated games with representation, the commodity form returned via the very structures that denied it, through the instability of the image in the modern period and its ambiguous role in the society of the spectacle.

The 'return of the repressed' is a psychoanalytic concept whereby what is unresolved or denied is bound to reappear, generally as hysterical symptom. In fashion the hysterical symptom becomes a historical one, as what Rabaté has termed 'the ghosts of modernity' are endlessly called up by its most recent innovations.[33] For all its modernist experimentation, Chalayan's work invokes the duplicitous and sophisticated play of image and idea that began to underwrite capitalist production, consumption and, particularly, marketing from the mid-nineteenth century.[34] As early as the 1850s, Baudelaire wrote that 'all the visible universe is nothing but a shop of images and signs'.[35] Much as they looked forward experimentally, Chalayan's mirrors and computer animations, because they existed in the context of late capitalist fashion, also harked back to the duplicitous vitrines and mirrored windows of nineteenth-century Parisian department stores, whose dazzling displays reflected the image of the new consumer back to her or himself while simultaneously mul-

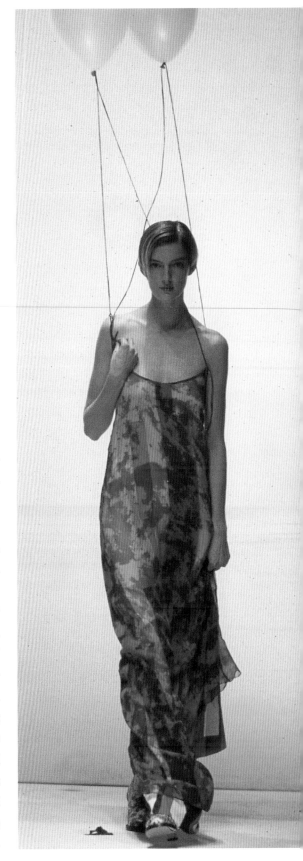

tiplying and fracturing the image of the goods on display.[36] Chalayan's catwalk experiments brought together the hard and shiny surfaces of the spectacle with the abysmal depths of the mirror.

Dérive

Like Chalayan's in London, the shows of Martin Margiela in Paris resembled fine art installations and performances and eschewed the conventional glitz of the catwalk. They were held in derelict urban spaces such as car parks, disused metro stations, warehouses and wasteland. For his Autumn–Winter 1997–8 collection free promotional maps of Paris with three locations and times for the show were sent to the journalists, many of whom threw them out, thinking they were junk mail rather than fashion show invitations. At 05.00 hours on the morning of the show, a bus carrying thirty-five brass band players left Brussels for Paris where it met another bus that carried thirty-five models to their first destination. This was an abandoned covered market, La Java, at Belville, at 10.30 hours. The second, at 11.45 hours, was a glass-covered loading bay of the huge Le Gibus building at République. The third, at 15.00 hours, was a 1930s dance school, Le Ménagerie de Verre, at Parmentier. At each venue the audience watched the models and band get out and then followed them into the show space as the band played a slow march. At the third, however, instead of going into the building the models simply paraded through the streets mingling with the public. They were accompanied throughout by Margiela's assistants clad in white laboratory coats, a tradition borrowed from the couture ateliers.

By departing from his pre-planned itinerary and allowing his models to 'drift' through the city streets rather than model on the more conventional catwalk, Margiela evoked two related tropes from the nineteenth and twentieth centuries: the flux of the crowd that was central to Baudelaire's city imagery and the Situationist concept of *dérive* that was supposed to counter the effects of the spectacle. Debord describes *dérive* as a form of drifting through 'the hidden wonders of urban space'.[37] Margiela, in all his shows, used the derelict urban spaces that, as Hal Foster has commented, were historically associated with the nineteenth-century literature and imagery of the ragpicker, another figure identified by Baudelaire as an index of modernity,[38] the scavenger who revitalises moribund material from city detritus and recycles it 'between the jaws of the Goddess of Industry.'[39]

In his Spring–Summer 1998 show Margiela made the models disappear completely and replaced them with 'fashion technicians'. The 'catwalk' had six tall white pedestals onto which were projected dictionary-style descriptions of the clothes, such as 'displaced shoulder . . . when not worn, the clothes are totally flat'.[40] The written descriptions were montaged with video shots of models wearing the clothes, to a soundtrack of thunderous applause. At the same time men in white coats (reminiscent of the white coats worn by master technicians of haute couture such as Hubert de Givenchy and Christobal Balenciaga) 'demonstrated' the clothes by carrying them around on hangers and pointing

36   Emile Zola, *The Ladies' Paradise*, trans. with an intro. by Brian Nelson, Oxford University Press, Oxford and New York, 1995, opens with one such description.

37   See Jay, *Downcast Eyes*: 424.

38   Baudelaire's poem, 'Le Vin des chiffonniers', or 'The Ragpickers' Wine', is discussed by Benjamin, *Charles Baudelaire: A Lyric Poet in the Era of High Capitalism*, trans. Harry Zohn, Verso, London and New York, 1997: 19.

39   Baudelaire quoted in ibid: 79.

40   *Women's Wear Daily*, 16 October 1997.

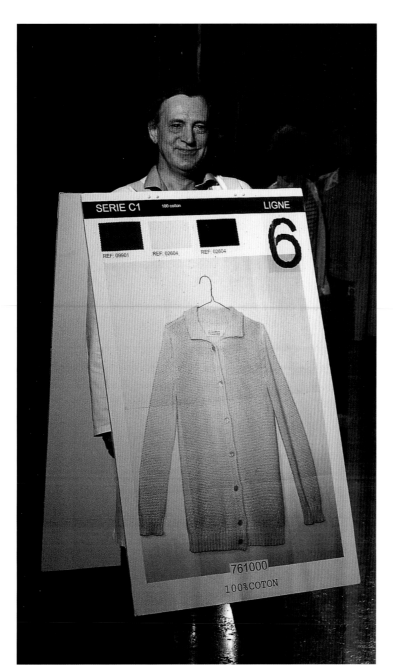

58   Martin Margiela, Spring–Summer 1999.
Photograph Niall McInerney

out their features. The following year, for Spring–Summer 1999, Margiela sent out models wearing sandwich boards with pictures of each garment rather than showing the actual clothes on the model (fig. 58). In *The Society of the Spectacle* Debord developed the notion of *détournement*, a way of turning the spectacle back on itself and 'reversing its normal ideological function'.[41] When Margiela's models paraded in the street alongside passers-by, mingling with the city crowds, or when he used technicians or sandwich-board men to 'demonstrate' his designs, Margiela could be argued to be turning the rules of the spectacle back on itself. Like the Situationist artist Asger Jorn in the 1950s, who bought flea market

41   Jay, *Downcast Eyes*: 424.

42 Ibid.

paintings and repainted or, as he termed it, 'modified' them as radical art, Margiela refabricated ancient thrift-shop clothing as avant-garde and modern. Martin Jay describes the 'detourned' paintings of Asger Jorn: 'elements from previous works were periodically devalued and invested with fresh meaning through their integration in a new ensemble'.[42] Margiela too, against fashion's newness, designed a collection that 'recycled' his earlier ones. One could also point to the repetition and deconstruction of design motifs that was repeated in many collections, as against fashion's clamour for perpetual newness and change.

Tap-dancing Capitalism

While Margiela's undoubtedly innovative show designs could be said to function as Situationist-style stratagems to evade the ubiquitous 'society of the spectacle', it could equally be argued that Margiela simply traded on a particularly exclusive kind of cultural capital which required insider knowledge of new fashion signs. For all their innovation, Margiela's shows expanded the repertoire of urban spectacle and fashion. The ambiguity as to whether a show can criticise the spectacle from a critical vantage point outside it or whether it is simply recuperated as just another spectacle, was raised in Viktor & Rolf's designs. Their early shows, before they moved from their native Amsterdam to Paris, trod a fine line between cynicism and innovation. Their Spring–Summer 1996 collection, L'Apparence du Vide, was made entirely from gold, a colour they associate with wrapping paper, in a criticism of the 'circus' surrounding the industry (fig. 77). But the ironic title

59a (*below left*) Viktor & Rolf, 'Launch', Spring–Summer 1997, maquette for miniature catwalk show, installation at the Torch Gallery, Amsterdam, November 1996. Art direction and styling Viktor & Rolf. Photograph Claudie Krommelin, courtesy Viktor & Rolf

59b (*below right*) 'Launch', Spring–Summer 1997. Poster for 'Le Parfum' advertising campaign, installation at the Torch Gallery, Amsterdam, November 1996. Art direction and styling by Viktor & Rolf. Photograph Wendelien Daan, courtesy Viktor & Rolf

"Viktor & Rolf on strike/en greve, winter/hiver '96/'97"

also recalls the artist Yves Klein's 1960 *Saut dans le vide*, a photograph of the artist apparently jumping from a window into the void which, in fact, is a fake.

Viktor & Rolf's knowing references to art, politics and commerce exhibit many of the polemical tactics of Klein who, in one performance piece, sold 'pure artistic sensibility' by giving the customer a certificate of his artistic sensibility in exchange for a piece of gold leaf which had ceremonially to be thrown into the Seine as 'payment'. Viktor & Rolf's seventh collection, Spring–Summer 1997, shown in an Amsterdam gallery, epitomised, they said, their hopes for the future, in miniature. As they had no money for a catwalk show they presented small maquettes, like theatre design models, of a minute catwalk (fig. 59a), shop, photography studio, atelier and a presentation for V&R perfume. This last consisted of a lightbox with miniature perfume bottles, a photograph for an imaginary advertising campaign and 250 life-size empty perfume bottles that cost £200 each, which mimicked the design and typeface of the classic Chanel perfume bottle from the 1920s (fig. 59b).

Their canny manipulation of the commercial context of both art and fashion in the 1990s had been highlighted by their Autumn–Winter 1996–7 collection when they produced no clothes at all and cheekily sent the fashion editors a poster which read 'Viktor & Rolf on strike' and fly-posted the streets of Paris with these images (fig. 60). Being 'on strike' as fashion designers and producing no clothes is to make a joke about production, arguably at the expense of the industry. Such tactics suggested that the designers were well aware that fashion is the ultimate product that emphasises consumption at the expense of production, making the latter invisible in classically Marxist fashion. Viktor & Rolf managed simultaneously to critique the industry and its spectacle yet to be part of them in an ironic and knowing way.

61 Viktor & Rolf Spring–Summer 1998.
Photograph F. Dumoulin/Java, courtesy Viktor &
Rolf

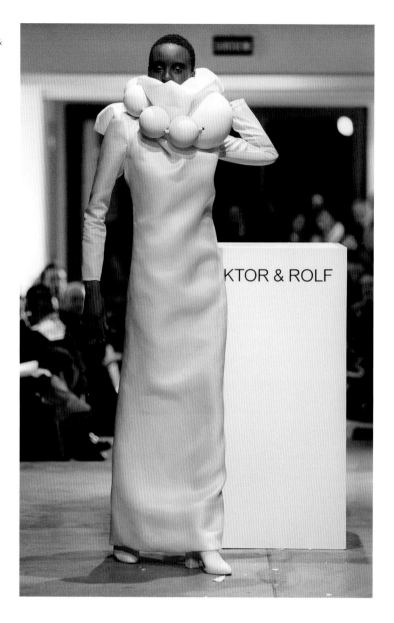

43 Amy Spindler in *Viktor & Rolf Haute Couture
Book*, texts by Amy Spindler and Didier Grumbach,
Groninger Museum, Gröningen, 2000: 8.

Nevertheless, as Amy Spindler has argued, their work is equally as informed by love of
the craft and business of fashion as it is by irony.[43] Their Spring–Summer 1998 couture
collection featured a white silk evening dress with a porcelain boater and a necklace made
of huge white porcelain beads, one of them as large as the model's head (fig. 61). During
the presentation the model threw both of them to the floor where they lay in shattered
fragments, supposedly to emphasise the importance of the garments over and above accessories. But the gesture was also a form of *potlach*, a bonfire of the vanities that could be
reconverted into capitalist spectacle even as it sought to destroy its emblems. While
Berardi's glass corset (see fig. 43) reified the spectacle of the catwalk without irony, it could
hardly be argued that Viktor & Rolf's catwalk destruction of their porcelain boater and
necklace was significantly different, simply that as a gesture it was more knowing.

62   Viktor & Rolf, Spring–Summer 2001.
Photograph Peter Stigter, Paris, courtesy
Viktor & Rolf

Viktor & Rolf's collections and early shows referred to capitalist production and the way it veils its origins, for example by fetishising the commodity, flooding it with meaning so that its image becomes an embodied form of what Judith Williamson has called 'congealed longing'. Williamson adapts Marx's description of the commodity as 'congealed labour' to describe our longing for it as 'congealed' in the seductive displays of retail and advertising.[44] Viktor & Rolf's work seems to nod to this and to undercut any notion of resistance to the spectacle by acknowledging that cultural producers and consumers today can be seduced and entranced by the spectacle even as they understand that they are being manipulated by it. Like Andy Warhol's soapboxes of the 1960s that seemed to 'love' capitalism, Viktor & Rolf's Spring–Summer 2001 ready-to-wear show was a homage to Hollywood musicals modelled by a troupe of Dutch tap dancers in Busby Berkeley line-ups rather than the usual fashion models. At the end, the two designers came on in white suits and pencil-thin moustaches to take their bow, only to be themselves willingly incorporated into a dance routine like twin Fred Astaires (fig. 62). Their version of tap-dancing capitalism made the spectacle of enjoyment into the subject matter of the show itself.

44   Judith Williamson, *Consuming Passions: The Dynamics of Popular Culture*, Marion Boyars, London and New York, 1986: 12.

four   phantasmagoria

Magic Delusion

Alexander McQueen's runway show for his fourth couture collection for Givenchy (Autumn–Winter 1999–2000) featured draped and cowl-necked devoré dresses, and was staged on a conventional catwalk. Its *coup de théâtre* was to replace the conventional parade of models on the runway by mannequins with clear, plexiglass heads (fig. 63). Springing from trap doors cut into the catwalk, they rotated slowly on wooden disks before sinking back down into the darkness from which they came (fig. 64). As the journalist Laura Craik wrote, 'the spectacle was riveting. Never have dummies looked so alive.'[1] Below the stage an elaborate system of scaffolding housed the mannequins and from this lower world the designer too rose up at the end like Mephistopheles to take his bow, before descending back into the darkness. The invisible designer, part-impresario, part-puppeteer, controlled the working of the show from behind the scenes, in a way reminiscent of the department store owner Mouret's Svengali-like behind-the-scenes manipulations in Zola's *The Ladies' Paradise*, based on the real Boucicault, creator of the Parisian department store in 1852, the Bon Marché.

For its Spring–Summer 1999 collection in Milan the design company Etro replaced the conventional runway with a conveyor belt on which the models posed like shop window dummies on revolving podiums, while an acrobat swung overhead. Like a photographic negative and a positive, these two shows made the same point: in the Etro show the living models looked like dummies, in the Givenchy show the dummies seemed to come alive. In both, the phantasmagoric figures created a bridge between animate and inanimate models, liveliness and deathliness. The term 'phantasmagoria' was first used in English in 1802 to describe another form of popular spectacle. Philipstal's Phantasmagoria in London consisted of a magic-lantern show in which skeletons, ghosts and other fantastical figures were made rapidly to increase and decrease in size in a darkened room veiled with gauze, unexpectedly advancing on the spectators, before finally appearing to sink into the ground and disappear, very like the mannequins in the Givenchy show. The term phantasmagoria thus came to describe back-lit optical illusions, usually those of the magic lantern, and metaphorically it came to connote some form of dramatic visual deception or display, in which shadowy and unreal figures appear only to disappear.[2]

In his analysis of Richard Wagner's operas, Theodor Adorno used the term to designate the tricks, deceits and illusions of nineteenth-century commodity culture, with its sleights of hand that peddled false desires.[3] Since its light source could not be seen by the spectators, the magic lantern provided Adorno with a metaphor for the way in which the working mechanisms of capitalist production were hidden from view by its marketing and retail stratagems.[4] In the same way, the workings of the Givenchy show were concealed below the catwalk, and the audience was distracted by the disconcerting substitution of the inanimate dummy for the living model. The concealed machinery beneath the catwalk was like the commercial transaction, while the ghostly mannequins rising out of, and falling back into, the darkness suggested the phantasmagoria or 'magic delusion'[5] of the dream

63 (*facing page*) Alexander McQueen for Givenchy, Autumn–Winter 1999–2000. Photograph Niall McInerney

64 (*below*) Alexander McQueen for Givenchy, Autumn–Winter 1999–2000. Photograph Niall McInerney

1 Laura Craik, *The Guardian*, 19 July 1999.

2 E.g. Scott's journal, 1808: 'in this phantasmagorical place [London] the objects of the day come and depart like shadows': Oxford English Dictionary.

3 Theodor Adorno, *In Search of Wagner*, trans. Rodney Livingstone, Verso, London and New York, 1981, ch. 6, 'Phantasmagoria': 85–96.

4 Karl Marx used the metaphor 'phantasmagoria' to describe commodity fetishism as 'a definite social relation between men themselves which assumes here, for them, the phantasmagoric form of a relation between things.' Karl Marx, *Capital*, vol. 1, trans. Ben Fowkes, Penguin, Harmondsworth, 1976: 165. This translation, however, substitutes the English 'fantastic' for 'phantasmagoric'. In Adorno's *In Search of Wagner*: 6, Rodney Livingstone translated Marx's term as 'phantasmagoric', more appropriately, since Marx's earlier references in the same paragraph are to the nineteenth-century science of optics. Marx's analysis informs Adorno's pejorative use of 'phantasmagoria' in his analysis of Wagner's operas.

5 Adorno, *In Search of Wagner*: 85.

65 (*facing page top*) Walter van Beirendonck for W&LT, Autumn–Winter 1998–9. Photograph Corina Lecca, courtesy Walter van Beirendonck

66 (*facing page bottom*) Alexander McQueen, Autumn–Winter 1998–9. Photograph Niall McInerney

world. When Galliano based his Autumn–Winter 1996–7 collection on the fantasy that the Princess Pocahontas went to Paris in the 1930s where she met Wallace Simpson, designed her own couture collection (which included beaded flapper dresses) and took it back to her tribe, he made a spectacle like the phantasmagoria described by Adorno, in whose narratives time is abolished and 'the near and the far are deceptively merged'.[6] Just as Galliano's shows could be said to evoke the seductive 'dreamworlds' of nineteenth-century department stores and world fairs, in which the consumer lost him or herself in fantasy and reverie, so, equally, could they be seen to operate like nineteenth-century phantasmagoria to conceal their commercial origins and aims.

Adorno wrote that 'where the dream is at its most exalted, the commodity is closest to hand' and in a series of 'exalted dreams' many European fashion designers played out this theme.[7] Walter van Beirendonck's Autumn–Winter 1998–9 collection for W&LT, titled Believe, was staged in a completely dark hall where members of the audience were given a flashlight to help them to see. The hall was empty apart from a wall covered with a fluorescent yellow curtain, an electric blue catwalk lit by white light, and benches either side for the audience. During the finale of the show, the curtain opened to reveal a fairy-tale scene of elves staring down at the audience, creating a fairyland like Adorno's account of nineteenth-century phantasmagoria (fig. 65).[8] Alexander McQueen's show of the same season was staged on a catwalk that simulated solidified black lava and culminated with a ring of flames springing up on the catwalk that trapped the red-sequinned model in the centre of 'a vast, magic conflagration', a phrase Adorno used to describe the apocalyptic effects of phantasmagoria (fig. 66).[9] He argued that Wagner's operas procured 'the occultation of production by means of the outward appearance of the product', a phrase that can aptly be applied to the 1990s fashion show, which concealed its production values behind ever increasingly theatrical sleights of hand.[10] In Martin Margiela's Autumn–Winter 2002–3 collection, shown in darkness that was briefly punctuated by rays of light, the models were escorted to their individual scaffolding catwalks by Margiela's lab-coated assistants who turned the light on before leaving them there. At one stage in the show the same lab-coated assistants carried round a perspex box containing a handbag covered in white cotton and displayed it to the audience in an ironic take on the vogue for designer handbags, so that, as Adorno wrote of late nineteenth-century commodity culture, 'the product presents itself as self-producing'.[11] In the same way, the late twentieth-century fashion show seductively presents its spectacle to the public while simultaneously diverting attention from the fact that, like luxury consumer goods on display in exclusive department stores, they are beyond the reach of all but a privileged few (for even money cannot buy a place in a fashion show, and yet only money can buy designer clothes). Margiela's parodic display of the handbag in his show highlighted the way in which such display is usually naturalised, and hence made invisible, through the everyday stratagems of contemporary consumer culture and the objects it fetishises.

* * *

6   Ibid: 86.
7   Ibid: 91.
8   Ibid: 86.
9   Ibid: 90.
10   Ibid: 85.
11   Ibid.

Phantasmic Dialogue

Like Margiela's, the Givenchy show that used mannequins made the commercial origins of fashion visible as spectacle, rather than veiling them entirely (see figs 63 and 64). As the plexiglass mannequins eerily rose and fell in the darkness, their turn-of-the-century draped evening dresses and static poses evoked both the wax dummies behind glass of the 1900 Paris exhibition (see fig. 13) and the reflective glass vitrines and shop-window dummies photographed by Eugène Atget (fig. 67). And the life-in-death nature of the ghostly mannequins struck a sombre note in the spectacle, highlighting the deathliness of the commodity form. Susan Buck-Morss has argued that 'in fashion, the phantasmagoria of commodities presses closest to the skin',[12] and there is something stifflingly oppressive about the way in which these phantasms return as the ghosts of modernity: the darkness of McQueen's show was supernatural. McQueen's chilly models and glassy mannequins sketched a darker, less euphoric, side of capitalist modernity as it re-emerged in the present. If, as Rabaté argues, the 'ghosts of modernity' return because modernism denied its own past in the interest of constructing a new and utopian future, they come back as chaotic and aberrant. They are the residue left by modernity.[13]

The drive to perpetual alteration and renewal that characterises fashion rejects or represses the past, ostensibly. 'But [the past] returns to disturb and unsettle the confidence of the modern. The present remains permanently engaged in a phantasmic dialogue with the past.'[14] This dialogue, however, is not a simple case of contrasting opposites (the past versus the present, for example) but a dialogue in which the ambiguities of both are deeply embedded. Martin Margiela's Spring–Summer 1992 collection was shown in a disused Paris metro station, Saint Martin, that had been out of use since 1939. Its three main stair wells down which the models paraded were lit by 1,600 beeswax candles, stuck by their own wax to the metal handrails (fig. 68). The presentation was entirely new, revolutionary for a catwalk show, yet also old in its evocation of pre-war dereliction and its use of poetic urban spaces. This complex dialogue of past and present also incorporated a vision of the future in that Margiela's innovative way of showing clothes broke new ground in mapping out future possibilities for the catwalk show.

This 'phantasmic dialogue', as Lynda Nead terms it, is not, however, a question of literal quotation or representation, for example a catwalk peopled by ghosts, although such shows have been staged. Imitation of Christ's Spring–Summer 2001 show was held in a New York funeral parlour. The performance mimicked a wake, the models marched at a funeral pace and were styled like the walking wounded, with bandages and bloody wrists. In Alexander McQueen's Autumn–Winter 1997–8 Eclect Dissect collection for Givenchy the models came back as ghosts to haunt their murderer (see fig. 114); here the conceit of a row of models representing a row of avenging ghosts perfectly exemplified both the spectacle of fashion, with its emphasis on drama, narrative and showmanship, and the ghostly presence at its metaphorical centre. However, the 'phantasmic dialogue' can also trace a less literal and more structural underlying connection between past and present. This is the status

12 Susan Buck-Morss, *The Dialectics of Seeing: Walter Benjamin and the Arcades Project*, MIT Press, Cambridge, Mass., and London, 1991: 97.

13 Lynda Nead argues in *Victorian Babylon*, Yale University Press, New Haven and London, 2000: 7, that 'there can never be a pure, clean modernity, for the discourses that constitute that historical temporality bear the ghosts of the past, of modernity's own other'. She cites Michel de Certeau: 'any autonomous order is founded on what it eliminates; it produced a "residue" condemned to be forgotten. But what was excluded re-infiltrates the place of its origin – now the present's clean [*propre*] place. It resurfaces, it troubles, it turns the present's feeling of being "at home" into an illusion, it lurks – this "wild", this "ob-scene", this filth, this "resistance" of "superstition" – within the walls of the residence, and, behind the back of the owner (the *ego*), or over its objections, it inscribes the law of the other.' Michel de Certeau, *Heterologies: Discourse of the Other*, trans. Brian Massumi, University of Manchester Press, 1986: 4. This argument is also made in Mary Douglas's aphorism 'dirt is matter out of place' and by Julia Kristeva's mobilisation of Douglas's writing on hygiene in Kristeva's account of abjection. See Mary Douglas, *Purity and Danger: An Analysis of the Concepts of Pollution and Taboo*, Routledge, London and New York, 1992 [1966]; Julia Kristeva, *The Powers of Horror: An Essay on Abjection*, trans. Leon S. Roudier, Columbia University Press, New York and Oxford, 1982 [1980].

14 Nead, *Victorian Babylon*: 8.

67 (*facing page*) Eugène Atget, avenue des Gobelins, 1925. The Museum of Modern Art, New York, The Abbot-Levy Collection. Photograph © Scala, Florence/The Museum of Modern Art, New York, 2003

68 Martin Margiela, Spring–Summer 1992. Photograph Niall McInerney

and role of the commodity itself, and its relation to human fears, desires and identifications. If there was a darkness surrounding the Givenchy glass mannequins, it was not the literal darkness out of which they rose, but the metaphorical darkness of capitalist enterprise itself, epitomised by the inanimate dummies standing in for human models. If they evoked anxiety, perhaps it was because living women had been replaced by prosthetic goddesses.

Lisa Tickner has argued that periods of new technology, such as the late nineteenth century, produce ambivalent responses, and perhaps her point helps to explain McQueen's ambiguous models in a different period of rapid technological change, the 'information revolution' of the late twentieth century. 'Technology held both a phantasmic promise and a phantasmic threat: men might become "prosthetic gods" or mere cogs in the machinery of modernity.'[15] A concern about the alienating effects of new technology also underlay Marx's concept of commodity fetishism, whereby human relations and feelings are displaced onto objects and people live out their relations via the commodity form rather than directly.[16] Thus the ghosts of both technological change and of the commodity could be argued to be invoked in McQueen's revolving mannequins; and the darkness of the Givenchy show to be not only literal but also metaphorical: neither the dark stage, nor the deathliness of the mannequin models, but the death-dealing nature of the commodity form as it impacts on social life. His reified, inanimate dummies recall the inverted relationships between objects and things of commodity culture, whereby, as people and things trade semblances, the commodity assumes an uncanny vitality of its own (' "dead labour" come back to dominate the living'[17]) while the human producer acquires some of the 'deathly facticity'[18] of the machine.

If the deathliness of the commodity form that reduces all human relations to a set of interactions between objects was evoked in McQueen's plexiglass mannequins for Givenchy, it was taken much further in his own Spring–Summer 2001 show, Voss, in London. McQueen had constructed a large mirrored box in the centre of his runway, so that as the audience took their seats they were obliged to sit and watch their own reflections in harsh lighting. As London shows regularly start anything from three quarters to an hour and a half late, the audience became progressively more uncomfortable as it was faced with its own reflection. Individuals had to choose between looking away, watching themselves or watching others watching themselves; after a while this self-scrutiny produced an intense and paranoid self-consciousness. The scenario was a cruel but particularly meaningful one because the audience consisted of fashion professionals or, as the journalist Sarah Mower described it, 'a gathering of the prime arbiters of vanity'.[19] Here McQueen reduced the observers to objects, turning their own sharp scrutiny of the models back on themselves, highlighting how much the model, as well as the clothes, are objectified in the gaze of the journalists, recalling Lukács's and Marx's descriptions of commodity fetishism whereby people live out their relations to each other via objects, displacing human emotions onto things, flooding them with meaning.

Having once reversed the spectacle, McQueen effected a further reversal by turning the audience into voyeurs when the show started. The lighting went down on the audience and came on inside the box, which proved to be made of reflective surveillance glass, mirrored inside as well as out. This time the models inside the box could not see the audience but they could clearly see their own reflections. Thus the audience could watch the models watching themselves. For ten minutes the models preened, strutted and admired their own reflections, staging a solitary performance before the mirror that in real life would only occur in the privacy of the bedroom, but with the additional frisson that their simulation of solitary pleasure was performed, like a sex show, to an audience of fashion voyeurs concealed behind a one-way mirror (fig. 69).

15   Lisa Tickner, *Modern Lives and Modern Subjects*, Yale University Press, New Haven and London, 2000: 191. Tickner takes the phrase from Freud, and refers to Hal Foster's use of it in his essay 'Prosthetic Gods', *Modernism/Modernity*, vol. 4, no. 2, April 1997: 5–38.

16   Marx, *Capital*: 176.

17   Hal Foster, *Compulsive Beauty*, MIT Press, Cambridge, Mass., and London, 1993: 129.

18   Hal Foster, 'The Art of Fetishism', *The Princeton Architectural Journal*, vol. 4, 'Fetish', 1992: 7.

19   Sarah Mower, 'Politics of Vanity', *The Fashion*, no. 2, spring/summer 2001: 162.

For models, a basic narcissism is part of the job; their bodies are their livelihood, their looks are the commodity. However, in this show, as the clothes became progressively more disturbing, this workaday narcissism started to look psychotic and dysfuntional. The models' heads were bandaged, their faces pallid. The clothes almost fetishised materials: feathers, brocade, shells, a wooden bodice, an outfit made from a jigsaw puzzle of a castle constructed three-dimensionally around the model's shoulders. Another had birds of prey swooping around her head. Two dresses were made of cuttle-fish and mussel shells, another clothed the model from neck to ankles in a sheath of razor shells (fig. 70). The tinkling and clattering of these dresses in motion was amplified in the final showpiece worn by the model Karen Elson, a simple dress made from a vintage silk kimono worn over a skirt of overlapping black oyster shells made from the pieces of a two-hundred-year old Japanese screen (fig. 71). In this garment McQueen destroyed a surviving dress while simultaneously fetishising and reifying it. As she walked the dress parted to reveal the skirt below whose scales clattered audibly against each other. It was worn with a neckpiece by the jeweller Shaun Leane. Although its filigree tracery and bunches of precious Tahitian peacock pearls

69 Alexander McQueen, Voss, Spring–Summer 2001. Photograph Chris Moore, courtesy Alexander McQueen

70 (following page) Alexander McQueen, Voss, Spring–Summer 2001. Photograph Chris Moore, courtesy Alexander McQueen

71 (page 97) Shaun Leane, necklace for Alexander McQueen, Voss, Spring–Summer 2001, made in collaboration with Perles de Tahiti. Photograph Chris Moore, courtesy Shaun Leane

72   Michelle Olley modelling for Alexander
McQueen, Voss, Spring–Summer 2001.
Photograph Chris Moore, courtesy
Alexander McQueen

looked delicate, its spiky silver branches that curled up the model's neck and over her cheek forced her head up like a restraining truss. The padded, white ceiling of the glass box in which the spectacle unfolded added to the overall effect of a padded cell in which the slow dance of schizoid vanity was enacted. Mower wrote: 'the creepy idea began to sink in that we were being treated to a performance by some of the world's top models about beautiful women driven insane by their own reflections.'[20]

After the last model had exited from the box, the sides of another box on the runway smashed down to reveal the naked figure of the fetish writer Michelle Olley reclining on a lace-covered sofa made from huge cow horns (fig. 72). Based on Joel Peter Witkin's photograph 'Sanitarium' of a twenty-stone middle-aged woman, connected via a breathing tube to a stuffed monkey, Olley's bandaged head was covered in a pig-mask in ghostly grey, a breathing pipe apparently protruding from her mouth, while her body was covered in large, fragile moths. Some were attached to her, others fluttered loose in the box. In the staging of this show McQueen oscillated between beauty and horror, turning conventional ideas of beauty upside down. Although the fashion world may embrace polymorphous perversity when it comes to sex, it is narrowly prescriptive about body shape and size. Above all

20   Ibid.

it does not tolerate fat, which, with some honorable exceptions, is taboo.[21] McQueen's presentation juxtaposed the so-called norm epitomised by the skinny psychotic models in the first box, with the large body that is usually anathematised in fashion, suggesting something of the horror it provokes by his use of the fluttering moths (moths which destroy clothes), the glass box, the breathing tube. Yet McQueen's presentation and the allure of the clothes themselves remained seductive. By putting beauty and horror together, the show exemplified the ambivalence that, in Adorno's account, was intrinsic to phantasmagoria: 'The conversion of pleasure into sickness is the denunciatory task of phantasmagoria'.[22] He argued that if Wagnerian phantasmagorias were 'dreamland brothels, these are simultaneously calumniated as places that no one can leave unscathed.'[23] There, simple pleasure is denigrated and anathematised as it is put on display, and thus 'the phantasmagoria is infected from the outset with the seeds of its own destruction. Inside the illusion dwells disillusion.'[24] The glass box made this visible by reflecting the audience back at themselves, firstly, and, secondly, by presenting the psychotic staging of the models' beauty inside a padded cell. The second box then inflected this so-called beauty with so-called horror, in the image of the rolling flesh of Michelle Olley.

Frivolity and Death

McQueen's Spring–Summer 2001 show lasted fifteen minutes and it cost more than £70,000.[25] Planned four months in advance, with McQueen's creative director Katy England, it had taken seven days to construct the set alone, built by teams of carpenters, electricians, metal-workers and model-makers. The clothes too, many of them showpieces that would never go into production, had been worked on by hand by teams of people sewing shells in individually and constructing headpieces. Before the show, the usual teams of hairdressers and make-up artists worked on the models. The show was produced by Sam Gainsbury and Anna Whiting, art directed by Joseph Bennett, the lighting was designed by Dan Landing, the music was by the DJ John Gosling. There was even an old man responsible for the exotic moths to ensure they did not come alive too soon before the show.

Like the phantasmagorias described by Adorno, this massive effort of production was never visible, and the show disguised its workings. It left, instead, a vivid, garish impression. Such strong imagery leaves a retinal afterimage in the mind that fades more slowly. Like the big top, the show was dismantled and put away after it was all over. The moths died, the models moved on to other shows. And, like the circus, this particular show combined celebration and menace. The annual round of international shows visited by fashion journalists is known as the 'fashion circus' and the metaphor is drawn from the circus's fly-by-night quality as much as from its tradition of spectacle and showmanship. In this it is like fashion: here today, and gone tomorrow. However, although the circus is a locus of spectacle, fun and abandon, it is also a twilight world of refuge, danger and loss of self.

21 See e.g. the photographer Nick Knight's website, www.showstudio.com, which has a feature from 2002 on high fashion for big women. For a discussion of late twentieth century fashion and Western culture's ambivalence towards large women, see 'Flesh' in Rebecca Arnold, *Fashion, Desire and Anxiety: Image and Morality in the Twentieth Century*, I. B. Tauris, London and New York, 2001: 89–95. On women and body size see Susan Bordo, *Unbearable Weight: Feminism, Western Culture and the Body*, University of California Press, Berkeley, 1993; and Naomi Wolf, *The Beauty Myth*, Vintage, New York, 1991.

22 Adorno, *In Search of Wagner*: 94.

23 Ibid.

24 Ibid.

25 It was sponsored by American Express. See Louise Davis, 'Frock Tactics', *The Observer Magazine*, 18 February 2001: 36–9.

74 (*above*) Alexander McQueen, What a
Merry-go-Round, Autumn–Winter 2001–2.
Photograph Roberto Tecchio,
courtesy Judith Clark Costume

73 (*facing page*) John Galliano,
Spring–Summer 1997. Photograph Patrice
Stable, courtesy John Galliano

75 (facing page) Alexander McQueen, What a Merry-go-Round, Autumn–Winter 2001–2. Photograph Roberto Tecchio, courtesy Judith Clark Costume

26   Walter Benjamin, *The Arcades Project*, trans. Howard Eiland and Kevin McLaughlin, Belknap Press of Harvard University Press, Cambridge, Mass., and London, 1999: 71.

27   Elizabeth Wilson, *Adorned in Dreams: Fashion and Modernity*, Virago, London, 1985: 13 [2nd ed. I. B. Tauris, 2003 forthcoming].

28   Marshall Berman, *All That is Solid Melts into Air: The Experience of Modernity*, Verso, London, 1983: 91.

29   See Baudelaire's review of the Salon of 1845 for the reference to 'the heroism of modern life' cited in ibid: 143. For the 'maelstrom' see 16.

30   E.g. Jean Baudrillard, *The Ecstasy of Communication*, trans. Bernard and Caroline Schutze, Semiotext(e) Autonomia, Brooklyn, New York, 1988.

31   There is a substantial body of writing on the relationship of fashion, consumption and identity from the eighteenth century to the twentieth. Notable among them are Alan Tomlinson (ed.), *Consumption, Identity and Style*, Comedia, London, 1990; Beverlie Lemire, *Fashion's Favorite: The Cotton Trade and the Consumer in Britain 1660–1800*, Oxford University Press, 1991; Stuart and Elizabeth Ewen, *Channels of Desire: Mass Images and the Shaping of America*, University of Minnesota Press, Minneapolis, 1992; Rob Shields (ed.), *Lifestyle Shopping; The Subject of Consumption*, Routledge, London, 1992; Daniel Roche, *The Culture of Clothing: Dress and Fashion in the Ancien Régime*, trans. Jean Birrell, Cambridge University Press, 1994; Philippe Perrot, *Fashioning the Bourgeoisie: A History of Clothing in the Nineteenth Century*, trans. Richard Bienvenu, Princeton University Press, 1994; Daniel Miller, *Shopping, Place and Identity*, Routledge, London, 1998; Christopher Breward, *The Hidden Consumer: Masculinities, Fashion and City Life 1860–1914*, Manchester University Press, 1999; Diana Crane, *Fashion and Its Social Agendas*, University of Chicago Press, 2000; Erika Rappaport, *Shopping for Pleasure: Women in the Making of London's West End*, Princeton University Press, 2000.

Fashion shows of the 1990s based on the circus and fairground picked up both these characteristics; some evoked the upbeat, energetic side of modernity (fig. 73) while others suggested that its residue consisted of melancholy and alienation (fig. 74).

The celebratory aspect of the circus was enacted in Julien Macdonald's Spring–Summer 2000 show, Frock & Roll, staged at London's Roundhouse in September 1999. To an audience of London celebrities perched in the front row, the lights dimmed and the shadows of hanging acrobats from the De La Guardia troupe played over the ceiling. Gradually it became clear that what sounded like pattering rain was a cascade of balloons and confetti falling onto the canvas ceiling. The acrobats burst through the ceiling, bungee-jumping, smoke-bombing and trapeze-flying. A member of the audience was swooped on and snatched away into the air, never to return. The show consisted of bubblegum colours, glitter and sparkle, epitomised by Macdonald's signature knitwear to which for the first time he added leather and suede, lattice-cut and silver-studded, in rainbow colours. At the show's finale, the canvas ceiling upon which balloons, confetti and styroform balls had been resting burst open, showering the audience with its contents. By contrast, Alexander McQueen's Autumn–Winter 2000–1 show articulated the darker side of the circus and fairground. Staging it on a merry-go-round in front of a Victorian toyshop, McQueen emphasised the sinister side of childhood toys, sampling the voice of the childcatcher from the film *Chitty Chitty Bang Bang* in the sound track. The models' make-up was based on the white clown to produce a mournful and alienated image (see fig. 74). In this show, the frightening and strange elements of the circus were made explicit, for example in the black-clad model with a golden skeleton dragging at her feet (fig. 75).

A German fashion magazine of 1925 declared, 'fashion consists only in extremes. Inasmuch as it seeks the extremes by nature, there remains for it nothing more, when it has abandoned some particular form, than to give itself to the opposite form.' Benjamin's comment was: 'its uttermost extremes: frivolity and death.'[26] Thus the fleshly body of the model is shadowed by the golden skeleton; the death-defying acrobat by the alienated clown. This is the double-sided nature of modernity identified by Marshall Berman, and associated specifically with fashion by Elizabeth Wilson: 'for fashion, the child of capitalism, has, like capitalism, a double face.'[27] In Berman's analysis, 'modernity' is characterised by the dynamism, 'reckless momentum' and 'breathless intensity' of modern life in a period of capitalist production and consumption.[28] This is the upbeat side of modernity that is evident in the excitement and theatricality of the spectacle, that returns in the present in the contemporary fashion show. Nineteenth-century modernity was a consequence of industrialisation and its impact on the social and economic life of peoples and cities. In 1845 Charles Baudelaire identified a heroism in everyday life that consisted of making oneself at home in what Berman calls 'the maelstrom of modern life'.[29] It is comparable to the way in which some late twentieth-century writers identified a post-modern euphoria or exhilaration.[30] More empirically minded cultural historians scrutinised the way in which individuals have been able to carve out identities for themselves through fashionable consumption in the modern period.[31] One of the ways in which individuals make a

changing world their own, and mark out their place within it, is through dress: Baudelaire described the epic quality of modern life that 'make[s] us feel how great and poetic we are in our cravats and our patent-leather boots.'[32] Just as it is today, fashionable dress was important in the nineteenth-century city: it emphasised the instability of the sign, signifying not only novelty but also choice and identity, giving men and women 'a way of becoming the subjects as well as the objects of modernisation.'[33]

Yet, Berman argued, modernity has a darker side. The excitement of the modern world, the will to change and desire for novelty that characterise it, is balanced by a terror of disintegration, a world in which 'things fall apart, the centre cannot hold'[34] and, in Marx's words, 'all fixed, fast-frozen relations, with their train of ancient and venerable prejudices and opinions, are swept away, all new-formed ones become antiquated before they can ossify. "All that is solid melts into air".'[35] Berman argued that a double-edged quality is a central feature of capitalism itself. For capitalist production depends on continual innovation, which fashion embodies, but innovation and novelty are the enemy of tradition and continuity; they produce a sense of instability and permanent dislocation. Furthermore, in order for things to be constantly built, they must be constantly pulled down, and the reverse of capitalist productivity is violent destruction.[36] Nietzschean nihilism has its roots in the 'banal, everyday workings of the market economy'[37] and vistas of capitalist production threaten constantly to turn into an abyss. This terror of disintegration invades the lively energetic side of modernity to produce a dark sensibility and aesthetic, visible in much fashion design of the 1990s. Veronique Branquinho's Autumn–Winter 1998–9 collection was based on the double life of Laura Palmer in David Lynch's *Twin Peaks*. In a range of just 'off' garments, that included mismatching colours, rabbit fur pullovers and heavily shrouded coats and capes, worn by models with white faces and teeth painted black, Branquinho's collection, shrouded in mystery and ambiguity, evoked a sense of unfathomable double meaning beneath the surface (fig. 76). Suggesting the secret life of girls and women as a subterranean world, this hidden undercurrent was brought to the surface in her collections and seamlessly blended with superficial appearances. Branquinho has said: 'the most important thing for me to recognise is that a woman is a very complex person . . . every woman has a mystery inside her . . . I like this black side of people. Black minds, black moods, black clothes: I like the word and I like the emotion. That's what I try to reflect. It's romance for the doom generation.'[38]

Both sides could be seen in a 1996 Viktor & Rolf collection that featured glittering golden clothes whose 'shadows' took the form of empty black equivalents of each of the golden outfits, laid out on the studio floor (fig. 77). These shadow clothes could be worn, just as the glittering ones could. Amy Spindler commented that 'a woman who wears flashy clothes to be noticed could wear the shadow clothes and be invisible . . . this collection, too, was the dark and light side of fashion . . . the fashion industry itself is polarised in just such a way. There are the editors who only wear black, shrinking away into the landscape, and the ones who dress to redress the rest of the world.'[39] This double-sided quality also relates back to the history of fashion in the modernist period. The euphoria and

32 Baudelaire's review of the Salon of 1845 cited in Berman, *All That is Solid*: 143.

33 Mica Nava, 'Modernity's Disavowal: Women, the City and the Department Store', in Pasi Falk and Colin Campbell (eds), *The Shopping Experience*, Sage, London, Thousand Oaks and New Delhi, 1997: 57.

34 W. B. Yeats, 'The Second Coming', l. 3, in *Selected Poetry*, ed. A. Norman Jeffares, Pan, London, 1974: 99.

35 Karl Marx and Frederick Engels, *The Manifesto of the Communist Party*, trans. Samuel Moore, Progress Publishers, Moscow, 1966 [1848]: 44–5. Also cited in Berman, *All That is Solid*: 21; see too Wilson, *Adorned in Dreams*: 60.

36 Berman, *All That is Solid*: 100.

37 Ibid.

38 Cited in Luc Derycke and Sandra van de Veire (eds), *Belgian Fashion Design*, Ludion, Ghent and Amsterdam, 1999: 85.

39 Amy Spindler in *Viktor & Rolf Haute Couture Book*, texts by Amy Spindler and Didier Grumbach, Groninger Museum, Gröningen, 2000: 10.

energy of nineteenth-century commodity culture shared the single-minded optimism of modernism, with its persistent denial of the past. Yet the ghosts of modernity return through the very structures that deny them, such as fashion, a cultural manifestation of modernity and change.[40] In more mainstream fashion production like Julien Macdonald's and John Galliano's we see the upbeat side of modernity, but at its heart, in the work of a few designers such as McQueen and Viktor & Rolf, the dark side erupts. It is at these moments that fashion is like a symptom, when the ghosts of modernity invade its space. Fashion produces images that oscillate between celebration and horror, sex and death, pleasure and terror, a juxtaposition that Colin Campbell has argued emerged in the Romantic movement of the late eighteenth and early nineteenth centuries as a mixture of the Puritan work ethic and the Romantic.[41] Elizabeth Wilson too, in her book on fashion and modernity, *Adorned in Dreams*, has argued that the intense individualism of the Romantic movement was at once a response and a counter-ideology to the advances of science and industrialisation.[42] Writing in 1985, Wilson drew analogies between the Romantic period and the present, an analogy which can still be drawn at the beginning of the twenty-first century.[43]

* * *

76 (*above*) Veronique Branquinho, Autumn–Winter 1998–9. Photograph Houbrechts/Daniels, courtesy Veronique Branquinho

77 (*left*) Viktor & Rolf, L'Apparence du Vide, Spring–Summer 1996. Galerie Patricia Dorfmann, Paris. Photograph Viktor & Rolf

40 Jonathan Dollimore, *Sexual Dissidence: Augustine to Wilde, Freud to Foucault*, Clarendon Press, Oxford, 1991: 279–325, uses the term 'transgressive reinscription' to describe the way that a quality or action can reverse into its opposite, so that, understood in psychoanalytic terms, what is repressed comes back via the very structures that repress it.

41 Colin Campbell, *The Romantic Ethic and the Spirit of Modern Consumerism*, Basil Blackwell, Oxford, 1987.

42 Wilson, *Adorned in Dreams*: 61.

43 E.g. Philippe Lacou-Labarthe and Jean-Luc Nancy, *The Literary Absolute: The Theory of Literature in German Romanticism*, trans. Philip Barnard and Cheryl Lester, State University of New York Press, Albany, N.Y., 1988, relates German Romanticism to post-modernism.

Pleasure into Sickness

The oscillation between extremes was identified in the nineteenth century as peculiar to its time. In 1856 Marx wrote:

> There is one great fact, characteristic of our nineteenth century, a fact which no party dares deny. On the one hand, there have started into life industrial and scientific forces which no epoch of former human history had ever suspected. On the other hand, there exist symptoms of decay, far surpassing the horrors recorded of the latter times of the Roman empire. In our days, everything seems pregnant with its contrary.[44]

While Marx linked progress inexorably with decay, Baudelaire linked the fashionable world with the criminal underworld.[45] And Elizabeth Wilson has argued that the myth of the artist as a bohemian was constructed in exactly this period as an imaginary solution to the problems posed by art and artists in industrial Western societies; the term 'bohemian' referred to a semi-criminal underworld until it was extended to impoverished artists and writers whose vocation thus 'became tainted with social and moral ambiguity.'[46] In her earlier study of fashion and modernity Wilson concluded that fashion in this period is necessarily ambiguous as it reflects 'the fissured culture of modernity': 'the daring of fashion speaks dread as well as desire; the shell of chic, the aura of glamour, always hides a wound.'[47]

It is this double nature of modernity that is bound up in the operation of phantasmagoria, so that everything becomes 'pregnant with its opposite' and progress is over-run with 'symptoms of decay'. In the late 1990s, fashion was the paradigm of this and it could express it so well for all the reasons for which it is frequently criticised: that it is superficial, obsessed with beauty, novelty and celebrity, the focus of continual change, conspicuous consumption and wasteful excess. It is in this sense that fashion can be argued to be at the very centre of the contemporary. As such, it is capable of expressing the underlying preoccupations of the culture, a route in to uncomfortable truths about the world.[48] Even in New York, an epicentre of commercial fashion, a few experimental designers began to work in an alternative vein, producing their version of American gothic. In one show the New York designer Elena Bajo had psychotic models staging breakdowns on the catwalk.[49] The American Jeremy Scott's first collection was shown in Paris in 1995 and was inspired by car crash victims. He said: 'I like the idea of this woman in a car accident, all chic'ed out in, like, a paper dress, like, couture and pleated, and totally, like, sexy. Instead of being, like, dowdy, like hospital.'[50] In common with the writer J. G. Ballard in his novel *Crash*, Scott imagined the car crash victim as erotic. This juxtaposition of glamour and horror was echoed, as seen earlier, in the British designer Andrew Groves's collection *Cocaine Nights* (see figs 48 and 49), of which he said: 'it was a collection that looked like the perfect collection, but had so many sub-currents . . . I wanted to show the horrors of perfection, how glamour is really the flip side of decay and destitution.'[51] For Adorno, the double-edged quality of nineteenth-century phantasmagorias, be they the operas of Richard

44   Karl Marx, speech made on 14 April 1856, London, printed in *People's Paper*, London 19 April 1856, repr. in *Surveys from Exile: Political Writings*, vol. 2, ed. and intro. by David Fernbach, Penguin in association with New Left Review, Harmondsworth, 1973: 299.

45   Berman, *All That is Solid*: 143.

46   Elizabeth Wilson, *Bohemians: The Glamourous Outcasts*, I. B. Tauris, London, 2000: 21.

47   Wilson, *Adorned in Dreams*: 246.

48   I am grateful for Elizabeth Wilson's comments which helped me to re-articulate my text here.

49   Ginger Gregg Duggan, 'The Greatest Show on Earth' in Ginger Gregg Duggan (ed.), 'Fashion and Performance', special ed. of *Fashion Theory*, vol. 5, issue 3, September 2001: 267.

50   *The New Yorker*, 30 March 1998: 108.

51   Martin Raymond, 'Clothes with Meaning', *Blueprint*, no. 154, October 1998: 31.

Wagner or the consumer goods on display in department stores, was that they converted pleasures into sickness, and sex into death.[52] Further, he argued that the 'dreamworld of Romantic protest' generated through phantasmagoria and other illusions was but a poor substitute for political consciousness.[53]

In the accelerated cycles of consumption of the late twentieth century, fashion was well placed to articulate the ambivalent nature of consumer capitalism. This juxtaposition was articulated in the nineteenth century in the way in which Baudelairean modernity produced a new definition of modern beauty as being bound up with horror.[54] The concept for Andrew Groves's Spring–Summer 1998 collection Status was based on disease. Like McQueen's collection featuring the mirrored box, Groves juxtaposed the external beauty of the supermodel against the internal decay of a society consumed with visual images of external perfection. The clothes were deconstructed, representing decay and disease. He conceived the idea of women beamed down from outer space who looked like beautiful, perfect, untouchable mannequins, but who were in fact rotting away inside, a contemporary echo of Baudelaire's *Les Fleurs du Mal* which is also echoed in the artist Mat Collishaw's cancerous orchids (fig. 78).

In Baudelaire's poem 'Les Métamorphoses du Vampire' from *Les Fleurs du Mal*, the sexually sated poet turns to kiss his lascivious and predatory lover, only to find she has turned into a puss-filled goatskin which, by morning, has become a pile of bones. Baudelaire's avant-garde aesthetic shares the structure of economic relations in consumer capitalism. Just as beauty is inflected with horror, and rags are the other of the commodity, so alienation is the other of spectacle, and wretched production is the other of extravagant consumption. The free-market economy of contemporary fashion brings nineteenth-century *laissez faire* economic policies into the present. While Andrew Ross, like Marx before him, has written of the cruelty and amorality of fashion as a system of production,[55] Gilles Lipovetsky has described its double nature. On the one hand, he has argued, fashion encourages us to be flexible modern people, ready for and open to change; for 'how could our societies fall into step with constant change . . . if individuals were wedded to intangible principles, if novelty had not won broad social legitimacy?'[56] On the other, fashion is also at the heart of some dysfunctional aspects of modern democracies: the reign of the market place encourages people to be greedy, demanding, selfish and uncharitable. Fashion society shares this conservatism. Where its self-preserving and self-seeking tendencies win at the expense of those less well-off or more disadvantaged, this can actually slow down social change. Lipovetsky argues that this conservative aspect of fashion is always at odds with its modernising potential.[57]

It is this darker side of capitalist enterprise that emerged phantasmagorically in a narrow range of more experimental fashion design of the late 1990s. While its preoccupation with death and decay might be dismissed as pretentious or gimmicky, it engages at least symbolically with the capacity of consumer capitalism to be wretched and destructive. As seen in previous chapters, with the exception of Galliano, it was largely the bleak moments of history, rather than romantic pastiche, that were rehearsed in the 1990s. Even Galliano's

52   Ibid: 94.

53   Adorno, *In Search of Wagner*: 95.

54   Christine Buci-Glucksmann, *Baroque Reason: The Aesthetics of Modernity*, trans. Patrick Camiller, Sage, London, Thousand Oaks and New Delhi, 1994 [1984]: 75.

55   Andrew Ross (ed.), *No Sweat: Fashion, Free Trade and the Rights of Garment Workers*, Verso, New York and London, 1997.

56   Gilles Lipovetsky, *The Empire of Fashion: Dressing Modern Democracy*, trans. Catherine Porter, Princeton University Press, 1994 [1987]: 149.

57   Ibid: 150–1.

celebratory shows can be interpreted as garish and overlit, the stuff of horror, the horror of the commodity form and its inherent darkness. In this way the fashion show, rather than being merely celebratory, can acquire a garish, hallucinatory quality, which Adorno identified as 'the absolute reality of the unreal'.[58] He attributed this quality to the way in which, in the nineteenth century, the commodity began to disguise its means of production through 'the inauthentic sense of theatrical illusion'.[59] Adorno argued that it was the nature of the illusion that changed in late nineteenth-century spectacle, so that, as the idea of authenticity was itself abolished, 'the concept of the illusion as the absolute reality of the unreal grows in importance'.[60] And, as seen, this was also the principal characteristic of the fashion show in the 1990s as it became increasingly spectacular – that its commercial operations were veiled by phantasmagoric spectacles.

58 Adorno, *In Search of Wagner*: 89.
59 Ibid: 90.
60 Ibid: 60.

78 (*facing page*) Mat Collishaw, Infectious Flowers (Metastases from a Malignant Melanoma), 1996. Lightbox with photographic transparency, 50 × 50 × 10 cm. Courtesy Modern Art/London

part two

five   glamour

Looking Rich

For his Spring–Summer 2001 collection, Julien Macdonald sent down his runway a black knitted mini-dress with a corsage on the shoulder embellished with more than a thousand hand-cut diamonds (fig. 79). The dress, worth a million pounds, was produced in collaboration with the diamond company De Beers, who housed it in their safe until it was brought to the show by ten security guards. According to Macdonald, it was the most expensive and glamorous ensemble he could devise, one that only the richest woman in the world would ever be able to afford; he planned to show it on a model whose eyelashes and shoes were also studded with diamonds.[1] From top to toe, she was to be value incarnate. But if the glitter seduced, it was the seduction of the commodity form.

Macdonald was not the only designer to parade excess and wealth for its own sake on the catwalks. In the same season, the London-based Maria Grachvogel sent out a £250,000 diamond dress at her show, and the previous year in Milan Antonio d'Amico showed a wedding dress encrusted with 350 diamonds that was worth two million dollars (£1.3 million). These showpieces raised the question of who or what exactly was commodified in fashion's spectacular excesses, the model or the garment. They evoked the showgirl's costume whose enormous feathered, wired and jewelled extensions spread many centimetres beyond her body, both framing and drawing attention to its near nudity like a jewel in an elaborate setting. The historical origins of the showgirl, like those of the fashion model, lay in the commodity culture of the late nineteenth century. The show-business razzmatazz of Macdonald's Spring–Summer 2001 fashion show referred explicitly to this connection, just as an earlier collection had featured a dress made from a chandelier, suggesting a woman dressed as an illuminated object. Macdonald's mobilisation of what Baudrillard has called 'the strategy of appearances'[2] to create a world of surface and illusion in his catwalk shows revealed him to be a showman and impresario quite as much as a fashion designer.

Alongside the one-million-pound dress, as if to affirm the transformative powers of status dressing, Macdonald transformed Anna Nolan from the British television series 'Big Brother' in a rags-to-riches conversion by plastering her grungy jeans with crystals. Anna wore them on the mirrored catwalk, alongside models in outfits scattered with crystals, while strobe lighting played on them and silver confetti fluttered down on the audience. Macdonald used glitter, crystal and mirrors alchemically to transform everything around him – women, clothes, his famous guests, the catwalk itself – into gold, metaphorically speaking. The use as a model of a person made into a celebrity by television demonstrated the values of celebrity and popular culture as the most obvious statement of money. Macdonald's subsequent recruitment to Givenchy as Alexander McQueen's successor consolidated a shift in French haute couture away from the old values of quality and cut, at least in terms of the imagery of 'old money', towards the endorsement of celebrity bad taste. Anna herself was almost the 'anti-Audrey', and by the 1990s the sort of salon

79 (facing page) Julien Macdonald, Spring–Summer 2001. Photograph Chris Moore

1 See Emine Saner, 'Designed in London: The £1m Dress', *The Sunday Times*, 24 September 2000.
2 Jean Baudrillard, *Seduction*, trans. Brian Singer, Macmillan, London, 1990 [1979]: 8.

80   John Galliano for Dior, Autumn–Winter 2001–2. Photograph Roberto Tecchio, courtesy Judith Clark Costume

elegance perpetuated in the 1950s by couture houses such as Balenciaga which had dressed Audrey Hepburn had become the province of austerely elegant minimalists like Jil Sander.

Haute couture imagery, by contrast, became detached from the idea of elite good taste and, as ever a loss leader, increased its mass market sales by perpetuating the imagery of mass culture, including the blandest kind of celebrity, on the catwalk. In 2001 the French conglomorate LVMH saw its profits rise by thirty per cent. Sales on cosmetics and fragrances alone went up by twenty-four per cent. Perhaps it was not surprising therefore that in much of the fashion imagery of this period the spectacle of woman herself began to be confused with the spectacle of the commodity, begging the question of what exactly was for sale in these images. From the same period there was a discernible shift in Dior's couture collections as Galliano's 'retro' historicism began to give way to a more magpie aesthetic, fusing 1980s club culture with the late 1990s 'bling bling' associated with hip-hop and pornography (fig. 80). This imagery suggested a changing idea of who the Dior customer might be, with the notion of Lil'kim as the woman of glamour, as opposed to the 'old' couture notion of taste and aristocracy that defined the lady of fashion, thus completing a process inaugurated in the 1960s by Yves Saint Laurent who introduced popular youth culture to a couture aesthetic.

In the late 1990s Italian fashion continued to produce its own brand of conspicuous consumption, commensurate with Milan's profile as the home of fairly traditional, high-glamour, luxury clothes, as opposed to the more avant-garde experimentation of London or Antwerp. Roberto Cavalli's Autumn–Winter 2001–2 used sumptuous materials to recreate the models themselves as luxury objects, dressed in fox fur and mink, corsets, feathers, brocade and gilt (fig. 81). These ambiguously commodified figures were haunted by their own historical origins. From the mid- to late nineteenth century, the actress, the showgirl, the fashion model and the prostitute were closely related figures whose images multiplied in tandem with those of the commodity in the display culture of the period. In Benjamin's descriptions of the nineteenth-century city the prostitute in particular was a key figure of modernity because she was, as he observed from his reading of Baudelaire, 'commodity and seller in one.'[3] Buck-Morss argued that 'as a dialectical image, she synthesised the form of the commodity and the content'.[4] Further, she co-existed with the woman of fashion, another emblem of reification: 'fashion has opened the business of dialectical exchange between woman and ware', he wrote.[5] For Benjamin, fashion concealed the natural processes of decay to which the body is subject, and remained as the fetishised fragment of the body. He linked women, commodities and consumption, for all three were 'surface and illusion'.[6] (Yet, paradoxically, he also suggested that fashion can be emblematic of social change.) When, alongside the one-million-pound dress, Julien Macdonald sent out a near-naked showgirl in an outfit made up of gold chains and a diamante and feather headdress, he made it clear that femininity itself could be commodified. And when a range of minor celebrities appeared in the press in his near-naked slithers of fabrics and sparkly knits, Macdonald brought the historical commodification of the showgirl up to date in the age of celebrity culture.

3   Walter Benjamin quoted in Susan Buck-Morss, *The Dialectics of Seeing: Walter Benjamin and the Arcades Project*, MIT Press, Cambridge, Mass., and London, 1991: 184. The same phrase is translated as 'seller and sold in one' in Walter Benjamin, *The Arcades Project*, trans. Howard Eiland and Kevin McLaughlin, Belknap Press of Harvard University Press, Cambridge, Mass., and London, 1999: 10.

4   Buck-Morss, *Dialectics of Seeing*: 184.

5   Benjamin, *Arcades Project*: 62 and 881.

6   See also Mica Nava, 'Modernity's Disavowal: Women, the City and the Department Store', in Pasi Falk and Colin Campbell (eds), *The Shopping Experience*, Sage, London, Thousand Oaks and New Delhi, 1997: 81.

The year before, Donatella Versace had produced a more nuanced, but no less obvious, modern version of the showgirl, moving beyond Macdonald's historical pastiche to recast the historical image in the twenty-first century. Her bamboo-printed chiffon dress, worn on the catwalk by Amber Valetta in the Versace Spring–Summer 2000 show, was split down the front, fastened only at the crotch with a huge jewelled pin, below which the dress flared open again to reveal jewelled knickers beneath (fig. 82). Like Macdonald's, her dress rapidly made the transition to the tabloid press. Whereas such show-stopping runway gestures, in the hands of an experimental designer, went no further than the pages of the newspaper, this dress, like many other Versace creations, was immediately worn by a range of major and minor celebrities and actresses, including the American Jennifer Lopez and the British Geri Halliwell. In Britain, the journalist Lisa Armstrong was invited to nominate a Dress of the Year for the Bath Museum of Costume. Having initially considered nominating Hussein Chalayan's experimental wooden table-dress, she instead chose this Versace dress because, she wrote, it seemed 'to represent some kind of high-water mark in the current symbiosis between fashion and celebrity.'[7] Armstrong went on to point out that we consume celebrity as avidly as any drug, so that certain designers have come to rely on tabloid images of celebrities to shift their garments off the rails.

In her Autumn–Winter 2000–1 collection Versace made wealth and status into the design motif of the collection. Both in the catwalk show (fig. 83) and in the advertising campaign shot by Steven Meisel (figs 84 and 85) Versace imagined a shamelessly wealthy-looking, opulent and self-assured woman whose status and sensibility could be read directly from her beautiful houses, precious jewellery and luxury clothing. On the catwalk, the col-

81 (*above left*) Roberto Cavalli, Autumn–Winter 2001–2. Photograph Ugo Camera, courtesy Roberto Cavalli

82 (*above centre*) Versace, Spring–Summer 2000. Photograph Dan Lecca, courtesy Versace

83 (*above right*) Versace, Autumn–Winter 2000–1. Photograph Dan Lecca, courtesy Versace

7 Lisa Armstrong, 'Frock'n'roll hall of fame', *The Times*, 24 July 2000.

84 Georgina Grenville in Versace advertising campaign, Autumn–Winter 2000–1. Styling Lori Goldstein. Photograph Steven Meisel, courtesy Versace

lection included fuschia-dyed and shaved fur coats and plunging necklines. The models' super-set hair-dos and high-glamour make-up evoked an early 1980s look; Meisel's accompanying advertising campaign captured it in rather more sedate images that hovered between deadpan conspicuous consumption and parody. The models' expensive hair, beige make-up and sleek, tanned legs complemented a camel, cream and navy collection of slick tailoring, 70s prints, neat knitwear and opulent fur coats, worn with simple but expensive chunky gold jewellery. But their glassy eyes and fixed gazes, unblinking in the flash of the shutter whose click one could almost hear in the silent, marble interiors, seemed so straight as to be tongue in cheek.

Versace's was a more complex take on conspicuous consumption than Macdonald's celebration of trashiness. Far from revelling in its own tackiness, it played with ideas of class and money through both European and American references, principally to a newly monied class whose taste could be read off the furnishings of their Swiss, Texan or Californian mansions. Although Donatella Versace defined the look as 'definitely high class'[8] it was a Eurotrash version of class that was delineated primarily by wealth, a look known to most people only through fictional images of the rich, beautiful and self-assured, as portrayed in Jackie Collins's blockbuster novels and the 1980s television series 'Dallas' and 'Dynasty'. In these designs of the late 1990s the double nature of the woman of fashion, in her affluent interior, as herself an *objêt de luxe*, harked back to the double nature of the nineteenth-century woman of fashion as both subject and object of a sexualised consumer

8   Quoted in Heath Brown, 'Donatella's Dynasty', *The Times Magazine*, 15 July 2000: 62.

85   Georgina Grenville and Amber Valetta in Versace advertising campaign, Autumn–Winter 20001–1. Styling Lori Goldstein. Photograph Steven Meisel, courtesy Versace

desire. The class dimension of female fashionable consumption in the mid-nineteenth century,[9] whereby middle- and upper-class women became active participants in the creation of their own fashionable images, reverberated again in Steven Meisel's luxury interiors for Versace. Lisa Armstrong identified the look as 'rich Palm Beach maven' and argued that the collection adroitly mirrored the aspirations and sensibilities of the period, epitomised by the sudden appearance of overnight internet billionaires and stock market buccaneers.[10] Certainly its adaptation of style references to the 1980s affluence of 'Dynasty' and 'Dallas', and to the pussycat bows of the Thatcherite 1980s in Britain, also mapped the decade in which the old certainties of welfare state and jobs for life began to be dismantled, a process that was accelerated after the fall of the Berlin Wall in 1989 by the collapse of the Soviet Union in 1991, and the spread of global capitalism.

*   *   *

9   See Philippe Perrot, *Fashioning the Bourgeoisie: A History of Clothing in the Nineteenth Century*, trans. Richard Bienvenu, Princeton University Press, 1994. Christopher Breward, *The Culture of Fashion*, Manchester University Press, Manchester and New York, 1995: 147–69.

10   Lisa Armstrong, 'Versace Seizes her Moment', *The Times*, 26 February 2000.

Reification

The motif of women for sale was captured by Vincent Peters in his photographs for *Big* magazine in 1999 of the Brazilian model Gisele Bundchen posing in a window against an anonymous cityscape of glass and steel. From the inside of the window we, the spectators, look past the model to see a series of window-shopping New York stereotypes – businessman, Latino family, street kids, uptown shopper – who scrutinise Gisele as if she were a luxurious commodity, apparently oblivious to the fact that this is a living woman posed in the window. She is costumed ambiguously, part showgirl, part prom queen, wearing a sash not normally part of the fashion wardrobe. Preening and apparently oblivious to her audience, the model appears like an exotic butterfly in the narrow space between the panes of glass. She is sandwiched between two parallel scopic regimes, the shop window through which the passing shoppers scrutinise her and the lens of the camera through which we, the viewers, perceive her. As spectators, our look echoes that of the window-shoppers, whose gaze in turn mirrors our own voyeuristic position. Despite the modernist design references that situate the image in the twentieth century, Gisele's sexualised posturing in the window recalls the 'parasexuality' of the late Victorian barmaid that Peter Bailey has argued was contained, rather than fully discharged, by the context and audience for whom it was performed.[11] Thus female sexuality in commodity culture is performative, mediated through the prism of the consumer gaze it solicits; and like the Medusa's head that is pictured on the Versace logo of the model's belt (see fig. 83), it can only be viewed through a glass if it is not to petrify the onlooker.

Vincent Peters' photograph encapsulated the way in which it was still the image of women that was largely associated with fashion, despite many welcome signs that men's fashion was progressively being incorporated into the 'fashion system'. The historical association of women with fashion is perhaps better perceived as an association of women with appearance, in which appearance becomes heavily symbolic and loaded with social meaning.[12] Lisa Tickner has argued that in the nineteenth century it was the image of woman that was the lynch-pin for social organisation.[13] Thus the image of woman became both normal and normalising, against which all deviation could be measured. And despite more than a century of movements for the emancipation of women, including the second wave of the feminist movement in the 1970s, the image of woman still resonates ambiguously today. Some of the repercussions of those nineteenth-century fears and concerns about gender and representation linger in the public domain and are played out on the catwalk and the magazine page where gender as a cultural construct can be interrogated as both image and idea.

The alienation and reification built into the fashion image nevertheless need not necessarily be female. The capacity to transform everything – even people – into commodities was described in 1923 by Lukács as 'reification' and he argued that it dominated all social relations.[14] The residual inequality, however, of gender relations, may be measured in the additional degree of discomfort elicited by a comparable picture of a man under scrutiny

11   Peter Bailey, *Popular Culture and Performance in the Victorian City*, Cambridge University Press, 1998; 'Parasexuality and Glamour: The Victorian Barmaid as Cultural Prototype', *Gender and History*, vol. 2, no. 2, 1990: 148–72.

12   Christopher Breward's *The Hidden Consumer: Masculinities, Fashion and City Life 1860–1914*, Manchester University Press, 1999, reintegrates men into this history, primarily through a consideration of men's engagement with fashion as a form of consumption, rather than as a form of making images of men as desired objects and desiring subjects. The historical association of women with fashion has been, by contrast, an explicit association with glamour, sex, availability and commodification.

13   Lisa Tickner, *The Spectacle of Women: Imagery of the Suffragette Campaign*, Chatto & Windus, London, 1987: 226. Elaine Showalter, however, has argued that the move towards female emancipation from the 1880s produced what was perceived as a 'crisis in gender', for men no less than for women, so that what was at stake, at the turn of the century, was a normative rather than 'aberrant' version of both genders. Elaine Showalter, *Sexual Anarchy: Gender and Culture at the Fin de Siècle*, Bloomsbury, London, 1991: 8–11.

14   Georgy Lukács, *History and Class Consciousness: Studies in Marxist Dialectics*, trans. Rodney Livingstone, Merlin Press, London, 1977 [1923].

in a glass box when in 2000 the artist Philip-Lorca diCorcia produced a spread for the
fashion magazine *W* that reversed the conventional codes of woman as spectacle (fig. 86).
In the sort of affluent milieu pictured by Meisel in his advertisements for Versace (see
figs 84 and 85) diCorcia posed a nude man behind a vitrine, calling into question his
status – whether performer, art object or naked commodity. To the well-groomed women
who survey him he is clearly a subject both of amused interest and of intense speculation,
while the uniformed guard, himself seen only in the mirror, looks on impassively. The
sexual charge of the image is generated in part by the way that the face of one woman is
framed between the principal figure's open legs, but the ambiguity of the image also resides
to some degree in the gendered dynamics of the gaze and its object; reversing the image
to imagine two clothed men examining a naked woman behind glass would produce a very
different reading, and one with many more historical precedents.

86   Philip-Lorca diCorcia for *W*, 2000.
Photograph © Philip-Lorca diCorcia, courtesy
Pace/MacGill Gallery, New York

15 Christine Buci-Glucksmann, *Baroque Reason: The Aesthetics of Modernity*, trans. Patrick Camiller, Sage, London, Thousand Oaks and New Delhi, 1994: 84–5 and 80. See too Tamar Garb, *Bodies of Modernity: Figure and Flesh in Fin-de-Siècle France*, Thames & Hudson, London, 1998.

16 Réka C. V. Buckley and Stephen Gundle, 'Fashion and Glamour' in Nicola White and Ian Griffiths (eds), *The Fashion Business: Theory, Practice, Image*, Berg, Oxford and New York, 2000: 53. Bailey, *Popular Culture*. See too the discussion of Bailey's article in Réka C. V. Buckley and Stephen Gundle, 'Flash Trash: Gianni Versace and the Theory and Practice of Glamour', in Stella Bruzzi and Pamela Church Gibson (eds), *Fashion Cultures: Theories, Explanations and Analysis*, Routledge, London and New York, 2000: 331–48, and Abigail Solomon-Godeau, 'The Other Side of Venus: The Visual Economy of Feminine Display', in Victoria de Grazia and Ellen Furlough (eds), *The Sex of Things: Gender and Consumption in Historical Perspective*, University of California Press, Berkeley, Los Angeles and London, 1996.

17 Bailey, *Popular Culture*, and Buckley and Gundle, 'Flash Trash': 335. See too Heather McPhearson, 'Sarah Bernhardt: Portrait of the Actress as Spectacle', *Nineteenth-Century Contexts*, vol. 20, no. 4, 1999: 409–54.

18 Buckley and Gundle, 'Fashion and Glamour' and 'Flash Trash'.

19 Steve Beard, 'With Serious Intent', *i-D*, no. 185, April 1999: 141.

20 In 'Womanliness as a Masquerade' [1929], repr. in V. Burgin, J. Donald and C. Kaplan (eds), *Formations of Fantasy*, Routledge, 1989: 38, Joan Rivière questioned the notion of an authentic womanliness, arguing instead that womanliness, or gender, could be read off the surface of feminine behaviour and appearance. 'Womanliness therefore could be assumed and worn as a mask, both to hide the possession of masculinity and to avert the reprisals expected if she was found to possess it – much as a thief will turn out his pockets and ask to be searched to prove that he has not stolen the goods. The reader may now ask how I define womanliness or where I draw the line between genuine womanliness and the "masquerade". My suggestion is not, however, that there is any such difference; whether radical or superficial, they are the same thing.' See Intro., n. 17 above. The concept also seemed to offer a clear explanation of instances of the manipulation of gender and identity in art and popular culture, such as the pop star Madonna's serial transformations of her image in the 1980s–90s and the artist Cindy Sherman's series *Untitled Film Stills* from the 1970s–80s.

Traditionally, it was the feminine body that was marked by the signs of modernity, persistently mythologised and allegorised in its representations. Indeed, Christine Buci-Glucksmann has argued that nineteenth-century modernity was 'haunted by the feminine'.[15] Peter Bailey and Réka Buckley and Stephen Gundle have argued that the association of women, glamour and the commodity form was, from the late nineteenth century, causally connected to the commodity culture of modernity, specifically through the expansion of visual culture through technological advances in printing, photography, lighting, techniques of display and packaging.[16] For Bailey glamour and modernity are allied through the visual seduction of the commodity form, which may be made manifest in the body of a woman as much as the seductive window displays of the period. Buckley and Gundle write that 'social status was important but so too were notoriety and photogenic beauty' and they argue that the origins of modern glamour lie in the turn-of-the-century figures of the *demi-mondaine* and the *grande cocotte*, courtesans whose spectacular appearances, promotion of make-believe and illusion, and commercialisation of sex combined to produce a 'glittering display of image, ostentation, sex, commerce and culture'.[17]

Medusa

Buckly and Gundle make a connection between these historical origins and modern glamour in the designs of Gianni Versace from the 1980s to his death in 1997.[18] At first glance, Versace's designs appeared an unproblematical image of glamour, a soothing balm or even a remedy against more disturbing images of an aggressive female sexuality. His designs for a golden goddess, often clad in figure-hugging evening gowns, based on old-fashioned Hollywood glamour, were modelled by the 'supermodels' that Versace had promoted since 1990, such as Linda Evangelista and Christy Turlington (fig. 88). Very different from the vogue for waif-like, even odd-looking, models, Versace's early 1990s promotion of curvaceous supermodels, complete with Californian suntans and workout regimes, might be understood as a 'healthier' or more progressive version of femininity than their pale and sickly looking successors. Yet in their very perfection the supermodels embodied an artificial and constructed version of femininity that was in itself so generic as to seem unhuman, even deathly,[19] an idea captured in Bryan Forbes's film *The Stepford Wives* (1974).

Furthermore, this version of femininity appeared so excessive as to parody itself. In these images of high-carat glamour, as in the psychoanalyst Joan Rivière's formulation of femininity as masquerade in the 1920s, gender can be understood as a matter of surface rather than depth, thus questioning the essentialist idea of an authentic femininity beneath the surface.[20] Gender itself stood revealed as a kind of drag act, an inference made explicit on the catwalk when Thierry Mugler employed Connie Girl to model in his 1992 show (fig. 87). And if men 'do' femininity better than women, what does that tell us about nature, gender and performativity? For all its old-fashioned characteristics, the hyper-femininity of

87 Connie Girl modelling
for Thierry Mugler,
Spring–Summer 1992.
Photograph Niall McInerney

88   Gianni Versace with supermodels Linda Evangelista, Christy Turlington and Naomi Campbell, Spring–Summer 1991. Photograph Beppe Caggli, courtesy Versace

89 (*facing page*)   Madame Yevonde, Mrs Edward Mayer, as Medusa, 1935. Vivex Print, private collection. Yevonde Portrait Archive.

21   In this context, the drag queen presents an example where, it is argued, his power is the power of the phallus beneath the surface of femininity. See Peter Ackroyd, *Dressing Up: Transvestism and Drag: The History of An Obsession*, Thames & Hudson, London, 1979, and Mark Simpson, *Male Impersonators: Performing Masculinity*, Cassell, London, 1994.

22   Louise J. Kaplan, *Female Perversions: The Temptations of Madame Bovary*, Pandora, London, 1991:262.

23   Freud, 'Medusa's Head' [1922], SE, vol. XVIII, 1959: 273–4.

24   Walter Benjamin, 'Paris – the Capital of the Nineteenth Century' [1935], cited in Buci-Glucksmann, *Baroque Reason*: 163.

25   Ibid.

26   Quoted in Robin Gibson and Pam Roberts, *Madame Yevonde: Colour, Fantasy and Myth*, National Portrait Gallery Publications, London, 1990: 36. She also commented that her sitter had 'eyes of the strangest and most intense blue': ibid.

27   See Jean Baudrillard, *Symbolic Exchange and Death*, trans. Iain Hamilton Grant, Sage, London, Thousand Oaks and New Delhi, 1993 [1976]: 103.

28   Marjorie Garber, *Shakespeare's Ghost Writers: Literature as Uncanny Causality*, Methuen, London, 1987: 109.

Mugler's red, rhinestone cowgirl may be more threatening than it is reassuring: Connie Girl's catwalk performance may reveal that womanliness is just about 'dragging up', thus destabilising any natural relationship between biological sex and gender, and between outer appearance and inner essence. If so, there is no reason why women too should not 'drag up' as women, perhaps even masking a dangerous masculinity below the surface.[21]

The Canadian psychoanalyst George Zavataros has described the parodying of one's own sex as 'homeovestism' (the opposite of transvestism). Women dragging up as women has an element of threat, rather than allure, even though, as Louise Kaplan has observed, 'in the fashion industry, a cornerstone of modern industrial economy, the female perversion of dressing up as a woman [is], like Poe's purloined letter, nicely disguised by being right out in the open.'[22] In the Versace canon, for all the apparently conventional femininity on display, the threat posed by this element of dragging up was acknowledged in the logo, a Medusa's head (see fig. 83). The Medusa in Western tradition has come to represent a woman as sexual lure, the sight of whose snaky locks turned men to stone. In Western art she frequently serves as an emblem of the dangerous power of women. In the original Greek myth, the Medusa was a hideous beast with bronze tusks, but by the late nineteenth century a far more sexualised version had become prominent in Western representation. The idea of the Medusa as a seductive temptress whose death-dealing attributes were somehow associated with her sexuality came to the fore in Decadent painting where she came to be represented, like Judith and Salomé, as a vampish *femme fatale*. Writing in 1922, Sigmund Freud saw the Medusa as the very emblem of the castrating woman,[23] whereas Benjamin used the metaphor of the Medusa to describe the reified nature of the commodity in nineteenth-century Paris: 'the face of modernity withers us with its look, as Medusa's did for the Greeks.'[24] Buci-Glucksmann argues, in her reading of Baudelaire, that 'the "female" look of the Medusa, petrifying and immemorial, is thus summoned up at the very heart of the modern.'[25]

In 1935 the society photographer Mme Yevonde described the way in which she had composed her portrait of Mrs Edward Meyer as Medusa (fig. 89) for her Goddess series: 'Medusa was a cold voluptuary and a sadist . . . we painted the lips . . . a dull purple and made her face chalk-white. The background was vaguely sinister and unevenly lit and over one light I put a green filter.'[26] This is the Medusa invoked in Versace's choice of the logo, the devastating power of beautiful women to slay, rather than the ugly beast with the boars' tusks of the original legend.[27] In her exploration of the uncanny in relation to Shakespeare, Marjorie Garber has argued that castration fear is expressed in the form of gender anxiety. The Medusa, like the murderous Lady Macbeth, becomes an emblem of gender ambiguity, neither purely masculine nor purely feminine, but a monstrous hybrid: 'With its gaping mouth, its snaky locks and its association with femininity, castration and erection, Medusa's head ends up being the displacement upwards of neither the female nor the male genitals but of gender undecidability as such.'[28]

It is this threat of gender undecidability that destabilises the hyper-feminine designs of Gianni Versace in a way not dissimilar to the ambiguities of diCorcia's reified image of a

naked man exhibited in a glass case (contrast figs 86 and 87). And the fact that the symbolic power of the phallus might actually be lurking behind the image of the glamorous woman, albeit veiled by a seductive femininity, is raised in the image of Ru Paul in a glittering red Stetson. In the Versace logo the Medusa and glamour combine as a form of same-sex drag; thus hyper-femininity can be associated with fear rather than allure. Mark Simpson describes the Medusa as 'the mother of all glamour and, therefore, of drag'.[29] Simpson argues that if glamour is constituted in women's magical power over men to enchant and allure, it is also a castration threat. In the image of the *femme fatale*, female power and female enchantment are one and the same. The etymology of the word 'glamour' is a Scottish variant of 'grammar' which, because of the association of learning with the occult, means a charm or a spell. It was first used by Walter Scott in the nineteenth century. Vamp (an abbreviation of vampire) was used as a verb in the early twentieth century. 'To vamp' suggests an active form of female display. As such female allure can be reconfigured as potentially threatening rather than reassuring.

Mary Ann Doane has argued that the cinematic *femme fatale*, and her *fin-de-siècle* precedent in art, is not a feminist image of female power so much as a symptom of male fears about feminism.[30] She too writes about ambivalence in relation to the *femme fatale*: 'she is not the subject of power but its *carrier*', with all its connotations of disease.[31] The same connection can be made to link Galliano's cinematic visions of vamps and sirens in his designs for Dior in the second half of the 1990s to their historical prototypes. If the vamp evokes desire, it is a desire that is tinged with dread. *The femme fatale* is a woman whose sexuality is fatal, who destroys men even as she entices and seduces them. Angela Carter proposed that the sexuality of the *femme fatale* could never be depicted as it might be in real life because it was a fiction, a libidinous projection of illicit male desires onto the figure of a woman who, subsequently, paid for them with her life.[32] In the late nineteenth century this ambivalence spilled out in the avant-garde painting of the time, in the Salomés and Judiths, where the spectacular displays of consumer capitalism were transposed from the world of goods to the woman herself. It is these images, for example of Aubrey Beardsley's designs or Gustave Moreau's *Dancing Salomé* (fig. 90) that are evoked in Galliano's modern decadence, as when he produced tattoo-printed body stockings worn under slip dresses for his Suzie Sphinx collection, for Autumn–Winter 1997–8 (fig. 91).

In this context, Galliano's fascination with sensational historical figures of the late-nineteenth and early twentieth centuries, and particularly with women who used their sexuality spectacularly to make their way in the world, evokes the ambiguous relation of sexuality, commerce and fashion in the modernist period.[33] His couture collection for Dior for Autumn–Winter 1997–8 reconfigured the *belle époque* and, specifically, Colette as a showgirl, evoking pre-war Paris as a city of spectacle and luxury. The next year his own collection for Autumn–Winter 1998–9 evoked post-war Berlin as a city of modernist experimentation and decadence. It referred to the paintings of Otto Dix and to the vampish and ambiguous sexuality of German cabaret in the Weimar period, implying that fashion is always about dragging up (fig. 92). Christian Schad's portrait from the same time and

29 Simpson, *Male Impersonators*: 178.
30 Mary Ann Doane, *Femmes Fatales: Feminism, Film Theory, Psychoanalysis*, Routledge, London and New York, 1991: 2–3.
31 Ibid: 2.
32 Angela Carter, 'Femmes Fatales' in *Nothing Sacred*, Virago, London, 1982: 132.
33 Showalter, *Sexual Anarchy*: 144–68.

90 Gustave Moreau, *Dancing Salomé* (detail), 1876, 92 × 60 cm, Musée Gustave Moreau, Photograph © RMN – R. G. Ojeda

91 John Galliano, Suzie Sphinx, Autumn–Winter 1997–8, Photograph Niall McInerney

93 Christian Schad, *Count St Genois d'Anneaucourt*, 1927.
Oil on wood, 86 × 63 cm, private collection. Photograph
© The Bridgeman Art Llibrary

92 John Galliano, Autumn–Winter 1998–9. Photograph
Niall McInerney

milieu (fig. 93) highlights the male cross-dressing that Galliano staged as a backdrop to his hyper-feminine designs, and shares some of his meticulous attention to surface detail, lingering on the textures of cloth and skin with the close-up focus of a lover.

Compared with Gianni Versace's exuberant celebration of femininity which endlessly recreated an iconic Hollywood version of feminine glamour, Galliano's depiction of feminine sexuality was slightly more ambiguous. Colin McDowell has commented on Galliano ambivalence in his projection of a libidinous female image, 'bringing echoes of hookers, geishas, hostesses in opium dens . . . John, we are told, loves women, but it is not easy to avoid the thought that, within that love lurks a fear which must be laid to rest by pastiche or, even more compelling, the suspicion that it is a love so intense it also encompasses a degree of hatred.'[34] Such interpretations suggest that the image of a *femme fatale* must be a misogynist one. Yet while Mugler's parodic versions of femininity do indeed suggest a misogynist and defensive image of woman, much fashion design seems more complicated than that, and ranges from the benign to the alarming. For example, Alexander McQueen's production of a post-modern *femme fatale* is at odds with the imagery of Versace and Mugler, for it configures the model on the catwalk as a terrifying subject, as opposed to an object of terror (as discussed in the next chapter). In 1985 Elizabeth Wilson argued that in its freakishness post-modern fashion questioned the imperative to glamour rather than simply playing out its tensions.[35] Indeed it seems appropriate to understand the contemporary *femme fatale* as the embodiment of ambiguity more than anything else. If Versace's modern Medusa, 'the mother of all drag', reveals femininity itself to be a kind of gender performance, akin to the artifice of the Decadent period, it is a representation which may be read as either celebratory or fearful, which oscillates between both poles, the very image of gender instability.

Sterile or Barren

Precisely because femininity is an unstable sign this imagery can segue from glamour into horror: tightly controlled femininity can flip into psychosis. This undercurrent ran through much film and fashion imagery of the 1990s, which suggested, at best, an uneasy equilibrium between horror and control over unruly femininity, an argument articulated in the 1940s by Simone de Beauvoir: 'If . . . woman evades the rules of society, she returns to nature and to the demon.'[36] In many fashion images of the 1990s women appeared either mad or dysfunctional: their sexuality could not be frank and straightforward but was always configured as complex, deviant, deranged or troubled. In particular two tropes of 'deviant' sexuality emerged, the lesbian and the vampire. Versace's 1999 advertising campaign for Versace couture, shot by Steven Meisel, which ran in Italian *Vogue* and the American *W*, showed a group of models in a claustrophobic Edwardian country-house interior. Dressed in evening gowns made from tulle, silk organza and hand embroidery, the models' hair was fluffed up madly, wilder than any bird's nest, to complement the array

34   Colin McDowell, *Galliano*, Weidenfeld & Nicolson, London, 1997: 117.
35   Elizabeth Wilson, *Adorned in Dreams: Fashion and Modernity*, Virago, London, 1985: 10; 2nd ed. I. B. Tauris, 2003 forthcoming.
36   Simone de Beauvoir, *The Second Sex*, trans. Howard Madison Parshley, Penguin, Harmondsworth, 1972 [1949]: 222.

of taxidermy that cluttered the baronial interior: stuffed peacocks, mounted antlers, flock
wallpaper and a chair made of deer horns. Stifling claustrophophia was suggested by a series
of closed rooms without natural daylight in which, whatever the time of day might be,
the models all wore formal evening wear. In these oppressive interiors they lounged together
in elaborate tableaux, with beaded décolletages or bare breasts, their intense, unsmiling
absorption in each other suggesting a form of lesbian solipsism.

In her analysis of Baudelaire and Benjamin, Buci-Glucksmann argues that 'woman is
not only [an] *allegory of modernity*. In the great anthropological utopias of bisexuality, and
in the two figures of the lesbian and the androgyne, she is also a *heroic protest against this*

modernity.'[37] For the image of the lesbian not only evades marriage and procreative sexuality but also embodies a 'protest against industrial modernity and the subjection of women to the reproduction of bodies and images.'[38] For *Pop* magazine in 2001, Terry Richardson photographed two gaunt, pallid and unhealthy looking models in a Hammer House of Horror gothic country house, aristocratic languor mixed with lesbian decadence. The extreme thinness of one model, her insouciant gaze (fig. 94) and her coupling with another woman in other pictures in the magazine story, suggested the staging of an image and an imaginary outside the reciprocal operations of 'the mass institutions of capitalism',[39] institutions such as marriage, maternity and prostitution that, like the commercial institutions of consumer culture, require either productivity or exchange.

Fashion images of lesbians and vampires imagine non-procreative forms of female sexuality; at the end of the nineteenth century the *femme fatale* was sometimes depicted as a lesbian, sometimes a vampire. [40] In Sean Ellis's 'Welcome to the Clinic', styled by Isabella Blow for *The Face* in March 1997 lesbian sexuality is pictured as 'decadent' and deathly, enacting the sexual death throes of the vampire in an act of non-procreative sex. Such images are the end product of the historical ambivalence and castration fear expressed in *fin-de-siècle* representations of the *femme fatale*. Between vamps and vampires lies the realm of gender ambiguity. In a spread called 'Neverland', by Martina Hoogland Ivanow androgynous models of indeterminate sex enacted suggestive vampire scenarios, recalling the derivation of the word 'vamp' from vampire (figs 95 and 96). Like the artist Jeff Wall's *Vampire Picnic* of 1991, these figures suggest an equivocal sexuality and a deviant form of kinship. Wall said of his image:

I thought of the picture as a depiction of a large, troubled, family. Vampires don't procreate sexually, they create new vampires by a peculiar act of vampirism. It's a process of pure selection, rather like adoption; it's based in desire alone. A vampire creates another vampire directly, in a moment of intense emotion, a combination of attraction and repulsion, or of rivalry. Pure eroticism. So a 'family' of vampires is a phantasmagoric construction of various, and intersecting, competing desires.[41]

The sexuality of the lesbian or the vamp recalls Virginia M. Allen's description of the *femme fatale* as the antithesis of the maternal: 'sterile or barren, she produces nothing in a society which fetishes production',[42] In such an analysis, the greatest perversion is not to produce, so the representation of non-reproductive sexuality becomes the representation of deviance.

Marx used the metaphor of the vampire for the voraciousness of capital: 'Capital is dead labour which, vampire-like, lives only by sucking living labour, and lives the more, the more labour it sucks.'[43] It seems, therefore, that this imagery returns one yet again to the ghosts and phantasmagoria of capitalist production and consumption that have haunted many other representations of the 1990s. Just as the *fin-de-siécle femme fatale* was indexically linked to capitalist modernity and its endlessly creative productivity, so too might the late twentieth-century vamp be connected to newly emergent forms of culture, image and technology, harnessing sexual 'deviance' to novel forms of commodity fetishism.

95 *(following page)* Martina Hoogland Ivanow, Neverland, *Dazed & Confused*, 1996. Styling Alister Mackie. Barnaby wears dress by John Galliano. Photograph courtesy Martina Hoogland Ivanow/Z Photographic

96 *(page 131)* Martina Hoogland Ivanow, Neverland, *Dazed & Confused*, 1996. Styling Alister Mackie. Barnaby wears dress by Helmut Lang and gold-plated silver fangs by Naomi Filmer for Hussein Chalayan, Autumn–Winter 1996–7. Photograph courtesy Martina Hoogland Ivanow/Z Photographic

37 Buci-Glucksmann, *Baroque Reason*: 104
38 Ibid: 108.
39 Ibid.
40 Bram Dijksra, *Idols of Perversity: Fantasies of Feminine Evil in Fin-de-Siècle Culture*, Oxford University Press, Oxford and New York, 1986: 145–59 and 333–51.
41 Cited in Thierry de Duve, Arielle Pelenc and Boris Groys, *Jeff Wall*, Phaidon, London, 1996: 21. See too Norman Bryson, 'Too Near, To Far', *Parkett*, 49, 1997: 85–9. for a discussion of Jeff Wall and vampirism. See also Showalter, *Sexual Anarchy*: 179–84.
42 Virginia M. Allen, *The Femme Fatale: Erotic Icon*, Whitson, Troy, New York, 1983: 4, quoted in Doane, *femmes Fatales*: 2. For an alternative interpretation of the vampire as a capitlaist trope that expresses the consumer ethos of young people (the vampire as an insatiable consumerwith a hunger for perpetual youth), see Rob Latham, *Consuming Youth: Vampires, Cyborgs and the Culture of Consumption*, University of Chicago Press, 2002.
43 Karl Marx, *Capital*, vol. 1, trans. Ben Fowkes, Penguin, Harmondsworth, 1976: 342. Other instances of the metaphor are: 'the prolongation of the working day . . . only slightly quenches the vampire thirst for the living blood of labour' (367), and 'the vampire [capitalism] will not let go' (416).

The Death of Beautiful Women

If fears of femininity out of control are expressed in the 'deviant' figures of non-productive sexuality, the representation of the death of beautiful women can be a form of mastery over this fear. In the late nineteenth century, Edgar Allen Poe wrote that 'the death of a beautiful woman is, unquestionably, the most poetical topic in the world.'[44] The morbid association of women with death was made in nineteenth-century art and literature, and there was something of the Victorian cult of the dead in the revival of waxen, morbid and beautiful images of women in fashion images at the turn of the following century. Luis Sanchis's 'The Lake' was a fashion spread based on the character of Ophelia in *Hamlet* (fig. 97). It showed a dreamy and romanticised Ophelia's death by drowning, converting her psychosis into watery ornament, reminiscent of John Everett Millais's portrait of Elizabeth Siddal as Ophelia in the mid-nineteenth century (fig. 98).

Foucault observed that for Baudelaire the modern painter was 'the one who knows how to make manifest, in the fashion of the day, the essential, permanent, obsessive, relation that our age entertains with death'.[45] The pairing of fashion and death are built in to the structures of modernity: in 'Fukasawa Elisa wears John Galliano' a beautiful and impeccably dressed actress lies dead, caught in the glare of camera lights on an abandoned film set in a kitsch Japanese theme park under Mount Fuji (fig. 99). Between approximately 1995 and 2001 the artist Izima Kaoru collaborated with a number of actresses and models to produce a series of photographs that imagined the conjunction of high fashion and violence in the staging of a perverse notion of the perfect death. The pictures have all the

44 Edgar Allen Poe, 'The Philosophy of Composition' [1846], cited in Elizabeth Bronfen, *Over Her Dead Body: Death, Femininity and the Aesthetic*, Manchester University Press, 1992: 59.

45 Michel Foucault, 'What is Enlightenment?' trans. Catherine Porter, in Paul Rabinow (ed.), *The Foucault Reader*, Penguin, Harmondsworth, 1984: 40.

beauty and high production values of a magazine shoot, as well as the roll call of designer dresses (Galliano, Paul & Joe, Yohji Yamamoto, Vivienne Westwood). In every case, the beauty of the model and her dress are counterpoised by the chilly violence of her end. Yet, as Chris Townsend has argued, Izima 'insists on both the wound and the name . . . That naming comes in part from fashion.'[46] The anonymity of inexplicable and violent death is countered by the clothes and the make-up of these beautiful women, accoutrements of high fashion which mark the body with a *griffe* or signature that armours it against annihilation.

A connection between fashion and death was made as early as 1824 by the Italian poet Giacomo Leopardi who personified them as sisters, 'both born of transience', in his 'Dialogue Between Fashion and Death.'[47] In his essay of 1916, '*On Transience*', Freud wrote that 'the idea that all this beauty was transient (gave) a foretaste of mourning'.[48] Within fashion's ceaseless preoccupation with change and alteration are inscribed the brevity of

98   John Everett Millais, *Ophelia*, 1851–2, oil on canvas, 76.2 × 111.8 cm, Tate, London 2003

youth and the ephemerality of beauty. Thus, to paraphrase Jonathan Dollimore, death is always interior to fashion.[49] However much it denies this, its very structure embodies the message. Yet the representation of 'the death of beautiful women' may, equally, gather new meanings of its own. In Philip Treacy's highly made-up woman, with a blood-red mouth, deathly pale with a skeletal profile, her waist cinched in by her corset, from which black lace fluttered like shredded flesh (fig. 100) the erotic link between sex and death is made. This image recalled Philippe Ariès's characterisation of the association of sex and death in the seventeenth century that resurfaced as a present-day concern: 'people play perverse games with death, even going so far as to sleep with her.'[50] The corsetted silhouette, too,

46   Chris Townsend, 'Dead for Having Been Seen', *Izima Kaoru*, fa projects, London, 2002: 6.
47   Giacomo Leopardi, 'Dialogo della Moda e della Morte' in *Operette Morali*, Rizzoli, Milan, 1951 [1824]: 30.
48   Sigmund Freud, 'On Transience' [1916], in *Works: The Standard Edition of the Complete Psychological Works of Sigmund Freud*, under the general editorship of James Strachey, vol. XIV, Hogarth Press, London, 1955: 306.
49   He argues that where death is eroticised, in Western culture, it is consequently bound into or 'interior to desire': Jonathan Dollimore, *Death, Desire and Loss in Western Culture*, Allen Lane, Penguin Press, London, 1998: xii.
50   Philippe Ariès, *The Hour of Our Death*, trans. Helen Weaver, Allen Lane, London, 1981: 406.

99   Izima Kaoru, Fukasawa Elisa wears John Galliano, 2001, C-print. Photographs courtesy fa projects, London

suggests the artifice of the inorganic that Benjamin identified as the defining feature of the woman of fashion, and the source of her death-dealing qualities. According to Benjamin, the woman of fashion herself was deathly:

> For fashion was never anything but the parody of the gaily decked-out corpse, the provocation of death through the woman, and (in between noisy, canned slogans) the bitter, whispered *tête-à-tête* with decay. That is fashion. For this reason she changes so rapidly, teasing death, already becoming something else again, something new, as death looks about for her in order to strike her down.[51]

Nineteenth-century modernity introduced a new term that modified the morbid image of the death of beautiful women, the idea of beauty inflected with horror that was inherently alluring. Baudelaire's poem 'Hymn to Beauty' praises 'horror, not the least charming of your jewels',[52] and his poem 'Danse Macabre' paints a picture of a slim-waisted dancing skeleton as a coquette in a ruched dress with pompoms on her shoes.[53] The image of woman as a death-inflicting coquette also occurred in Grandville's *Journey to Eternity* where a prostitute propositions a good bourgeois while hiding her death's head behind a fashionable mask (fig. 101). In the late twentieth century this type of imagery resurfaced in the form of a decadent and self-fulfilling female desire that no longer depended on male approbation or disapprobation. One has only to contrast Moreau's *Salomé* (see fig. 90) with an Alexander McQueen *femme fatale* (see fig. 106) or Nick Knight photograph of Rebekka Botzen that lingers in delicious close-up on the black lips, the black pearl, the white teeth (fig. 102). Buci-Glucksmann argues that 'love gives rise to . . . "funereal strategies" of which Salomé holds the key.'[54] If the love and death drives collide in *fin-de-siècle* images of women, in Nick Knight's modern Salomé the deathly body is turned into its opposite: a living fragment.

51   Walter Benjamin cited in Buck-Morss, *Dialectics of Seeing*: 101.

52   'De tes bijoux l'Horreur n'est pas le moins charmant': 'Hymne à la Beauté' from Charles Baudelaire, *Spleen et Idéal, Complete Poems*, trans, Walter Martin, Carcanet, Manchester, 1997: 59.

53   'Danse Macabre' from *Tableaux Parisiens* in ibid: 251.

54   Buci-Glucksmann, *Baroque Reason*: 156.

100 (*above*)   Philip Treacy, Autumn–Winter 1996–7. Photograph Niall McInerney

101   J. Grandville, *Journey to Eternity* (*Voyage pour l'éternité*), c. 1830, lithograph by Langlume. Beinecke Rare Book and Manuscript Library, Yale University

102 (*facing page*)   Nick Knight, Rebekka Botzen with black pearl. Photograph courtesy Nick Knight
© VOGUE/The Condé Nast Publications Ltd

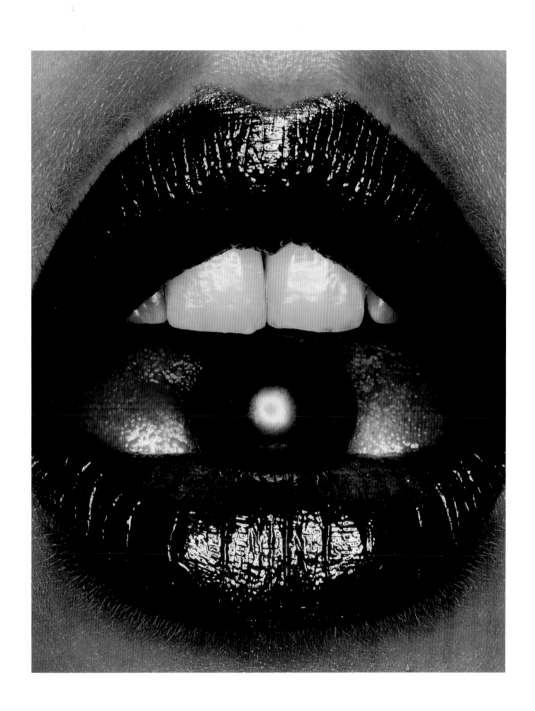

six   cruelty

Victimisation

Alexander McQueen graduated from the Fashion Design MA course at Central Saint Martins in London in February 1992. His first collections were Victorian in inspiration, drawing on the dark side of the nineteenth century, rather than its picturesque representations. His graduation collection (fig. 103) was based on Jack the Ripper and Victorian prostitutes who sold their hair to be made into locks which were bought by people to give to their lovers: he stitched locks of human hair under blood-red linings. Here, as in so much of McQueen's subsequent work, the themes of sex, death and commerce intertwined. He also encased locks of his own hair in perspex, creating an object which was both souvenir and *memento mori*; as he conceived it, he was giving himself to the collection.

Through the mid-1990s McQueen developed his aesthetic in a series of spectacular fashion shows. His first show after his graduation collection took place in March 1993 and was inspired by the film *Taxi Driver*. The models were inadequately wrapped in clingfilm and were styled to look bruised and battered. His second show, Nihilism, was staged in October 1993. It featured Edwardian jackets in corroded gilt, over tops apparently splattered with blood or dirt (see fig. 47). The *Independent* newspaper's report of this collection was entitled 'McQueen's Theatre of Cruelty': 'Alexander McQueen's debut was a horror show . . . McQueen, who is 24 and from London's East End, has a view that speaks of battered women, of violent lives, of grinding daily existences offset by wild, drug-enhanced nocturnal dives into clubs where the dress-code is semi-naked.'[1] The review spoke of violence and abuse, but not of the historical eclecticism which also permeated the show. This collection set the tone for others over the next few years. Their mood was doomy and lost, savage and melancholic, yet also darkly romantic. In them McQueen developed an aesthetic of cruelty culled from disparate sources: the work of sixteenth- and seventeenth-century anatomists, in particular that of Andreas Vesalius; the photography of Joel-Peter Witkin from the 1980s and 90s; and the films of Pasolini, Kubrick, Buñuel and Hitchcock.

The second collection attracted shocked, if not universally hostile, press coverage[2] which McQueen continued to garner in subsequent collections. The aesthetic shock tactic continued in the fourth, The Birds, featuring hard tailoring which was based on the idea of road kill (see fig. 48).[3] The models at the show were bound in sticky tape and streaked with oily tyre marks; these tyre marks were also printed on some of the jackets to look as if the model had been driven over. However, it was the styling and presentation of McQueen's fifth collection, Highland Rape, shown in March 1995 and his first to be staged under the aegis of the British Fashion Council in its official tent during London Fashion Week, which attracted the greatest criticism (fig. 104). The collection mixed military jackets with McQueen tartan and moss wool, contrasting tailored jackets with torn and ravaged lace dresses and ripped skirts. On a runway strewn with heather and bracken, McQueen's staggering and blood-spattered models appeared wild and distraught, their

103 Alexander McQueen, graduation collection show, Central Saint Martins College of Art and Design, 1992. Photograph Niall McInerney, courtesy Alexander McQueen

facing page Detail of fig. 106

1 Marion, Hume, 'McQueen's Theatre of Cruelty', *The Independent*, 21 October 1993: 29.
2 Ibid.
3 Ashley, Heath, 'Bad Boys Inc', *The Face*, vol. 2. no. 79, April 1995: 102.

breasts and bottoms exposed by tattered laces and torn suedes, jackets with missing sleeves, and skin-tight rubber trousers and skirts cut so low at the hip they seemed to defy gravity.

The show was described as 'aggressive and disturbing'.[4] Much of the press coverage centred on accusations of misogyny because of the imagery of semi-naked, staggering and brutalized women, in conjunction with the use of the word 'rape' in the title. But McQueen claimed that the rape was of Scotland, not the individual models, as the theme of the show was the Jacobite Rebellion. 'I'd studied the history of the Scottish upheavals and the Clearances . . . Highland Rape was about England's rape of Scotland'.[5] The harsh styling was intended to counter romantic images of Scottish history: 'I wanted to show that the war between the Scottish and the English was basically genocide.'[6] This was also the period of considerable coverage of atrocities in Bosnia and Rwanda in the Western press, when the historical word genocide acquired contemporary meaning.

Criticisms of McQueen's work as misogynist, however, tended to obscure its defining characteristic, the theatrical staging of cruelty. Although most apparent in the styling of his collections, his aesthetic of cruelty also extended to his designs where it was not only thematic but also intrinsic to his cutting techniques and his methods of construction. In the early collections cloth was usually slashed, stabbed and torn, and each garment was a variation on the theme of abuse. When he arrived at Givenchy in Paris in 1997 as principal designer the staff described their terror as they saw him approach a garment with the scissors, knowing he was about to cut up the couture model they had just produced, like a malevolent Edward Scissorhands. 'I'm intent on chopping things up', he said in an interview early in 1997.[7] Apart from the slashed garments, McQueen also developed a distinctive style of tailoring for which he became famous: razor sharp, its seams traced the body's contours like surgical incisions, skimming it to produce pointed lapels and sharp shoulders.

The stylist Isabella Blow, who became his patron, commented on the way his cutting techniques and his practice of historical collage came together:

What attracted me to Alexander was the way he takes ideas from the past and sabotages them with his cut to make them thoroughly new and in the context of today. It is the complexity and severity of his approach to cut that makes him so modern. He is like a Peeping Tom in the way he slits and stabs at fabric to explore all the erogenous zones of the body.[8]

4 Women's Wear Daily, 14 March 1995: 10.
5 Lorna V., 'All Hail McQueen', Time Out, 24 September–1 October 1997: 26.
6 Womens Wear Daily, 14 March 1995: 10.
7 Cited in 'Cutting Up Rough' (The Works series, produced by Teresa Smith, series editor Michael Poole), BBC2, broadcast 20 July 1997.
8 Cited in Sarajane Hoare, 'God Save McQueen', Harpers Bazaar (USA), June 1996: 30 and 148.
9 'Cutting Up Rough'.

Blow, who said McQueen combined 'sabotage and tradition, beauty and violence',[9] referred here to Michael Powell's film Peeping Tom (1960) in which the protagonist is a photographer who murders women in the act of photographing them by means of a bayonet attached to his tripod so that the camera becomes the instrument of the death it records.

In McQueen's 1996 catwalk show for his Spring–Summer 1997 collection La Poupée the black model Debra Shaw walked contorted in a metal frame fixed to her wrists and ankles by manacles (fig. 105). Denying the obvious connotation of slavery, just as he denied the accusations of misogyny in Highland Rape, McQueen claimed he wanted the restricting

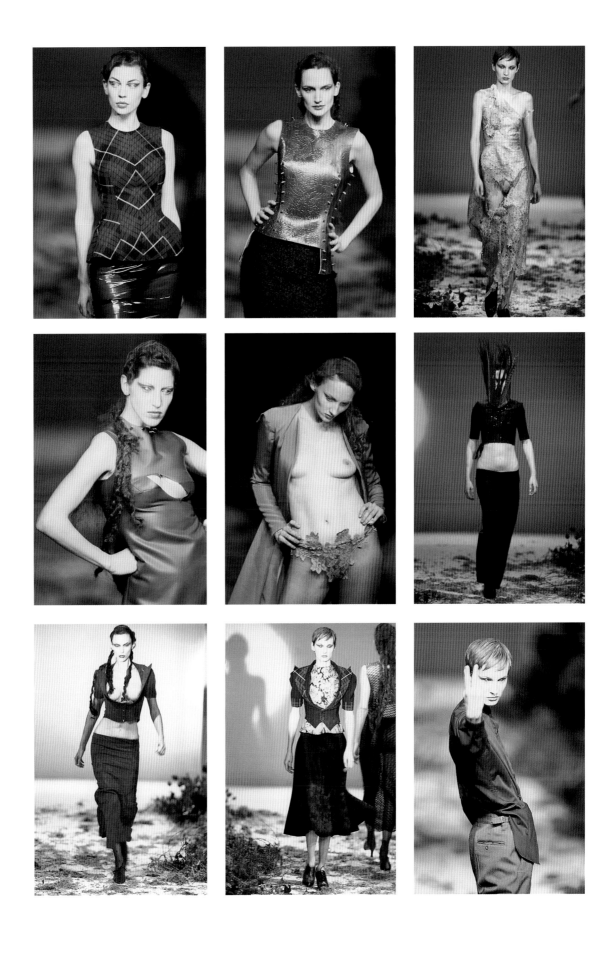

105 Debra Shaw in Alexander McQueen,
La Poupée, Spring–Summer 1997. Photograph
Niall McInerney

10 Lorna V., 'All Hail McQueen', 26.
11 Rosalind Krauss, 'Corpus Delicti', in Rosalind
Krauss and Jane Livingston, *L'Amour fou: Photography
and Surrealism*, Abbeville, New York and Arts
Council of Great Britain, London, 1986: 86.
12 Peter Webb, *Hans Bellmer*, Quartet, London,
1985: 29–30.

body jewellery to produce the jerky and mechanical movements of a doll or puppet.[10] The
collection was based on Hans Bellmer's dolls of the 1930s which the artist compulsively
took apart and reconstructed for a series of photographs, a process described by Rosalind
Krauss as 'construction through dismemberment'.[11] Although McQueen's collection was
not a literal reinterpretation of Bellmer's *poupée*, in all his work of this period he revealed
a similar compulsion to dissect and probe. Bellmer's 1933 doll had six miniature panoramas fitted inside her stomach; illuminated by a torch bulb, operated by a button on her
left nipple, and viewed through a peep-hole in her navel, the tiny panoramas displayed a
collection of bric-à-brac which represented 'the thoughts and dreams of a young girl'.[12]
Going beneath the skin of conventional fashion, McQueen's first collections explored the
taboo area of interiority, breaching the boundaries between inside and out. The fantasy of

exploring and probing the interior of the body, although commonplace in contemporary art, is habitually disavowed in fashion by its emphasis on surface, perfection and polish. McQueen, by contrast, actively explored the female body in relation to the tropes of abjection. In a television interview while he was working on the collection It's a Jungle Out There, he held up to the camera a piece of cloth with blond hair trailing from it like a pelt and said 'the idea is that this wild beast has eaten this really lovely blond girl and she's trying to get out.'[13]

Femme Fatale

The cruelty inherent in McQueen's representations of women was part of the designer's wider vision of the cruelty of the world, and although his view was undoubtedly bleak it was not misogynist. And this was not because the designer often talked of the 'strong', uncompromising women for whom he designed,[14] but because of his fascination with an uncompromising and aggressive sexuality, a sexuality which in his Dante collection shown in March 1996 (fig. 106), came to resemble that of the *fin-de-siècle femme fatale*, the woman whose sexuality was dangerous, even deathly, and for whom, therefore, male desire would always be tinged with dread. In this context McQueen's fascination with lesbian 'decadence' was significant in his production of the *femme fatale*: 'Critics who labelled me misogynist got it all wrong, they didn't even realise most of the models were lesbian.'[15]

> I'm not going to say my clothes are for lesbians, but a lot of my best friends are strong lesbians and I design with them in mind. If anyone's going to say my shows are out of order or anti-women it's going to be them, not some dainty housewife sitting in the front row. You can't please everyone when you design.[16]

For the Dante collection McQueen used well-known 'blue-blooded' models (Honor Fraser, Elizabetta Formaggia and Annabel Rothschild) whose make-up emphasised their chiselled features with pale skin and dark lips. The collection featured fine boning and military embroidery, braid-trimmed hussars' jackets and an eighteenth century style gold brocade admiral's coat worn with a shredded lace dress and a black jet-encrusted headpiece made by the jeweller and art director Simon Costin (see fig. 106e). Costin's previous jewellery, which McQueen had used in his graduation show in 1992, employed the techniques of taxidermy and dissection (figs 107 and 108). The deathly references were explicit in this collection in which fashion became the locus of darker meanings. The jet headpiece made the *memento mori* imagery explicit, as did a McQueen lace top which extended over the head to cover the face like a hangman's hood (see fig. 106b). Costin was also responsible for the figure of a plastic skeleton seated in the front row of the audience (see fig. 106i). Further references to death included models wearing masks set with crucifixes, imagery which McQueen 'appropriated' from the *grand guignol* photography of Joel-Peter Witkin;

13 'Cutting Up Rough'.

14 E.g., 'I don't like frilly, fancy dresses. Women can look beautiful and wear something well without looking fragile': Alexander McQueen quoted in Jennifer Scruby, 'The Eccentric Englishman', *Elle American*, July 1996: 154; of the type of model chosen for McQueen shows, his assistant Katy England said 'They must be able to carry off the clothes, as well as being beautiful. Some of the really young girls are gorgeous, but are not ready to do McQueen yet, they just haven't got enough attitude. We need strong, ballsy girls': Katy England in Melanie Rickey, 'England's Glory', *The Independent* Tabloid, 28 February 1997: 4.

15 Cited in Lorna V., 'All Hail McQueen', 26. McQueen was referring here to his sixth show after graduation, The Hunger, Spring–Summer 1996.

16 Cited in Heath, 'Bad Boys Inc', 102.

a

b

c

d

e

f

g

h

106 (right and previous pages)   Alexander McQueen, Dante, Autumn Winter 1996 7. Photographs Niall McInerney

17   Suzy, Menkes, 'The Macabre and the Poetic', *The International Herald Tribune*, 5 March 1996: 10. Menkes cited McQueen's comment on this collection that 'it's not so much about death, but the awareness that it is there.'

18   Bram Dijkstra, *Idols of Perversity: Fantasies of Feminine Evil in Fin-de-siècle Culture*, Oxford University Press, Oxford and New York, 1986; Elaine Showalter, *Sexual Anarchy: Gender and Culture at the Fin-de-Siècle*, Bloomsbury, London, 1991.

19   Ibid. See too Christine Buci-Glucksmann, *Baroque Reason: The Aesthetics of Modernity*, trans. Patrick Camiller, Sage, London, Thousand Oaks and New Delhi, 1994; Mary Ann Doane, *Femmes Fatales: Feminism, Film Theory, Psychoanalysis*, Routledge, London and New York, 1991; Elizabeth Bronfen, *Over Her Dead Body: Death, Femininity and the Aesthetic*, Manchester University Press, 1992.

20   E.g. these eponymous exhibition catalogues: Jeffrey Deitch, *Post Human*, Musée d'Art Contemporain, Pully/Lausanne, 1992, Museo d'Arte Contemporanea, Turin, 1992, Desle Foundation for Contemporary Art, Athens, 1992–3, Deichtorhallen, Hamburg, 1993; Mike Kelley, *The Uncanny*, Gemeentemuseum, Arnhem, 1993; *Abject Art: Repulsion and Desire in American Art*, Whitney Museum of American Art, New York, 1992–3; *Biennale*, Venice, 1994; *Elective Affinities*, Tate Gallery, Liverpool, 1993; Stuart Morgan (ed.), *Rites of Passage: Art at the End of the Century*, Tate Gallery, London, 1995; *L'Informe: mode d'emploi*, Centre Georges Pompidou, Paris, 1996; *The Quick and the Dead: Artists and Anatomy*, Royal College of Art, London, Warwick Arts Centre, Coventry and Leeds City Art Gallery, 1997–8. The exhibition 'L'Amour Fou: Photography and Surrealism' at the Corcoran Gallery of Art, Washington D.C. in 1985 and then at the Hayward Gallery, London in 1986 was an important predecessor.

Costin's earrings of dangling bird claws; arms caught in silver crowns of thorns; and Victorian jet beading. Stella Tennant modelled a mauve and black lace corset which drew on the collection's mourning palette of black, bone beige, mauves and greys (fig. 106c).[17] The model's berry-coloured lips against her pale flesh were vampiric and deathly. The high, constraining lapels of the corset, like an exaggerated wing collar, forced her chin up in a pose which also suggested an orthopaedic brace or truss. But in its dark sexuality her image also recalled the *femme fatale* of the *fin-de-siècle* whose terrifying allure was fatal to men.

The nineteenth-century *femme fatale* was, arguably, a fearful representation which configured female sexuality as perverse, even deathly, and which echoed fears about the social, economic and sexual emancipation of women at the turn of the century.[18] Turn-of-the-century fears about syphilis were also articulated specifically in images of women whose sexuality was toxic, tracing a link between contagion and sexuality by suggesting that such women were the carriers of disease.[19] Like her nineteenth-century counterpart, the late twentieth-century *femme fatale* could be thought of in relation to fears about illness, death and sexuality, fears which were raised in relation to HIV and AIDS from the mid-1980s onwards. The ubiquitous rise of 'the body' as a subject for artists and cultural theorists in this period was partly linked to this. Specifically, the imagery of both art and fashion was permeated by Kristeva's concept of the abject, Freud's uncanny and Bataille's *informe*, each of which was the subject of major exhibitions in the USA and Europe in the 1990s.[20]

What differentiated McQueen's late twentieth-century representation of the *femme fatale* from the turn-of-the-century counterpart was that the figure was no longer depicted as an object of fear: rather, she became a frightening subject. Her highly sexualized appearance was a defence, but one which shaded into a form of attack. Medusa-like, McQueen's woman was designed to petrify her audience, dressing if not actually to repel or disgust,

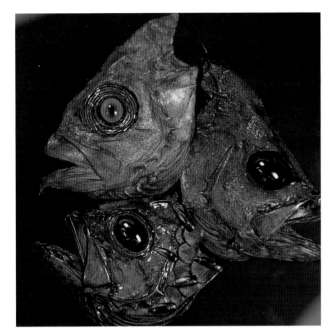

at least to keep men at a distance, rather than to attract them. In the Dante show a model wearing Philip Treacy's headpiece of stag's horns (fig. 109) created an image of a feral woman, only half human, recalling Baudrillard's phrase in *Fatal Strategies*: 'imagine a thing of beauty that has absorbed all the energy of the ugly: that's fashion.'[21] Her spiky, hybridised beauty and deathly pallor recalled the etymology of the words 'glamour' and 'vamp' as something potentially terrifying and bewitching rather than reassuring. Allying glamour with fear rather than allure, McQueen's avowed intent was to create a woman 'who looks so fabulous you wouldn't dare lay a hand on her', a statement which was illuminated by the knowledge that one of his sisters had been the victim of domestic violence.[22]

> I design clothes because I don't want women to look all innocent and naïve, because I I know what can happen to them. I want women to look stronger.[23]

> I don't like women to be taken advantage of. I disagree with that most of all. I don't like men whistling at women in the street, I think they deserve more respect.[24]

> I like men to keep their distance from women, I like men to be stunned by an entrance.[25]

> I've seen a woman get nearly beaten to death by her husband. I know what misogyny is . . . I want people to be afraid of the women I dress.[26]

In the Dante show in particular, the chilly elegance of the models, with their accessories of shaved feathers, antlers and thorns was combined with McQueen's razor-sharp cutting techniques to produce an image tinged equally with desire and dread – an image intended, like the Medusa's head emblazoned on a shield, to act as a talisman to protect its bearer in an uncertain world.

107 (*above left*) Simon Costin, pin, 1998. Dried lacquered fish skin with Venetian glass beads, taxidermy glass eyes, haematite, Victorian beetle-wing cases and 9-carat gold pin. Photograph courtesy Simon Costin

108 (*above right*) Simon Costin, Adam and Eve tiara, 1987. Baby iguanas, peridot eyes, copper, gold, thrushes' wings and citrines. Photograph Andy Fulgoni, courtesy Simon Costin

21 Jean Baudrillard, *Fatal Strategies*, Semiotext(e), New York, 1990: 9.
22 Marion Hume, 'Scissorhands', *Harpers & Queen*, August 1996: 82.
23 Cited in ibid.
24 Cited in Tony Marcus, 'I am the resurrection', *i-D*, 179, September 1998: 148.
25 Cited in *The Sunday Telegraph Magazine*, 22 September 1996: 36.
26 Cited in *Vogue* (USA), October 1997: 435.

Terror

The representation of female sexuality as terror has a long history in which the power of female display, or allure, is pictured as terrifying, sometimes deathly.[27] Like the artist Cathy de Monchaux's wall-mounted *vagina dentata* from the 1990s (fig. 110), it reveals a triumphant perversity and an exuberant sexuality. It substitutes for the frozen immobility of the Medusa the obscene laughter of the Baubo, a primitive and obscene female demon, according to the Oxford Classical Dictionary, who 'flashes' her genitals, recalling Freud's phrase in 'the devil fled when the woman showed him her vulva' (fig. 111).[28] For all the links to the *fin-de-siècle femme fatale*, this form of female terror differentiated the 1990s from the 1890s. In the early designs of McQueen it emerged as the trope of cruelty and female domination.

Many representations of the *femme fatale* are ambivalent, both fearful and fascinated, from late nineteenth-century paintings to early twentieth-century cinema. Mary Anne Doane has pointed out that most of these come to a sticky end, for the *femme fatale* is

111 Charles Eisen, *The Devil Deterred.* Illustration for La Fontaine's 'Le Diable de Papefiguière', *Contes*, 1750s

110 *(left)* Cathy de Monchaux, Once upon a Fuck, 1992. Brass, leather, velvet, 17 × 14 × 6 cm. Courtesy Cathy de Monchaux

109 *(facing page)* Philip Treacy, headpiece, Alexander McQueen, Dante, Autumn–Winter 1996–7. Photograph Chris Moore, courtesy Alexander McQueen

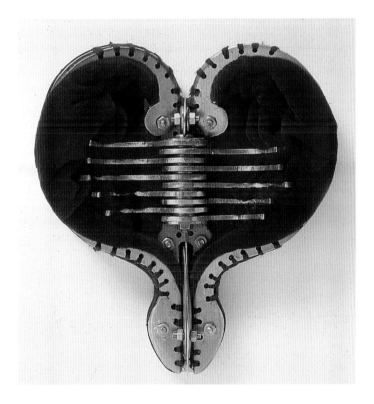

frequently an articulation of male fears about the social and sexual mobility of women in transitional periods.[29] Yet McQueen's images of a woman so powerfully sexual that no one would dare to lay hands on her, a woman who used her sexuality as a sword rather than a shield, also drew on an earlier and more dissident representation than the *fin-de-siècle* vamp or her early twentieth-century cinematic successor. Both in the cruelty of McQueen's

27 Efrat Tseëlon, *The Masque of Femininity: The Presentation of Woman in Everyday Life*, Sage, London, Thousand Oaks and New Delhi, 1995.

28 Sigmund Freud, 'Medusa's Head' [1922] in *Works: The Standard Edition of the Complete Psychological Works of Sigmund Freud*, under the general editorship of James Strachey, vol. XVIII, Hogarth Press, London, 1955: 273–4.

29 Doane, *Femmes Fatales*: 2.

cut and in the choice and styling of his catwalk models, he recalled the great female libertines of the Marquis de Sade, with their repertoires of savage dominance and mastery.
Sade's dangerous females were superwomen so exceptional that they were almost beyond
gender; their power to terrify lay precisely in the distance between their purely biological
femininity and their trans-gender actions. McQueen's first ready-to-wear collection for the
house of Givenchy, shown in March 1997, featured extraordinarily tall models, whose long
coats and micro-minis emphasised their height, which was further augmented by especially
tall wigs and high stiletto heels (fig. 112). These terrifyingly tall amazons stalked the cobbles
of an old Parisian stable and posed like streetwalkers against its metal poles. In Luis
Buñuel's film *Belle de Jour* (1976), the *haute bourgeoise* bored housewife played by
Catherine Deneuve spends her afternoons working in a brothel dressed in Chanel. The

film suggested a connection between Parisian chic and prostitution; but McQueen's association of the two made Parisian chic aggressive rather than languid. The bruised and battered models of the earlier collections had given way, by about 1997, to a regiment of superwomen. McQueen, like Sade, was fascinated by a dialectical relationship between victim and aggressor, and the parade of women he created on the catwalk resembled Sade's aggressors rather than their victims. They were far removed from, say, the parodic humour of Thierry Mugler's use of actual drag queens as models in his Spring–Summer 1992 collection (see fig. 87). McQueen's runway suggested a world without men, not because men were absent from it (they were not), but because it was a world in which gender was unsettled by women who were both hyperfeminine and yet in some respects terrifyingly male.

In his collections of this period McQueen began to manifest a fascination with the dynamics of power, in particular with a dialectical relationship between predator and prey, between victim and aggressor. In Dante, Stella Tennant modelled with a hooded and tethered bird of prey on her wrist; in Eclect Dissect McQueen came onto the runway for his bow with a tethered bird of prey on his. In his visual imagination there operated an economy very like that of double-entry book-keeping: every instance of goodness was balanced by one of cruelty, every gesture of dominance also sketched a gesture of subservience. As his shows progressed the victimised model gave way to a more powerful image, as prey became predator. In It's a Jungle Out There, shown in February 1997 in London's Borough Market, McQueen meditated on the theme of the Thomson's Gazelle and its terrible vulnerability to predators. He used the idea of animal instincts in the natural world as metaphor for the dog-eats-dog nature of the urban jungle, staging the show against a forty-foot-high screen of corrugated iron drilled with imitation bullet holes and surrounded by wrecked cars, adding dry ice and crimson lighting for drama. In a television interview he said:

> The whole show feeling was about the Thompson's Gazelle. It's a poor little critter – the markings are lovely, it's got these dark eyes, the white and black with the tan markings on the side, the horns – but it is the food chain of Africa. As soon as it's born it's dead, I mean you're lucky if it lasts a few months, and that's how I see human life, in the same way. You know, we can all be discarded quite easily . . . you're there, you're gone, it's a jungle out there![30]

Yet the design and styling of a hide jacket with pointed shoulders from which a pair of twisting gazelle horns stood up, worn by a model whose metallic contact lenses made her look like an alien (fig. 113), subverted the fatal passivity of the Thompson's Gazelle. Although the animal was referred to in the model's dramatic black and white face makeup, the horns and the hide jacket, McQueen repositioned its parts and added the huge shoulders and metallic contact lenses to create a woman more like the protagonist in Rider Haggard's *She*: predatory, scary, powerful and only half human. These were the characteristics of McQueen's *femme fatale*, a figure who suggested the terrifying power of women rather than their soft vulnerability.

113 Alexander McQueen, It's a Jungle Out There, Autumn–Winter 1997–8. Photograph Chris Moore, courtesy Alexander McQueen

30 Cited in 'Cutting Up Rough'.

Angela Carter's *The Sadeian Woman*, first published in 1979 by the feminist press Virago, was a late twentieth-century interpretation of the problems Sade raised about the culturally determined nature of women. She wrote that Sade's heroines healed themselves of their socially inflicted wounds through sexual violence, for 'a repressive society turns all eroticism into violence.'[31] Sade, she said, 'cuts up the bodies of women and reassembles them in the shapes of his own delirium'.[32] Four women – the ruthless and self-serving Juliette, the aristocratic man-hater Clairwil, the microbiologist, poisoner and magician Durand and the voluptuary Princess Borghese – are merely four examples of what Angela Carter called 'a museum of woman-monsters'[33] that Sade conjured up, because, she wrote, 'a free woman in an unfree society will be a monster.'[34]

McQueen created his own 'museum of woman-monsters' in his second couture collection for Givenchy, Eclect Dissect, shown in July 1997 (fig. 114). In the period leading up to the show, his art director Simon Costin combined the late Victorian costumes McQueen was then looking at with a series of animated skeletons and muscle men from the sixteenth-century anatomical plates of Andreas Vesalius in a series of collages (fig. 115). The cut of some of the dresses in the collection was influenced by the figures from these anatomical plates in which the skeletons appear to 'vogue' or model their own bodies. The concept behind the theme of the show was a paragraph written by Costin who dreamed up a fictional *fin-de-siècle* surgeon and collector who travelled the world collecting exotic objects, textiles and women, whom he subsequently cut up and reassembled in his laboratory. The 'scenario' of the catwalk show staged the return of these gruesomely murdered women who came back to haunt the living. It was shown in a Paris medical school, swathed with blood-red velvet curtains and decorated with medical specimens. The models impersonated the ghosts of the long-dead women, dressed in the exotica collected by their murderer on his foreign journeys. Spanish lace, Burmese necklaces, Japanese kimonos and Russian folk dresses were jumbled with the art of the taxidermist – stuffed animals and birds, and animals' skulls. Baudelaire wrote that

> fashions should never be considered as dead things; you might just as well admire the tattered old rags hung up, as slack and lifeless as the skin of St Bartholomew, in an old-clothes dealer's cupboard. Rather they should be thought of as vitalized and animated by the beautiful women who wore them.'[35]

His explicit comparison between skin, or flesh, which clothes the body and fashionable dress; was made through a gruesome comparison to St Bartholomew, who was flayed alive and the passage suggests that there is something ghostly in the idea of a beautiful woman animating a lifeless corpse in the pursuit of fashion. When in Eclect Dissect the fashion models impersonated the ghosts of long-dead women come back to haunt their murderer, the conceit was animated on the catwalk. The models, tall and imposing, were not, however, victims but vengeful ghosts. One strode out in an outfit which fused *Madame Butterfly* kitsch with an imposing dominatrix look: the Japanese *obi* became a corset, the kimono a tight, Western skirt, in a late twentieth-century interpretation of Mirabeau's turn-

114 Alexander McQueen, Eclect Dissect for Givenchy, Autumn–Winter 1997–8. Art direction Simon Costin. Photographs Niall McInerney

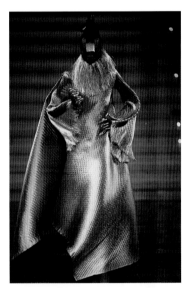

31 Angela Carter, *The Sadeian Woman: An Exercise in Cultural History*, Virago, London, 1979: 26.

32 Ibid.

33 Ibid: 25.

34 Ibid: 27.

35 Charles Baudelaire, *The Painter of Modern Life and Other Essays*, trans. Jonathan Mayne, Phaidon, London, 2nd ed., 1995: 33.

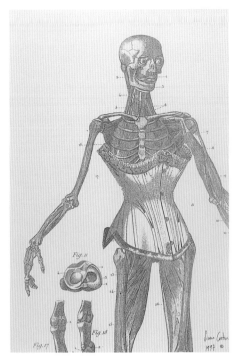  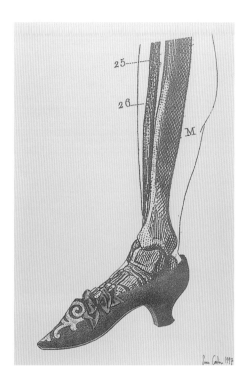

115   Simon Costin, photocopied collages
for Alexander McQueen, Eclect Dissect for
Givenchy, Autumn–Winter 1997–8. Courtesy
Simon Costin

of-the-century text *The Torture Garden*. The analogy between the doctor and the designer
as anatomist was clear. McQueen himself could be seen as a kind of anatomist, dissecting
and flaying conventional fashion to show us the death's head beneath the surface and, particularly, the link between eroticism and death which permeated much of the fashion
imagery of the 1990s.

Angela Carter made the case for Sade as a 'terrorist of the imagination', a 'sexual guer-
rilla', who revealed that everyday social, economic and political relations were mirrored in
sexual relations. In Sade's writings, the cruelty of statesmen, princes and popes exceeded
that of all other men. Yet his great women were more cruel still, as they used their
sexuality in an act of vengeance in a world which otherwise condemned them to a life of
passive endurance – a life of victimisation without power or autonomy, like that of Sade's
virtuous Justine. So although the 'pornographer as terrorist' may not think of himself as a
friend of women, he is always their unconscious ally because he approaches some kind of
emblematic truth about gender relations and power.

Carter described Sade's late eighteenth-century writing as being at the threshold of the
modern period, looking simultaneously back to the *ancien régime* and forwards to a revolutionary future. A hundred years later, at the beginning of the twentieth century, the
French poet and critic Guillaume Apollinaire equated Sade's undoubtedly monstrous
Juliette with the New Woman, writing – admiringly – that Juliette was the woman whose
advent Sade, at the beginning of the nineteenth century, could only anticipate.[36] Yet Carter
herself qualified her original assertion that Sade's women were free women. In his darkly
mechanistic world women were either sacrificial victims or ritual murderesses, but in either

36   Carter, *Sadeian Woman*: 75.

case always overseen by men, a world in which every instance of freedom was balanced by one of repression. This dialectical structure can be mapped onto McQueen's visually plotted universe in which victims mutated into amazons, a shield became a sword, the woman's body an emblematic Medusa's head. However, Sade's female libertines or McQueen's amazonian models cannot be classified simply as New Women for a new age, for the woman as aggressor is no freer from the trammels of gender relations than her dialectical sister, the woman as victim. If one is a pawn and the other a queen, free to go where she will, nevertheless there is always a king elsewhere on the board, a Lord of the Game.[37] Sade's free-wheeling Juliette was as locked into a dialectic of gender, power and sexual violence – even as she transcended them – as the enslaved and miserable Justine.

Yet Sade's pornographic narratives were also a critique of the nature and exercise of power, in particular of political oppression, in his own time and, like McQueen's, his vision was singularly dark. As Carter wrote, for Sade 'all tenderness is false . . . all beds are minefields.'[38] Similarly, for McQueen there could be no sanctified view of history, culture or politics. The past was neither picturesque nor romantic. Such views merely served to mask vicious realities, and a desire to strip history of its romance defined McQueen's imagery. Whereas a designer such as Galliano romanticised history and culture, McQueen made it harsh and painful to watch, as in the Highland Rape collection (see fig. 104). In building McQueen's 'yob' reputation, journalists stressed his working-class upbringing, his education in a 'sink' school in East London, and his taxi-driver father, but under-emphasised the fact that his mother was a local historian and former lecturer. As a child, he was taken with her to a London archive where she researched the McQueen family origins, discovering that they had been Spitalfields Huguenots, which influenced McQueen's choice of venue for the Dante collection, Hawksmoor's Christchurch, Spitalfields. McQueen's mother has recounted how, while she researched the family origins, her young son investigated the story of Jack the Ripper, a theme which subsequently informed his graduation collection.[39]

Disenchantment

The violence of McQueen's vision was fuelled by 'a desire to strip romance to the truth'[40] as he saw it, just as the violence of Sade's writing was fed by his own political disaffection, his disappointed utopianism. Among the chilly *femmes fatales* of McQueen's Dante collection, with its male models styled to look like Los Angeles gang youths, were jackets photo-printed with images of Don McCullin's war photographs (fig. 116). The collection was about religion as the cause of war throughout history. It was staged on a candle-lit cross-shaped runway, against a backdrop of flashing, back-lit stained-glass windows, and had a soundtrack of Victorian church music which, as the show started, was drowned by the sound of gunfire, and then by a hard-core club track. Against this backdrop, the harshness of McQueen's images of women shifted and began to resignify.

37 Ibid: 80.
38 Ibid: 25.
39 Judy Rumbold, 'Alexander the Great', *Vogue* (UK), July 1996, catwalk report supplement.
40 Hume, 'Scissorhands': 82.

41   Simon Schama, *Citizens: A Chronicle of the
French Revolution*, Viking, London and New York,
1989: 742–6.

Beyond the surface cruelty which patterned both Sade and McQueen's work lay a deeper structural connection which united these apparently disparate figures in the same tradition. McQueen's lurid and *grand guignol* displays on the catwalk conjure up the artist Jacques-Louis David's revolutionary spectacles in the 1790s and his elaborate staging of the assassinated Marat's funeral in the church of the Cordeliers in Paris.[41] The darkness of McQueen's view of history and culture echoed that of Sade's utopian, yet despairing, political idealism. More than half the extraordinarily violent and pornographic *Philosophy in the Boudoir* consists of a political treatise entitled 'Just one more effort, Frenchmen, if you would become republicans'. This treatise was extracted from its pornographic context and reprinted as a pamphlet in the revolution of 1848 by the followers of the utopian Saint-Simon. Sade's library, inventoried at his death, included the complete works of Rousseau and Voltaire; yet his pornographic vision renounced both reason and enlightenment in favour of a view of the world as fundamentally driven by relations of power. For Sade, freedom only existed in opposition to, and was defined by, tyranny. Propelled by this seemingly Manichean dualism, Sade's contradictions extended to his sexual choices and his political ideals equally. Despite the extreme cruelty of his sexual writings he claimed the smell of blood from the guillotine made him feel sick. Although a supporter of the revolution he was opposed to the death penalty and, as a judge during the Terror, was briefly imprisoned on the charge of 'moderatism'.[42]

It is Sade's nihilism that makes him modern, as well as the proximity of sex and politics in his sensibility. Indeed, we might ask why it is that cruelty re-emerged as a trope of the late twentieth century, be it in the 1990s turn to a fashionable sado-masochism or the cruelty of, for example, films like *Fight Club* and *American Psycho*, in which the hard bodies of cinema meshed with the fetishised body beautiful of consumer culture. Both Sade's and McQueen's worlds are post-Edenic. Each paints a picture of a tragic universe, an alienated world of Baudelairean modernity in which, as John Rajchman has written, sexuality becomes the ruination of harmonious, 'centred' love: 'There has arisen in the modern period a literature of a sexuality that is not about love, happiness or duty but about trauma, otherness and unspeakable truth.'[43] This literature is not new: it runs from Sade through Baudelaire to Genet and Bataille, and is now two hundred years old. What was new, however, at the close of the twentieth century was that these ideas found expression in the work of a fashion designer, perhaps for the first time since the inception of this literature, the late eighteenth century, which ushered in the post-Revolutionary French fashions *à la victime* in which, for example, women wore a red ribbon round the neck in reference to the cut of the guillotine. In a fashion plate of 1798 these scarlet *croisures à la victime* have moved down from the neck to traverse the bodice to signify that their wearer would sacrifice everything for her lover (fig. 117).[44] As in many of McQueen's designs today, political trauma has become eroticised; Terror bleeds into Eros.

The art historian Ewa Lajer-Burcharth has argued that in the Directoire period trauma was played out in the way the body was represented. If the body is a historically privileged cultural representation of the self, Directoire fashions represented an effort to come to terms with the Terror, a moment of historical trauma that had subsequently to be accommodated through a series of bodily practices. However, although the Directoire body was, according to Lajer-Burcharth, 'marked by trauma', the same period saw a resurgence of bodily narcissism that was mobilised to heal trauma through pleasurable display: the public parading of fashion, the rise of gymnasia and swimming pools, and the development of an entirely new industry of bodily care and pleasure through the development of unguents and creams.[45] It is precisely this balancing of competing forces in the one body – marked on the one hand by trauma yet characterised on the other by an entirely hedonistic cult of the body beautiful – that makes this post-revolutionary body modern. Anthony Giddens has referred to identity as self-conscious and self-reflexive in modernity, and this process of continual self-scrutiny and self-creation takes place through the

117 *Croisures à la victime*, fashion plate in *Journal des dames et des modes*, 1798. Bibliothèque nationale de France, Paris.

42 Carter, *Sadeian Woman*: 32.
43 John Rajchman, 'Lacan and the Ethics of Modernity', *Representations*, 15, Summer 1986: 47.
44 Aileen Ribeiro, *Fashion in the French Revolution*, Batsford, London, 1988: 124.
45 Ewa Lajer-Burcharth, *Necklines: The Art of Jacques-Louis David after the Terror*, Yale University Press, New Haven and London, 1999: 2.

thoroughly banal daily rituals of beautification, exercise and the pursuit of the toned body.[46] Yet it was on that very same body that designers like McQueen staged their late twentieth-century images of trauma and anxiety, and it is entirely due to the fact that Western consumer capitalism fetishes the toned body that experimental designers have had a canvas on which to paint its abject counterpart.

Sade's books had been banned to the general public for the best part of two hundred years; they are in print now, as they were at the time of the French Revolution, both periods of instability and oscillation, between revolutionary freedom and state or corporate oppression. If, in Angela Carter's phrase, 'our flesh arrives to us out of history'[47] (her more poetic formulation of Foucault's concept of sexuality as historically determined) perhaps such fashions gesture towards moments of cultural trauma which we can only just begin to describe. The philosophical nihilism of the late twentieth century, the dark fact of *intifada*, genocide and torture in Palestine, Rwanda and the Balkans, and the prurient accounts of murder, child abuse and street crime in both the British and the American press, seem glib, even tasteless images to cite in this context. Yet in the 1990s McQueen's fictional visions of beautiful women, like Andrew Groves's collection based on the Troubles in Northern Ireland, were easily as dark, while they masqueraded under the lightness of 'fashion'. And the same newspapers that brought lurid news accounts of contemporary horrors extended their coverage to fashion and beauty. In American fiction of the 1990s, both Jay McInerney and Brett Easton Ellis connected fashion to pathological violence. Ellis's *American Psycho* (1991) linked sadistic murder and designer accessories, while his *Glamorama* (1998) drew parallels between the American obsession with fame and fashion and European terrorism and sadistic torture. Ellis's horror scenes are masked by a veneer of fashionability of which the model becomes the very emblem, while the novel is punctuated by references to brands and labels: Gucci, Prada, Comme and Versace. Indeed, as the heart of darkness gradually comes closer to home, the references to more avant-garde European labels are gradually replaced by American ones such as Brooks Brothers and Gap. In *Bright Lights Big City* (1984) Jay McInerney directly assimilates a model to a mannequin, highlighting the dead gaze of capitalism. In his *Model Behaviour* (1998) the author contrasts the protagonist's ambitious 'dumb blonde' model girlfriend with his intelligent, educated, beautiful but anorexic sister who, unable to go to work, spends her days watching videotapes of witnesses' testimony of Bosnian atrocities from the United Nations' War Crimes Tribunal. Her boyfriend works in the trauma department of a large public hospital. Like the characters in the American television series 'ER' who oscillate continually between 'trauma and techno-speak, cardiac arrest and broken hearts',[48] McInerney's characters mimic the endless repetition of trauma itself against the backdrop of fashionable uptown New York chic.

It is precisely this oscillation between beauty and horror in the fashion and fiction of the late twentieth century that recalls earlier moments of beauty shot through with darkness. Again, Baudelaire's avant-guarde aesthetic in the mid-nineteenth century resurfaces in the late twentieth, highlighting the connection between Baudelairean modernity and late

46 Anthony Giddens, *Modernity and Self-Identity: Self and Society in the Late Modern Age*, Polity Press, Cambridge, 1991. If the idea of modernity connotes a certain self-consciousness or self-scrutiny measurable in the social sciences, T. J. Clark has identified a similar self-consciousness or, rather, self-reflexivity, in the field of representation rather than social praxis. Clark has argued for self-reflexivity in art as a defining moment of modernism, first in relation to Manet and the Paris of the 1860s and subsequently to David and Paris of the 1790s: *The Painting of Modern Life: Paris in the Art of Manet and his Followers*, Knopf, New York, 1984; *Farewell to an Idea: Episodes from a History of Modernism*, Yale University Press, New Haven and London, 1999.

47 Carter, *Sadeian Woman*: 9.

48 Mark Seltzer, 'Wound Culture: Trauma in the Pathological Public Sphere', *October*, 80, spring 1997: 26.

twentieth-century post-modernity. But in McQueen's work the ghosts of the period after the French Revolution of 1789, rather than those of the 1840s–50s, provide a comparable model of historical trauma and rupture. The art historian T. J. Clark traced this 'moment of modernity' first to Paris of the 1860s[49] but subsequently revised his argument to move this date further back to the period immediately after the French Revolution, in his analysis of David's painting *The Death of Marat*.[50] For Clark, artistic modernism is associated with politics and contingency, and he argued that modernism's engagement with politics is a way of 'coming to terms with the world's disenchantment'.[51] In McQueen's work too a warped engagement with politics as trauma sketches a strong sense of disenchantment with the world through the expression of a rough sensuality and refined cruelty.

49 Clark, *Painting of Modern Life*.
50 Clark, *Farewell*.
51 Ibid: 22.

seven   deathliness

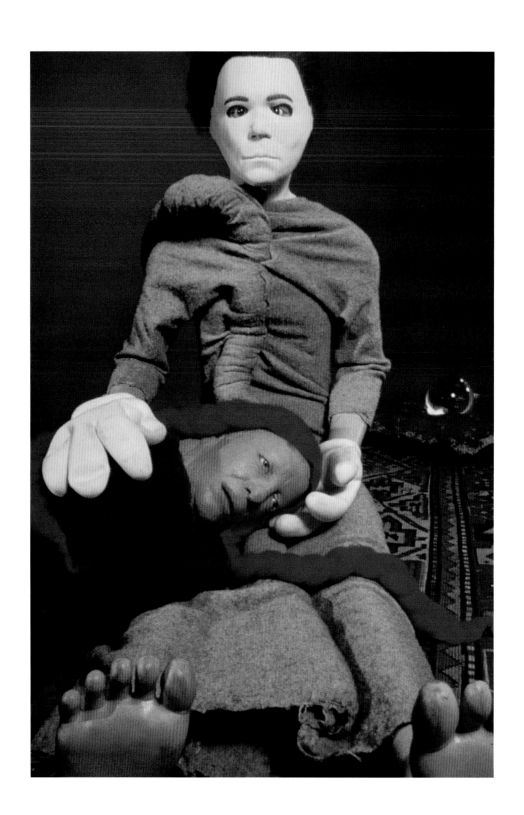

Living dolls

In 1981 the German pop group Kraftwerk released a song, 'Das Model', in which they sang 'she shows off her body for consumer goods', highlighting the ambiguous status of the fashion model, whose own body becomes an object in the course of modelling clothes.[1] The film-makers The Brothers Quay made 'Street of Crocodiles' in 1986, based on the novella by Bruno Schultz, in which tailors' dummies come alive and take over the tailor's shop. They capture their former master and dismantle him like a doll; treating him like a Stockman dummy, they measure him up, go through samples of fabric and trimmings and sew an outfit to dress him in. Comme des Garçons' Metamorphosis collection for Autumn–Winter 1994–5 was photographed by the artist Cindy Sherman for the designer's direct-mail campaign on slumped, dysfunctional dolls (fig. 118). In the late 1990s, European designers like Martin Margiela, Hussein Chalayan and Alexander McQueen effected a similar reversal by substituting dummies for fashion models on the catwalk, or by playing on the robotic qualities of the model, stressing the inorganic at the expense of the organic. Their dummies or dolls echoed the ambiguous subject – object status of the model since the nineteenth century, recalling the opening pages of Zola's novel about a nineteenth-century department store, *The Ladies' Paradise.* The young country girl Denise arrives in Paris and is seduced by a shop window full of dummies, mirrored to infinity, dressed in the most sumptuous and elaborate fashions. The infinitely reflecting mirrors of the shop window seem to fill the street with 'beautiful women for sale with huge price tags where their heads should have been'.[2] Zola's image forces the commodity fetishism that figures prominently in his novel; and the 'swelling bosoms' and 'beautiful women' of the passage point to the complexity of the spectacle of femininity in Paris of the 1880s when women were both subjects and objects of consumer desire.[3]

Julie Wosk has argued that in the nineteenth century

artists' images of automatons became central metaphors for the dreams and nightmares of societies undergoing rapid technological change. In a world where new labor-saving inventions were expanding human capabilities and where a growing number of people were employed in factory systems calling for rote actions and impersonal efficiency, nineteenth-century artists confronted one of the most profound issues raised by new technologies: the possibility that people's identities and emotional lives would take on the properties of machines.[4]

And in the twentieth century, Hillel Schwartz has noted, this is the prevailing view of modernism: 'modern life, with its essentially industrial momentum, has processed our worlds and our bodies into dissociated, fetishised, ultimately empty and machinable elements.'[5] These elements resurface in contemporary fashion imagery which substitutes dolls for models or makes models look like androids (see fig. 9). For one of her collections Shelley Fox researched the Victorian dolls section of the Bethnal Green Museum of Childhood in London. For the show, the jeweller Naomi Filmer created porcelain chin plates

118 (*facing page*) Cindy Sherman, Untitled #304, 1994, C-print. Courtesy Cindy Sherman/Metro Pictures

1 Caroline Evans, 'Living Dolls: Mannequins, Models and Modernity', in Julian Stair (ed.), *The Body Politic*, Crafts Council, London, 2000: 103.

2 Emile Zola, *The Ladies' Paradise*, trans. with an intro. by Brian Nelson, Oxford University Press, Oxford and New York, 1995: 6.

3 Janet Wolff, 'The Invisible *flâneuse*: Women and the Literature of Modernity', *Feminine Sentences: Essays on Women and Culture*, Polity Press, Cambridge, 1990: 34–50; Mica Nava, 'Modernity's Disavowal: Women, the City and the Department Store', in Pasi Falk and Colin Campbell (eds), *The Shopping Experience*, Sage, London, Thousand Oaks and New Delhi, 1997: 56–91. Christopher Breward, *The Culture of Fashion*, Manchester University Press, Manchester and New York, 1995: ch. 5, 'Nineteenth Century: Fashion and Modernity': 145–79.

4 Julie Wosk, *Breaking Frame: Technology and the Visual Arts in the Nineteenth Century*, Rutgers University Press, New Brunswick, 1992: 81.

5 Hillel Schwartz, 'Torque: The New Kinaesthetic of the Twentieth Century', in Jonathan Crary and Sanford Kwinter (eds), *Incorporations, Zone 6*, Zone Books, New York, 1992: 104. Schwartz himself, however, disagrees with this interpretation of modern life.

and dipped the models' hands in wax to make them more doll-like. Martin Margiela based a collection on scaled-up dolls' clothes with huge machine knitting and giant poppers (fig. 119). In a fashion spread from 2000 called 'Dolly Mixture' models dressed and made up to look like Victorian dolls were juxtaposed against images of real Victorian dolls dressed in similar clothes (figs 120 and 121). The spread played with scale, reproducing the dolls in the same size as the human models. All were styled to look creepily dysfunctional, with bald foreheads, hair askew and jerky poses, disturbingly reminiscent of Hans Bellmer's doll from the 1930s. In a short accompanying text, Gaby Wood cited Freud's essay on the uncanny to explain 'the hovering uncertainty between animate and inanimate' that makes dolls inherently uncanny:

> But what does doll history, this little set of parables, threaten for women? Is 'living doll' still a compliment? Why are fashion models still called mannequins? What these wonderful, unsettling photographs seems to say is: if you want your women to look like dolls, this is what that reality would be like – a mad, decaying, decadence, full of about-to-snap jointed limbs, dangling paranormal dances and balding Jills-in-the-box, ready to spring into horrible, inhuman laughter.'[6]

The doll of these fashion pictures is a 'familiar', the structural inversion of the humanist subject, an alienated other.[7] But it is not gender-neutral: as Wood's text implies, the female doll or cyborg in particular can also be linked to the search for the perfect body in Western culture, often played out in the idealised images of women in fashion, as well as in the ubiquitous Barbie doll. 'The desire for the right image . . . alienates women from themselves, turning them into automatons.'[8] Sadie Plant has argued that the association of women, modernity and the machine dates at least from the early twentieth century when the first telephonists, operators and calculators were women, 'as were the first computers and even the first computer programmers.'[9] But her utopian vision of women as instruments and images of progress and a better future is shadowed by a darker image of women as commodities in the age of mass production. This shadow goes back earlier, to the Paris of the Arcades, and the fear of the shadow is discernible in Benjamin's writing. His jottings include this fragment: 'No immortalizing so unsettling as that of the ephemera and the fashionable forms preserved for us in the waxworks museum', a reference to André Breton's *Nadja* in which the poet loses his heart to a wax mannequin of a woman adjusting her garter in the waxworks museum in Paris, the Musée Grevin.[10]

In 1993 at Viktor & Rolf's first staged show the models climbed onto a pedestal and posed like classical sculptures. Annette Kuhn stated that 'women are dehumanised by being represented as a kind of automaton, a living doll,'[11] yet such images can be construed as a kind of ghosting of the alienating effects of modernity, specifically in relation to the female image. This point was implicit in the Imitation of Christ show in New York in which the more usual procession of live women on the catwalk was replaced by a fictional auction of clothes displayed on dummies. Benjamin's notes include the phrase 'Emphasis on the commodity character of the woman in the market of love. The doll as wish

6 Gaby Wood, 'Dolly Mixture', *The Observer Magazine*, 27 February 2000: 36–41.

7 V. Sobchack, 'Postfuturism', in G. Kirkup *et al* (eds), *The Gendered Cyborg: A Reader*, Routledge in association with the Open University, London, 2000: 137.

8 R. Fouser, 'Mariko Mori: Avatar of a Feminine God', *Art Text*, nos 60–2, 1998: 36.

9 Sadie Plant, 'On the Matrix: Cyberfeminist Simulations', in Kirkup *et al.*, *Gendered Cyborg*: 267.

10 Walter Benjamin, *The Arcades Project*, trans. Howard Eiland and Kevin McLaughlin, Belknap Press of Harvard University Press, Cambridge, Mass., and London, 1999: 69.

11 Annette Kuhn, *The Power of the Image: Essays on Representation and Sexuality*, Routledge, New York and London, 1985: 14.

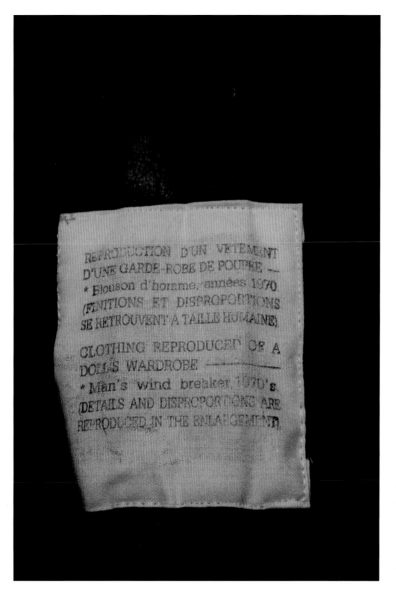

119 Label for scaled-up dolls' clothes (enlarged by 5.2 times to human size). Martin Margiela, Autumn–Winter 1994–5. Photograph Anders Edstrom, courtesy La Maison Martin Margiela

120 (following page) Michael Baumgarten, Dolly Mixture, The Observer Magazine, 2000. Styling Jo Adams.dress and underskirt by Yohji Yamamoto. Photograph courtesy Michael Baumgarten

121 (page 169) Michael Baumgarten, Dolly Mixture, The Observer Magazine, 2000. Styling Jo Adams, skirt by Chanel, underslip doll's own. Photograph courtesy Michael Baumgarten

symbol.'[12] For Theodor Adorno, too, in his 1931 lecture on Dickens's *The Old Curiosity Shop*, the waxworks museum, the puppet theatre and the graveyard were all equally 'allegories of the bourgeois industrial world.'[13] In Dickens's *Our Mutual Friend*, Jenny Wren, the tiny dolls' dressmaker, is contrasted with Mr Venus, taxidermist and 'articulator of human bones' who assembles human skeletons for sale from miscellaneous body parts.[14] By inference, Jenny Wren's dolls are the equivalent of Venus's skeletons constructed out of dead fragments and body parts. The figure of the 'anatomist' who recycles human remains is the shadow of the ragpicker (a figure who also appears in the novel, and is one of its few benign characters, the Jew Riah). To emphasise the madness of this world of inversions, Jenny Wren refers to her father as her child, to Riah as her god-mother, to dolls as human and to humans as dolls. And in a final dark touch, as if to underline the capitalist base of the enterprise, and to remind us that this is a novel about money and its

12 Benjamin, *Arcades Project*: 895.

13 See Esther Leslie's discussion of Adorno's lecture in *Walter Benjamin: Overpowering Conformism*, Pluto Press, London and Sterling, Va., 2000: 10–11.

14 Charles Dickens, *Our Mutual Friend*, ed. with an intro. by Stephen Gill, Penguin, Harmondsworth, 1985 [1864–5]: 128.

influence and, therefore, about the rot and the dead matter at the heart of capitalist life: human teeth continually drift into the change in Mr Venus's till.[15]

In 1894 *Scientific American* showed an illustration of a French talking doll who sings and laughs 'in a clear childish voice' and recounts how her mother will take her to the theatre.[16] It also shows the American equivalent being manufactured in the factory of Thomas Edison, who invented the phonograph in 1877 and half of whose factory was given over to the manufacture of phonographic dolls (fig. 122). The central image shows us the young woman recording the doll's utterance onto a wax cylinder. On either side we see the doll, dressed on the left and undressed on the right, to reveal the talking mechanism inside. The image below shows Edison's factory, in which a great number of people are at

15   Ibid: 125.
16   Reprinted in *Der Natuur*, 26 April 1894, trans. and reproduced in Leonard de Vries, *Victorian Inventions*, John Murray, London, 1971: 183.

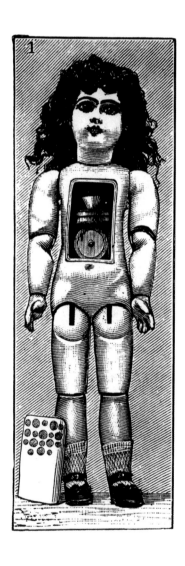

122 (*above and right*)   Edison's phonographic doll, from *Der Natuur*, 26 April 1894, reprinted from *Scientific American*, 1894

work producing the dolls. The text accompanying this illustration perfectly describes the alienating effect of the modern production line:

> Edison has no less than 500 people employed in manufacturing phonographs and half of them work in the doll department. Walking through the factory, one is filled with admiration for the order which prevails everywhere. Everything is done in the American way and the principle of the division of labour is most extensively applied . . . About 500 talking dolls ready to play can be supplied every day. In the centre of the picture a female employee can be seen speaking the words on to the wax cylinders one by one.[17]

Thus in the most up-to-date modern factory we witness the young woman robotically speaking each individual utterance, five hundred times a day, onto the wax cylinders in order to produce the living or, at least, talking simulacrum of the human female. The animated doll acquires some of the lifelike qualities of the living girl, while the girl trades semblances with the doll in her mechanical and repetitive utterances, to invoke Marx's description of commodity fetishism whereby workers are increasingly dehumanised and consumers begin to live out their lives in and through commodities.[18] As people and things trade semblances the commodity assumes an uncanny vitality of its own ('"dead labour" come back to dominate the living'[19]) while the human producer acquires some of the 'deathly facticity'[20] of the machine. All is done in the name of progress, 'the American way', which was exemplified by Henry Ford's production line in the early twentieth century. In figure 122 Marx's concept of the worker's alienation through the processes of industrial production is fused with the image of the woman as spectacle and commodity; and, in the age of mass production, the commodity is no longer unique but endlessly repeatable.

The image finds an echo in the Tiller Girls of, for example, the Weimar period in Berlin and the Rockettes of New York's Radio City Music Hall in the 1930s, whose identical heights, synchronised dance routines and uniform costumes denied the material difference of sixty-four female bodies (fig. 123). Siegfried Kracauer in his article of 1927 'The Mass Ornament', written while working as a journalist for the *Frankfurter Zeitung*, described the patterns made by chorus lines as 'building blocks and nothing more . . . only as parts of a mass, not as individuals who believe themselves to be formed from within, do people become fractions of a figure.'[21] Kracauer argued that the chorus line was a symbolic form of representation of 'the capitalist production process', singling out the Taylor system and the worker on the production line, for the massed forms of the cabaret entertainer are ways of visualising 'significant components of reality' that have become 'invisible in our world'. 'The mass ornament is the aesthetic reflex of the rationality to which the prevailing economic system aspires.'[22] In other words the industrial aesthetic of modernity pictures its economic origins, and this is true no less of the fashion model than of the chorus girl. At the end of the twentieth century, as much as at the beginning, the uncanny replication and standardisation of the female form, in the shop window dummy, the showgirl or the fashion model, brings together two ideas: the idea of femininity commodified in an age of

17 Ibid.

18 Karl Marx, *Capital*, vol. 1, trans. Ben Fowkes, Penguin, Harmondsworth, 1976: 165.

19 Hal Foster, *Compulsive Beauty*, MIT Press, Cambridge, Mass., and London, 1993: 129.

20 Hal Foster, 'The Art of Fetishism', *The Princeton Architectural Journal*, vol. 4 'Fetish', 1992: 7.

21 'The Mass Ornament' [1927] in Siegfried Kracauer, *The Mass Ornament: Weimar Essays*, trans. Thomas Y. Levin, Harvard University Press, Cambridge, Mass., and London, 1995: 76.

22 Ibid: 76–9.

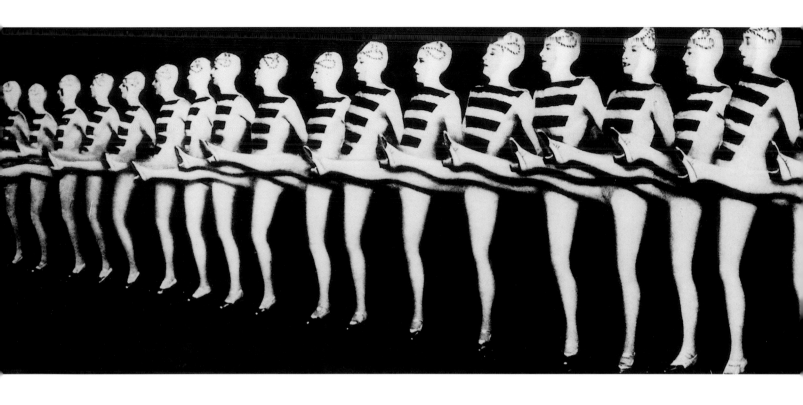

123   The Rockettes, Radio City Music Hall, New York, 1930s

mass production, and that of the Fordist production line in which human beings function as cogs in a machine.

The same visual shock tactic is often deployed at the end of the contemporary fashion show when all the models parade down the runway: fashion, supposedly about individuality, is actually about uniformity, and designers like Issey Miyake have fruitfully exploited this to dramatic ends (fig. 125). The body which is produced is a disciplined, streamlined and modernist body, in which the outer discipline of the corset has given way to the inner disciplines of diet and exercise. In the 1920s the designers Coco Chanel and Jean Patou designed for a body which conformed with the modernist aesthetic, which was functional and anti-decorative; this body was, and continues to be, 'produced', through diet and exercise, very much along the lines of Fordist production.[23] In the same way the uncanny cloning of Busby Berkeley's musicals of the 1930s echoes Henry Ford's production line in the early years of the century. Today one might find the same echo in Donna Karan's 'uniforms' for working women, the toned models of her shows or in Adel Rootstein's dummies, which are modelled from the bodies of real individual models to produce generic types.

A photograph of 1990 shows the model Violetta in profile next to the Adel Rootstein dummy modelled on her (fig. 124). They are posed in double profile, the one echoing the other, her hand resting on her Doppelgänger's shoulder. The two identical profiles are striking: which is the real woman, which the copy? The double portrait demands a double take. If the economic transactions of mercantile capitalism are uncanny, it is because they enable this slippage between animate and inanimate, life and death, subject and object. The image suggests the living model is merely an up-to-date variant of the inanimate dummy; and

23   Peter Wollen, *Raiding the Ice Box: Reflections on Twentieth Century Culture*, Verso, London and New York, 1993: 20–1 and 35–71.

the process of fetishism – in this case commodity fetishism – enables the displacement of meanings and motifs from the living woman onto the doll. Or does it? The theory of fetishism, be it commodity or sexual fetishism, is predicated on there being an original, organic, object of desire, from which feelings are displaced, but the entire relationship of model and mannequin and their historical origins call into question the nature of an original, especially when the two together appear almost indistinguishable.[24]

In the seventeenth and eighteenth centuries the fashion doll was the plaything of adult women, in the sense that dolls dressed in the latest fashions were sent from Paris to guide dressmakers towards fashion trends. Immediately after the Second World War the French Syndicat de la Couture Française created the Théâtre de la Mode, a collection of dolls dressed by Parisian couturiers that was sent round the world to promote French couture. Thus even if clients did not initially go to Paris themselves the dolls wore the clothes instead, something that Viktor & Rolf may well have had in mind in their 1996 miniature show with dolls dressed in hand-made outfits (see fig. 59a).[25] Susan Stewart describes how, after the death of Catherine de' Medici's husband, eight fashion dolls were found in the inventory of her belongings, all dressed in elaborate mourning garb. Stewart also reminds us that 'the world of objects is always a kind of "dead among us"' and that the toy is a reminder of this: 'as part of the general inversions which that world presents, the inanimate comes to life.'[26] Freud believed that children expect their dolls to come to life: 'the idea of a "living doll" excites no fear at all.'[27] His essay on the uncanny (*unheimlich*)

124 (*right*)   Model Violetta next to a mannequin by Adel Rootstein (released in 1990). Photograph courtesy Adel Rootstein

24   For a discussion of doubling, see Hillel Schwartz, *The Culture of the Copy*, Zone Books, New York, 1996.

25   *Viktor & Rolf Haute Couture Book*, texts by Amy Spindler and Didier Grumbach, Groninger Museum, Gröningen, 2000: 8.

26   Susan Stewart, *On Longing: Narratives of the Miniature, the Gigantic, the Souvenir, the Collection*, Duke University Press, Durham, N.C. and London, 1993: 57.

27   Sigmund Freud, 'The Uncanny' [1919] in *Works: The Standard Edition of the Complete Psychological Works of Sigmund Freud*, under the general editorship of James Strachey, vol. XVII, Hogarth Press, London, 1955: 223.

125 Issey Miyake, Spring–Summer 1999. Photograph courtesy Fashion Group International

opens with a discussion of E. T. A. Hoffmann's 'The Sandman' which contains the original of the doll Olympia that appears in the first act of Offenbach's opera *Tales of Hoffmann*, the biddable and charming fiancée who turns out to be an automaton. Although Freud goes on to play down the significance of the doll, in order to bring forward the theme of castration, nevertheless he opens his discussion by referring to the uncannyness of waxworks, dolls and automata in their resemblance to living figures, and vice versa.[28]

The fashion dummy posed next to the real mannequin in the photograph is both a doll, uncannily posed against her human, and a double. Freud discusses the double too as uncanny in that it is simultaneously a reassurance against the threat of death and annihilation and a terrifying challenge to human individuality.[29] He recalls his own uncanny dream of a red-light zone ('nothing but painted women') to which he inexplicably doubles back at every turn.[30] Despite Freud's disavowal of the themes of femininity and dolls, the *unheimlich* figure of the painted woman is the figure to which all roads return. And after canvassing several more examples he concludes his discussion with the suggestion that 'to some neurotic men' femininity itself might be uncanny: the female body, in particular its internal and external sexual parts, are both *heimlich* and *unheimlich*.[31]

In the shadow world of capitalist excess, the contemporary model is the uncanny double of the historical mannequin, in both her inanimate and her animate incarnations. The uncanny doubling that recreates the model in the dummy's image also multiplies on the catwalk, endlessly replicated in the models' generic beauty, 'mirrored to infinity' like the dummies in the shop window described by Zola in *The Ladies' Paradise*. The uncanniness of the double is fused with the uncanniness of twins in Alexander's McQueen's red-headed twins in his snowstorm show (fig. 126). Thus the fashion model invokes the twin themes of doubling and deathliness. Mark Selzer has identified the late twentieth-century model with trauma and deathliness, linking the uncanny doubling and repetition of the model's body on the catwalk (fig. 127) to the structure of trauma itself, with its acts of compulsive repetition. He describes

the stylized model body on display, a beauty so generic it might have a bar code on it; bodies in motion without emotion, at once entrancing and self-entranced, self-absorbed and vacant, or self-evacuated: the superstars of a chameleon-like celebrity in anonymity.[32]

Selzer comments on the way in which 'the public dream spaces of the fashion world' reduce the model to an object with deathly connotations, assimilating the animate to the inanimate, citing Benjamin that fashion 'couples the living body to the inorganic world', 'it asserts the rights of the corpse', and that 'this is the sex appeal of the inorganic'.[33] In the period in which Selzer made this analysis the supermodels were being displaced by more waif-like figures such as Kate Moss. This imagery was given added potency by the publicity given to the lifestyle of many models in the 1990s, in which substance abuse and eating disorders were prevalent, and in which enormous pressures were put on already slender models to remain thin. And in July 2001 *The Face* featured a fashion spread by Sean Ellis that actually used a skeleton posed like a dressmaker's dummy.

28 Ibid: 226.
29 Ibid: 235–7.
30 Ibid: 237.
31 Ibid: 245.
32 Mark Seltzer, *Serial Killers: Death and Life in America's Wound Culture*, Routledge, New York and London, 1998: 271.
33 Benjamin, *Arcades Project*, cited in ibid.

If the fashion model at the end of the twentieth century was deathly this was not based on superficial resemblance of lifestyle or body shape but, rather, on an underlying structural connection to her industrial origins, the connection I have traced to doubling and mass production in nineteenth-century consumer capitalism. Girls may come and girls may go; in the 1990s the fashion for waifs replaced the fashion for supermodels.[34] Yet, despite the deathly connotations of 'grunge' and 'heroin chic', as these visual styles were termed, in the 1990s the sheer perfection of the supermodel remained the more deathly version, because more generic, than the singularity and quirky imperfections of the models who followed in their place, such as Devon Aoki and Karen Elson. Recognising this, the cultural commentator Steve Beard looked back, at the close of the decade, in the British style magazine *i-D*:

Kristeva argues that the ultimate abject body is the human corpse. The human corpse aestheticised and galvanised then comes very near to conjuring the aura of the catwalk model. The supermodels of the last ten years have been compared to assembly-line cyborgs, sci-fi posthumans and wannabe transsexuals but perhaps the likes of [Cindy] Crawford and Claudia Schiffer were always closer to walking corpses than anyone dared to imagine.[35]

34   For a discussion of the relation among fashion, women and fluctuating body ideals, see Rebecca Arnold, 'Flesh', in *Fashion, Desire and Anxiety: Image and Morality in the Twentieth Century*, I. B. Tauris, London and New York, 2001: 89–95.

35   Steve Beard, 'With Serious Intent', *i-D*, no. 185, April 1999: 141.

Modelling Alienation

The temporal relays of modernity were played out in Alexander McQueen's Spring–Summer 1999 collection that explored the relationship between the nineteenth-century Arts and Crafts movement and what he called 'the hard edge of the technology of textiles' (fig. 128). Segueing between pre-industrial craft imagery and post-industrial urban alienation, the collection combined moulded leather body corsets with frothy white lace, punched wooden fan skirts and Regency striped silk. The show was opened by the athlete and model Aimee Mullins (figs 128a and b) in a pair of hand-carved prosthetic legs designed by McQueen (the model was born without shin bones and had her legs amputated below the knee at the age of one), and closed by the model Shalom Harlow (figs 128k and l) who revolved like a music-box doll on a turntable as her white dress was sprayed acid green and black by two menacing industrial paint sprayers which suddenly came to life on the catwalk. Juxtaposing the organic with the inorganic (a model that mimicked a doll, a paint sprayer that mimicked human motions and an artificial leg that enhanced human performance), the collection skewed the relation of object and subject to evoke Marx's commodity exchange in which 'people and things trade semblances: social relations take on the character of object relations and commodities assume the active agency of people.'[36] In the figures of these two young women the ghosts of Marx and Lukács seemed to flutter up and live again at the end of the twentieth century, as the embodied forms of alienation, reification and commodity fetishism.

Thus the contemporary model's historical origins lie in the urban modernity of nineteenth-century Europe, a modernity characterised by Marshall Berman in his re-reading of Marx as on the one hand bustling, lively and endlessly productive but on the other as destructive, voracious and heartless.[37] Elizabeth Wilson argued that fashion and modernity share a double-sided quality, because they were both formed in the same crucible, that of 'the early capitalist city'.[38] It is in this sense that I have suggested that the model is a capitalist Doppelgänger, a kind of corporeal ghost, or a form of embodied mourning that haunts consumer relations, specifically through the forms and transactions of commodity fetishism. In Diesel's Winter 2001 advertising campaign, photographed by Jean-Pierre Khazem, the return of the ghosts of modernity was literally pictured in a series of advertisements showing models with their heads replaced by transluscent silicone masks with glassy eyes and dead expressions (figs 129 and 130). Accompanied by a fictional text attributing a history and a personality to each one, the advertisements suggested a figure preserved from the past who had been frozen in time into an uncanny simulacrum of a living human. In 'Breathless', the figure is titled 'Maria Deroin, born 1891'. Her modern hair style and contemporary dress and bag contrast with her retro choker and lacy gloves; her waxy face and glassy stare recall the dummies of the 1900 Paris exhibition, a ghost of feminine beauty that has returned to haunt the present. The text attributed to her says: 'I limit my breathing to just a few times a day. It helps me to stay as beautiful as I was a century ago. After living so long, I may smell, but why should I care – I look absolutely breathtaking.'

36   Foster, 'Art of Fetishism': 7.
37   Marshall Berman, *All That is Solid Melts into Air: The Experience of Modernity*, Verso, London, 1983; Marshall Berman, *Adventures in Marxism*, Verso, London and New York, 1999.
38   Elizabeth Wilson, *Adorned in Dreams: Fashion and Modernity*, Virago, London, 1985: 9.

a

b

c

d

e

f

g

h

i

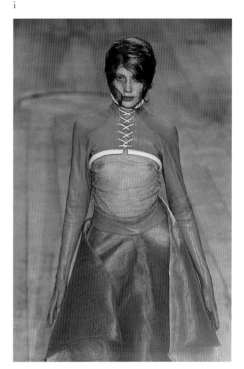

j

k

l

128 Alexander McQueen
Spring–Summer 1999.
Photographs Niall McInerney

129 and 130 Diesel, Stay Young/Save Yourself, advertising campaign, Autumn–Winter 2001. Photograph Jean-Pierre Khazem, courtesy Diesel

39 The installation 'Pause' was a collaboration between Khazem and New York architect Andreas Angelidakis', held at the Färgfabriken Arts Centre, Stockholm, March–May 2002. *Independent on Sunday*, Review, 10 March 2002: 12.

In Khazem's photographs the generic beauty of the contemporary model's body invokes not only her historical predecessors but also the history of woman as spectacle, be it nineteenth-century luxury and ornamentation or the more regulated, modernist body of the twentieth century. In his art installation 'Pause' in Stockholm's Färgfabriken Arts Centre five local women in a mirrored space posed nude in transluscent waxy masks recalling 1920s dummies, their mirrored images also recalling the serial repetition of capitalist display. Further fetishised and reified, their photographs were displayed separately in plexiglass mounts.[39] The installation suggested that the generic female body of modernism was a body that was manipulated, produced and standardised, like the model's body, through the canons of beauty that determine its representation.

The ghosts of modernity haunted this fashion-body, and returned as a hysterical symptom, an object-mannequin-model in a number of late twentieth-century catwalk shows and fashion photographs. For Autumn–Winter 1999–2000 three designers played on the theme of the dummy in their runway shows, tracing a connection between mannequin and model, living doll and inanimate dummy. Margiela substituted life-size wooden artic-

131 Martin Margiela, rehearsal for marionette presentation, Autumn–Winter 1999–2000. Photograph Anders Edstrom/London, courtesy La Maison Martin Margiela

ulated puppets for living models. Styled by Jane How, who had also worked closely with Chalayan, each was operated by two puppeteers dressed in black, who moved them along the catwalk (fig. 131). Margiela's presentation played with notions of scale, as the carved wooden mannequins seemed if anything slightly larger than the black-clad pupeteers who controlled them, sinisterly overgrown dolls on the runway that were shadowed by their living counterparts. McQueen showed his couture collection for Givenchy on mannequins with Plexiglass heads that rose and fell from the dark catwalk (see figs 63 and 64). Viktor & Rolf seated their audience in a small room with a pedestal at the centre of a square stage, on which lay a single pair of shoes. The petite, doll-like model Maggie Rizer appeared in a short, frayed hessian slip, followed by the two black-clad designers, Viktor Horsting and Rolf Snoeren. They guided her into the shoes on the pedestal on which she then revolved like a toy ballerina in a music box while the designers disappeared, to return with a lace and crystal dress that they placed on her, tweaking the hem, adjusting the bow at her neck. While she revolved on her pedestal, Victor & Rolf went to get her next outfit, a diamanté pepper-pot shaped dress, which they put on over the previous layers. The col-

40 Christine Buci-Glucksmann, *Baroque Reason: The Aesthetics of Modernity*, trans. Patrick Camiller, Sage, London, Thousand Oaks and New Delhi, 1994 [1984]: 84–5 and 93–4: 27.

41 Ibid: 79. Buci-Glucksmann argues that woman herself becomes 'an article that is mass-produced' in the Arcades.

lection was sponsored by the crystal company Swarovski, and nearly every outfit featured crystal against jute. There followed a stiff dress embellished with gigantic jewels, a matching floor-length waistcoat, a flounced baby-doll dress and a gigantic bejewelled coat, all of which were fitted to the revolving model like the layers of a Russian doll. Gradually the model was clad in a total of nine outfits, each placed on top of the previous one. The tenth layer consisted of a giant canvas overcoat with fifteen-foot-long sleeves (fig. 132). The whole presentation was an exercise in the sedimentation of fashion, making formal the way in which it continually expands on existing currency.

These designers worked nearer the experimental edge of fashion than most. Their use of dummies or other inanimate forms of display gestured towards experimentation but also fixed their work firmly in the field of fashion – with its links to industry and commerce – rather than art. For the dummies only made sense in the context of the tradition in fashion of using living women to display clothes, a tradition which draws attention to the commodification of the body through fashionable consumption in nineteenth-century Paris. These uncanny images invoke the historical origins of the fashion model herself, the alienated status of the worker in capitalist production and the ambiguous status of the nineteenth-century woman of fashion as both subject and object. Thus, again, contemporary images of alienation in fashion can be seen to evoke the alienated body of early industrial production described by Marx. Just as the nineteenth-century *flâneur* embodies the estrangement of the nihilistic observer[40] and the industrial worker embodies the alienation of labour, so the fashion model or dummy embodies the uncanny ambivalence of the woman-object, an ambivalence that was made clear in the Surrealist mannequins, for example, of the 1938 Surrealist exhibition in Paris.[41] If alienation was a key trope of literary and philosophical modernism, it fuses with Marxist alienation in industrial production to return as the repressed in fashion, the archetypal commodity form, specifically through the reified and estranged figure of the mannequin, dummy and model. These themes were elo-

132 Viktor & Rolf, Autumn–Winter 1999. Photograph Peter Tahl, courtesy Viktor & Rolf

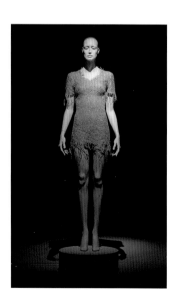

quently invoked in a series of photographs by Tim Walker for Italian *Vogue*, which showed the model being delivered to a warehouse as if she were an industrial product (fig. 133). Immaculately dressed in each shot, in couture evening gowns fit for a princess by Gaultier, Versace, Valentino and the like, she is nevertheless styled to look like a scaled-up doll or toy. Variously transported on pallets and fork-lift trucks, mimicking the packaging of Barbie and other dolls, she comes bubble-packed, shielded in a pre-moulded plastic form (figs 134 and 135), surrounded by styrofoam balls or wrapped in clingfilm.

Dead Things

Hussein Chalayan's runway show Still Life for Autumn–Winter 1996–7 showed models who emerged onto the catwalk by way of a revolving platform, and incorporated the theme of the mannequin as a 'still life': in Chalayan's words, the show's title meant 'still life as in a still *from* life, or still as in dead.'[42] The similarity between make-up and death mask was clear in the waxen, pale and bloodless faces of the Versace 1998 advertising campaign, based on historical images, in which the models were made up to look like figurines (fig. 136). Waxy and bloodless, the highlights on their flesh are like those on smooth, plaster shop dummies; their hair is styled to look like wigs; and their stiff and formalised poses and lifeless gazes evoke the clumsy displays of dummies in period costume of local history and waxworks museums. Here too, one could argue, the woman of fashion is turned into an object, just as the commodity form converts social relations into objects. Efrat Tseëlon has elaborated the concept of the 'mortality-fetishist' who regulates the body through surgery and diet. She observes the similarity of beauty and death rituals (cosmetic surgery which resembles embalming and make-up which resembles a death mask, for

42   Jon Ashworth, interview with Hussein Chalayan, *The Times*, London, 2 March 1996.

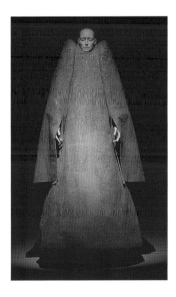

133–5 Tim Walker, Couture Delivery, Italian *Vogue*, 1999. Photographs courtesy Tim Walker and Condé Nast Milan

43 Efrat Tseëlon, *The Masque of Femininity:
The Presentation of Woman in Everyday Life*, Sage,
London, Thousand Oaks, New Delhi, 1995: 108,
103–4.

44 Cited in Susan Buck-Morss, *The Dialectics of
Seeing: Walter Benjamin and the Arcades Project*,
MIT Press, Cambridge, Mass.,, and London,
1991: 101.

example). 'In both cases the mask of permanence replaces undesirable temporality while drawing attention to it.'[43]

When Walter Benjamin proposed that fashion, unlike biological woman, was both deathly and unreproductive, he used the metaphor of the mannequin to make the point: 'the modern woman who allies herself with fashion's newness in a struggle against natural decay represses her own reproductive powers, mimics the mannequin, and enters history as a dead object.'[44] Benjamin's translator uses the term mannequin in the modern sense to signify 'dummy'; but this usage is comparatively new. When fashion was first shown on living women rather than wicker mannequins, from the mid-nineteenth century, the term mannequin was used to describe the living model; and 'model' designated the garment, although now this term is used for the living woman. This linguistic switch echoes Marx's concept of commodity fetishism, on which Benjamin draws. In his analysis, the woman of fashion is an emblem of the way in which all fashion is deathly, spectral and wraith-like, a kind of ghost in the machine of late capitalism. Benjamin's analysis identifies a death-in-life quality in modernity itself, the spectre at the heart of the spectacle. In linking modernity, fashion, the spectacle and death, Benjamin's discussion of the term death becomes a metaphor for alienation; it describes the death of the spirit under capitalism. It is not, therefore, about the terrifying and death-dealing powers of the sexualised *femme fatale* described at the end of Chapter 5, but another kind of deathliness: the alienation inherent in technological modernity. It mourns a fantasy of pre-industrial human relations which are unmediated by the commodity form. Bound up in Benjamin's references to the deathliness of fashion in the modern period is Lukács's concept of reification, where all human relations are commodified.

Marx's association of fashion and death was more literal, and though it was articulated through searing descriptions of the brutality of nineteenth-century fashion and textile production, it may still be invoked in relation to the sweated labour of modern-day production across the world of Western fashion items.[45] In Marx's account, 'the murderous, meaningless caprices of fashion' have a literal connection to death on two counts. Firstly, the unpredictability of fashion led to fluctuating markets whose sudden gluts were ruinous to the workforce. Secondly, it was linked to the factory system through the textile industry in whose cotton mills women and children were ruthlessly exploited to spin the cotton that was itself grown and harvested by American slaves. Esther Leslie has argued that

> *Das Kapital* supplies a materialist core for Benjamin's idea of the fashionable body as, symbolically and concretely, intimate with death . . . The connection between products and death alerts Benjamin to the fact that everything consumed has been produced under conditions that occasioned suffering. Capital's rule – exercised through its technologies and techniques – fractures and fragments bodies, and these are bodies that have been remade as prostituted, dehumanised commodities. Through the reifying operation of commodity fetishism, capital's organisation murderously consumes life.[46]

By adding a different gloss to Marx's concept of commodity fetishism, Benjamin describes fashion as an attempt to defeat, or transcend, death by making the inorganic commodity itself the object of human desire. Clothes mimic organic nature (as, for example, in the decorative use of fruit, flowers and feathers), whereas the living human body mimics the inorganic world (cosmetics with 'satin' finishes, for example). This swapping between organic and inorganic alive and death possessions and death was played out in Margiela's use of mannequins in his 1997 exhibition at the Museum Boijmans Van Beuningen in Rotterdam. The clothes were displayed on inanimate mannequins and then 'grew' mould and bacteria; the mannequin, rather than the living woman, modelled the organic, in the form of the yeasts, moulds and bacteria. Although a mannequin cannot reproduce, here the dress itself was weirdly fecund, having acted as a growing medium for the moulds and bacteria, so that in a spectacular reversal of the normal situation in which the living woman wears the inorganic dress, the living dress was worn by the tailor's dummy (fig. 137).

* * *

127 Martin Margiela, installation view of the exhibition '9/4/1615', Museum Boijmans Van Beuningen, Rotterdam, 1997. Photograph Caroline Evans

45 See e.g. Andrew Ross (ed.), *No Sweat: Fashion, Free Trade and the Rights of Garment Workers*, Verso, New York and London, 1997.
46 Leslie, *Walter Benjamin*: 10.

138 Nick Knight, Aimee Mullins, Access-Able, *Dazed & Confused*, 1998. Wooden fan jacket by Givenchy Haute Couture, suede T-shirt by Alexander McQueen, crinoline from Angels and Berman. Concept Alexander McQueen, styling Katy England. Photograph courtesy Nick Knight

139 (*facing page*) Nick Knight, Aimee Mullins, Access-Able, *Dazed & Confused*, 1998. Concept Alexander McQueen, styling Katy England. Photograph courtesy Nick Knight

Transformation

I have argued in this chapter that these designers' and photographers' exploitation of the uncanny equivalence between model and dummy harks back to the fashion model's commercial origins in the nineteenth-century city, and to the image of woman as spectacle. Yet while this figure continues to haunt the contemporary catwalk as the historical ghost of modernity's past, perhaps these dummy-mannequins also presage a shift in attitudes. In the September 1998 issue of the London magazine *Dazed & Confused*, guest edited by Alexander McQueen, Nick Knight photographed the model and athlete Aimee Mullins as a fragile and pretty doll, her prosthetic legs reminding us of her phantasmagoric predecessor, the shop-window dummy and its uncanny ghosting of the corporeal woman (fig. 138). For this image she applied her own chipped nail varnish to, and smudged dirt on, her moulded plastic legs to echo the chipped polish and grime of her 'real' fingernails. The picture evoked a run-down mechanical doll, the ghost of the past wound down and come to a halt, appropriately frozen in the deathly gaze of the camera. One might think that the woman as spectacle and commodity had returned full force, were it not for the contradictory image on the cover of the magazine (fig. 139) of the model in her running shorts and the flexed metal sprinting legs with which she won the Paralympics – sporty, alert and ready to race, an allegorical image of the future at the turn of the century.

eight   disconnection

Disaster Pictures

Shot in dramatic chiaroscuro, the marionette-like figure of a young woman in a tutu and leotard lies on the leaf-strewn ground in front of an abandoned open-air café, her open eyes staring. Is she dead, mad, unconscious or play-acting? How long has she been lying there, and in what circumstances? Two mugs lie upturned on a table but the troubling narrative is not resolved. Violence or death may be suggested but the picture itself is seductive, in its dark, gloomy beauty. This enigmatic fashion spread from *The Face* in 1999 by Mario Sorrenti recalled Dena Shottenkirk's descriptions of Robert Maplethorpe's photographs in the 1980s:

> The exact circumstances are to us, the viewer, unknowable . . . we know the ambience of the situation but never its pertinent facts. We sense the luxury, the sensuality, but the plot is rarely spelt out to us. The pose remains frozen in a narrative purgatory. Free of confining specifics, it is lost in that dream world where reality is negotiable. The fashion photograph becomes the image of promises. Through contextual ambiguity, the viewer (consumer) is seduced.[1]

Similarly equivocal, Peter Lindbergh's fashion photograph for Italian *Vogue* in 1999 of Amber Valetta in Los Angeles showed the model walking dramatically out of a disaster zone (fig. 140). She leaves behind her a scene of devastation that includes an upturned car, several policemen reacting violently to the photographer's flash and an undifferentiated jumble of debris. Beyond this, the strong chiaroscuro of the picture impedes further interpretation. She is strangely dressed; it is unclear whether some of the brownish red tones of her clothes are blood stains. Her image evokes Rebecca Arnold's words: 'Fashion photographs produce simulacra of the body, of beauty and even of death, removing the traces of mortality, ageing and decay, to become sites of conflict and ambiguity, rather than of resolution.'[2]

However disturbingly indeterminate Lindbergh's narrative, the photograph's historical antecedents are clear. It draws on the 1940s scene-of-crime imagery of Weegee as reinterpreted by Guy Bourdin in his advertisements for Charles Jourdain shoes in 1975. In the 1970s Guy Bourdin, with Helmut Newton and Bob Richardson, introduced an entirely new darkness into fashion photography. Bourdin and Newton in particular both developed a narrative photographic style in their fashion work that played with images of excess, decadence, glamour and danger. The harder, darker edge to their photographs caused the American critic Hilton Kramer to comment in 1975 that fashion photography was becoming a subdivision of pornography, 'with some photographs indistinguishable from an interest in murder, pornography and terror . . . fashion photography as we know it is over, and something else – murder, terror and violence as viable subjects – is taking its place.'[3] And Susan Sontag in 1979 described the 'moral letdown of recent decades', and contrasted earlier photographic ideals of purity and timeless beauty, for example in the work of Edward Weston, which she associated with the optimistic and utopian modernism of the early twentieth century, with the dark themes of 1970s fashion photography:

140   Peter Lindbergh, Amber Valetta, Los Angeles, Italian *Vogue*, 1999. Styling Karl Templer. Photograph Peter Lindbergh

1   Dena Shottenkirk, 'Fashion Fictions: Absence and the Fast Heartbeat', *ZG*, 'Breakdown Issue', 9, 1983: n.p.
2   Rebecca Arnold, *Fashion, Desire and Anxiety: Image and Morality in the Twentieth Century*, I. B. Tauris, London and New York, 2001: 81.
3   Hilton Kramer cited in Nancy Hall-Duncan, *The History of Fashion Photography*, Alpine Book Company, New York, 1979: 196–7.

In the present historical mood of disenchantment one can make less and less sense out of the formalist's notion of timeless beauty. Darker, time-bound models of beauty have become prominent, inspiring a reevaluation of the photography of the past; and, in an apparent revulsion against the Beautiful, recent generations of photographers prefer to show disorder, prefer to distill an anecdote, more often than not a disturbing one, rather than isolate an ultimately reassuring 'simplified form'.[4]

In the 1990s many fashion photographs looped back to those of the 1970s, in a strand of imagery that Rebecca Arnold has categorised as 'fashion noire'.[5] Fashion photography became permeated by the themes of decay, decadence and death in an elaboration of what the critic D. A. Miller presciently named 'morbidity culture' in 1990.[6] A cinema advertisement for the London tailor Richard James showed a dandyish man dressing with extreme precision and careful consideration, only to be seen committing suicide in the final shot. The British retailers Jigsaw's menswear catalogue for Autumn–Winter 1997–8 consisted of a narrative sequence of twenty images by Juergen Teller, alternating sludgy colour with grainy black-and-white photography. Over several pages, a series of well-dressed men appear to fall, jump, bounce and tumble against a backdrop of London rooftops, high-rise buildings and derelict underpasses (fig. 141). With the art director Phil Bicker, Teller used professional stuntmen rather than models for the shoot. Teller claimed he was interested in the idea of his subjects doing something visually interesting, rather than in how they looked, and over a three-day shoot his subjects performed their professional stunts using fire, high buildings and bicycles.

When edited into the Jigsaw catalogue the images created an ambiguous narrative, seeming to be linked but without conviction or resolution. Is this a story of suicide, murder or accident? Broken glass flies, a burning jacket hangs mystifyingly from a hanger in a concrete garage or warehouse. Figures who should be dead appear to rise again, as if rewound on film. The narrative is told by cut-up and collage, disrupted by the modernist ploys of discontinuity and fragmentation; its jumpy nervousness shares Jean-Luc Godard's jump-cutting technique in the film *A Bout de Souffle* (1960). The tale of death, of fragmentation and of style is simultaneously layered and unresolved. If it is a mystery story, it is the mystery of how best to sell menswear. The sharp cut of a trouser leg, or the shine on a shoe, are never in doubt. Indeed, the only clues are sartorial ones. As so often in the city, dress marks identity, recalling the cult of distinction which differentiated Baudelaire's dandy from the ordinary man.[7]

4 Susan Sontag, *On Photography*, Penguin, Harmondsworth, 1979: 102.

5 Arnold, *Fashion, Desire and Anxiety*, ch. 2, 'Violence and Provocation': 32–62.

6 D. A. Miller cited in Peggy Phelan, *Mourning Sex: Performing Public Memories*, Routledge, London and New York, 1997: 17.

7 Charles Baudelaire, 'The Painter of Modern Life' [1863], *The Painter of Modern Life and Other Essays*, trans. Jonathan Mayne, Phaidon London, 2nd ed. 1995: 26–9.

In Jigsaw shops across Britain in autumn 1997 the image of the falling man, staged like Yves Klein's *Saut dans le vide* of 1960, was replayed on a video loop, falling again and again and again. It operated as a fragmented biography of unknown disasters, recounting in episodic filmic images a tale of anonymous death rather than a life story, recalling the artist Robert Longo's project from the 1980s, 'Men in the Cities', in which smartly dressed men were posed on city rooftops at the moment of death. Chris Townsend has argued that for Longo 'the city might be interpreted as potentially lethal, a space where death might happen at any time . . . death bequeathed anonymity . . . Longo's murder victims were generic "yuppies", smart city kids in suits and sharp dresses.'[8] In Longo's photographs, as in the Jigsaw pictures, the narrative of fashion was fractured, punctured with references to violent death, and redolent with inexplicable trauma and anxiety.

A Diesel advertisement in the early 1990s that seemed to parody American excess showed a multiple car crash with dead models implausibly strewn across the road, or spreadeagled across the cars' shiny surfaces and luxurious interiors; one figure in white leather boots has one leg propped on the dashboard, the other over the side of the car (fig. 142). To the left, three men in sharp suits are engaged in photographing the dead (journalists? tourists? forensic scientists?). To the right, a group of tubby suburban Americans sit and eat popcorn while surveying the scene. Verbal clues of 'American-ness' are provided by the 'popcorn' on the vendor's stand and, at the bottom of the page, the '1.800. SUE THEM' on an abandoned briefcase. The scene is shot diagrammatically from above, again like Weegee's New York scene-of-the-crime shots from the 1940s. Infused with kitsch excess, the image is different from, but nevertheless evokes, Andy Warhol's *Saturday Disaster* of 1964 from his 'Death in America' series (fig. 143). In contrast with the stiff corpses improbably posed in classic cars in the Diesel picture, Warhol's *vérité* image shows the limp bodies of the dead spilling from the everyday American automobile. Screen-printed, doubled and aestheticised on a matt silver ground, the cheap newsprint photograph is both distancing and brutally close, 'both affective and affectless', the doubling and repetition of Warhol's re-arrangement mimicking the repetition of trauma itself.[9] Thomas Crow has characterised these car crash pictures as 'a stark, disabused, pessimistic version of American life, produced from the knowing rearrangement of pulp materials'[10] and Hal Foster has identified them as specifically American too, describing the staging of traumatic reality as one element of the 'forging of a psychic nation through mass-mediated disaster and death.'[11]

If the Warhol image is shocking in part because it flatly shows a traumatic reality, the shock of the Diesel image is very different. It is stagey and kitsch (the white leather boot); it is prepared to mock a disaster scene, and then to parody grotesque public voyeurism (the seated popcorn eaters); most of all, it is a fashion photograph. Elliott Smedley has discussed this Diesel image in relation to a quotation from an article by Cecil Beaton entitled 'I am Gorged with Glamour Photography' published in 1938:

> I want to make photographs of very elegant women taking the grit out of their eyes, or blowing their noses, or taking lipstick off their teeth. Behaving like human beings in other words . . . it would be gorgeous instead of illustrating a woman in a sports suit in a studio, to take the same woman in the same suit in a motor accident, with gore all over everything and bits of the car here and there. But naturally that would be forbidden.[12]

In this quotation, Beaton, who had used London bomb sites during the Blitz as a location, seems like an unlikely J. G. Ballard *avant la lettre*. Yet, as Smedley argued, in the 1990s such desires were no longer forbidden.[13] Designer roadkill and brutalised bodies

141 (*following pages*) Juergen Teller, Jigsaw menswear advertising campaign, 1997. Art direction Phil Bicker, styling David Bradshaw. Photographs courtesy Juergen Teller

8 Chris Townsend, 'Dead for Having Been Seen', catalogue essay for *Izima Karaou*, fa projects, London, 2002: n.p.

9 Hal Foster, 'Death in America', in Annette Mitchelson (ed.), *Andy Warhol, October* Files 2, MIT Press, Cambridge, Mass., and London, 2001: 72–5.

10 Thomas Crow, 'Saturday Disasters: Trace and Reference in Early Warhol', in ibid: 60.

11 Foster in ibid: 82.

12 Cecil Beaton, 'I am Gorged with Glamour Photography' [1938], cited in Hall-Duncan, *History of Fashion Photography*: 202.

13 Elliott Smedley, 'Escaping to Reality: Fashion Photography in the 1990s', in Stella Bruzzi and Pamela Church Gibson (eds), *Fashion Cultures: Theories, Explorations and Analyses*, Routledge, London and New York, 2000: 143.

JIGSAW MENSWEAR

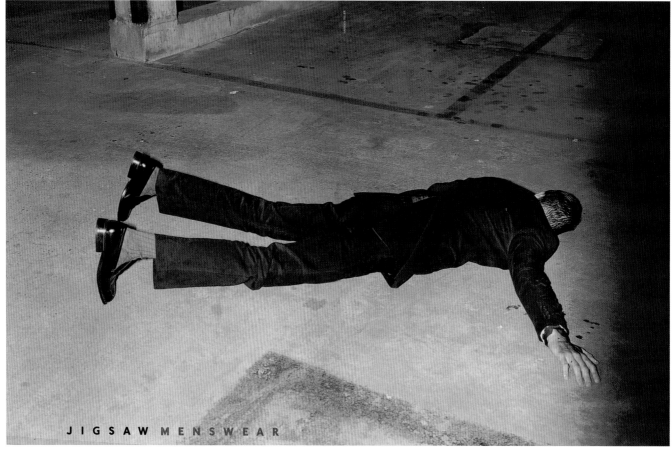

JIGSAW MENSWEAR

JIGSAW MENSWEAR

JIGSAW MENSWEAR

142   Diesel advertising campaign,
early–mid-1990s. Styling Liz Botes.
Photograph Pierre Winthe, courtesy Diesel

14   On the 'brutalised body' of 1990s fashion, see
Arnold, *Fashion, Desire and Anxiety*: 80–9.

15   Anthony Giddens, *Modernity and Self-Identity:
Self and Society in the Late Modern Age*, Polity Press,
Cambridge, 1991.

patterned the pages of magazines like *The Face* and *Dazed & Confused*, just as real life disaster images pervaded the modern media.[14]

Anthony Giddens has drawn attention to specific forms of anxiety and risk as peculiar to modernity.[15] He has identified in particular: the risk of massively destructive warfare (nuclear and chemical weapons); ecological catastrophe; the collapse of global economic mechanisms; and the rise of totalitarian superstates. In addition, one could argue that the fear of death permeated the affluent West on a grand scale in the 1990s, particularly as media reports proliferated: cancer, AIDS, terrorist explosions, Gulf War syndrome, 'ethnic cleansing' in Bosnia, genocide in Rwanda. Aeroplanes fell out of the sky, ferries sank within sight of land, and space shuttles exploded on live television. These disaster images, in the tradition of Ballard's *Atrocity Exhibition* (1970) or Warhol's 'Death in America' pictures, were experienced as apocalyptic visions on flickering screens and in fuzzy newsprint.

In this context, the Diesel advertisement or the Jigsaw catalogue are part of a field of representations of disasters that seem specifically modern. Although not likely to happen to us as individuals, distant events are more and more part of everyday consciousness as mass communications bring these remote possibilities into our homes via TV and radio, and electronic communication meshes self-development with global systems (in the inter-

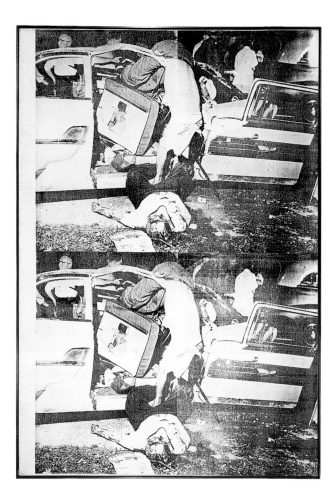

143 Andy Warhol, *Saturday Disaster*, 1964.
Silkscreen ink on synthetic polymer paint on
canvas, 301.9 × 208 cm. Rose Art Museum,
Brandeis University, Waltham, Massachusets,
Gift of Mr. and Mrs. Eric Estorick, London
© The Andy Warhol Foundation for the Visual
Arts, Inc./ARS, NY and DACS, London 2003

net, for example). Giddens argues that, because in everyday life we have little or no material knowledge or direct experience of death and disaster, these media representations do
not just mirror realities but in some part form them and change the nature of our 'reality'.[16] It is this phenomenon that Diesel and Jigsaw so adroitly exploited. Both borrowed
the visual language of a new strand of experimental fashion publishing that developed
in London, Paris and New York in the late 1990s in small, directional micro-zines such
as *Big*, *Purple*, *Tank*, and *Sleaze/Nation*, harnessing the imagery of disaster to mainstream advertising.

Looking Wasted

Teller's Jigsaw shoot also highlighted contemporary concerns about how to represent men and masculinity in fashion. Menswear spreads that drew on themes of street
crime, surveillance and urban angst, set in derelict city streets, amid tower blocks or public
lavatories, told tales of everyday disenfranchisement. The photographer Rankin's 1996
spread for the magazine *Dazed & Confused* was called 'Surveillance'. Mimicking the poor

16   Ibid: 27.

resolution and unreal colour of CCTV cameras, it showed two urban lads hanging around the streets, in and out of council estates, having a go at breaking into a car and larking around on the bus (fig. 144). Another *Dazed & Confused* spread from 1996 called 'Cottage in the City' photographed by Henrik Halvarsson was shot in a public lavatory and, while keeping the models scrupulously clothed throughout, made it very clear that they were engaged in various sexual encounters (fig. 145).

All these spreads theatricalised a kind of urban knowledge and street savvy, drawing on the idea of hard men who knew how to look after themselves on the mean streets of the city.[17] While these images of men may relate to the idea that the 1990s produced a crisis in gender for men, they might equally be understood in the context of a street culture where drug use and crime was rampant. In a decade that produced a fashion magazine called *Pil* and a restaurant owned and designed by the artist Damien Hirst called 'Pharmacy', whose interior reproduced the clinical look of the chemist's counter, a cool druggy look was not confined to so-called heroin chic imagery.

The wasted look started in the early 1990s with Wolfgang Tillmans' images for *i-D* magazine and Corinne Day's pictures in *The Face*. Barely fashion images at all, Day's showed her friends looking thin and dishevelled in seedy flats in the inner London zones of Soho, Brixton or Notting Hill. Often dressed in cheap bras and knickers, or thin T-shirts and jeans, 'Georgina', 'Rose', 'Tania' and 'Jesse' were shown slumped on scruffy sofas, or against scuffed walls, under windows covered in greying net curtains, in rooms lit by neon strips. Surrounded by beer cans and ashtrays, they stared apathetically into space, their eyes rolled, or they slept. Critics found suggestions of all kinds of abuse in Day's pictures, not least drug abuse. And when she photographed her friend the model Kate Moss wearing tacky underwear in her own apartment for *Vogue* (fig. 146), Hilton Als wrote in the *New Yorker* that 'the photographs are a first testimony to the fashion industry's now

17 Arnold comments more broadly on the allure of violence and provocation in contemporary fashion imagery, covering gangers, gangstas, skinheads and punks. See too her discussion of the differing representations of men and women in the fashion shoots of this period: *Fashion, Desire and Anxiety*: 32–47 and 86.

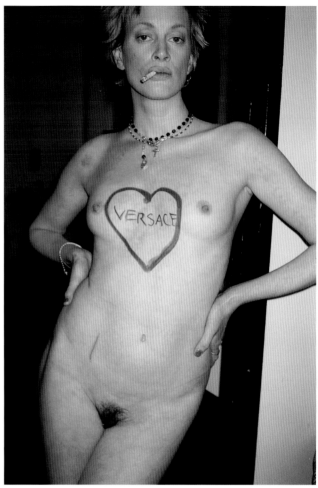

146 (*above left*) Corinne Day, Under-
exposure, British *Vogue*, 1993. Styling Cathy
Kasterine. Kate Moss wears a Liza Bruce vest
and Hennes briefs. Photograph courtesy
Corinne Day © VOGUE/The Condé Nast
Publications Ltd

147 (*above right*) Juergen Teller, Kristen
McMenamy, *Süddeutsche Zeitung* supplement,
1996. Photograph courtesy Juergen Teller

18   Hilton Als cited in Val Williams (ed.), *Look
at Me: Fashion Photography in Britain 1960 to the
Present*, British Council, London, 1998: 114.

19   Richard Billingham, ' *Untitled I, II and III*',
Inependent Fashion Magazine Spring 1998: 10–14.

20   For a longer discussion of this image see
Arnold, *Fashion, Desire and Anxiety*: 86.

pervasive flirtation with death. The naked, bruised look in Moss's eyes was an apt expression of the brutality that Moss was beginning to experience in the fashion world.'[18] It is
not known, in fact, whether Moss experienced the fashion world as brutal, but Als's
comment does convey both the influential look of the imagery and the critical response
to it. The look was by now commonplace in *The Face* but its appearance in the more conventional British *Vogue* caused a furore that centred on accusations that the images made
Moss's slight frame look anorexic.

Like the kitchen-sink style of documentary of the British photographer Richard
Billingham – who also did a fashion shoot featuring 'some of the kids on his block' dressed
in brands such as Polo Ralph Lauren and Ellesse, ironically called 'Untitled I, II and III)'
– this school of fashion publishing suggested that there was an element of truth or honesty
in its images, which were, however, as artful as more formal representations of fashion.[19]
In similar vein in 1996 Juergen Teller's photographs of the model Kristen McMenamy
showed her in a seedy-looking studio (fig. 147).[20] Her naked, mottled torso had a lipstick
heart crudely drawn on it containing the word 'Versace', and she had a cigarette stuck to
her lower lip. Commissioned by the magazine supplement to the German newspaper *Süd-*

deutsche Zeitung to illustrate the theme of fashion and morality, Teller felt that his pictures revealed a truth about the model in a world in which the construction of the fashionable woman was always a lie. But, again, suggestions of abuse were made. Controversy was sparked in particular by the 'scar' or mark on her abdomen, the suggestion of abuse and violence, as opposed to the simpler alternative explanation, that she had caught her flesh in a zip in one of the rapid backstage costume changes of a fashion show.

In 1997 a spate of fashion photography and advertising images was christened 'heroin chic' by the media, after President Clinton's criticism of the industry.[21] This was provoked by the death from a heroin overdose of Mario Sorrenti's brother Davide and the ensuing campaign against drug use in the industry by their mother Francesca, also a fashion photographer. Pioneered by a small group of photographers, the look rapidly crossed over to influence the make-up and styling of a range of fashion shows from Vivienne Westwood's to Ann Demeulemeester's (figs 148 and 149). Proposing that 'sex, death and ambiguity are the key signifiers of our times', Rebecca Arnold argued that the healthy, toned body of the early 1980s was increasingly replaced through the 90s by one that had given in to decay.[22] Arnold's analysis rejected any simplistic reading of heroin chic, and she suggested that fashion images that portrayed the body as a site simultaneously of perfection and decay were images of internalised violence: 'the creation of the perfect fashionable body has been refused, and that body has been wilfully brutalised, destroyed.' However

21 For a nuanced account and critical commentary on the moral scare see ibid: 48–55.

22 Arnold, '*Heroin Chic*', *Fashion Theory*, vol. 3, issue 3, September, 1999: 285 and 295.

148 (*far left*) Model backstage, Vivienne Westwood, Autumn–Winter 1996–7 Photograph Niall McInerney

149   Ann Demeulemeester Spring–Summer 1997. PhotographNiall McInerney

150 (*above left*) Jil Sander advertising campaign, 1996. Photograph Craig McDean, courtesy Jil Sander, Germany

151 (*above right*) Paolo Roversi (based on Egon Schiele), Italian *Vogue*, 1996. Stella Tenant wears dress, tights and shoes by Prada. Photograph Paolo Roversi/Streeters

23 Arnold, *Fashion, Desire and Anxiety*: 290.
24 Arnold, 'Heroin Chic': 285.
25 Katharine Wallerstein, 'Thinness and Other Refusals in Contemporary Fashion Advertisements', *Fashion Theory*, vol. 2, issue 2, June 1998: 129–50.
26 Ibid: 140.

she went on to say that these images were ambiguous and complex, for they were also about pleasure and control.[23] As she wrote in 1999:

> The nihilistic gamble of living more intensely by chancing death in the pursuit of pleasure is a dark vision that haunts these photographs. Whether they reflect actual drug-taking or not, they are conveying a mood that crystallises a contemporary notion of excess as the most real experience, the most immediate sensation.[24]

Katharine Wallerstein also rejected the idea that this type of imagery was straightforwardly connected to anorexia or heroin chic, arguing instead that it was an aesthetic of abjection.[25] She suggested that the imagery of spent and exhausted people with burnt out and numbed expressions and lethargic poses connoted the lows after the highs of extreme experiences, not just drug highs but also emotional ones:

> That look of hunger, of aching emptiness, that look of having been up all night, of feverish fatigue, of having flirted with danger, with death, a look associated with drugs, with fasting, with sex, with intense emotional experiences, and with the dangerous excitement of the night, speaks of the highest experience of living.[26]

While such imagery started in magazines like *The Face* and *Dazed & Confused*, it was rapidly taken up in the advertising photography of large directional houses such as Prada, Miu Miu and Jil Sander (fig. 150). Their models were variously thin, faux-scruffy, alienated and withdrawn. In this type of advertisement, the dysfunctional, the depressed or the disaster-prone made the crossover to commercial advertising from minority magazines. Make-up in particular created the effect. Paolo Roversi's photograph for Prada shows the model infantilised like a 1960s picture, but also made up and coiffed in the then fashionably scruffy style, shoulders and cheeks glossed with Vaseline slicks and tufty hair framing the face (fig. 151).

Insofar as this imagery constituted an iconography of affect it seemed to contradict writers on post-modernism who argued for a 'waning of affect', an inability to feel or care strongly about anything. In its passionate self-absorption, and for all its emphasis on image and aesthetics, this style of photography counteracted the argument that in the late twentieth century everyday life had become progressively aestheticised, or that the 'real' was effaced in post-modern society.[27] As Arnold argued, it was the brutalised body that came to signify the real. Jean Baudrillard might have said that such images functioned as a substitute for authentic feeling ('artifice is at the very heart of reality'[28]) but one could equally argue that they were a spur to empathy, and Wallerstein suggested that the genre constituted an aesthetic of passionate intensity in the same vein as the nineteenth-century cult of consumptive beauty.[29]

Blank

The images of urban angst and alienation nevertheless also bring to mind the alienation associated with nineteenth-century industrialisation and urbanisation, just as the 1990s fashion show recalled the spectacle of nineteenth-century luxury consumption. As manifest in the euphoria of display and fantasy in the newly commercialised leisure spaces of nineteenth-century Paris, the exuberance of the spectacle has as its counterpoint alienation, loss and despair which are, similarly, played out on the stage set of the modern city. In the most banal of forms, they may even be encountered in the city, as in the blank and pretty image of Kate Moss in a Calvin Klein underwear advertisement on a telephone booth in New York City (fig. 152). From modelling in her own apartment for her photographer friend to the bland anonymity of advertisements is New York City, Moss made the transformation, as Smedley has observed, from 'friend' to 'commodity' via 'model'. As described by Day, 'We were poking fun at fashion. Halfway through the shoot, I realized it wasn't fun for her and that she was no longer my best friend but had become a model. She hadn't realized how beautiful she was and when she did, I didn't think her beautiful any more.'[30]

The transition, from grungy London flats to sleek New York or Californian apartments, was part of a bigger move made by this genre of photography as the decade progressed.

152   New York Street, early 1990s. Photograph Niall McInerney

27   Mike Featherstone, *Consumer Culture and Postmodernism*, Sage, London, Newbury Park and New Delhi, 1991. Michel Maffesoli, *The Time of the Tribes: The Decline of Individualism in Mass Society*, trans. Mark Ritter, Sage, London, Thousand Oaks and New Delhi, 1996.

28   Jean Baudrillard, *Simulations*, trans. Paul Foss *et al*, Semiotext(e), New York, 1983: 151.

29   Wallerstein, 'Thinness and Other Refusals': 131.

30   Corrine Day of Kate Moss, cited in Robin Muir, 'What Katie Did', *Independent, Magazine*, 22 February 1997, quoted in Smedley, 'Escaping to Reality': 151.

153 Philip-Lorca diCorcia for *W*, 1997.
Photograph © Philip-Lorca diCorcia, courtesy
Pace/MacGill Gallery, New York

Wallerstein proposed that imagery which had started in experimental fringe magazines crossed over into more established magazines easily because its aesthetic – of grainy, black-and-white pseudo-realism – corresponded to the new emphasis on streamlined minimalism in fashion and design of the mid-1990s. When high fashion brands produced cheaper, diffusion lines, they needed this edgier black-and-white style to sell it to a younger audience and began to use it in their advertising campaigns (see fig. 150). In the *New York Times* Amy Spindler analysed Calvin Klein's late 1990s style of pared-down minimalism as being about alienation. Of his 1998 campaign, photographed by Steven Meisel, she wrote that Meisel had 'tapped into the latest spirit of the times: disconnection.'[31] Although the Calvin Klein company produced the images as an antidote to so-called heroin chic, wanting to inject some healthy, happy images into its publicity, they are nevertheless, as Spindler points out,

> images depicting the height of isolation, figures in close physical proximity but with eyes never meeting . . . That is appropriate for a modern luxury goods campaign, introspection today being a luxury few can afford . . . What if nothing was happening, and we finally had time to sit and think, but our minds were as minimalistic as the room, as blank as our faces, and as empty as our eyes?[32]

In Philip-Lorca diCorcia's image for *W* magazine, a well-heeled couple seem trapped in amber, sealed in the luxury glass box of a modern apartment, as disconnected from each other as we are from their lives (fig. 153). Like a Rorschach blot, the claustrophobic picture is resonant with undisclosed meaning: affluent American ennui or the existential loneliness of the couple? Either will do. In this modern, landscaped, Garden of Eden there is no possibility of either fall or redemption to put an end to its endless present. The woman's floral dress echoes and mimics the lush growth outside. The glass box is stifling, airless, and she herself is like a hothouse flower that can never leave its artificial environment. The paradisal imagery is merciless: too bright, too clear, nowhere to go and nowhere to hide.

Depression

> The euphoria of fashion has its counterparts in dereliction, depression and existential anguish. We encounter more stimulations of all sorts, but also more anxiety; we have more personal autonomy, but also more personal crises. Such is the greatness of fashion, which always refers us, as individuals, back to ourselves; such is the misery of fashion, which renders us increasingly problematic to ourselves and others.[33]

With this melancholic description of fashion at the end of the twentieth century Gilles Lipovetsky closes an account in which he argues that fashion has made a significant contribution to the development of modern bureaucratic and democratic society. Lipovetsky argues that modern society requires modern individuals; the instability of fashion in our

31 Amy Spindler, 'Critic's Notebook: Tracing the Look of Alienation', *New York Times*, 24 March 1998.
32 Ibid.
33 Gilles Lipovetsky, *The Empire of Fashion: Dressing Modern Democracy*, trans. Catherine Porter, Princeton University Press, 1994 [1987]: 241.

time trains us to be flexible and adaptable so that modern fashion is socially productive of such individuals and not, as some would argue, irrational and wasteful. 'Fashion socializes human beings to change and prepares them for perpetual recycling.'[34] There is a 'revolution in subjectivities embodied in . . . fashion.'[35] Thus the person who is best at 'doing' fashion is the person who can endlesssly re-invent themselves through surface reconstruction.

Yet at the end of his book Lipovetsky introduces a note of doubt, a melancholy chord that unravels some of the earlier threads with which he draws together his arguments. The dissonance that he detects in fashion – between euphoria and hopelessness – is identifiable in this strain of design, photography and styling which emerged in the more experimental fashion magazines of the 1990s. It ranged from the dysfunctional, traumatised or deathly to a certain gloom, alienation or *anomie*. But rather than understanding its imagery simply as wasted pictures of a wasted generation of apathetic slackers, as depicted by Douglas Coupland in his 1991 novel *Generation X*,[36] perhaps the alienation of such images points to something larger. Perhaps it makes explicit the essential relationship of fashion to alienation in commodity culture, a relationship that is more frequently naturalised and made invisible in colourful and glossy consumerist fashion imagery.

The body of so-called heroin chic photography, for example, may come out of an alienated youth culture but it is theatricalised through extreme representation, using the photograph as a theatrical space in the way that urban subcultures such as punk used the street in 1976. In fashion shows and fashion shoots, the emphasis on a certain type of derelict urban space such as the warehouse or run-down council estate in the late 1990s could be understood as a post-Romantic moment in which truth and urban beauty could not be reconciled. What could be achieved, however, was the staging of this disillusion as a 'truth', its shabby locations and grungy models the alienated other to the enchantment and magic spectacle of fashion phantasmagoria in the late 1990s.

Lipovetsky argued that fashion is at the leading edge of superficial experience. This is not to say that fashionable people are shallow as individuals, but that consumer culture mediates social relations so as to encourage shallowness. In his introduction to Lipovetsky's book Richard Sennett wrote: 'democracy works better the more superficial the social relations between people in it. The less deeply people feel about one another, the better they will get on.'[37] Fashion diminishes social conflict by helping people to achieve such indifference by not engaging deeply with the world. At the same time, however, as it diminishes social conflict it contributes to increased personal despair, because dispute is also a form of social gel, confirming a common language and common cause between people. Perhaps this relates to the 'disconnection' that Amy Spindler associated with late-1990s minimalism such as Calvin Klein's, and to diCorcia's images of alienated couples who are unable to connect.

Fashion helps us to take on new and mobile identities, argued Lipovetsky, but to connect less with each other:

34 Ibid: 149.
35 Ibid: 152.
36 Douglas Coupland, *Generation X*, Abacus, London, 1996 [1991].
37 Foreword to Lipovetsky, *Empire of Fashion*: viii.

Through the pursuit of fashion, people become complex selves, though this complexity differs radically from the interior, soulful selfhood of the past . . . the impersonal is the realm of fantasy and desire, structured in such a way that masses of people can get along with one another, whereas the personal is a realm of social rupture, a lack of connection . . . the only way to make diversity work in a society is to make people less interested, and so less interfering, in the lives of people unlike themselves.[38]

Yet some of these images from earlier in the 1990s did seem to mark a return to an 'interior, soulful selfhood' (see figs 146 and 147 for example). Their insistence on existential world-weariness is depicted as part of lived experience. Lipovetsky writes that there is a 'tragic lightness' to fashion; it 'pacifies social conflict but deepens subjective and intersubjective conflict: allows more individual freedom but generates greater malaise in living',[39] and this sense of malaise is born out by this imagery. Richard Sennett asks, therefore: 'What does this "existential anguish" tell us about democracy? Does a politics of mutual toleration require privatised suffering? Could the political sphere possibly do something about that anguish?' Implicit in his question, and Lipovetsky's analysis, is the idea that alienation is not exclusively a personal but is also a social and political matter, not only subjectively determined but also produced by the modernising and bureaucratising tendencies of modern society. Perhaps, then, the alienation implied in diCorcia's photographs, when they are made for fashion magazines, is not so much the alienation of the individual as that of modern consumer culture. Fashion and alienation are, on the face of it, incompatible, even an oxymoron. Yet the relationship between the two might become apparent by tracking the connection between contemporary fashion and the free market, and the way that this relationship evokes the ghosts of nineteenth-century *laissez-faire* economic policies.

If the style of late 1990s fashion photography discussed in this chapter chimes with Lipovetsky's characterisation of late twentieth-century fashion as inherently melancholic, this connection between alienation and contemporary fashion can also, and equally, be traced to the harsh realities of the business of fashion photography in the period. Changes in fashion magazine publishing in the 1990s incorporated new risks and uncertainties but also new possibilities for photographers who were prepared to take those risks.[40] New opportunities were provided by micro-zines that tended to be financially independent and were run on a shoestring, with a very different system of commissioning and paying for fashion shoots. A micro-zine might sell six to seven thousand copies, whereas an established magazine such as *Vogue* had target sales of a minimum of two-hundred thousand copies a month. Thus the micro-zines had greater editorial freedom but also greater financial restraints. Arguably, the established magazines would never have permitted such ground-breaking work, which could then cross over to commercial advertising campaigns. The new magazines did not commission fashion shoots so much as publish them in exchange for the photographer bearing all or most of the costs of the shoot. It was relatively easy to build up a book, but each shoot would put the photographer further into debt, perhaps for years. Although these experimental micro-zines were hawkishly watched

38   Ibid: ix.
39   Ibid: 241.
40   On risk and modernity see Ulrich Beck, *Risk Society: Towards a New Modernity*, trans. Mark Ritter, Sage, London, Newbury Park and New Delhi, 1992.

by established companies such as Valentino and Prada, a photographer might wait in vain to be discovered and commissioned to do a campaign for them. Thus, if the past returns through cultural production in order to disturb and unsettle the idea of the modern, perhaps it is the alienated form of labour itself that haunts these contemporary images. For the fierce economy of nineteenth-century *laissez-faire* economic policies were exactly reproduced in the economy of so-called cutting-edge fashion photography and publishing in the late 1990s. In them the alienated labour that went into their production is mirrored by their subject matter, and that makes them into images of alienation for fashionable consumption.

Digitalisation

In Brett Easton Ellis's 1998 novel *Glamorama*, a dark fable about fashion and alienation which incorporates, even equates, European terrorism and American capitalism, much of the plot hinges on the creation through digital photography of a new history for the central character, a history which he cannot refute even though it never happened.

> Bentley starts tapping keys, landing on new photos. He enhances colors, adjusts tones, sharpens or softens images. Lips are digitally thickened, freckles are removed, an ax is placed in someone's outstretched hand, a BMW becomes a Jaguar which becomes a Mercedes which becomes a broom which becomes a frog which becomes a mop... licence plates are altered, more blood is spattered around a crime-scene photo, an uncircumcised penis is suddenly circumcised. Tapping keys, scanning images, Bentley adds motion blur (a shot of 'Victor' jogging along the Seine), he's adding lens flair (in a remote desert in eastern Iran I'm shaking hands with Arabs and wearing sunglasses and pouting, gasoline trucks lined up behind me), he's adding graininess, he's erasing people, he's inventing a new world, seamlessly.[41]

The protagonist Victor sees himself on screen having sex with people he never slept with, sitting in the audience of fashion shows he never attended, and modelling on shoots he never did. As Bentley goes on to say, 'you can move planets with this... you can shape lives. The photograph is only the beginning.... Were you there, or were you not? It all depends on who you ask, and even that doesn't really matter any more'.[42]

If pictures can be seamlessly altered and blended anything is possible, which introduces a new dilemma for the 'photographer': if anything is possible, what is she or he going to do? The art director Robin Derrick argued that the new technology shifted the focus to ideas and visions 'not hampered by reality',[43] while the photographers Nick Knight and Inez van Lamsweerde regarded digital photography as a liberation from the idea that photographs tell the truth, and from their connection with real time.[44] It allows the photographer to incorporate other media fictions and facts into her or his imagery. Vincent Peters's shoot 'The Riot' for *Arena* magazine in 1999 juxtaposed the model Gisele with lantern-

41 Brett Easton Ellis, *Glamorama*, Picador, London and Knopf, New York, 1998: 357.

42 Ibid: 358.

43 Mark Sanders, Phil Poynter, Robin Derrick (eds), *The Impossible Image: Fashion Photography in the Digital Age*, Phaidon, London, 2000: intro. [p. 2].

44 Charlotte Cotton, *Imperfect Beauty: The Making of Contemporary Fashion Photographs*, Victoria & Albert Publications, London, 2000: 17 and 134–5.

jawed male models dressed as riot police brandishing batons. 'The magazine called me on Sunday night when I was watching riots in Korea on TV and asked me if I'd do a shoot with Gisele. The idea is how you bring fashion and reality together'.[45] It was, however, a digitally imagined 'reality', no different from the sub-plots of *Glamorama*. For the digital image can turn the clock back, scramble time, fast forward, reverse and then cut to the chase. It can impose a riot on a fashion scenario or a fashion scenario on a riot. Digitalisation reduces the image to a scrapyard, a jumble of shards and fragments to be cannibalised and made into new forms. The darkness at the heart of *Glamorama* is the disappearance of the real as a photographic referent in a world that still believes that pictures tell the truth.

Freed from the meta-narrative of 'truth', the late twentieth century can be understood as a period of experimentation in identity, in which the self was a project, something to be negotiated and constructed as an ongoing and permanent process. Celia Lurie looked specifically at the role of photography in constructing modern sensibilities, arguing that 'vision and self-knowledge have become inextricably and productively intertwined in modern Euro-American societies'.[46] Seeing and knowing are meshed in specific formations in what Lurie dubbed 'prosthetic culture'. Pictures are no longer 'out there' as distinct entities, representations that mirror our images back to ourselves; rather, the photographic screen or image becomes a prosthetic extension of the self, allowing the individual to reconfigure his or her identity experimentally.

In Mike Thomas's 'The Difference is Clear' for *Dazed & Confused* in 1998 the model's coat is pictured as transparent; through it we see the modernist slab block behind, but refracted and distorted as if seen through textured glass (fig. 154). The effect is comically tweedy too. The image refers to the fact that we live in an increasingly technological and urban environment; this is reflected in urban images of the body splintered and refracted in space. Amelia Jones has coined the phrase the 'technophenomenological body' to describe the high-tech means of presenting the body used by artists in the 1990s, for example in digital imagery installations or using sophisticated video techniques.[47] This particular form of return to the body has a clear bearing on fashion and the development of digital techniques of the image in fashion photography (though that was not Jones's object of study). It is in this way that the body returns as a ghostly trace or fragment, stubbornly reinvesting the digital image with the melancholy of the analogue image, a poignant ghosting of the physicality of fashion.

That this could happen was due in part to the commercial availability of software packages that allowed photographers to manipulate their images of disaster or urban alienation, and in part to new kinds of fashion publishing. Fashion and advertising in particular were able to pioneer digital photography because the market as well as the means of production enabled them to be at the vanguard of new sensibilities. By the mid-1990s image manipulation software was cheap enough to be available outside specialist laboratories, and fashion photographers working for less mainstream magazines were quick to exploit their possibilities. Fashion photography in particular was in the forefront of this trend, firstly

45 Vincent Peters quoted in Katherine Flett, 'Altered Images', *The Observer Magazine*, 28 May 2000: 20.

46 Celia Lurie, *Prosthetic Culture: Photography, Memory and Identity*, Routledge, London and New York, 1998: 3.

47 Amelia Jones, *Body Art/Performing the Subject*, University of Minnesota Press, Minneapolis and London, 1998: 17 and 235.

because the infrastructure of the publishing industry enabled this development, secondly because by definition fashion is concerned to represent the body, and thirdly because the shallow space of the fashion image creates a fictive space that is particularly appropriate to a post-modern, post-humanist, model of identity. No longer fixed, centred and universal, the post-humanist subject is deracinated, urban, decentred, dispersed, fragmented, various and plural, in ways that are pictured in Mike Thomas's photograph. Celia Lurie wrote, for example, of 'non-dimensional personalities', the transformation of reality into images through virtual reality, and the aestheticisation of everyday life, all in relation to identity and new technologies of the image.[48] And digital fashion photography, precisely because it is not predicated on a humanist model of 'truth', was a particularly fruitful medium for experimenting with the pleasures and pains of modern identity.

48 Lurie, *Prosthetic Culture*: 157.

154 (*facing page*) Mike Thomas, 'The Difference is Clear', *Dazed & Confused*, 1998. Styling Cathy Edwards, clothes by Hussein Chalayan. Photograph courtesy Mike Thomas

part three

nine   trauma

Symptom

In the early 1990s the Italian fashion company Benetton ran an advertising campaign that featured images of copulating horses, dying AIDS patients, human hearts and sexualised priests – striking imagery that was at odds with the company's design aesthetic of brightly coloured jumpers and jeans for Euro-teenagers. The small but influential London magazine *The Face* in June 1994 featured a fashion spread by Jean-Baptiste Mondino in which models posed with guns to their temples, blood dripping from their mouths and thighs. Some looked wounded, others dead. In 1995 another Mondino spread in *The Face* showed the model Kristen McMenemy looking bruised and beaten, with multiple scars. A Dolce e Gabbana advertisement from the Autumn 1997 campaign used a black-and-white photograph of a woman lying on glistening tarmac, limbs stiff enough to suggest *rigor mortis*. Sean Ellis's gothic fashion spread in *The Face* in 1997, 'The Clinic', subtitled 'Welcome. We'll tear your soul apart', pictured dark and dystopian fantasies of abject and terrorized bodies (fig. 155).

The 'brutalised body', in Rebecca Arnold's phrase, that characterised fashion imagery and styling of the 1990s was marked by signs of trauma and violence.[1] Arnold drew attention to the way Quentin Tarantino's films *Reservoir Dogs* (1992) and *Pulp Fiction* (1994) self-referentially combined stylised violence and sartorial cool to inspire numerous fashion shoots in menswear magazines.[2] Describing the ways in which 1990s fashion imagery and design drew selectively on film noir images of vamps and gangsters of the 1940s, Arnold pointed out that the glamorised violence and trailer-trash aesthetic of the mid-1990s showed a fascination with the underbelly of consumer society, and concluded that 'such images represent dark dreams of taking control of the chaos of contemporary life by resorting to violence'.[3] Contemporary artists also appropriated the imagery and iconography of murder and atrocity from media images, for example the artist Marcus Harvey's 1995 portrait of the child killer Myra Hindley, which was included in the Royal Academy 'Sensation' exhibition in London in 1997. Harvey's enormous monochrome oil painting consisted of thousands of children's hand prints that simulated the dot matrix effect of newsprint photographs to replicate Hindley's face. In recognition of the way in which media imagery of death and disaster began to permeate cultural production, in 2001 the touring exhibition 'Trauma' brought together a range of artists whose work was concerned with the 'immediate experience of traumatic events and situations'.[4]

The original meaning of the word 'trauma' was 'wound'; it has a precise medical meaning, as well as a psychoanalytic one, but in the late 1990s the term also came to be used more loosely to describe a psychic or emotional shock so great as to amount to a form of dislocation. It is in this sense that one could designate the more unsettling fashion imagery and design of the 1990s as traumatic. In both mainstream and minority imagery, fashion came frequently to be construed as pathological: the distressed body was marked by trauma, and many of its themes became correspondingly darker in the 1990s, to include death, disease and dereliction. Yet the field of representations of traumatised bodies

155 (*facing page*) Sean Ellis, The Clinic: Welcome. We'll tear your soul apart, *The Face*, 1997. Styling Isabella Blow, jacket by Hussein Chalayan and knickers by Alexander McQueen. Photograph courtesy Sean Ellis

1 Rebecca Arnold, *Fashion, Desire and Anxiety: Image and Morality in the Twentieth Century*, I. B. Tauris, London and New York, 2001: 80–9. On p. 87 she analyses Sean Ellis's spread 'The Clinic'.
2 Ibid: 37.
3 Ibid: 32.
4 For the catalogue, see *Trauma*, Hayward Gallery Publishing, London, 2001.

was wide enough to extend to images of transformation, in which the body might be 'brutalised' but also constructively and critically opened up for speculation.

Melancholic Incorporation

The idea that such themes could be appropriate to fashion was developed in photography, but also by a range of small-scale London fashion designers whose market and small-scale production freed them to think and work experimentally, even as they were hampered by lack of cash. Boudicca, established in 1996, produced moulded leather breast-plates, layered dirty white organdie dresses, body-restrictive pieces, deconstructed ballgowns and 'renegade winged blouses' that all made up a 'strange emotional armour'.[5] For Boudicca's two designers, Zowie Broach and Brian Kirby, inspiration came from what they saw around them and often from the radio and television news. They felt that clothes should express feelings, even if they were miserable ones. Their Spring–Summer 1999 collection, Immortality, first shown in Copenhagen in late 1998, dealt with emotions, they claimed, especially those concerning life and death, and was partly inspired by the Princess Diana car crash – leaving flowers was not so much to do with grieving but with 'acquiring fame and immortality'.[6] The collection was accompanied by a video of their 'muse' Julia Ain-Kruper discussing her feelings on the suicide of a family member. For the collection she modelled pieces with titles such as the 'Cut Me Out' jacket and the 'Miss Ugly' top. The collection included boots made from antique ice-skates inspired by the phrase 'skating on thin ice'. The cut of the garments was bleak and angular; each came with a notebook in which the owner of the garment could record where and when she wore it. If the piece was sold or given away, the book would live on. The idea came from Milan Kundera's phrase 'immortality is when people remember you who don't know you', only here it was the history of the clothes, rather than the person, that would become immortal.

Boudicca's next collection, Autumn–Winter 1999–2000, was inspired by the reclusive lifestyle of Howard Hughes. Called System Error, the show featured only thirteen pieces and one model. The long gaps between her appearance on the catwalk, while she changed backstage, produced painful moments as the audience fretted in uncomfortable silence, wondering if something had gone wrong (fig. 156). The designers claimed they intended simply to slow down the frenetic pace of the fashion show, to give people time to think about the clothes, to look closely, but fashion time does not normally permit this degree of scrutiny. Of the thirteen dresses, the 'Embrace Me' jacket in rich, tactile fabric, had pockets at each shoulder so that admirers could hug the wearer inside her clothes. The 'Solitary Dress' was slashed at both sides of the waist so the wearer could hug herself. Zowie Broach of Boudicca said: 'We are increasingly single – we work alone, travel alone, live alone – but we'd rather be part of a couple, we'd rather have company.'[7] In the same collection were the 'Distress Dress', in high-visibility orange nylon ('people always talk about

5   Stephen Gan, *Visionaire's Fashion 2001: Designers of the New Avant-Garde*, ed. Alix Browne, Laurence King, London, 1999: [n.p.].

6   Naomi Stungo, 'Boudicca', *Blueprint*, no. 154, October, 1998: 34.

7   Zowie Broach quoted in Susannah Frankel, 'We want to be', *Independent* magazine, 8 May 1999: 30.

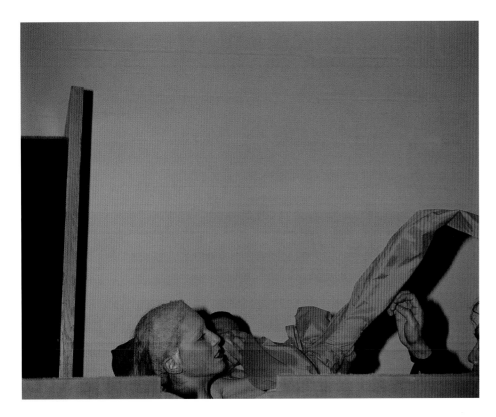

156 Boudicca, model putting on Distress Dress backstage, Autumn–Winter 1999–2000, Photograph courtesy Robert Wyatt

the black box after a plane crash but in fact it is orange. We thought it was interesting because it contains the pilot's last words') and 'Howard's Coat', a tissued black dress, because 'Howard Hughes covered the floor with tissue before he walked on it'.[8]

The Distress Dress had a particularly modern resonance in a period in which the technologies of the black box and the mobile telephone brought the moment of death into the public realm as something capable for the first time of being represented, or pictured, as it happened. The artist Johan Grimonprez' piece *dial* H-I-S-T-O-R-Y, made in 1997, was a seventy-minute long collage of used television news coverage of aeroplane hijacks set against the artist's soundtrack that mixed newsreel reports, 1970s soul and funk tracks and excerpts from Don DeLillo's *White Noise* and *Mao II*.

Voice over 1

All plots tend to move deathwards. This is the nature of plots. Political plots, terrorist plots, lovers' plots, narrative plots, plots that are part of children's games. We edge nearer death every time we plot. It's like a contract that all must sign, the plotters as well as those who are targets of the plots.

Voice over 2

It is a curious knot that binds novelists and terrorists. What terrorists gain, novelists lose. Years ago, I used to think it was possible for a novelist to alter the inner life of the culture. Now, bomb-makers and gunmen have taken that territory. They make raids on human consciousness. What writers used to do before we were all incorporated.[9]

8   Ibid: 28.
9   Voiceover from *dial H-I-S-T-O-R-Y*, cited in *Trauma*: 36.

Shocking though the suggestion may be, if novelists have lost the high ground, the pure visuality of modern spectacle makes it fertile terrain for anyone, fashion designer, terrorist or visual artist, to 'alter the inner life of the culture.'

Other designers configured trauma more literally on the surface of the body. Andrew Groves's MA graduation collection from Central Saint Martins in 1997 was called Ordinary Madness and was inspired by turn-of-the-century drawings by the mentally ill. There were pieces studded with four-inch nails whose points projected outwards from the garments and a skirt covered in two thousand dressmakers' pins. Groves's first runway presentation after graduation, his Spring–Summer 1998 collection, was called Status and was based on the idea of disease, specifically on the internal decay of a society consumed with visual images of external perfection epitomised by the beauty of the supermodel. It featured 1980s shoulder lines and complicated threadwork to simulate decay. Groves said 'I wanted to show what was inside that was eating the clothes away'.[10] The narrative of Groves's show was based on the idea of women who were beamed down from outer space and looked like perfect, untouchable mannequins but who were in fact rotting inside: the clothes were deconstructed, representing decay and disease. As a final gesture, a model opened her cotton wadding jacket to release a swarm of five hundred flies over the fashion journalists seated in the front row, causing horror and outrage (fig. 157). 'Flies trapped inside a Jacket' contained within it the disturbing idea that the flies were feeding on the model. It was a self-conscious homage to the artist Damien Hirst's *A Thousand Years* (1990), a piece consisting of maggots which hatched in a hatchery, fed on a rotten cow's head, grew into adult flies, mated, laid eggs and died in an insectocutor, while the eggs hatched to continue the cycle. Although the piece gestured towards the immortality of art and the cycle of life, it seemed to be as much about death, as the insectocutor and the rotting cow's head suggested.

The abject and uncanny elements of Groves's runway shock tactics were part of a contemporary move to disrupt and expose the contained, classical body of conventional art and fashion. Hal Foster argued that for many people in the 1990s the truth resided in the traumatic or abject subject, in the discarded or damaged body: 'if there is a subject of history for the cult of abjection at all, it is . . . the corpse.'[11] Both Groves's and McQueen's collections, such as the latter's Dante and Eclect Dissect collections that featured human bones, used the idea of the interior of the body to flirt with dark and deathly themes, and worked to reinstate the category of the *memento mori* in contemporary practice.[12] Running through the art and fashion of the 1990s were images of the body opened up, fissured and traumatised, a body at odds with the idealised nude of classical art and mainstream fashion. These cultural practitioners returned to the imagery of the first anatomists: Olivier Theyskens's Autumn–Winter 1998–9 collection featured a translucent white polo-necked body stocking traced with a pattern of red veins and arteries that ran from a red lace appliquéd heart over the right breast and trailed away towards the edges of the body like the wintry branches of a tree silhouetted against a pale sky (fig. 158). Photographed against a solid grotto wall of human skulls and bones, the model's white face make-up, dark panda

10   Gan, *Visionaire's Fashion 2001*: [n.p.].

11   Hal Foster, *The Return of the Real: The Avant Garde at the End of the Century*, MIT Press, Cambridge, Mass., and London, 1996: 166. Foster gives his reasons: firstly, he argues that there is disillusionment with earlier artistic stratagems, and with ideas about the subject; secondly, he cites despair about AIDS, disease and death, poverty and crime, and the destruction of the welfare state; and thirdly, he argues that there is a broken social contract: the rich drop out from the revolution and the poor are dropped out.

12   On the revival of *memento mori* themes in contemporary art see 'Allegories of Life and Death: Tradition Revisited and Transformed' in Margit Rowell, *Objects of Desire: The Modern Still Life*, Museum of Modern Art, New York and Hayward Gallery, London, 1997: 122–5. For a discussion of Alexander McQueen's work as a form of *memento mori* see Arnold, *Fashion, Desire and Anxiety*: 59.

157 Andrew Groves, Spring–Summer 1998.
Photograph Niall McInerney

eyes and emaciated frame, with her wilting pose, combined to suggest an intense fascination with the juxtaposition of death and extreme youth.

The image suggested the body itself as a crypt, a form of melancholic incorporation of trauma into the body. The psychoanalysts Nicholas Abraham and Maria Torok have argued that 'inexpressible mourning erects a secret tomb inside the subject . . . the loss is buried alive in the crypt as a full-fledged person, complete with its own topography. The crypt also includes . . . actual or supposed trauma.'[13] Here the topography of the body is charted on a fictionalised map of veins and arteries. Where fashion designers and photographers drew on the imagery of the interior of the body, whether the emotional interior of Boudicca's designs, the anatomical imagery of Theyskens or Groves's more literal idea of the inside of a beautiful woman rotting away, they suggested the idea of the body as

13 Abraham and Torok saw the symptom as a 'telltale memory trace of latent or unavailable promptings or trauma'. They were concerned with language as a system of expressive traces and in their work on trauma produced a series of bodily metaphors to describe how their patients could transcend or surmount traumas that were obstacles to their functioning. They were concerned with the ways in which people sealed off their trauma, using the metaphors of crypt and incorporation to describe the individual's 'forcible creation of a psychic tomb'. Nicholas Abraham and Maria Torok, *The Shell and the Kernel*, vol. 1, trans. and intro. by Nicolas T. Rand, University of Chicago Press, Chicago and London, 1994: 6, 22 and 130.

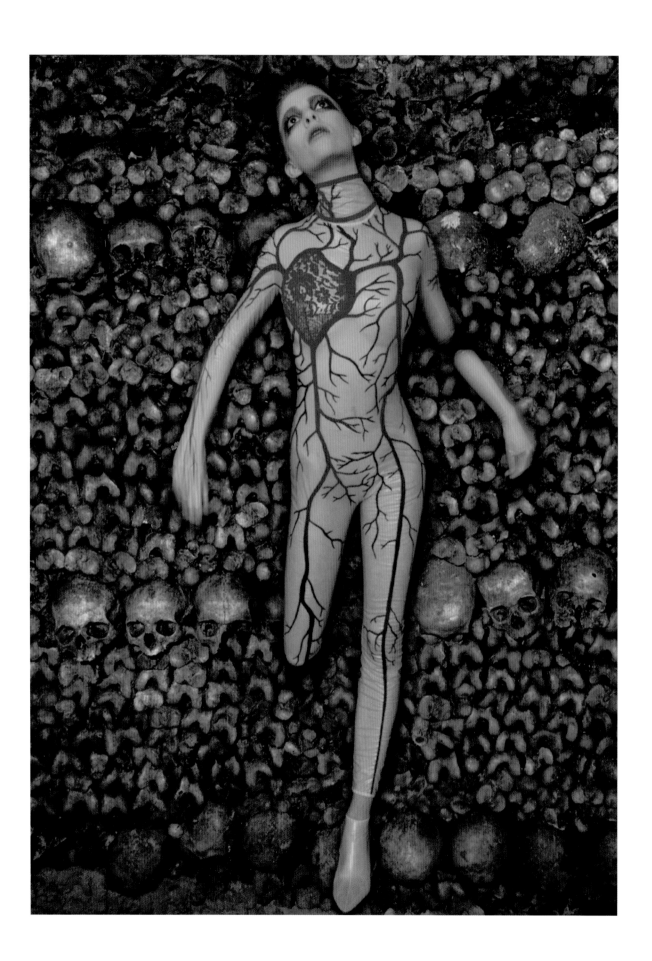

a crypt, or a psychic tomb, which was theatricalised in the space of the runway and the fashion magazine. These images drew on the iconography of death and interiority to picture the body from the inside. They suggested that fashion can take us to the inside, either emotionally (Boudicca) or corporeally, as in the images of the 'brutalised' body that opened this chapter.

158 (*facing page*)   Olivier Theyskens, Autumn–Winter 1998–9. Photograph Les Cyclopes, courtesy Olivier Theyskens

Memento mori

Charles Dana Gibson, the illustrator who in the early years of the twentieth century created the Gibson Girl, the epitome of upbeat and lively modernity, also produced a *memento mori* in the form of a fashionably dressed young woman seated at her dressing table whose image converts into a death's head (fig. 159). The mirror in which she is contentedly surveying herself forms the skull, her head and its reflected image the eye sockets, and the cosmetic preparations on the table before her become a row of teeth. From a distance the image reads unequivocally as a skull, and it is only closer scrutiny that reveals the alternative vision of the young woman at her toilette, confirming the notion that death and decay are the privileged terms here, to which youth and beauty are merely temporary destabilising supplements.

Gibson drew on an old tradition.[14] All fashion has a structural affinity with the *memento mori*, even where death itself is not in any way represented in the image. In the 1970s, Susan Sontag commented on the 'perfect complementarity' between Richard Avedon's flattering fashion photographs and the series of 'elegant, ruthless portraits Avedon did in 1972 of his dying father.'[15] In the 1990s, a certain strand of fashion design, photography, make-up and styling was pervaded by explicit references to death. It was a minority strand that revealed the melancholy death's head beneath the skin. Meanwhile the highly glossy, optimistic images of much Italian, French and American mainstream fashion, with their emphasis on healthy, toned bodies, continued to deny the pain of loss and to seek to hold death and decay at bay. The two kinds of imagery co-existed, in different magazines and on different runways, like the paired figures of the living and the dead in the medieval Dance of Death – one celebratory and life-affirming, the other inexorably signalling its opposite.

Many of them drew on a range of visual symbols from the *memento mori* tradition, particularly its use of human hair, bones or decay. François Berthoud photographed a high-heeled ankle boot like an X-ray image for *Amica* in 1997/8 (number 22). Alexander McQueen lined the garments of his 1992 Central Saint Martins graduation collection with human hair, a reference to the use of human hair in mourning jewellery. For his Spring–Summer 1998 collection a model wore over her black dress an aluminium ribcage corset by the jeweller Shaun Leane cast from a real human skeleton (fig. 160). Also for McQueen, Dai Rees made a hairpiece in 1998 out of human hair; photographed by the artist Mat Collishaw for the Judith Clark Costume Gallery, the model was styled with waxy

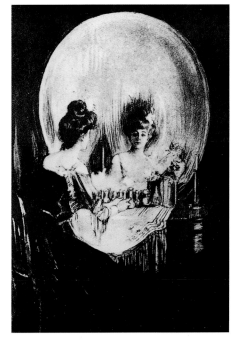

159   Charles Dana Gibson, from a German postcard, c. 1908. Private collection

14   Many seventeeth-century paintings showing women at their toilette also contain symbols of ephemerality and are really vanitas portraits. See Liana de Girolami Cheney, 'Dutch vanitas paintings: the skull' from Liana de Girolami Cheney (ed.), *The Symbolism of* Vanitas *in the Arts, Literature and Music*, Edwin Mellen Press, Lewiston, Queenston, Lampeter, 1992: 128.

15   Susan Sontag, *On Photography*, Penguin, Harmondsworth, 1979: 104–5.

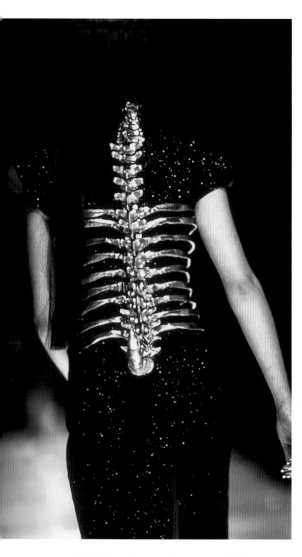

160 Shaun Leane, ribcage corset for Alexander McQueen, Untitled, Spring–Summer 1998. Aluminium, cast from real skeleton. Photograph Chris Moore, courtesy Shaun Leane

161 (facing page) Dai Rees, hat, 1998. Pheasant quills, duck feathers, human hair, styrofoam, collar felt. Photograph Mat Collishaw, courtesy Judith Clark Costume

16 Jonathan Sawday, *The Body Emblazoned: Dissection and the Human Body in Renaissance Culture*, Routledge, London and New York, 1995: 13–14.

17 Efrat Tseëlon, *The Masque of Femininity: The Presentation of Woman in Everyday Life*, Sage, London, Thousand Oaks and New Delhi, 1995: 8.

pallor in a bleak and derelict setting (fig. 161). In contemporary art too the theme of mortality surfaced – in Damien Hirst's sculptures that preserved animal parts in formaldehyde, in Marc Quinn's *Head*, a mould of the artist's head made from eight pints of his refrigerated blood, and in Collishaw's 1994 installation of a female and a male finch encased in blocks of ice (fig. 162). Even the pretty butterfly prints of the London designer Matthew Williamson in 1997 (fig. 164) recalled the flowers and insects of Dutch still-life flower paintings which, in the seventeenth century, were symbols of ephemerality, whose imagery resurfaced in Quinn's deathless flowers frozen for ever in silicon (fig. 163).

Jean-Baptiste Mondino's 1997 spread in *The Face*, titled 'Internal Affairs', juxtaposed black-and-white photographs of the models with their X-ray images. Paired over five pages, in each spread the living body was contrasted with the skeleton beneath, evoking the Dance of Death in which each living figure was paired with a deathly one. But in this modern version, death is not conceived of as an external figure who comes to take away the living but as an internal one: the X-ray imagery goes 'beneath the skin' in its references to medical technology. In this fashion spread, as in much late twentieth-century art that used medical references or technology to image the artist's body (Hannah Wilke, Mona Hatoum, Orlan and Bob Flanagan, for example), video and photography present us with a trace of the body, but it is a body threatened by technology and science as much as by its own mortality.

Before the advent of modern medicine, with its new technologies for imaging the body, the sight of the inside of the body was always an encounter with death. Today, despite medical advances, it still retains some of that charge, and a visual encounter with the inside of the body may be an encounter with disease and pathology. In addition to its association with mortality, the inside of the body has been linked particularly to women in the Judaeo-Christian tradition. Jonathan Sawday has argued in his history of anatomy that in Western culture the body's interior is a Medusa's head that 'speaks directly of our own mortality' and that, regardless of the sex of the body, 'interiority' is first feminised and then sexualised in representation.[16] It is women's bodies, their internal and external parts, that have come to represent the space of danger, desire and unconscious fears about both sexuality and mortality.[17] This scenario is invoked only to be rescripted in David Sims's fashion photograph for *The Face* in 1995, where a young woman seated on a stool holds a skull in her lap, one thumb resting idly over an eye socket (fig. 166). The positioning of the skull between her open legs suggests the historical connection between sex, death and women, and reminds us that when the Medusa's head of interiority is coded as female it is also, inevitably, sexualised. Yet this is not an image of a vampish *femme fatale* so much as a picture of a young woman whose own contemplation of life is almost casually predicated on the proximity of sex and death. Her transluscent skin and fine bone structure make palpable the 'skull beneath the skin', which is also symbolised by the skull she holds in her hands. The photograph invites a comparison between her skimpy lace dress and her own skin under which her slight frame seems more like an armature than flesh and blood. The melancholy contemplation of death is re-gendered in this image: whereas Shakespeare's

Hamlet looks at the skull and soliloquises on death and transience, the model here does not seem to be contemplating the skull in any way. Perhaps she herself is the skull, posed for our contemplation. Perhaps this type of image suggested an attraction to images of death, decay and hybridity as a way of finding out what was socially ignored or anathe-

164   Matthew Williamson, Electric Angels,
Spring–Summer 1998. Photograph courtesy
Matthew Williamson

matised. The fascination with the dark side of life is the other side of the coin of fashion's emphasis on idealised bodies. These norms and stereotypes are only half the picture, so we are drawn to the negated or neglected other side, be it cultural otherness or death. In these images fashion functions as a symptom to evoke its opposite, so that glamour masks decay, but the latter returns as the repressed of the former. Just as in Lucas Furtenagel's portrait

166 (facing page) David Sims, Play for Today, *The Face*, 1995. Styling Anna Cockburn, dress by Giorgio Sant Angelo. Photograph courtesy David Sims

165 Lucas Furtenagel, *The Painter Hans Burgkmair and his Wife Anna*, 1529, oil on panel, 60 × 52 cm, Kunsthistorisches Museum, Vienna. The frame of the convex mirror bears the inscription 'Erken dich selbst/ o Mors/ Hoffnung der Welt'

18 Walter Benjamin cited in Christine Buci-Glucksmann, *Baroque Reason: The Aesthetics of Modernity*, trans. Patrick Camiller, Sage, London, Thousand Oaks and New Delhi, 1994: 67–9, and on the corpse in the *Trauerspiel*: 71.

19 Walter Benjamin cited in Susan Buck-Morss, *The Dialectics of Seeing: Walter Benjamin and the Arcades Project*, MIT Press, Cambridge, Mass., and London, 1991: 181.

20 For a discussion of 'trauma' culture see Foster, *Return of the Real;* for a sociology of fear in contemporary society see Frank Furedi, *Culture of Fear: Risk-Taking and the Morality of Low Expectation*, Cassell, London, 1997; and for a characterisation of 'wound culture' see Mark Seltzer, *Serial Killers: Death and Life in America's Wound Culture*, Routledge, New York and London, 1998, which discusses anxiety, change, fear and trauma. See too Sarah Dunant and Roy Porter (eds), *The Age of Anxiety*, Virago, London, 1996, and Jeffrey Weeks, *Inventing Moralities: Sexual Values in an Age of Uncertainty*, Columbia University Press, New York, 1995.

from 1529 the mirror (a traditional symbol of female vanity) reveals death to the living (fig. 165), so Sims's fashion photograph of a model holding a skull inscribes death at the heart of life, decay as the corollary of youthful perfection, darkness as the inevitable consequence of light.

In its return to *memento mori* and vanitas imagery, the second half of the 1990s was haunted by an earlier moment of modernity, the development in the seventeenth century of European mercantile capitalism. For Walter Benjamin, the fragmented nature of the German Baroque mourning play (a play about loss, ruination and transience) mourned the off-stage transition to capitalist modernity.[18] In his analysis, there was a link between nineteenth-century consumption and the rise of mercantile capitalism in the seventeenth century. As such, it helps us to understand the fragmented nature of modernity in the nineteenth century when, he writes, 'the emblems return as commodities.'[19] The culture of the Reformation was formed in the early stages of capitalist transition; that of the nineteenth century when capitalist production was consolidated, expanded and modified through the processes of industrialisation and urbanisation. Both were cultures of transition in which all fixed points seemed to have been removed; the late twentieth century, a period of globalisation and fast-changing technology, exhibited the same characteristic, which may account for some writers' fascination with the themes of abjection, trauma and anxiety in the present.[20] Certainly, these themes were pictured in a range of fashion imagery, spanning Sean Ellis's and David Sims's photography, Shaun Leane's jewellery and Theyskens's, McQueen's and Groves's traumatised bodies on the runway.

Corporeality

21   Naomi Filmer quoted in Alexandra Bradley and Gavin Fernandez (eds), *Unclasped: Contemporary British Jewellery*, essay by Derren Gilhooley, afterword by Simon Costin, Black Dog, London, 1997: 105.

22   See Rand in Abraham and Torok, *The Shell*: 102–4.

In the 1990s Naomi Filmer designed jewellery that occupied negative space in and around the body, rather than adorning it decoratively. Her 1993 'Hand manipulation piece' and her 'Finger and Toe Betweens' were like small abstract modernist sculptures that, once inserted in the voids between fingers and toes, suddenly made sense as they miraculously assumed a relationship with the living body (fig. 167). For Hussein Chalayan's Spring–Summer 1996 collection Filmer designed mouth pieces, such as a 'Mouth Bar' that was inserted vertically behind the front teeth to keep the mouth open (fig. 168a), and a 'Mouth Light' that illuminated the open mouth from inside, glowing like a furnace; it was made from resin casting set with red LEDs and a single cell battery that filled the inside of the mouth, substituting an incandescent red core for the shiny gloss of lipstick on the outside of the mouth (fig. 168b). Filmer has said that 'my work is not about what goes on the body but about the body itself.'[21] If the polished surfaces of conventional make-up and fashion can constitute a carapace to hold the horror of death and decay at bay, the inside of the body, with its connotations of mortality, are the flip side of that denial. Yet when Filmer opened up the spaces in and around the body in unconventional ways, the traumatised fashion body was no longer a sealed grave; in her work, and in that of her fellow jewellery designers in the same period, the body, however deathly its representation, could, like Romeo and Juliet's crypt, be creatively opened and entered.

Just as the inside of the body can be represented as a crypt, so, too, may the spaces around it, in and between its parts, be creatively revealed. In their work on trauma, Torok and Abraham also looked at the concept of self-creation and sexuality, arguing that if trauma is unresolved it hinders the creative fashioning of the self of which sexuality is a part.[22] Introjection might involve projecting the trauma onto the self as a screen, casting light on it, however painfully, rather than incorporating trauma and then sealing it off as a secret. Then erotic death might be staged as part of the process of introjection. Thus, in their formulation, a traumatic event that cannot be accommodated will be incorporated,

167   Naomi Filmer, 'Tulip Finger Between', 1993, cast silver. Photographs Tim Brightmoore, courtesy Naomi Filmer

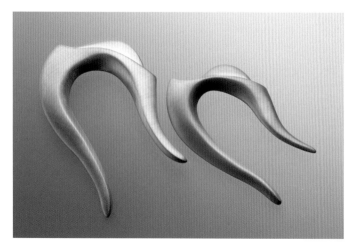
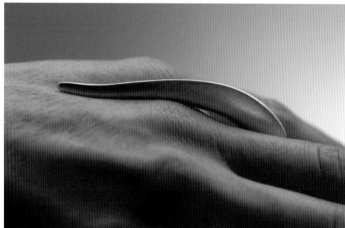

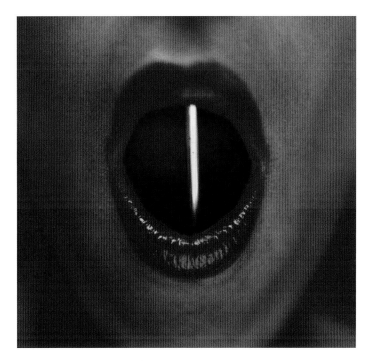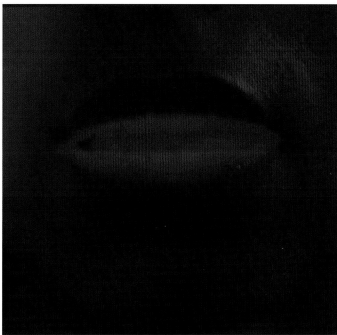

turning the body into a living tomb, or crypt; but if the traumatic event can be addressed through the process of 'introjection' the subject will be able to move on and refashion the self.[23] Introjection, which Torok and Abraham use differently from other psychoanalysts, is thus the opposite of incorporation, but the metaphor still suggests the notion of an interior self that can be used to think about the relation between body and identity.

Thus the traumatised body of 1990s fashion can be further explored via this metaphor of incorporation as it applies to jewellery design in the period. Jewellery has a special relationship to the body, and in the 1990s fashion designers began increasingly to draw on the work of jewellers on the runway. As well as spiky metal knuckle-dusters for Fabio Piras's Autumn–Winter 1995–6 collection, Lars Sture produced a necklace made from patinated brass and human hair (fig. 169). Hussein Chalayan's collection featured Naomi Filmer's gold vampire teeth (see fig. 96); Scott Wilson's dangling veils of beads and ethereal beaded horns were commissioned by Thierry Mugler and Karl Lagerfeld in Paris and Hussein Chalayan, Antonio Berardi and Julien Macdonald in London. Lesley Vic Waddell's designs for Galliano for Dior combined delicate tracery with Goth sado-masochism. The use of jewellery as part of catwalk shows, allied to a particular designer's name, became symptomatic of the way fashion display and marketing developed in the 1990s. As London fashion shows became increasingly theatrical, many designers relied on the work of stylists, jewellers, make-up artists and accessories designers to augment their extreme effects. This theatricality extended to the set design and stage effects of the shows, but the emergence of jewellery in this period was different because it pinpointed a relationship with the body rather than the space surrounding it.

168   Naomi Filmer, 'Mouth Bar' and 'Mouth Light', for Hussein Chalayan, Spring–Summer 1996. Resin casting, red LEDs. Photographs Jeremy Foster, courtesy Naomi Filmer

23   Ibid: 100–2.

169 (*facing page*)   Lars Sture, patinated brass and human hair necklace, 1996. Photograph courtesy Gavin Fernandes

170   Shaun Leane, sterling silver mouthpiece for Alexander McQueen, Spring–Summer 1997. Photograph courtesy Gavin Fernandes

Indeed, often the style of the jewellery came to summarise the style of the designer in a kind of pictorial shorthand. Shaun Leane's designs for McQueen's Spring–Summer 1997 collection mirrored the elegant cruelty of McQueen's razor-sharp cutting techniques, in a series of lethal-looking pieces that wrapped a single, long, silver spike round the models' heads in a range of ways. One circled the space around the model's head like a halo; another wrapped round the front of the neck, its two sharply pointed ends streaming horizontally backwards from the model's neck. Another pierced an ear, only to loop round to the front again, its two potentially fatal tips projecting far beyond the model's cheeks and chin; a fourth snaked across the model's face, slotting in and out of her mouth like a horse's bit before curving upwards round her ears to project its long, shiny tips up and away from her temples like fierce antennae (fig. 170). Sean Ellis chose to show this piece in a vam-

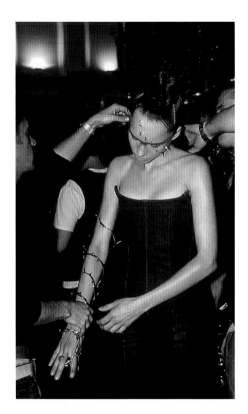

171 Shaun Leane, Thorn Arm Vine, solid silver, for Alexander McQueen, Autumn–Winter 1996–7. Photograph Maya Kardun/© V&A Images

172 (*facing page*) Sarah Harmanee, finger horns for Alexander McQueen, Autumn–Winter 1997–8. Photo-etched silver plates with horns and leather armband. Photograph courtesy Sean Ellis

24 Derren Gilhooley in Bradley and Fernandez, *Unclasped*: 10.

piric lesbian scenario in a story for *The Face* called 'The Clinic': one woman lowers her head so the tips of the spikes are pushed into the receptive neck of her partner whose smiling silhouette reveals a head thrown back in pleasurable anticipation.

For McQueen's Autumn–Winter 1996–7 collection Leane made silver rose thorns which were stuck to the model's faces (see fig. 106d) and thorn necklaces and bracelets that spiralled up the model's arm like rampant barbed wire (fig. 171). These pieces pinpointed what Derren Gilhooley has called 'the inherent sexual violence' of jewellery: 'violence is implicit in jewellery's very mechanisms of fastening, piercing clasping and buckling'.[24] It is these mechanisms that became the decorative motifs in Leane's elegant, spiky and menacing jewellery for McQueen.

A year later, for McQueen's Autumn–Winter 1997–8 show, It's a Jungle out There, Sarah Harmanee incorporated threatening animal horns with intricately patterned silver, photo-etched with lace patterns, fitting her contraptions onto unexpected parts of the body such as elbows or fingers, often wrapping them on with cross-laced black leather straps; the results postulated a delicate yet decadent form of beauty, mixing subcultural Goth sensibility with fashionable sado-masochism (fig. 172). Her 'Knife Head Piece' from this collection fitted the head like a conventional Alice band but extended round the ears, from where a series of metal 'knives' splayed out over the cheeks (fig. 173). Etched with delicate lace patterns and spread like a flirtatious fan against the face, the piece also suggested a lethal weapon that might whirr into life at any minute like Edward Scissorhands' hands, and seemed dangerously unstable. For this collection Dai Rees produced head pieces made from shaved pelican and turkey quills that the designer first stripped and sanded, then mounted so that his spiky structures framed the air round the model's head. They looked heavy and sharp like metal but were in fact airy and light to wear; the pieces were then flocked so that the joins were concealed.

In 1992 McQueen had used the jewellery of Simon Costin in his graduation collection. Trained in stage design rather than jewellery, and without traditional craft skills, Costin used unconventional materials such as fish skin, animal bones, birds' feet and human fluids (see figs 107 and 108). These pieces had attracted controversy in the late 1980s when they were made, largely because Costin's Incubus Necklace of 1987 (fig. 174) had been impounded by the police and Costin threatened with prosecution. The Necklace incorporated five glass vials of human sperm, each with a Baroque pearl dangling from it, set against a filigree of copper wire with snaky silver sperm entwined over its surface. Surmounted by a little metal plaque that said 'vice and virtue', the piece invoked the dark sensibility of Elizabethan and Jacobean literary imagery, suggesting an attraction of opposites that characterised much of the fashion sensibility of the following decade: vice and virtue, beauty and horror, sex and death. Costin was also interested in Decadent literature and art of the late nineteenth century, and in all his jewellery he played on the tension between attraction and repulsion, prefiguring many fashion designers' concerns in the 1990s.

173 Sarah Harmanee, 'Knife Headpiece', for
Alexander McQueen, Autumn–Winter 1997–8.
Silver-plated brass with photo-etched lace
detail. Photograph courtesy Gavin Fernandes

174 (*below*) Simon Costin, Incubus Necklace,
1987. Copper, baroque pearls, silver, human
sperm and glass. Photograph courtesy Simon
Costin

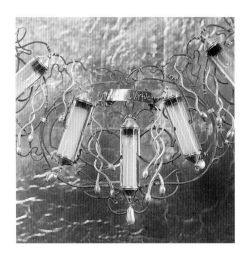

25 Julia Kristeva interviewed by Charles
Penwarden in Stuart Morgan (ed.), *Rites of Passage:
Art at the End of the Century*, Tate Gallery
Publications, London, 1995.

Costin's Incubus Necklace is linked in theme to the work of the New York based artist
Andrès Serrano whose large cibachrome photographic images often drew expressly on
Roman Catholic and Baroque imagery, for all the contemporaneity of their subject matter.
Serrano's imagery included sexual acts, fragments of corpses in the morgue, and body fluids
such as blood, milk and sperm. His *Ejaculation in Trajectory* was made in 1989, two years
after Costin's Incubus Necklace, and flirts similarly with the notions of sex, death and life,
destabilising the boundaries between them. Just as Philippe Ariès and Norbert Elias have
related fourteenth-century *danse macabre* imagery to the plague of that time, so Julia
Kristeva has related the return of images of bodily decay and distress in the late twentieth
century to HIV and AIDS.[25] In the late 1980s images of bodily fluids such as blood and
semen were highly cathectic due to their relation to HIV and AIDS; semen, associated with
pleasure and the beginning of life, was also deathly, toxic, potentially fatal. In the work of
Costin and Serrano it thus connoted both life and death, growth and decay, a contemporary *memento mori* image which was inextricably linked to sexuality, pleasure and danger.

*   *   *

The Armoured Body

When Alexander McQueen drenched his models with 'golden showers' (actually water lit with yellow light) as they came down the catwalk, fashion exemplified the way that trauma was turned into spectacle through the theatrical staging of transgression (fig. 175). In a show sponsored by American Express and art-directed by Simon Costin, McQueen harnessed the idea of the 'money shot' of pornography to fashion promotion; when American Express vetoed the show title Golden Showers he renamed it Untitled, an ironic parody of art titles. McQueen's shows, in common with other London-based designers' shows in the mid-1990s, demonstrated a fascination with artifice, drama, spectacle, transformation and occasionally horror, enacted on and by the figure of the fashion model on the catwalk. Their staging of these events in the artificial space and time of the fashion show suggested a relationship to what Mark Selzer has called 'wound culture'. Selzer has attributed the contemporary American fascination with wounded and traumatised bodies in film, novels and media to a collapse of the difference between public and private registers, as a result of which the public sphere itself became, he argues, 'pathological'.[26] He described the 'deer-in-the-headlights look of the model on the runway' in Donna Karan's Autumn–Winter 1994–5 show in New York as a form of anti-female violence, and posited that fashion and the fashion model are exemplary modes in which 'wound culture' and trauma are staged 'in the pathological public sphere' of contemporary American culture. He connects the repetition of the model's body to the compulsion to repeat of trauma, arguing that this compulsion is evident in the 'toggling between signs and bodies' in contemporary culture, signalled by the 'return of the body' and the 'return of the real' in recent cultural studies:

> For if the toggling between signs and bodies is nowhere clearer than in the rhythms of the fashion industry, this is not to dismiss these claims, but to indicate their contemporary force. The relays between bodies and signs could not be more explicit than in the model body as leading economic indicator (its bioeconomics) and as mass-mediated spectacle (the excitations of the body–machine–image complex). The fashion victim has, beyond that, emerged as something of a model trauma victim. I am referring in part to the traumatized look of the fashion model on the runway.[27]

Selzer understands the fashion show as a relay 'between vulnerably exposed, fetishised, bodies and the witnessing and wounding crowd, between the seduction of public dream spaces and fantasies of violence'.[28] Yet in McQueen's show Untitled, for all its abject connections, the fashion body could also survive pathology and abjection through the very process of reification, armouring itself through clothes, make-up and styling on the catwalk. Unlike the vulnerable art bodies of Cindy Sherman (her late 1990s vomit pictures, for example), McQueen's fashion body is armoured through glamour. This armouring converts it into a fierce fetish, or charm: for if the fetish is an object it is nevertheless a powerful one, like the atropeic Medusa's head. Even where glamour shades into abjection, or oscil-

175 (following page) Alexander McQueen, Untitled, Spring–Summer 1998. Photograph Chris Moore, courtesy Alexander McQueen

176 (page 239) Alexander McQueen, The Hunger, Spring–Summer 1996. Photograph Niall McInerney

26 Seltzer, *Serial Killers*: 254.
27 Ibid: 270–1.
28 Ibid: 271.

177 Transi: recumbent figure at former Abbey of Saint-Vaast, Arras, showing worms feeding on corpse.

lates between attraction and repulsion, between beauty and horror, those contradictions assist the protective charm that makes the Medusa's head a powerful talisman.

Thus in McQueen's collection The Hunger (Spring–Summer 1996) a model wore a clear plastic bustier in which actual worms were sandwiched against her skin (fig. 176). McQueen's polychrome worms have the colour and vermicellated form of intestines, and are not far different in colour from the pink flesh and red satin against which they are set. They are framed by a skin-tight jacket that exemplifies McQueen's razor-sharp cutting, with its exaggerated shoulders and lapels, drawn back like a surgical incision to reveal the model's body beneath the textile skin. His bustier recalls an earlier image from the fifteenth and sixteenth century, the *transi*, a representation of a semi-decomposed corpse in whose intestines worms can be seen to be feeding (fig. 177). The visceral disgust such an image can evoke is at odds with the idealising and aestheticising tendency of mainstream fashion in the late twentieth century. Yet despite its deathly connotations, the aggressive vitality of McQueen's modern *transi* asserts the right of the living to commandeer the iconography of the dead. The jacket may be drawn back like the flesh in a surgical incision, the worms may evoke the grave, but the plastic bustier aggressively frames the model's bare breasts, overlaid with their tracery of worms, and the razor-sharp brooch worn at her groin resembles a whip. If anything, the image gestures towards defilement rather than death. McQueen's *transi* suggests a robust defiance, and a pleasure in defilement and transgression, over and above straightforward horror, or terror. The designer evokes a certain perverse pleasure in bringing together sexuality, death and transgression in an image in which 'disgust . . . bears the imprint of desire'.[29]

This oscillation between opposites is characterised psychoanalytically as splitting. Hal Foster identified it as 'a moral splitting, the paradox of disgust undercut by fascination, or

29   Peter Stallybrass and Allon White, *The Politics and Poetics of Transgression*, Methuen, London, 1986: 191.

of sympathy undercut by sadism; and splitting of the body image, the ecstasy of dispersal rescued by armouring.'[30] For Foster, the modern, or post-modern, self was constituted precisely in and through such repeated splitting in which the self was constantly made and unmade, like Bellmer's doll of the 1930s which formed the theme of McQueen's Poupée collection. And compulsive repetition is also a characteristic of trauma. The oscillation between opposites which Foster identified as typifying the intellectual concerns of artists in the 1990s constituted, he wrote, 'the very riddle of the subject'[31] and – although fashion was the last of Foster's concerns – where better than in the compulsive instability of fashion design and jewellery of the 1990s to locate this riddle?

Instability and Baroque Reason

These images are unstable, swinging between desire and repulsion, and instability is the very characteristic of fashion. As Cecil Beaton wrote in the supposedly staid 1950s, 'Those who live or work or are involved in fashion breathe the air of instability: they are like the Mexican farmer who several years ago discovered a volcano growing in his cornfield.'[32] This instability, which may at times be explosive, means that fashion can never be purely deathly, even when its imagery is at its most sombre, because its meanings are never static. It can shift suddenly from darkness to celebration of the here and now, of youth, beauty and pleasure, and it can oscillate between the two. It is in the nature of fashion to transform everything, a characteristic which Walter Benjamin attributed to Baroque art.[33] Benjamin acknowledged that this trait is not confined to the seventeenth century but argued that it is 'an unambiguous indication of Baroque qualities in later periods.'[34] The late twentieth century could be argued to have been a 'Baroque moment', in the sense that Christine Buci-Glucksmann has identified modern modes of capturing beauty as Baroque. Bryan S. Turner argues that her analysis gives us 'an archaeology of the modern from within':

> Baroque culture was a conservative culture that sought to manipulate the masses through fantastic images, colour and elaborate music . . . just as Baroque culture created the spectacle as a means of suborning mass populations in order to induce them into conformity through pleasure, so the modern world of consumerism can also be seen as a spectacle . . . the culture industry of modern society is thus a new version of the culture industry of the Baroque.'[35]

Thus Baroque instability may be understood as an intrinsic part of the spectacle. It is the emphasis on transformation and the instability of the Baroque image that resonated in late 1990s fashion, as much as its more *grand guignol* imagery. The fashion image, or spectacle, like the Baroque emblem, always signals its opposite and its imagery slips easily from darkness into light and back again. It is like the imagery of Baroque allegory in which, for example, Benjamin argued that a harp becomes an executioner's axe, 'the throne room is

30 Foster, *Return of the Real*: 222.

31 Ibid: 223.

32 Cecil Beaton, *The Glass of Fashion*, Cassell, London, 1954: 330.

33 Walter Benjamin, *The Origin of German Tragic Drama*, trans. John Osborne with an intro. by George Steiner, New Left Books, London, 1977: 229.

34 Ibid: 229–30.

35 Bryan S. Turner, introduction to Buci-Glucksmann, *Baroque Reason*: 22–5.

36 Walter Benjamin, *The Origin of German Tragic Drama*: 231.

transformed into the dungeon, the pleasure chamber into a tomb, the crown into a wreath of bloody cypress.'[36] Likewise, in fashion, bones are transformed into elaborate jewels (Shaun Leane), human hair is made into hats (Dai Rees) and microscopic images of viruses, mouse testicles or rabbit intestines are blown up into decorative floral prints (Suture). The designer Marjan Pejoski's pale pink knitwear in 2000, embellished with delicate beaded and embroidered skulls, drew on the embroidery of Elsa Schiaparelli and the Mexican Day of the Dead to produce imagery that moved beyond *grand guignol* to celebrate 1980s trailer trash as well (fig. 178). Much contemporary fashion imagery and design, like these examples, are saturated with a melancholy awareness of the uncertainty of life, but also suffused with a passionate attachment to material goods, which takes the form of a delight in materials, luxury, artifice and ornamentation and shares the Baroque taste for bizarre and fantastical creations.[37]

The instability of the image is modern too; Buci-Glucksmann has argued that 'to have the corpse inside oneself . . . demolishes the certainty of the subject.'[38] Sims and Mondino's photographs, or Leane and McQueen's catwalk imagery, while harking back to a Baroque aesthetic, are also singularly modern, precisely in the way they locate the corpse at the heart of the self, within fashion. Transforming life into death, light into darkness and pleasure into trauma, and back again, they disrupt the idea that these are fixed and stable antitheses.

As Marshall Berman argued in 1983, modernity depends on sustaining chaos and crisis because change comes from these; so disturbance, far from subverting modern capitalist society, actually strengthens it. Catastrophes are made into lucrative possibilities for redevelopment and renewal and thus 'to say that society is falling apart is only to say that it is alive and well'. The 'modern' person thrives on mobility and renewal.[39] This volatile quality enables modern fashion designers endlessly to transform, 'constantly ringing the changes' on modernity, flipping from the impenetrable fashion body to an open, fissured one, but then turning this imagery back on itself from horror to pleasure. Hence the affiliation of dark glamour to sex and death. If fashion is an embodied practice, as both Lajer-Burcharth and de Certeau suggest,[40] it can work through memory and trauma in the past to re-articulate them as pleasure and sex in the present. Even when such images were evoked through imagery and styling, rather than in actual fashion design and worn clothes, nevertheless it was a memory of the body and fashion as embodied practice that were invoked.

Modernity fundamentally decentres and deracinates the modern subject, Buci-Glucksmann argues, paving the way for new, uncertain identities; thus the alienation tracked in Chapters 7 and 8 can also be reinterpreted as a 'loosening of the self'.[41] Such instability runs like an undercurrent through the work of Dai Rees: his jewelled head piece of 1998 could be a hat, a mask or a piece of jewellery, all three or none (fig. 180). A sheep's pelvis found on the beach is covered with Swarowski crystals. It is worn high on the head, above the face which its mask-like form echoes with two 'eyes'; from it hangs a reticulated veil of silver and crystal beads which does not obscure so much as transform the model's face. If the bones are a *memento mori* the piece is not a simple reminder of death but a transformation of it. First, death transformed the living body of the sheep, then the elements stripped it down to a bleached image of decay which Rees transformed again, into an image of artifice, life, luxury and masquerade. The transformations run from life into death and back into life, from animal to human to other worldly, from degeneration

37 Philippe Ariès, *The Hour of Our Death*, trans. Helen Weaver, Allen Lane, London, 1981: 330.

38 Buci-Glucksmann, *Baroque Reason*: 76 and 103.

39 Marshall Berman, *All That is Solid Melts into Air: The Experience of Modernity*, Verso, London, 1983: 95–6.

40 Ewa Lajer-Burcharth, *Necklines: The Art of Jacques-Louis David after the Terror*, Yale University Press, New Haven and London, 1999: esp. 181–204. Michel de Certeau, *Cultural Practices of Everyday Life*, trans. Stephen Rendall, University of California Press, Berkeley, 1984.

41 Buci-Glucksmann, *Baroque Reason*: 97.

180 (*facing page*) Dai Rees, mask, 1998.
Sheep's pelvis, Czech crystal, Swarovski crystal,
silver. Photograph Mat Collishaw, courtesy
Judith Clark Costume

42 Jennifer Higgie, catalogue essay in *Dai Rees:
Pampilion*, Judith Clark Costume, London, 1998: 15.
43 Benjamin, *The Origin*: 232, where the phrase
is translated as 'a death's head will be an angel's
countenance', and Buck-Morss, *Dialectics of Seeing*:
174, where the phrase is translated as 'a death-skull,
become an angel's face'.

to regeneration, nature to culture, bare bones to masquerade. Like Philip Treacy's unicorn hat for 1994 (fig. 179), through decoration and artifice a woman's head is transformed into something mythic, magical and animal. Rees's crystal mask has the eloquent sadness of the *commedia dell'arte* with its undercurrent of travesty and tragedy, yet it is also sinister and vaguely decadent. Its unexpected transformation turns the sheep's pelvis into an image of a goat's head, with its two horns connoting devil worship and the black mass. It is both veiled and erotic, bridled and suggestive. Jennifer Higgie discusses Rees's transformation of materials as metamorphosis into a magical realm where nothing is quite what it appears to be: 'Like predatory apparitions, Dai Rees' millinery manages to intimate what a merger between the spirit world and the human one might be like.'[42] *Memento mori* imagery may initially show us the skull beneath the skin, but Rees's Baroque process of transformation turns it again into something else: 'a death-skull, become an angel's face'.[43]

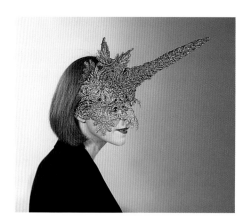

179 Philip Treacy, Spring–Summer 1994.
Photograph Niall McInerney

ten   dereliction

Rags

In the 1980s Rei Kawakubo for Comme des Garçons produced fabrics with flaws in them by loosening a screw here or there on the looms that produced them; she left the same piece of linen out in the sun to dry in a crumpled heap over several days, submitting it to the ravages of the elements; and she produced hand-knitted black sweaters with lacy holes like moth holes. By these means she introduced the idea of patina and ageing into Paris fashion. In the 1990s the aesthetic of *boro boro*, meaning ragged, tattered, worn out or dilapidated, was also developed by the Japanese textile company Nuno. Their textiles were boiled, shredded, dropped in acid or slashed with blades. Comme des Garçons's Autumn–Winter 1994–5 collection used muted colours and threadbare woollens with frayed edges to bundle the models up in their clothes like Balkan refugees from a phantasmic Eastern Europe (fig. 182). For Autumn–Winter 2001–2 the first issue of *Another Magazine* featured a photograph by Richard Burbridge of five models dressed and posed to look like bales of old clothes awaiting collection from a depot (fig. 181). From the late 1980s Martin Margiela cut up and reassembled old clothing to give it a new life and history. Tea dresses of the 1940s were cut in half and spliced together asymmetrically; a 1950s ball gown was cut down the front and worn open as a long waistcoat over a man's singlet and faded jeans; military socks were remade as jumpers (fig. 183). Margiela's 'raw materials' were fashion detritus when he started with them; second-hand or army surplus clothing is the commodity form with the lowest exchange value in the fashion system. Second-hand dress has historically been associated with low economic status and class; long before there was a ready-to-wear industry, the second-hand trade clothed the poor, often in third-, fourth- and fifth-hand clothing. From the eighteenth century, if not earlier, it dealt in 'need and aspiration' and was frequently 'a symbol of poverty and lower class oppression and patronage', not least in the form of an enforced 'gift' from a mistress to her servant, often with the trimmings removed to render the clothes more suitable to the humbler station of their new owner.[1]

Margiela's refabricated rags, however, did the reverse, bestowing on their wearers the cachet recognised only by a discreet, and élite clientele. Like the nineteenth-century rag-picker who gathered scraps for recycling, Margiela converted the low status of second-hand clothing into the high status of a unique fashion piece. Similarly, when he made T-shirts out of plastic carrier bags and waistcoats of broken crockery, he converted urban refuse into something of rare value.[2] Dickens's *Our Mutual Friend* starts with the inheritance of a dust heap and tells the tale of its inheritor, Boffin, the Golden Dustman, who converted rubbish into cash.[3] Margiela's transformations of 'abject' materials in the world of high fashion mark him out as a kind of golden dustman or ragpicker, recalling Baudelaire's analogy between the Parisian ragpicker and the poet in his poem 'Le Vin des chiffonniers' (The Ragpickers' Wine). Like Baudelaire's nineteenth-century poet-ragpicker who, although 'marginal to the industrial process . . . recovered cultural refuse for exchange value', Margiela scavenged and revitalised moribund material and turned rubbish back into

181 (*facing page*) Richard Burbridge, *Another Magazine*, Autumn–Winter, 2001–2. Styling Sabina Schreder. Clothes by Vintage Yves Saint Laurent, Miguel Adrover, As Four, Calvin Klein Jeans, Jill Stuart, Yohji Yamamoto, Plein Sud, Carol Christian Poell, Ralph Lauren, William Reid, Tommy Hilfiger, Vivienne Westwood. Photograph courtesy Richard Burbridge/ Art and Commerce

182 (*below*) Comme des Garçons, Autumn–Winter 1994–5. Photograph courtesy Comme des Garçons

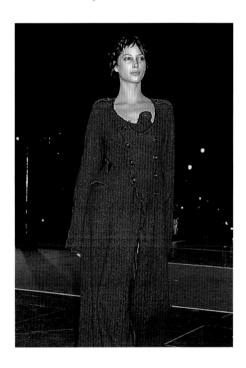

1 Madeleine Ginsburg, 'Rags to Riches: The Second-Hand Clothes Trade 1700–1978', *Costume: Journal of the Costume Society of Great Britain*, 14, 1980: 121 and 128.

2 Purchased by the Museum Boijmans Van Beuningen in Rotterdam on the occasion of Margiela's exhibition there in 1997.

3 The dust heaps that towered over suburban London in the nineteenth century were a lucrative business, often employing a considerable number of people. Stephen Gill suggests that Boffin may be based on the real figure Henry Dodd who owned a dust-yard in Islington and who was said to have given his daughter a wedding present of a single dust heap which afterwards fetched £10,000: see Charles Dickens, *Our Mutual Friend*, ed. with an intro. by Stephen Gill, Penguin, Harmondsworth, 1985 [1864–5]: 898 n. 3.

4   Hal Foster, *Compulsive Beauty*. MIT Press, Cambridge, Mass., and London, 1993: 134–5.

5   Ibid: 269.

6   Karl Marx, 'Economical and Philosophical Manuscripts' [1844], *Early Writings*, trans. Rodney Livingstone and Gregor Benton, Penguin, Harmondsworth, 1975: 292. Karl Marx, 'Review of *Les Conspirateurs* par A. Chenu, and *La Naissance de la république en Février* 1848, par Lucien de la Hodde' [1851] in Karl Marx and Friedrich Engels, *Collected Works*, vol. 10, Lawrence & Wishart, London, 1978: 311–25. Karl Marx, *The Eighteenth Brumaire of Louis Bonapartes* [1852], trans. from the German, Progress Publishers, Moscow, 3rd rev. ed. 1954 [2nd rev. ed. 1869]: 63. Charles Baudelaire, 'Le Vin des chiffonniers' [1851] from *Le Vin* in Charles Baudelaire, *Complete Poems*, trans. Walter Martin, Carcanet, 1997: 272. Peter Quennell (ed.), *Mayhew's London: Being Selections from 'London Labour and the London Poor'* [1851], Spring Books, London, 1964: 306. Dickens, *Our Mutual Friend*. Edmond de Goncourt, *Pages from the Goncourt Journal* [24 September 1870], trans. Robert Baldick, Oxford University Press, 1978. Eric de Maré and Gustave Doré, *The London Doré Saw* [1870], Allen Lane, London, 1973.

For a review of further primary sources and a commentary on Atget's photographs of ragpickers and their milieu see Molly Nesbitt, *Atget's Seven Albums*, Yale University Press, New Haven and London, 1992: 175. For further comments on the nineteenth-century ragpicker see Walter Benjamin, *Charles Baudelaire: A Lyric Poet in the Era of High Capitalism*, trans. Harry Zohn, Verso, London and New York, 1997: 19; Foster, *Compulsive Beauty*: 134; Susan Buck-Morss, 'The Flaneur, the Sandwichman and the Whore: The Politics of Loitering', *New German Critique*, 39, Fall 1986: 99–140; Elizabeth Wilson, *The Sphinx in the City: Urban Life, the Control of Disorder, and Women*, Virago, London, 1991: 54–5.

7   Richard Martin and Harold Koda, 'Analytical Apparel: Deconstruction and Discovery in Contemporary Costume' in *Infra-Apparel*, Metropolitan Museum of Art, New York, 1993: 105.

the commodity form.[4] Thus the connection can be made between cultural practices in a post-industrial period, such as collage, mixing and cut-up, and their early modernist counterparts in the newly industrialised cities of the nineteenth century. As Hal Foster asks, rhetorically, 'are postmodern *pasticheurs* any different from modernist *bricoleurs* in this ambiguous recuperation of cultural materials cast aside by capitalist societies?'[5]

The Autumn–Winter 1992–3 Margiela collection was shown in the Salvation Army sales depot where a discerning fashion clientele sat surrounded on all sides by racks of used clothing destined for thrift shop resale. The analogy between the ragpicker and the poet, artist or designer can be chased into many other urban spaces that Margiela went on to use to pioneer a new form of fashion show. The earliest spaces in which he showed included an old theatre, an area of wasteland, a warehouse corridor, a disused hospital and an empty supermarket. These derelict Parisian spaces echoed the chaos and marginality of the nineteenth-century ragpickers' milieu in the *zone militaire* and beyond the *barrières*, and remind us of the ragpicker's literary provenance in texts and images of urban *dérives* and derelict spaces.[6]

As well as cutting up and reassembling old dresses, Margiela played more complex games when for Spring–Summer 1996 he exactly reproduced the lining of a 1950s cocktail dress as a contemporary dress, and then photographed the original lining of the dress inside out and screenprinted this image onto the new dress (fig. 184). He made dressmaking and couture techniques into design motifs when he designed garments based on the flat pattern pieces that dressmakers store on hangers (see fig. 19) and recreated the tailor's dummy as a linen waistcoat, so that foundation became underwear, the body became the dress (see fig. 18). Over this waistcoat Margiela showed a 'study' for the half front of a draped dress in silk chiffon that would normally be pinned to a Stockman dummy in the course of cutting and sewing the dress. Although Margiela made the chiffon study wearable by fitting it to the waistcoat with corset bones and elastic bands, nevertheless the look was of a garment in progress, and the design gestured to a garment that would remain forever unfinished, like a deconstructed work in progress (fig. 185). In all these collections Margiela questioned the logic and techniques of tailoring, pattern cutting and garment construction that are fetishised in the couture *atelier*.

A similar interest in deconstruction characterised the very different work of Helmut Lang who, from the early 1990s, created complex layers with minimal net T-shirts, often flesh-coloured, a 'poor' aesthetic that transformed the transparency of filmy blouses into structural questioning (fig. 186). Both designers sought, like the philosophical project of deconstruction, to rethink the formal logic of dress itself, which Rei Kawakubo had also achieved in her earliest collections from the 1980s, where skirts might have, for example, a pair of extruded arms to wrap and tie at the back like a bustle. The costume curators Richard Martin and Harold Koda located the origins of these 1990s trends in the 1980s and argued that deconstruction was a 'mode of thought current to our times'.[7] However, in the early to mid-1990s the term 'deconstruction' or *la mode Destroy* was used more loosely by fashion journalists to describe a trend towards frayed hems, recycled fabrics and coming-

183 Martin Margiela, hand-sewn sweater made from military socks, Autumn–Winter 1991–2. Photograph Tatsuya Kitayama, courtesy La Maison Martin Margiela

184 (*below left*) Martin Margiela, Spring–Summer 1996. Photograph Marina Faust, courtesy La Maison Martin Margiela

185 (*below right*) Martin Margiela. Photograph Ronald Stoops, courtesy La Maison Martin Margiela

8 For a summary and contextualisation of these sources see Alison Gill, 'Deconstruction Fashion: The Making of Unfinished, Decomposing and Re-assembled Clothes', *Fashion Theory*, vol. 2, issue 1, March 1998: 25–49.

apart seams.[8] Towards the end of the 1990s this trend gained pace, and the use of vintage fabrics was added to second-hand ones. Olivier Theyskens's first collection featured Edwardian dresses made out of old linen sheets. In London Jessica Ogden used second-hand fabrics, saving their stains, darns and hand-sewn seams to incorporate these vestiges of the past in her contemporary designs (fig. 187). The design company Fake London cut up and recycled cashmere jumpers in jokey pastiche themes; and Russell Sage revamped trademark fabrics like Burberry's in his So Sue Me collection. Viktor & Rolf's first collection in 1993 had featured a ball gown made from old shirts and a dress constructed out of an old jacket and trousers. In Paris in 1993 Junya Watanabe showed ball gowns made out of old football shirts. Viktor & Rolf's tenth collection, shown in Paris in 1998, featured vintage 1960s Chanel and Pucci fabrics.

In New York Susan Cianciolo produced one-offs from vintage fabrics, and for his first collection (Autumn–Winter 2000–1) the New York-based Spanish designer Miguel Adrover presented a 'garbage collection' that recycled, among other things, Quentin Crisp's old mattress. The expatriate British writer who had made his home in New York in old age claimed never to have cleaned his apartment, and that after a period of time the dust simply drifted from the centre to the edges of the room and ceased to bother him.[9] Adrover dredged his own cellar for comparable abject pickings and converted them into darkly elegant high-fashion items on the catwalk. Like a rags-to-riches fable of the American Way, Adrover's New York scraps were recuperated by the very industry that might be expected to reject such abject leavings. As a result of this first show his work came to the attention of influential journalists at American *Vogue* and *Women's Wear Daily* and he was invited to be part of the American luxury goods group Pegasus. His story approximates an American myth of enterprise and success conjured out of nothing; and commercially America constitutes one of the biggest consumer markets in the world, one in which even recycling is an industry. Here again is a trope of the instability of fashion that can as easily convert darkness into light as light into darkness.

For their Autumn-Winter 2000–1 collection, which made the cover of the *New York Times* magazine's fashion issue, Viktor & Rolf acknowledged their anxiety about commercialism by using the Stars and Stripes as fabric. Dedicated to the 'the art of commercial-sell out', it could be seen as a first-strike collection that got the point in before its detractors could. The label Imitation of Christ also showed in New York; the polemical, anti-fashion slogans they inscribed on their one-off productions made from cut up and recycled second-hand clothes rejected arrant consumerism and claimed to occupy an oppositional space outside it. Yet all these designers' work has a relation to the myth of the American Way: Adrover via mainstream American consumption, Cianciolo as art, Imitation of Christ through politics and polemic and Viktor & Rolf through irony. While they could be said to have brought a voguish European aesthetic to New York City, their work also suggested a symbolic context for its success in New York as America teetered on the edge of a major recession.

Patina

The graduation collection of Hussein Chalayan in 1993 called The Tangent Flows incorporated fabric that Chalayan had buried with iron filings in a friend's garden. When it was dug up six weeks later the rusted iron had sunk into and saturated the crevices and folds of the cloth creating a rich patina of golden brown (fig. 188). In 1997 Martin Margiela worked in collaboration with a microbiologist on an exhibition of his work at the Museum Boijmans Van Beuningen in Rotterdam. Margiela recreated in white one outfit from each of the eighteen collections he had designed to date. The clothes were then saturated with agar, a growing medium, and sprayed with green mould, pink yeast or fuchsia or yellow bacteria, and housed in specially constructed greenhouses in the museum's grounds for four days while the moulds and bacteria grew on the clothes. They were then displayed on Stockman dummies in a row along the outside wall of a glass and steel modernist pavilion in the museum, ranged along the external glass wall like melancholy ghosts, their textiles fluttering in the breeze, giving new life to garments that were, paradoxically, reviv-

9 Quentin Crisp, *The Naked Civil Servant*, Fontana, London, 1977.

ified by the deathly process of mould and decay. Benign sentinels in their tattered, second-hand clothes, the eighteen mannequins along the glass wall evoked a ghostly presence that brought the past into the present (fig. 189). Although Margiela's deconstructions often made his clothes look completely modern, in this installation there were curious and unexpected historical resonances. Many of the styles were surprisingly Napoleonic, adding to the ghostly impression of a troop of people from a previous age: a pea jacket, thigh boots, Empire-line dresses (fig. 190 and see fig. 137). A more Victorian connotation was evoked by the 1950s ball gown split down the front: tattered, mouldy, blowing gently in the breeze, it suggested what could have been Miss Haversham's wedding dress given a new and unexpected life (see fig. 21).

When first exhibited in June the garments were still wet and fluffy with new mould; by August the wind and sun had bleached and weathered them, leaving a mottled tracery of decay on their surface, as if they had just been disinterred from a rusty trunk and hung up to air. Spots of mildew, mould and bacteria traced patterns on the two 1940s tea gowns stitched together, a false patina of age grown in a few days on fifty-year-old dresses. In these garments Margiela changed the rules of time, grew something 'old' overnight (the moulds), made something new and modern (the deconstructed dress) out of old things and then layered one on top of the other.

189 Martin Margiela, installation view of the exhibition '9/4/1615', Museum Boijmans Van Beuningen, Rotterdam, 1997. Photograph Caroline Evans

A number of other designers also at the end of the twentieth century began to introduce the theme of patina into their more avant-garde designs. Unlike Galliano or McQueen, there were no obvious historical references in their work. Rather, the theme of decay evoked the passage of time. Grant McCracken has argued that patina and fashion are inimical: in his analysis patina was a signifier of social status until the eighteenth century when it was eclipsed by the consumer revolution that formed the bedrock of the modern fashion system in which status is marked by novelty rather than by the signs of longevity and age. Thus, he states, fashion is the 'terrible rival' of patina.[10] But in the work of a significant minority of designers in the late 1990s the signs of ageing and the idea of a history were replicated in fashion designs that drew on motifs of refuse, detritus, remnants from the past which were transformed in the present.

The London designer Robert Cary-Williams also re-used old garments and transformed them into something new, in particular when he used army surplus clothing and made dresses out of reflective thermal blankets, clingfilm or crumpled foiled, and fishnet aprons with bondage straps, which he accessorised with an army medical truss. But frequently his design process only started with a finished garment and he, like Margiela, gave his garments a history and a life of their own through the very processes of production. Once made, he then took his scissors to them, transforming a recognisable object into a strange one (fig. 191). The final act involved slashing or taking apart a garment, dismembering and deconstructing it. Pattern pieces of latex and leather jackets, dresses and full skirts were cut away to leave only the armature of a garment: seams, cuffs and trailing zips that sketched the ghostly presence of an earlier garment in space. Flesh-coloured leather was soaked, moulded to the body, then baked or shredded before being ruched or plaited into strands.

190 Martin Margiela, Pea jacket, view of the exhibition '9/4/1615', Museum Boijmans Van Beuningen, Rotterdam, 1997. Photograph Caroline Evans

The idea of the fragment or trace inhabited the work of Shelley Fox too. Fox made her own fabrics through the process of ruination: by felting, shrinking, burning and laser-treating textiles she gave her them a patina of decay and age. Leather was sanded-blasted, wool felted and scorched, elastoplast fabric and bandaging were heat-treated and burnt. Gauze and wadding were sprayed with industrial car paint, lambswool and merino burnt with a blow torch, and fine woollen twin-sets were 'sealed' with wax candle drippings (fig. 192).

10 Grant McCracken, *Culture and Consumption: New Approaches to the Symbolic Character of Consumer Goods and Activities*, Indiana University Press, Bloomington and Indianapolis, 1990: 31–43.

Harold Koda has attributed a specific 'poor' aesthetic in conceptual fashion to the Japanese concept of *wabi sabi* in relation to Rei Kawakubo of Comme des Garçons, and the same analysis could be applied to Fox's aesthetic of melancholy and dereliction.[11] In Japan, *wabi sabi* attributes a superior value, based on enlightened recognition, to the flawed artefact and to poor materials. The aesthetic was pioneered by Comme des Garçons in the early 1980s when its first Paris collections were shown on solemn models who walked, swift and unsmiling, up and down the catwalk, their faces bare of make-up or with alienating, misapplied make-up, smudges of eye shadow decorating their cheekbones like a bruise, blotchy lipstick resting on a jawbone as if applied by a child. The clothes, largely grey and black, had shredded seams and extra sleeves that flapped like scarecrows as the models walked.

Fox's wrecked textiles and Cary-Williams's shredded military uniforms, like Margiela's tracery of mould and decay, summoned up the nineteenth-century ragpicker who scavenged cloth for recycling, recuperating cultural detritus cast aside by capitalist societies. His figure permeates these doelful returns to a derelict and run-down past that harks back to the melancholy dereliction that is the obverse of capitalist excess. The idea that there is an element of decay built into capitalist modernity was suggested by Fox who said of her Autumn–Winter 2000 collection:

This collection of clothes has been based around the idea of lack of balance . . . it is modernity not in the purest form but in a state edging on decay . . . often seen in the corrupting and burning of certain fabrics. In this collection I have included sequinned pieces that are not pure but burnt and frayed, the felt is twisted and pressed.[12]

11   Harold Koda, 'Rei Kawakubo and the Aesthetic of Poverty', *Costume: Journal of the Costume Society of America*, 11, 1985: 5–10.

12   Shelley Fox hand-out for 'Fashion in Motion', Victoria & Albert Museum, London, 13 September 2000.

Narrative

Rather than simply configuring images of dereliction, these designers frequently used these motifs to introduce the idea of narrative and history into their clothes. Margiela and Cianciolo described their re-use of second-hand clothing as giving it a new life, as did Ogden whose clothes, made from second-hand fabrics patterned with biography, bore the trace of the past in their stains, darns and hand-sewn seams. She described her garments as if they were sentient, capable of bearing memory traces. Her installation for the fashion shop The Pineal Eye, 'A Dozen Dresses', consisted of twelve dresses in graduated sizes, from 6 inches long to a standard size 12, each dress in between increasing by exactly ten per cent (fig. 193). Although intended to be shown in a line, Ogden also had the idea that they might be displayed inside each other, like a series of Russian dolls, with the light shining through them. She tea-stained the muslin dresses, not to make them look antique but to 'imbue them with feeling'. The graduated dresses might suggest the passage from childhood to adulthood, but the smallest dress could never have been worn by a baby; rather, it was fitted to a doll. The largest was fitted to Ogden herself. The empty forms were ghostly, waiting to be filled, suggesting histories that were either yet to be written or irretrievably lost. Intending to suggest a memory and create a space that had feeling, Ogden resisted over-precise interpretation of this and other pieces, preferring viewers to bring their own histories to bear on the installation.

In his collections Cary-Williams too created a stage setting for the history and the life of a garment:

> My kimono dress is tattered so it will leave pieces behind everywhere it is worn until there is only a little bit left at the top, then it has had its life . . . some pieces will be at a party and others will be at someone's house, like some of the spirit of the garment is left everywhere.[13]

These designs recall the nineteenth-century clothes-makers' and repairers' term for the wrinkles in the elbow of a jacket or a sleeve: 'memories'.[14] As Peter Stallybrass observes, the wrinkles record the body that inhabited the garment, but to the pawnbroker every wrinkle or 'memory' devalued the commodity and, since seventy-five per cent of the goods pawned in the mid-nineteenth century were articles of clothing, 'memories were thus inscribed for the poor within objects that were haunted by loss. For the objects were in a constant state of being-about-to-disappear.'[15]

The sense of melancholy in all these designs recalls the Romantic cult of ruins, for example in Piranesi's prison etchings or the eighteenth-century English vogue for artificially constructed ruins in the grounds of country houses. This sensibility permeated the objects in the 1998–9 'Stealing Beauty' exhibition at London's Institute of Contemporary Arts that showed the work of young designers who made a virtue of the contingency of city life by drawing on its run-down industrial quarters, such as the work of the industrial designer Torde Boontje or the fashion designer Ann Sophie Back. The cult of the past, in

193 Jessica Ogden 'A Dozen Dresses', installation, Pineal Eye, London, 1999. Photograph courtesy Jessica Ogden

13 Robert Cary-Williams interviewed by Lou Winwood, *Sleazenation*, vol. 2, issue 11, December 1998: 22.
14 Peter Stallybrass, 'Marx's Coat', in Patricia Spyer (ed.) *Border Fetishisms: Material Objects in Unstable Spaces*, Routledge, New York, 1998: 196.
15 Ibid.

which objects are imbued with a fragile sense of loss, might perhaps be construed as a response to the rapid onslaught of change and of technological novelty that this carefully hand-crafted type of fashion rejects. Thus the loss that is evoked is the loss of fixedness and stability in the recent past, qualities which are supposedly the enemies of fashion with

its emphasis on perpetual renewal; and this too sets this type of fashion design outside the mainstream. In A. F. Vandervorst's first collection shown in Paris, Autumn–Winter 1998, the melancholy of the Second World War was traced in a collection based on Joseph Beuys's account (which after his death was revealed to be itself a fiction created by the artist) of his wartime experiences of being saved by Tatars who wrapped him in felt and fat, saving his life, when his plane was shot down in the snow over the Soviet Union (fig. 194).

In differing ways, these designers imbued cloth with narrative and memory. By inscribing on them the marks of the past, they gave the clothes a new life, perhaps even a second chance of a better life. But of course the narrative and memory that

saturated the cloth were not real but fictional. There was no real history imbued in these clothes, just a simulated mark or trace of the past. In the work of these designers fashion becomes a space of fiction to create new stories and embroider on old ones. Sontag described in the 1970s the way the collage aesthetic of twentieth-century artists recycled rubbish to make new meaning: 'As Kurt Schwitters and, more recently, Bruce Connor and Ed Keinholz have made brilliant objects, tableaux, environments out of refuse, we now make a history out of our detritus.' She argued that American consciousness is 'built, *ad hoc*, out of scraps and junk. America, that surreal country, is full of found objects. Our junk has become art. Our junk has become history.'[16] Whether this is a specifically American characteristic of twentieth-century culture is debatable; perhaps junk is as much a part of what Sontag called 'the beauties and squalors of the European city' as it is of the American consciousness.[17] Still, Miguel Adrover's first collection demonstrated how junk could be recycled into profit, and his second collection shown in New York (Spring–Summer 2001) made more explicit American references by trawling through recent American history, making a 'tiger's leap' back to the Vietnam War and to hip-hop and rap culture, drawing on a mish-mash of American motifs that included native American and prairie styles as well as urban street culture and baseball references. It featured a strong military look that was influential until the events of 11 September 2001 effectively put an end to the military

16   Susan Sontag, *On Photography*, Penguin, Harmondsworth, 1979: 68–9.

17   Ibid: 69. Among many post-war European artists who have used detritus in their work are Jean Tinguely, Daniel Spoerri and Arman. In 1960 Arman filled the Galérie Iris Clert in Paris with rubbish for his installation 'Le Plein'. Among Arman's many sculptures of consumer goods and domestic rubbish embedded in acrylic, the 'Poubelles' and 'Accumulations', is a plexiglass dummy embedded with dressmakers' objects like buttons, now in the collection of Tate Modern, London.

look that Adrover, like the better-known Marc Jacobs, had shown on the catwalk a year before. The unforeseen 'developer of the future' that Benjamin argued can change the meaning of imagery in the future did its work. Adrover's two collections immediately prior to 11 September took traditional Middle Eastern dress as their theme. In figure 195 three motifs can be seen: worn clothing, the archetypal American Coca Cola logo, and Middle Eastern dress. Adrover all but lost his business after his Spring–Summer 2002 collection was shown in New York on 9 September 2001 as his backer the Leiber Group (formerly Pegasus) sought a buyer for the company. Perhaps appropriately, for a designer whose fortunes went mercurially from rags to riches and back to rags again in only two years, Adrover had claimed 'the American way of life' as his inspiration for Spring–Summer 2001, and Saks on Fifth Avenue had claimed that the collection marked a turning point in 'American street couture'.[18] And these articulations of 'American-ness' were not incompatible with the patriotism invoked in the New York fashion industry that followed a year later in the wake of 11 September 2001.

Speculation

In a world that seemed to many to be rotting and wasting environmentally, a few designers made rotted and wasted clothes, recycling old fabrics and distressing new ones to make them look old and derelict, salvaging junk and converting it into high fashion. This type of experimental work by a small group of niche-market designers seemed to articulate local anxieties that were crystallised in the Kyoto treaty on carbon emissions, which the US government notoriously refused to ratify, and in anti-globalisation protests in, among other places, Seattle (1999), Washington, Quebec and Prague (2000) London (2001 and 2002) and Gothenburg and Genoa (2001). Jessica Ogden, for example, was trained as a fine artist and only came to fashion design through participating in the Oxfam Recycling Scheme. She was one of several small-scale urban designers in London whose production runs, if they existed at all, were tiny; whose collections might consist of as few as seven pieces; and who might work to private commission, selling samples through their studios or exhibiting in experimental spaces.

Just as the anti-globalisation movement was closely linked to anti-capitalism, so too did this type of designer reject the business practices of the large conglomerates in favour of an artisanal way of working. These designers' minuscule production runs existed in a business based on mass production. In terms of orthodox fashion production the craft-based nature of their practice was anachronistic; yet it demonstrated an understanding of the significance of craft techniques in the age of mass production. The garments played with the notion of an urban gothic and a poor aesthetic by looking back at yesterday through the eyes of today. Why else, in an age of mass production and global distribution, would notable young fashion designers so painstakingly revive craft methods? Their artistic approach to craft signalled a complex form of consumer address that more orthodox forms

18   Cited in Hilary Alexander, *Daily Telegraph*, 19 September 2000.

of fashion production could not make. In contrast to high street fashions, these designers' avant-garde fashion designs that recycled old textiles and imbued them with the traces of the past were highly crafted pieces that bore the mark of their maker, like a trace or an evocation.

This aesthetic of ruination made a specific appeal to a discerning customer whose cultural capital allowed them to perceive the added value of these clothes whose avant-garde aesthetic was distinct from the look of shiny newness, luxury and excess of mainstream fashion. As such, this constitutes a distinct, if minority, tradition of international fashion, running from Kawakubo's earliest designs for Comme des Garçons in the 1980s to Margiela in the 1990s. Designs like this appealed to a bohemian notion of poverty as inherently aesthetic in a way that could never be matched by the ostentatious display of wealth. Indeed, Andrew Ross has criticised Margiela for precisely this, that his poor aesthetic was limited to the realm of aesthetics and consumption, without ever addressing the very real issues of exploitation and sweated labour in fashion production to which his work referred.[19]

If in traditional Japanese aesthetics *wabi sabi* attributes a superior value, based on enlightened recognition, to the flawed artefact and to poor materials, in a modern consumer economy the style of *wabi sabi* only becomes valuable when it is used to create a consumer discourse of the avant-garde. Although these clothes were rarely made from luxury fabrics, their cut was often innovative and their production extremely labour-intensive. One garment might have been worked on as intensely as an artist's canvas and have something of the value of the unique piece in an age of mechanical reproduction. Through over-accentuating hand-made methods that could now be achieved with machines, these designers connoted a poor aesthetic, and their symbolic communication through craft addressed a sort of chic that the stylish and the rich could recognise only too well.

When such designers fetishised craft techniques, emphasising the beauty of the flaw and the value of the mark of the hand, they performed a kind of alchemy, not dissimilar to the magical equations Marx worked out between 'a coat and ten yards of linen' in his discussion of commodity fetishism in the nineteenth century.[20] Marx argued that 'The value of a commodity represents nothing but the quantity of labour embodied in it.'[21] And, 'as values, commodities are simply congealed quantities of human labour'.[22] Human labour 'has been accumulated in the coat': the coat 'counts as embodied value, as the body of value'.[23] In these designers' work, the heavily hand-crafted nature of the clothes imbues them with human traces. The burning and scarring motifs of Fox's or the shredded nature of Cary-Williams's carried the association of dereliction in the midst of luxury. These shredded, toasted, scorched, felted and scarred materials bore the trace of the hand, and were sold as luxury goods in specialist shops, a poor aesthetic produced out of hard labour in the East End of London for West End consumption. Emblematic of the extreme nature of such fashion were Cary-Williams's T-shirts on sale in the Hoxton Boutique that had been peppered with lead shot blasted at them through their vinyl packaging.[24]

The alchemy that converts mass-produced cloth into crafted one-off contains resonances from Marx's conversion of the 'ten yards of linen' into first a coat, secondly a form of

19 Andrew Ross (ed.), *No Sweat: Fashion, Free Trade and the Rights of Garment Workers*, Verso, New York and London, 1997.

20 Karl Marx, *Capital*, vol. 1, trans. Ben Fowkes, Penguin, Harmondsworth, 1976: 131–63.

21 Ibid: 136.

22 Ibid: 141.

23 Ibid: 143.

24 I am grateful to Alistair O'Neill for this observation.

embodied labour and then, dizzyingly, its equivalent in tea, coffee, corn and gold.[25] Marx's creative confusion of energy with matter has a material reality in the haywire economy of Cary-Williams's and Fox's production. Yet for all their pre-modern production practices, in their aesthetic these designers can be understood as taking themselves out of history into a pre-industrial past which was, however, commercially connected to a post-industrial present. High fashion, since the nineteenth century, has sought to differentiate itself from mass production and consumption through its use of expensive craft techniques. These give it cultural capital so that fetishised production acquires a symbolic value through a consumer discourse of art. Thus the coat becomes, in Marx's phrase, 'the body of value'.[26] These designers' design and selling stratagems that depended on the hand-crafted made specific sense in the context of the history of the commodity, tied as it is to the history of both craft and mass production. Poverty and riches were rendered proximate in a 'poor' aesthetic that fetishised production, in hand-made clothes in which 'human labour . . . becomes value in its coagulated state'.[27]

There is a paradox inherent in this type of design: however oppositional or experimental it might be, it remains locked, like the foraging of the nineteenth-century ragpicker, into the very capitalist system whose cycles of production and consumption it might be seen to be criticising.[28] If images of decay masked the failure of environmental politics and global protest, one interpretation of this material is that it was a despairing re-enactment of the spoiling of the world's resources through the production of symbolically spoiled clothes. Just as we worry about the world rotting and wasting so our most avant-guard designers and photographers use this imagery in cutting-edge fashion design and images. This type of fashion design makes theatre out of material that spoke to us, reaching parts that most polemicists cannot reach, but only in the realm of the symbolic.

Yet, as Marx wrote, 'in history as in nature, decay is the laboratory of life',[29] and the work of these designers was fertile and creative rather than simply derelict and destitute. The contingency of everyday life was reflected both in their aesthetic and their working methods. Working almost invisibly in the cracks and interstices of the fashion industry, they managed with whatever came to hand in a flawed and fragmented world, turning errors and faults to their advantage. Fox's rippled and scarred wool originated from mishaps in the studio when she left a heat press on too long and accidentally scorched the fabric. The ripples and scars resemble the scarred bodies suggested by the medical themes she researched in the Wellcome Museum of Medicine in London, such as Victorian bandaging techniques, but there was also a healing connotation in her use of muslin and wadding, and her signature felted wool was reminiscent of Beuys's use of felt and fat. Although she burnt white, loom-state elastoplast fabric with a blow torch, she made it up into delicate and ethereal garments. She used bandaging too, but to drape rather than wrap the body, in the metre-wide strips in which it is woven before being cut into ten-centimetre widths for bandages. Similarly, although Cary-Williams's distressed fabric might have violent connotations, particularly when torn, slashed and cut clothes were modelled on the catwalk by young and beautiful women, the results were not inherently violent, only poetic and

25 Marx, *Capital*: 157.
26 Ibid: 142.
27 Ibid.
28 For an analysis of the relation between environmental politics and fashion in the 1990s and a discussion of its ethics see 'Eco' in Rebecca Arnold, *Fashion, Desire and Anxiety: Image and Morality in the Twentieth Century*, I. B. Tauris, London and New York, 2001: 26–31.
29 Karl Marx Cited in Georges Bataille, *Visions of Excess: Selected Writings, 1927–1939*, ed. and trans. Allan Stoekl, University of Minnesota Press, Minneapolis, 1985: 32.

strange. Even where his slashed leather resembled scar tissue Cary-Williams made it delicate and beautiful. Like Fox's, his work was not about deconstruction so much as transfiguration. Apparent deconstruction turned out to be a novel form of enquiry. For Freud, adult creativity is a continuation of childhood play which is, therefore, always creative, even where it appears destructive, because it is an attempt to interpret and understand the world, even to acquire a degree of control over it through 'describing' it.[30] There was an element of the intense curiosity of the child in Fox's exploration of the limits of materials, or Cary-Williams's compulsive taking apart of objects, that produced flawed beauty out of aberration.

30 Sigmund Freud, 'Creative Writers and Day-dreaming' [1908] in *Works: The Standard Edition of the Complete Psychological Works of Sigmund Freud*, under the general editorship of James Strachey, vol. IX, Hogarth Press, London, 1959: 141–53. See too 'Beyond the Pleasure Principle' [1920], vol. XVIII, 1955: 7–64.

eleven   exploration

Telegrams from the Future

If the imagery of rags and bones was dark, it reflected the way in which designers who used that visual language worked in the dark in an uncertain world, trying to map the future without much to guide them. The fashion designer Roland Mouret said: 'In the seventies and eighties we knew the enemy, i.e. the establishment, whereas now it is less tangible. Technology, chaos, genetic engineering, the dystopian worlds of Ballard and Banks, Vonnegut and Branzi? All these things, yes, but also the body itself – AIDS, BSE, hidden cancers, androgyny, genetic engineering, changing notions of sex and sensuality.' And he excoriated commercial fashion for what he called 'the Faust Syndrome', in which fashion sells its integrity: 'if fashion is the mirror which reflects what is taking place in society at present, then it is telling us we are bland, the same, concerned with the surface of things rather than the underbelly. And I think these designers – myself included – are trying to counter this by saying, yes, fashion is a mirror, but this is what is really happening, here is what you should really be seeing, and perhaps that makes us ugly, disturbing, a threat – but if that is the case then all the better. If Faust could see what's in store for him, really in store for him, would he have made the pact he made? I think not.'[1]

Several small-scale London designers in the late 1990s seemed able to articulate current concerns, making themselves artists not just of spectacle but of social comment through dress. Boudicca's inspiration, for example, was drawn from unlikely sources such as the news, death, technology, chaos, genetic engineering, illness and sexuality. An early collection was inspired by genetically misshapen clothing forms, producing beauty from aberration. Instead of an aesthetic of the ugly, however, Boudicca's shattered tailoring, with jacket parts grafted onto coats and dresses, simply redefined the category of the 'normal'. Boudicca's designs were a testament to the idea that life in the modern world is not perfect and that this should be read off the imperfect surface of its fashion imagery. In a story in a 1998 issue of the British magazine *Dazed & Confused*, guest edited by Alexander McQueen and titled 'Fashion Able?', innovative designers collaborated with models with disabilities to produce clothes, some made specifically for individuals (see fig. 138). Photographed by Nick Knight, the story, titled 'ACCESS-ABLE', was not intended to be controversial so much as a 'a joyful celebration of difference'. Opening with the statement that 'in a world where the mainstream concept of what is and isn't beautiful becomes increasingly narrow – you have to be young, you have to be thin, you should preferably be blond and, of course, pale skinned', the story and the collaborations it documented issued a challenge to these preconceptions.[2] A 1997 fashion story in *The Face* magazine by Sean Ellis entitled 'Tissue: A Portfolio of Scars' showed six individualistic looking young people, none of them professional models, who each had a scar (fig. 196). The imagery was glamorous and affirmative; it did not draw on grunge or heroin chic, nor did it connect with the contemporary fashion for body piercing and scarification. In presenting the scar as part of the individual geography of the body, a map of the life, rather than as a disfigurement, the spread underlined how narrow definitions of beauty are in the fashion industry, where

196 *(facing page)* Sean Ellis, Tissue: A Portfolio of Scars, *The Face*, 1997. Styling Mark Anthony. Tomi wears barbed-wire necklace by Agent Provocateur. Photograph courtesy Sean Ellis

1 Roland Mouret quoted in Martin Raymond, 'Clothes with Meaning', *Blueprint*, no. 154, October 1998: 31.
2 *Dazed & Confused*, Alexander McQueen guest editor issue, 'Fashion Able?', no. 46, September 1998: 'ACCESS-ABLE', 68.

197 Comme des Garçons, Dress Becomes
Body Becomes Dress, Spring–Summer 1997.
Photograph courtesy Comme des Garçons

3   Linda Evangelista was reputed to have a long
scar on her left side, the result of a collapsed lung in
the early 1990s: Ruth Picardie, 'Clothes by Design,
Scars by Accident', *The Independent*, Tabloid, 2 May
1997: 8–9.

it is common for the model's body to be subtly altered digitally in its images. For a person
with a scar, however beautiful they are, cannot easily work in fashion.[3]

Comme des Garçons's Spring–Summer collection of 1997, called Dress Becomes Body,
consisted of long, fitted dresses in stretch fabrics, some in red, white or black, others in a
range of ginghams: black, pale blue, pink or red and white. They were padded, with goose-
down pads arranged asymmetrically to run over a shoulder, diagonally across a hip, down
the back, or coil round the torso to form half-bustles, raised necks or prominent backs
(fig. 197). The curator Richard Martin described the look of the 1997 Comme collection

as one of 'perturbed beauty'. The shop assistants at the Comme retail outlet in New York reputedly called them 'tumor pieces' between themselves, while fashion journalists made Quasimodo references in articles called 'Like It Or Lump It' and 'Padded Sell'.[4] Yet in this collection Kawakubo did seem able to rethink the body. If industrialisation inevitably produces a traumatised body, Kawakubo valiantly tried to re-see that body from another perspective, to invent it from scratch and to envisage multiple possibilities for such a body, fashioning fabulous creatures on the catwalk, fashion itself being the 'enchanting spectacle' of signs.[5] 'Creature' and 'creativity' have the same etymological root; the Latin noun *creatura*, a creature, is 'a thing created'.[6] The padded designs from this collection, each of which was a variation on a theme, could be seen as speculative prototypes, or an experiment in rethinking the human creature. Kawakubo, in her 'thought laboratory', set up this experiment by refashioning the relationship between subject and object, between body and dress and between human flesh and soft, goose-down pads. In these fabulous creatures the boundaries between body and dress were blurred, and subject and object, or self and other, were no longer posited as mutually exclusive terms.

The Comme press release for the collection stated: 'the theme . . . is body meets dress, body becomes dress, dress becomes body.' In the nineteenth century bodies became dress via the corset; in the twentieth, cosmetics 'became body' in the form of liposuction and cosmetic surgery. The 'post-industrial' body was further reconfigured by the technology of the 1980s: the personal computer, the Sony Walkman, portable telephones, soft contact lenses. These 'harmless devices' contributed to a new body, 'one thoroughly invaded and colonised by invisible technologies'.[7] The question, therefore, was not whether the wearer was a subject or an object in Comme des Garçons's padded collection, but what kind of a new subject, or future subject, she might be. It was not so much that the new technologies forced a reconsideration of the relationship between body and identity; rather, they had already invisibly extended the parameters of the body and, it follows, of consciousness. One could speculate that Comme's padded extensions, which 'morphed' the body into new forms, were simply a series of poetic speculations on the theme of embodiment in the modern age. They began to sketch new possibilities of subjecthood, a subjecthood which was not concerned with containing the body but with extending it, via new networks and new communications. Perhaps the best way to regard Comme's designs is as an exploration, an early foray into space, or a probe.

Both as designers and businessmen and women, fashion designers are always, in their heads at least, sending out probes, prospecting in the future while they echo the concerns of the present. They are trained to think ahead, and the production schedules of their business require it. Walter Benjamin's fanciful suggestion that fashion can foretell the future as a way of describing its drive to perpetual alteration and renewal,[8] also describes the way that designers project themselves forward in time. Writing about new London designers, photographers, stylists and retail outlets in 1998, the journalist Martin Raymond quoted Deidre Crowley who argued that they had created a kind of science fiction in their work, 'a narrative not of the now but of the future'. Crowley developed the theme to argue that

4   See Caroline Evans, '"Dress Becomes Body Becomes Dress": Are you an object or a subject? Comme des Garçons and self-fashioning', *032c*, 4th issue, 'Instability', Berlin, October 2002: 82–7.

5   'Fashion, or the Enchanting Spectacle of the Code' in Jean Baudrillard, *Symbolic Exchange and Death*, trans. Iain Hamilton Grant, Sage, London, Thousand Oaks and New Delhi, 1993 [1976]: 87–100.

6   Oxford English Dictionary.

7   Tiziana Terranova, 'Posthuman Unbounded: Artificial Evolution and High-tech Subcultures', in George Robertson *et al* (eds), *FutureNatural: Nature, Science, Culture*, Routledge, London and New York, 1996: 166.

8   Walter Benjamin, *The Arcades Project,* trans. Howard Eiland and Kevin McLaughlin, Belknap Press of Harvard University Press, Cambridge, Mass., and London, 1999: 63–4.

'you should think of their garments as one-line concepts, their collections as telegrams from the future; telegrams that refer to things other than fashions and trends.'[9]

Monuments to Ideas

Hussein Chalayan explored ideas about nature, culture and technology, often drawing on themes of nomadism, exile and alienation in the process. In three consecutive collections between 1999 and 2000, he developed one concept through three dresses made by the industrial designer Paul Topen using technology from the aircraft industry, out of a composite material created from glass fibre and resin cast in specially designed moulds.[10] Chalayan described them as 'monuments' not because of their rigid form but because they were 'monuments to ideas', as opposed to other pieces in the collections that expressed the same idea in a much more diluted, and wearable, form.[11] These monumental dresses were mirrored, or repeated, with subtle differences in a series of equivalents in cloth that followed them a little later onto the catwalk like an echo. The hard resin dresses were a blueprint for a set of experiments and comments in cloth, experiments which in some cases Chalayan also conducted in film and computer animations.

For Geotropics (Spring–Summer 1999) Chalayan started with ideas about the meaning of a nation, linking the concepts of nature, culture, nationalism, expansion and disputes over boundaries. He also explored the idea of an itinerant existence, in the idea of carrying a chair with you that you can sit on wherever you are (figs 198 and 199). This collection featured the first resin dress, in the same greenish grey as the chair dress, fastened with

9   Raymond, 'Clothes with Meaning': 28.

10   Chalayan made a fourth resin dress that was not part of a specific collection, and not intended to be worn by a fashion model. Instead, it was a remote-control dress commissioned by the curator Judith Clark for the 'Mind' section of London's Millennium Dome, designed by the architect Zaha Hadid. The dress never went into the Dome but was exhibited at Judith Clark Costume. Made of pale green resin with a stand, it could be controlled from the floor and moved around the room on its own.

11   Melissa Starker, 'Chalayan UNDRESSED', Columbus Alive, 25 April 2002.

198 and 199   Hussein Chalayan, Geotropics, Spring–Summer 1999. Photograph Chris Moore, courtesy Hussein Chalayan

chrome catches made for the motor industry. It was bigger than the model, with an off-centre slit and subtly asymmetrical shell that created a cavity around her body as she walked, suggesting a protective cocoon.[12] Its form was echoed on the catwalk a short while later, first by a white cloth dress and then a black one.

Behind Echoform (Autumn–Winter 1999–2000) lay Chalayan's premise that everything we do is an external vision of the body. He looked at the body's natural capacity for speed and the way it can be enhanced by technology, focusing on ergonomics and the interior design of cars (fig. 200). Moving on to flight, his second resin dress, in white, the Aeroplane Dress, contained a concealed battery, gears and wheels that were activated by a tiny internal switch operated by the model on the catwalk. Like the moving flaps of aeroplane technology, the section at the waist slid down and a side flap came up as the flap under the chin moved horizontally across. This dress, like the first one, was shadowed later on the catwalk by others in soft olive cloth that echoed its form.

In collaboration with Chalayan, Marcus Tomlinson made a film of the dress (fig. 201) that was first shown at the Hyères festival in France in May 1999.[13] In the film the panels of the dress slid open and shut as the model spun round like a mechanical top, at first slowly and then gathering speed, before slowing down and coming to rest again, her rate of acceleration and deceleration mimicking the experience of aeroplanes taking off and coming in to land. The film was accompanied by an atmospheric soundtrack of a muezzin's call to prayer combined with the sound of a propellor building up speed, a soundtrack that combined the 'no place' of airports and jet travel with the specificity of older cultural forms. Chalayan, who grew up in Northern Cyprus where the muezzin played all the time, and found the sound of the call to prayer both beautiful and 'slightly scary',[14] was struck by the combination of a threatening image with a beautiful thing in the background. Made at a time when, as the designer was aware, parts of Iraq were being bombed by Western planes enforcing the 'No Fly Zones' in the north and the south, Chalayan's soundtrack gestured beyond fashion to subjects it normally eschews.

The third monumental dress also had moving parts but was operated by remote control rather than a battery and switch inside the dress. Cast in pink, its rear section and side flaps opened to reveal a mass of frothy pink tulle below. It was shown in Chalayan's Before Minus Now collection (Spring–Summer 2000), staged on a Constructivist white set in London's Sadler's Wells Theatre. The collection was based on the idea of using 'the intangible as a means to create form.'[15] The intangible forces included gravity, expanding forces, the weather, technological forces and wave and wind detecting objects. A vermilion dress had an electrically wired hem with a 'memory' so that, once the current was passed through it, its skirts spread and lifted, seeming to hang in the air against the force of gravity. The show invitation contained a photograph with the absurd image of a small boy in a yellow T-shirt trying to control a jet plane flying overhead with his remote control (fig. 202). The show programme contained an even more absurd proposition: a photograph of the same boy at the edge of a lake fringed with reeds trying to control a swan on the water (fig. 203). When, in the course of the show, the same boy in a yellow T-shirt walked across

200 Hussein Chalayan, Echoform, Autumn–Winter 1999–2000. Photograph Chris Moore, courtesy Hussein Chalayan

12 Bradley Quinn suggests Chalayan's hard resin dresses evoke the protective shells of snails and crustaceans, and cites Gaston Bachelard's 'inhabited shells . . . that invite daydreams of refuge' in Bradley Quinn, *Techno Fashion*, Berg, Oxford and New York, 2002: 30.

13 The film was also shown in London at the Atlantis Gallery and in New York at the Anchorage, under Brooklyn Bridge.

14 Hussein Chalayan, lecture at the Wexner Centre, Ohio, 25 April 2002

15 Hussein Chalayan, 'On Recent Works', lecture given at the Architectural Association, London, 27 November 2000.

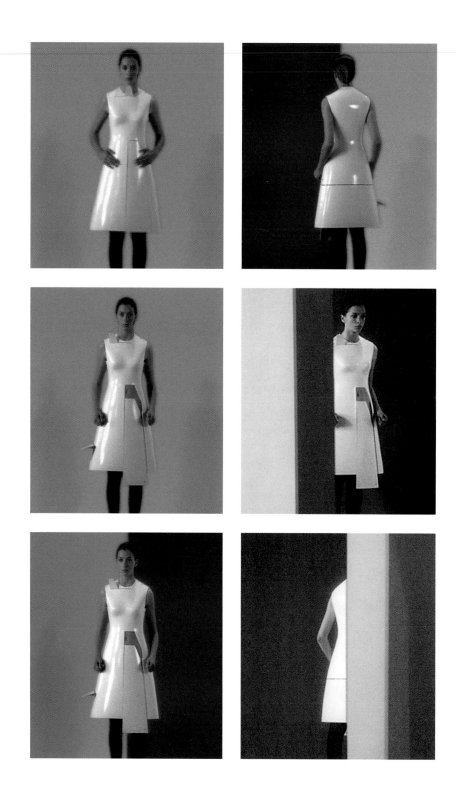

201   Marcus Tomlinson, film of Hussein
Chalayan's Aeroplane Dress, 1999. Film
stills courtesy Marcus Tomlinson

202 (*far left*) Hussein Chalayan, invitation for Before Minus Now, Spring–Summer 2000. Photograph Marcus Tomlinson, courtesy Hussein Chalayan

203 Hussein Chalayan, programme for Before Minus Now, Spring–Summer 2000. Photograph Marcus Tomlinson, courtesy Hussein Chalayan

the stage with his remote control in front of a row of five models in white shifts printed with architectural wire-frame drawings, it suggested that he might believe it possible to operate a human being with his remote control. The boy returned when a model in the pink resin dress came on stage and, to the sound of a solo violinist accompanying the solo pianist who had played until that moment, the boy again operated his remote control and this time the panels of the model's dress rose serenely (fig. 204). The juxtaposition of aeroplane and swan came together in the one garment on the catwalk: when the dress, whose rigid hem dipped at the front, opened its aeronautical side and back flaps to reveal the tulle below it became swan-shaped, the frothy tulle standing up like a raised swan's wing.

These images of the boy in the yellow T-shirt with the remote control posited the futility of the idea of human mastery over either nature or technological modernity. The

204 Hussein Chalayan, remote control dress, Spring–Summer 2000. Photograph Niall McInerney

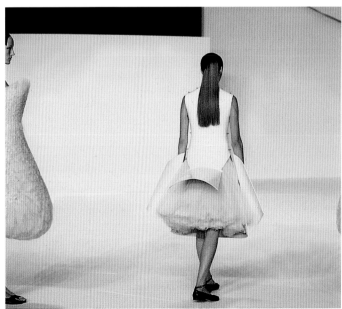

absurdity of his being able to control a jumbo jet, a swan or a living woman suggested some equivalence between all three, which evoked an uneasy relation of nature, technology and alienation. As the flaps closed on both the frothy tulle and the soft flesh of the model, nature was again contained inside the machine and the dress reverted to its aerodynamic appearance and once more became a kind of Cartesian machine, or container for the person. A similar polarisation was suggested by the chair dress (see figs 198 and 199). On the one hand the flesh-coloured underwear and the model's bandaged head reinforced the idea of her human vulnerability and near-nudity. On the other, the hard carapace of the neck and arm rest suggested the modernism of hard-edged precision engineering. The contrast between frail humanity and rigid technology emphasised the difference between organic and inorganic, recalling the historical image of the woman as a kind of 'mechanical-commodified' doll or robot, (as explored in Chapter 7).[16] All three aerodynamic dresses were shadowed by images of nature and the organic world. This fusion of human flesh and hard mechanical form evokes again the reversals of commodity fetishism where 'people and things trade semblances: social relations take on the fantastic form of a relation between things . . . and the commodity becomes our uncanny double, ever more vital as we are ever more inert.[17]

Bradley Quinn has written that the 'aeroplane dress', whose panels slide open to reveal the model's navel, 'suggests technologised sexualisation of the body. It reveals and conceals erogenous zones while also equipping and manipulating the body to conform [to] ideals of sex appeal.'[18] But the hard shell that contains the soft human flesh of the model also suggests the reified surfaces of the dolls and dummies of consumer display whose appearance conflates sexual and commodity fetishism. Marcus Tomlinson's film of the aeroplane dress suggested a hard, technologised body shell in an uncanny fusion whereby a woman came to resemble an aeroplane, a great emblem of modernist progress in engineering and technology. The idea of the mechanised human body suggests the uncanny switching between human and machine of modern industrial production. Hal Foster has argued that whereas the earliest machines were thought of as tools in the service of humankind, as industrial production grew apace people became the slaves rather than the controllers of the machine:

> As the worker resembles the machine, it begins to dominate him and he becomes its tool, its prosthetic. The modern machine thus emerges not only as an uncanny double but as a demonic master. Like the commodity, it is uncanny both because it assumes our human vitality and because we take on its deathly facticity. Both machine and commodity thus draw out human labour and will, animation and autonomy, and return them in alien forms, as independent beings; both are thus other yet not other, strange yet familiar – 'dead labour' come back to dominate the living.[19]

Whereas early twentieth-century modernism effaced history in its revolutionary pursuit of the new, at the end of the century it was possible to glimpse the ghosts of modernity in Chalayan's thoughtful and poetical modernism. If we overlay his experimental forms

16   On the 'mechanical-commodified', the mannequin and the automaton see Hal Foster, *Compulsive Beauty*, MIT Press, Cambridge, Mass., and London, 1993: 126 ff.
17   Ibid: 129.
18   Quinn, *Techno Fashion*: 51.
19   Foster, *Compulsive Beauty*: 129.

with shadows from a previous moment of commodity culture we can see traces of earlier reified, technologised and fetishised bodies. Chalayan took the tropes of modernist progress (travel, technology, aerodynamics) and inflected them with modernist trauma (alienation, reification and the uncanny). The model in his aeroplane dress was generic, robotic, and mechanical in her gestures. His eloquent technological modernity was haunted by the ghosts of commodity fetishism and modernist alienation. At the same time, he made modernist design complex, by patterning it with echoes and whispers – of soft dresses mimicking hard ones, of morphs in time and space, of correspondences between virtual and real environments. Thus while his work was abstract and pure in formal terms, it was also complex and nuanced in terms of its suggestive possibilities, shadowed by history and time. It raised the question of how a late twentieth-century designer might draw on the aesthetics and language of early twentieth-century modernism, even though the historical conditions that gave rise to the early optimism and utopianism of modernism were long gone, without falling back on a contemporary sense of cynicism and ennui or on millenarian visions of apocalypse.

New Technology

Some designers explored the possibilities of new textiles technology. Whereas Shelley Fox used labour-intensive and pre-industrial craft techniques in her treatment of felting, many designers such as Issey Miyake reversed this process, using advanced textile technology to create fabrics that looked labour-intensive as well as innovative, such as holographic cloth.[20] Miyake developed his A-POC concept in collaboration with the textile engineer Dai Fujiwara, which was first produced in 1999.[21] Short for 'a piece of cloth', the A-POC was a bolt of cloth in bright green, scarlet, white or navy from which the purchaser could construct their own wardrobe. Constructed from raschel-knit tubes produced from computer-programmed industrial knitting machines, the fabric did not require stitching when cut. The A-POC was patterned with a series of serrations, rather like the lines on a traditional paper pattern. The owners chose from a range of possible garments and cut out and constructed their own garment. The options included a dress, either full or three-quarter length, with either short or three-quarter length sleeves, or sleeves that extended into mittens; a shirt and top, a hood, a drawstring bag, a purse, knickers, socks, a bra and a water bottle holder. The date the A-POC was made and the instructions were woven into the cloth, including a tiny pair of scissors that indicated where to cut. Once cut, the unsewn edge had tufted fringing which became a decorative motif.

Fashion and textile design that was driven by the possibilities of new technological processes recalled the way that modernist designers earlier in the century experimented with utopian ideas, speculatively mapping the future through imagined technological Utopias, resolutely turning their back on the past. By the end of the century, however, for a designer to fetishise technological progress and novelty suggested a double ghosting; a

20 Amy de la Haye, 'A Dress is no longer a Little, Flat, Closed Thing: Issey Miyake, Rei Kawakubo, Yohji Yamamoto and Junya Watanabe', in Claire Wilcox (ed.), *Radical Fashion*, Victoria & Albert Publications, London, 2001: 32. See too Sarah E. Braddock and Marie O'Mahony, *TechnoTextiles: Revolutionary Fabrics for Fashion and Design*, Thames & Hudson, London, 1998.
21 De la Haye in Wilcox, *Radical Fashion*: 34. And see M. Kries and A von Vegesack (eds), *A-POC making: Issey Miyake & Dai Fujiwara*, Vitra Design Museum, Weil am Rhein, 2001.

205 Yohji Yamamoto, secret dress, Spring–Summer 1999. Photographs Niall McInerney

return to heroic modernism that refused the sedimentation of history, seeking to expunge the insistent past-in-the present of modernity.

This denial haunted the work of a range of designers who explored the possibilties of new technology or new types of clothing. Some designers, however, eschewed such a strictly technologically determinist aesthetic and instead played on the contradictions between an old- and new-fashioned look. Yohji Yamamoto's Spring–Summer 1999 collection was inspired by the crinoline, but the hooped skirts came with pockets that carried different accessories for different occasions (fig. 205). For all that they seemed to evoke the ghosts of modernity, Yamamoto inventively used the construction of the crinoline, rather than playing with it as surface decoration, to imagine new uses for historical costume. Junya Watanabe's Spring–Summer 2000 collection called Function and Practicality made an ironic play on the modernist rubric that form follows function because it featured ostensibly impractical ruffled party dresses made in smart fabric that became waterproof on contact with liquid. As the models paraded on the catwalk artificial rain showered them from above (fig. 206). Although the collection used the sort of new textile technology that many i-wear (intelligent wear) designers were interested in, the aesthetic was widely different from the hoods and pollution masks and the defensive urban camouflage that echoed the muted colours of the city streets of much i-wear.[22] Watanabe's designs eschewed the modernist aesthetic in which garments are engineered to suit a purpose; rather, he combined ideas and functions poetically to make a waterproof dress decorative, elegant and frilly, more Audrey Hepburn that urban warrior – indicating, perhaps, a way out of the impasse of modernist design aesthetics that continued to fetishise the new.

22   Andrew Bolton, *The Supermodern Wardrobe*, Victori & Albert Museum, London, 2002, and Quinn, *Techno Fashion*. Both document and comment in different ways on the engagement of late twentieth-century designers with new technology. The term i-wear designates clothing with information technology embedded in it, such as Levi's ICD+ range. It was coined by Walter de Brouwer who used it to describe prototype garments designed in collaboration with Walter van Beirendonck in the Belgian research laboratory Starlab (1996–2001). See Quinn, *Techno Fashion* 100–6.

206 Junya Watanabe, Function and Practicality, Spring–Summer 2000. Photograph J. François Jose, courtesy Junya Watanabe

The Spring–Summer 2001 collection by Watanabe was called Digital Modern Lighting for the Future. Watanabe sent plain white clothes onto the catwalk that began to glow in vibrant colours as the lights dimmed (fig. 207). Made from naturally glowing powdered minerals pressed onto the surface of the fabric, the aesthetic was high-tech and modern due to the clean cuts and vibrant colours of the collection. The inspiration came from the glow of digital machinery. However, the collection's title was misleading in that the production did not rely on any radical technological processes; unlike the previous collection that had used new technology but made it look decorative, this collection looked high-tech but was actually based on craft. Watanabe described his clothes as 'techno couture'[23] but they were, like conventional couture garments, painstakingly produced, the hand-made nature of the materials making them extremely expensive and the crushed minerals evoking the decorative trimmings and beads of historical haute couture.

23 Junya Watanabe quoted in de la Haye in Wilcox, *Radical Fashion*: 37.

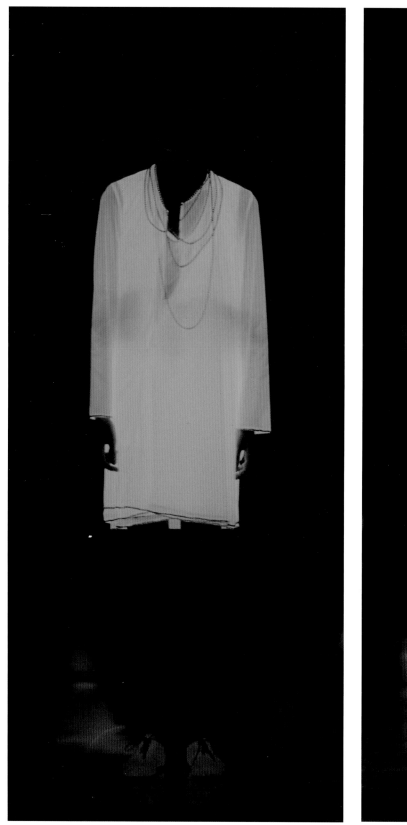

208 (*above*)   Simon Thorogood, with Spore, 'White Noise', installation at Atlantis Gallery, London, February 1998. Photograph Timothy John, courtesy Simon Thorogood

207 (*facing page*)   Junya Watanabe, Digital Modern Lighting for the Future, Spring–Summer 2001. Photographs J. François Jose, courtesy Junya Watanabe

Simon Thorogood showed his poetical exploration of redundant technology as a mixed media installation for his first 'couture' collection in February 1998, entitled White Noise (fig. 208). He chose the form of a dialogue with adjacent areas of culture, collaborating with the digital art group Spore and the electronic music duo Barbed. In a cavernous and dimly lit late Victorian music hall in Brick Lane in London's East End, shop mannequins in duchesse silk of aeronautical greys inset with brightly coloured panels were suspended by wires from the ceiling a foot above the floor. The stiffness of the silk evoked the formality of seventeenth-century Spanish court dress, but the contemporary cut and the insertion of coloured panels into the garments recalled the futuristic aesthetic of television space adventure series. This impression was augmented by the mannequins, a range by Adel Rootstein called 'woman' which Thorogood chose because they approximated a generic woman rather than imposing another style or period on his designs. Presented without wigs or make-up, the unsmiling pure white figures with downcast eyes seemed android. The influence of early 1960s computer graphics and stealth aircraft technology – an evocative and melancholic nod to the old-fashioned look of recent culture – was echoed in the surrounding installation. Spore's contribution consisted of 40 'vintage' Apple Mac computers (SE30s and ClassicIIs, machines from the 1980s which had already become 'techno-junk') arranged round the room. Spore exploited their minimal memory and, by contemporary standards, slow processing speeds and low resolution, and programmed them to produce a series of random images which mimicked the chance procedures exploited in musical composition in the 1960s and 70s by experimental musicians such as John Cage and Brian Eno.

The installation as a whole composed a melancholy elegy to dead technology, in which the computer screens' flickering and fuzzy images, without definition or colour, mirrored the grey silk clothes of the suspended mannequins which revolved slowly in the aural landscape of sampled electronic sounds. Thus the link between fashion and technology was articulated poetically, not as an up-to-the-minute, state of the art, hyper-modern use of digital imagery but, rather, to acknowledge the spectre at the heart of the spectacle, and the role of history nestling in the heart of the 'now'. As Guy Debord wrote, 'history itself haunts modern society like a spectre'.[24] For Walter Benjamin, too, the angel of history looks backwards rather than forwards, contemplating destruction rather than progress. Thorogood's and Spore's use of redundant technology in their installation was melancholy and thoughtful rather than breezily optimistic. Its vision of future fashion also looked backwards, tracing links between the history of computing and of the textiles industry. The binary punch card of the early nineteenth-century Jacquard loom inspired Babbage,[25] and these binary threads were exploited by Spore's computer programmes, which wove random texts in an asynchronous cycle as the gently and unevenly revolving mannequins looked down with solemn eyes.

*   *   *

24   Guy Debord, *Society of the Spectacle*, trans. Donald Nicholson-Smith, Zone Books, London, 1994 [1967]: para. 200.

25   Sadie Plant, *Zeros and Ones: Digital Women and the New Technoculture*, Fourth Estate, London, 1997.

Scripting the Self

The ghosts of modernity haunted this installation, just as they haunted Chalayan's aircraft dresses and indeed his entire aesthetic, yet they also granted these designers a certain freedom of imagination. Because we are alienated and unrecognised we have the freedom to reinvent ourselves: in these designs alienation can begin to be interpreted as a 'loosening of the self'.[26] When Chalayan repeated a design motif, like a set of musical variations, he posited a series of experiments in constructing the self. The plane technology was about engineering, and suggested that perhaps it is not only the dress but also the self that can be engineered, fine-tuned, technologically adjusted and played with. In her introduction to Benjamin's *One Way Street* Susan Sontag wrote that 'the self is a text . . . a project, something to be built.'[27] To paraphrase Sontag, fashion designers, photographers and stylists 'spatialise' the world, expressing ideas and experiences not as narrative but as spatial stories and ruins.[28] Thus while the spectacle of fashion veils commercial transactions at the same time it can be a blueprint for the design of the self. The 'story' of fashion is just one of the many stories in which we map our relation to others and tell ourselves our own stories: as Mark Poster has argued, 'in an increasingly hyper-aestheticised everyday life it is through various fictions that we endeavour to come to know ourselves'.[29]

Christopher Lasch argued that global risks are so huge that we no longer imagine we can combat or diminish them and, since we cannot control the global environment, we retreat to the control of the self, through therapy, diet and other forms of self improvement.[30] In Foucault's words, 'man is an invention of recent date, and one perhaps nearing its end.'[31] But if we are nearing our end, we are endlessly capable of reinventing ourselves in the present, not least through self-fashioning. Anthony Giddens has identified this 'reflexivity' as intrinsic to modernity: 'the altered self has to be explored and constructed as part of a reflexive process of connecting personal and social change.'[32] He cites the role of self-help manuals and therapeutic guides in the making of modern identity as something self-conscious and critical, something to be forged.[33] Dress and appearance too are central elements of the reflexive project of the self[34] and while fashion in the 1990s was haunted by a particular historical imagination it was also concerned to picture the future in the present. Some designers, instead of endlessly revisiting the past, either nostalgically or through dark and alienated images of Victoriana, mapped out a new language of design for the modern world. This categorical refusal of nostalgia or any of the themes of the past is invoked in Viktor & Rolf's phrase 'anti-memory'. Their notes for their second couture collection in 1998 read like a parody of Marinetti's First Futurist Manifesto of 1909: 'this is the high couture of anti-memory. Couture without any limits of form – all nostalgia pulverised . . . styles' acid rain destroying all forms of nostalgia, to put an end once and for all to this waning century.'[35]

The phrase 'anti-memory' is surely a temporal equivalent of the idea of 'anti-matter' in the physical world. If the splitting of the atom threatens to blow up the world, Michel Houellebecq has implied that we already live in an atomised society as family and com-

26 Christine Buci-Glucksmann, *Baroque Reason: The Aesthetics of Modernity*, trans. Patrick Camiller, Sage, London, Thousand Oaks and New Delhi, 1994:1.

27 Susan Sontag, intro. to Walter Benjamin, *One Way Street and Other Writings*, trans. Edmund Jephcott and Kingsley Shorter, Verso, London, 1985: 14.

28 Ibid: 15.

29 Mark Poster, 'Postmodern Virtualities', in Mike Featherstone and Roger Burrows (eds), *Cyberspace/Cyberbodies/Cyberpunk*, Sage, London, Thousand Oaks and New Delhi, 1995: 13.

30 Christopher Lasch, *Culture of Narcissism: American Life in an Age of Diminishing Expectations*, Abacus, London, 1980.

31 Michel Foucault cited in C. Springer, *Electronic Eros: Bodies and Desire in the Post Industrial Age*, Athlone Press, London, 1996: 79.

32 Anthony Giddens, *Modernity and Self-Identity: Self and Society in the Late Modern Age*, Polity Press, Cambridge, 1991: 33.

33 Ibid: 2.

34 Ibid: 100.

35 Viktor & Rolf show notes cited in Tamsin Blanchard, 'Haute New Things', *The Independent Magazine*, 1 August 1998: 22.

munity fragment.[36] Yet as older forms of community are threatened, new forms of community are forged. In the 1970s Daniel Bell argued that in a post-industrial age reality itself would have to be rethought; since then developments in information technology and changing patterns of work and leisure made that task even more pressing. Bell wrote:

> In the salient experience of work, men live more and more outside nature, and less and less with machinery and things; they live with, and encounter, only one another . . . In the daily round of work, man no longer confronts nature, either as alien or benificient, and few handle artefacts and things . . . in post-industrial society, men know only one another, and have to 'love one another or die.' Reality is not 'out there', where man stands 'alone and afraid in a world [he] never made'. Reality is now itself problematic and to be remade.[37]

Bell drew a line between the reified, fetishised world of industrial production and the post-industrial age:

> For most of human history reality was nature . . . in the last 150 years reality has been technics, tools and things made by men, yet with an independent existence, outside men, in a reified world. Now reality is becoming only the social world, excluding nature and things, and experienced primarily through the reciprocal consciousness of others, rather than some external reality.[38]

In imagining social life as unmediated, Bell failed to take into account the way computers would simply become the tools of the future. Today we engage with the technics of texting and e-mailing, for example, and these things structure our social reality. It seems that 'things' inhere in Western culture and we are reluctant to let go of them. However, Bell was right too in that these new forms have a profound impact on the social world and on 'reciprocal consciousness'. New technology has redefined what human community might be, so that to be networked could be more important than being grounded in space and time.

Nomadism

For the British designer Julian Roberts, the process of fashion design itself began to exclude the material object – in the sense of a designed collection – in favour of a series of conceptual pieces on the nature of fashion. Roberts's first design label was called 'nothing nothing' and for his first two shows in 1998 he simply launched invitations to non-existent shows. Yet Roberts, who planned to write a book called 'Pattern Cutting and Short Stories', invested an almost painful quantity of emotion in the processes of pattern cutting and garment construction. He communicated his clothing through video, drawing and text, postulating clothing as an object of imagination that has to be dreamt up and somehow brought to life, on the basis that the pleasure of thinking and making clothes

36   Michel Houellebecq, *Atomised,* trans. Frank Wymm, Heinemann, London, 2000 [1999].

37   Daniel Bell, *The Cultural Contradictions of Capitalism,* Heinemann, London, 2nd ed. 1979 [1975]: 148–9.

38   Ibid: 149.

was actually lost in the process of presenting them as products. His work echoed Daniel Bell's assertion that we have lost contact with human artefacts and that, instead, in the spheres of work and leisure, we deal with each other and bring ourselves into being through the ways we present ourselves.

Thinking about how to live in the modern world involved for many designers thinking about how to live flexibly, imagining new forms of urban nomadism, in which the differences between dress and architecture would diminish and cladding and clothing would become, equally, flexible membranes that respond to their environment.[39] The suitcase company Samsonite produced a range of clothing for modern travel. The Italian CP Company made wind and rain-proof transformables in rubberised nylon mesh such as a parka that converted to a sleeping bag and a cloak that became a tent, a jacket with a built-in backpack for a scooter and a top that incorporated a hood with a visor. Levi's worked with the electronics firm Phillips to produce its ICD+ range (ICD stood for Industrial Design Clothing) that included a jacket with a voice-recognition mobile telephone and MP3 player, a microphone in the collar and earphones built into the hood, all of which could be removed from the machine-washable jacket. It was produced in response to market research from which Levi's identified 'a group we call nomads, who are constantly on the move, always in taxis or airports and need to be wired.'[40] Andrew Bolton documented and explored the moment in his book on i-wear using Marc Augé's concept of 'supermodernity' to describe a sense of placeless-ness, and taking the airport as a metaphor for the 'no-places' of modernity.[41] If in reality most people inhabited their homes and used airports only for travel, nevertheless the metaphor of the airport as a 'no-place' was one that pointed, at the level of the symbolic, to a contemporary desire for nothingness, annihilation or 'non-being', whereby Sigmund Freud's idea of the 'oceanic' was re-articulated as the bland and stylised spaces of international travel, in the style of the British interiors magazine *Wallpaper**.

Samsonite, CP Company and Levi's IDC+ range all used a new-tech aesthetic, as well as actual new technology. These were clothes, as Richard Martin wrote of the New York based designer Yeohlee, for the 'fifth season' of the controlled urban environment,[42] a world in which nature is effaced (for example through Vexed Generation's use of phase-change fabrics that regulate body temperature, first developed for NASA) and the metaphors of jungle and desert are played out in the urban landscape. The fifth season might be urban and technological; it certainly existed in a parallel universe to the natural one. What perfume would one wear during the fifth season? Perhaps Comme des Garçons's eau de toilette Odeur 53, marketed as 'an abstract anti-perfume' that claimed to contain the scents of metal, cellulose, nail polish, sand dunes, washing drying in the wind and burnt rubber. It contained no flower or vegetable essences, recalling Coco Chanel's comment on her perfume Chanel Number 5 in its 1920s plain modernist bottle and sans serif typeface: 'women are not flowers. Why should they smell like them?'[43] However, Odeur 53 was a perfume for both men and women, perhaps a significant difference between the modernism of the 1920s and that of the 1990s.

39   Deborah Fausch *et al* (ed.), *Fashion in Architecture*, Princeton Architectural Press, 1994.

40   Massimo Osti, the designer of the ICD+ range, quoted in Dominic Murphy, 'Would You Wear a Coat that Talks Back?' *The Guardian*, Weekend, 21 October 2000: 36.

41   Bolton, *Supermodern Wardrobe*.

42   Richard Martin, 'Yeohlee: Energetics: Clothes and Enclosures', *Fashion Theory*, vol. 2, issue 3, September 1998: 291.

43   Coco Chanel cited in Edmonde Charles-Roux, *Chanel and Her World*, trans. Daniel Wheeler, Weidenfeld & Nicolson, London, 1982 [1979]: 127.

209 Lucy Orta, *Nexus Architecture × 50*,
Nexus Intervention in the City Space,
Cologne, 2001. Photograph Peter Guenzel,
courtesy Lucy Orta

Other, more polemical, designers looked specifically at the inequality, the risks and the dangers of modern urban life. The Japanese designer Kosuke Tsumura set up his sportswear label FINAL HOME in Tokyo in 1994. Based on an urban and ecological ethos, he produced collections made of paper and nylon, stuffed with newspaper for warmth. Many of his designs were for clothing that had several functions and were based on the concept of survival and protection, because clothing is our ultimate home.[44] The artist Lucy Orta's *Refuge Wear* project combined clothing and urban space to make polemical points about poverty and homelessness in the city. Her *Survival Kits* had pockets for cutlery and other basic tools; *Flexible Clothing* converted from a parka-like garment into a tent; another version expanded to fit a hundred people, raising issues of community and communality in the city. Orta's hybrid dress-shelters were a polemical form of defensive armour, or urban survival gear. Her *Nexus Architecture* project of 2001 (fig. 209) consisted of individual workers' overalls that could be joined one to another in a modular grid by sixty-five-centimetre zip connections, which converted the individual garment into a social one, potentially linking hundreds of people through material connections. The inscriptions printed on the connecting fabric links consisted of words such as 'heart', 'link', 'nexus'.

44 Liz Farelley (ed.), *Jam: Tokyo–London*, Booth-Clibborn, London, 2001.

Although made as art pieces, Orta's work had much in common with street and club wear in this period. The London company Vexed Generation exhibited a concern with the late twentieth-century metropolitan experience, such as pollution, surveillance and police powers of arrest. Their Ballistic Parka was made from knife, fire and bullet-proof material developed by the military (fig. 210). Their Shark Jacket had a hood that could be zipped up over the face, highlighting the erosion of civil liberties in the 1998 Crime and Disorder Act which, among other things, made it illegal to hide the face in a demonstration. Vexed's response was to say 'you put up a surveillance camera – I'll put up a collar!'[45] If increased surveillance and powers of arrest helped to erode community and breed paranoia in late 1990s London, Vexed Generation's agitprop streetwear simultaneously communicated these issues and protected their wearers from their worst effects. Beneath the turned-up collar was an anti-pollution mask. While not being part of the fashion establishment, Vexed was a commercially viable company whose designers Joe Hunter and Adam Thorpe highlighted social and political questions in response to their own experience of London street life: surveillance (a hood that zipped up to conceal the face), the environment (a sleeve pocket for an anti-pollution mask), and the quick change (a skirt that zipped into a pair of trousers).

For the collection Between (Spring–Summer 1998), Hussein Chalayan explored the ways in which we define our cultural and geographic territory in space, using a range of design motifs from non-European dress codes to the negative space around the body. He covered the models' heads in opaque wooden pods, or translucent plastic ones, because, he said, he wanted to get away from the emphasis in fashion on personality and individuality. They were worn with clean-cut, unadorned modernist dresses in an austere pallet of black, white and scarlet. But, shockingly, a naked model emerged between a run of clothed ones, her face partially concealed by a chador. The trope was repeated, and Chalayan developed the theme as a series of models appeared, all with covered faces, their bodies progressively uncovered from the feet upwards, ranging from entirely swathed to entirely naked. The covered faces and bare bodies reversed Western protocols. It is hard not to interpret this imagery as a form of imperialist appropriation, drawing on the well-worn territory of Eastern women as exotic and mysterious other presences onto which Western image makers can project, as onto a screen, the idea of lascivious Eastern sexuality. Yet Chalayan intended the collection to be about being in the gaps between spaces, places and cultures, something that could be said to characterise the post-colonial fusions and hybridity of modern urban life. The show was held in a part of the East End of London with a large Bengali population, long before the majority of London designers used out of the way locations, and on the day of the show the fashion journalists walked through a local religious festival to get to the venue.

In After Words (Autumn–Winter 2000–1), a show designed when the news was full of items about people in Kosovo having to flee their homes, Chalayan started with the idea of having to leave one's house in times of war. He imagined how people could carry away their possessions with them (a pocket shaped like an umbrella, for example), and also of

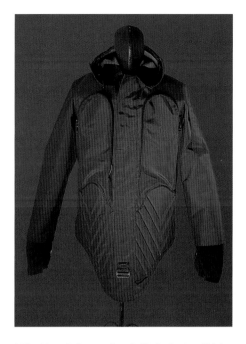

210 Vexed Generation, Ballistic Parka, 1994. Ballistic nylon, neoprene coating, UK Ministry of Defence specification. Photograph Jonny Thompson, courtesy Vexed Generation

211 (following pages) Hussein Chalayan, After Words, Autumn–Winter 2000–1. Photographs Niall McInerney

45 Adam Thorpe, Vexed designer, 1999.

how they can transform and hide them (dresses turned into chair covers). Bound into this was the idea of carrying one's environment with one, an idea that had first surfaced with the chair dress (see figs 198 and 199). Chalayan also had in mind the history of turmoil in Cyprus where he grew up, in particular the Turkish military invasion that divided the island in half in 1974 and displaced both Turkish and Greek Cypriots. 'I come from a part of the world that's turbulent. The collection was about leaving your house and hiding your possessions. Kosovo was a reminder of what happened in Cyprus.'[46] On a theatre stage, Chalayan created a bare white room sparsely furnished with a low, circular coffee table, four chairs, a television and a shelf with a few ornaments on it (fig. 211). As the show opened a generic 'family' of five, ranging from an old man to a young girl, sat facing the audience. They rose and exited, the women changing their pinafores into capes, leaving an empty room into which the models came one by one. After three models in black dresses – the bad omens – had come and gone, four models came on and took off the chair covers transforming them into dresses, followed by another model who transformed the table into a skirt. The show closed with the image of all five facing out, the chairs folded up and transformed into the models' suitcases. Outside the room a Bulgarian choir sang; their vague shadows could be seen dimly through the 'window' covered by a muslin screen. A monitor showed them clearly on the television screen in the room, while the sound came from behind the window.

The table and chairs were made by the Scottish maker and product designer Paul Topen. When Chalayan replaced the tailor with the furniture maker in his designs he rethought fashion as 'portable architecture', drawing on ideas of urban nomadism. As well as his Tyvek air mail dress, Chalayan had designed dresses printed with the flight paths of aeroplanes, and paper suits embedded with lights that flashed like aeroplanes at night, tracing flight path patterns on the paper. Gilles Lipovetsky has proposed an optimistic analysis of the connection between fashion and psychological flexibility, arguing that modern fashion has produced a new individual, 'the fashion person, who has no deep attachments, a mobile individual with a fluctuating personality and tastes.'[47] Thus the fashionable person is an avatar of modernity. Such social agents who are open to change constitute 'a new type of kinetic, open personality' on whom societies undergoing rapid transition depend.[48]

For Lipovetsky's argument that fashion trains the modern subject to be flexible, mobile and psychologically adaptable, Chalayan provided the physical cladding and the meta-physical speculation about identity in the twenty-first century. The blurring of the boundaries between the traditional functions of clothing and dress in Chalayan's Table skirt brings to mind furniture designers who have thought of furniture as a flexible membrane, possibly an intelligent one, that mediates between the body and the built environment.[49] And concerning fashion, J. G. Ballard imagined a definition for the twenty-first century: 'Fashion. A recognition that nature has endowed us with one skin too few, and that a fully sentient being should wear its nervous system externally.'[50]

Yet, as has been noted, Chalayan's design motifs of technological progress were shad-owed by the darker motifs of displacement, exile and uprootedness. This shadow gener-

46   Hussein Chalayan quoted in Tamsin Blanchard, 'Mind Over Material', *The Observer Magazine*, 24 September 2000: 41.

47   Gilles Lipovetsky, *The Empire of Fashion: Dressing Modern Democracy*, trans. Catherine Porter, Princeton University Press, 1994 [1987]: 149.

48   Ibid: 149.

49   E.g. Sorrel Hershberg and Gareth Williams, 'Friendly Membranes and Multi-Taskers: The Body and Contemporary Furniture', in Julian Stair (ed.), *The Body Politic*, Crafts Council, London, 2000: 58–70.

50   J. G. Ballard, 'Project for a Glossary of the Twentieth Century', in Jonathan Crary and Sanford Kwinter (eds), *Incorporations*, Zone Books, New York, 1992: 275.

ated a bleak beauty that haunted the modernist purity of his installation-like shows. In After Words in particular, dislocation and rootlessness were evoked through the sparse interior, the image of the refugee family and the existential bleakness of the harsh, Bulgarian singing, so that the show could not, by any stretch of the imagination, be understood solely (if at all) as a paean to the infinite flexibility of the modern subject. Iain Chambers has argued that alienation is part of the post-modern condition, citing Heidegger's aphorism 'Homelessness is coming to be the destiny of the world'.[51] And in fashion, we are all migrants, for there is no such place as home. The fashionable being is constantly in the process of re-imagining and re-creating him or herself in a rootless world. This process of self-fashioning may be simultaneously pleasurable and alienating. Modernist alienation allows the 'unloosening of the self' that Buci-Glucksmann referred to and can facilitate a shift towards new definitions of culture and identity as fluid, mobile and portable. Deirdre Crowley described this type of fashion design as an 'intimate technology which reproduces itself via human intervention'.[52]

There is a risk that design which is led solely by technological innovation may fetishise the new and invoke redundant myths of progress that no longer have validity in the early twenty-first century, following the dark history of the twentieth. In work in which, however, the ghosts of modernity are permitted to trouble the present, although without falling back into pastiche, its complexity and nuances can be acknowledged. This dialectic underpinned Chalayan's technologically themed collections. Janus-headed, they were shadowed by the urban alienation or estrangement that are a part of the modern condition, while articulating a new design language that did not resort to excessive historicism or nostalgia for the past. For history is also, as Iain Chambers describes it, citing Benjamin's concept of the 'now-time', 'a perpetual becoming, an inexhaustible emerging, an eternal provocation . . . to the linear flow of historicist reason with the insistent now, the *Jetzt*, of the permanent time of the possible'.[53]

51 Iain Chambers, *Migrancy, Culture, Identity*, Comedia/Routledge, London and New York, 1994: 1.
52 Deirdre Crowley cited in Raymond, 'Clothes with Meaning': 31.
53 Chambers, *Migrancy*: 135.

twelve   modernity

Now-Time

In the previous chapter I surveyed the way in which I thought some designers were 'mapping the modern' in their practice, turning estrangement to their advantage. In this final chapter I should like to pull together some of the threads which have patterned the entire book in order to speculate on the conjunction of the modern and the specific type of fashion surveyed in this book. It should be stressed at the outset that this type of fashion is not typical, and my more generalised assertions must be read with that proviso in mind.

The connection between fashion and Baudelairean modernity is highlighted by Christine Buci-Glucksmann:

> modernity is this theatricality *which is constantly eroticising* the new. For if the eye func-
> tions here as the organ of the passions and of their aggravation, the theatre for its part
> is unreal and lacking in affect – masquerade and artifice which Baudelaire's apology for
> appearances and fashion makes quite manifest. In fact, unlike all the philosophemes of
> traditional aesthetics of the beautiful, Baudelaire's critical texts never fail to associate
> modernity with fashion, and more generally with an aesthetic of appearances, artifice
> and play which promotes the Baroque values *par excellence* of spectacle, unexpectedness,
> ephemerality and mortality.[1]

Many of the themes rounded up in this passage have been the themes of this book: unexpectedness, ephemerality and mortality, but also masquerade, artifice and play, in a consumer domain which eroticises the visual, where it goes without saying that seduction is the realm of the commodity as much as of the person. Abigail Solomon-Godeau describes the uncanny fusion of the female and the phantasmagoria of consumer culture where the two collapse into each other and the image of femininity is 'a supplementary emblem of the commodity itself'. She writes: 'In becoming not only the commodity's emblem but its lure, the feminine image operates as a conduit and a mirror of desire, reciprocally inten-sifying and reflecting the commodity's allure.'[2] Although she is describing the late nine-teenth century, in the late 1990s this confusion haunted the 'if you've got it, flaunt it' aesthetic of Versace and Julien Macdonald, for what was flaunted was not simply a body but also a body of wealth, so the two continued to be confused.

What is at work in the association of femininity, modernity and the commodity is, as Solomon-Godeau describes it, 'an economy of desire operating on the register of the visual – which is itself commodity culture's primary and privileged mode of address.'[3] And it is an economy: this is what McQueen underscored in his linkage of sex, death and com-merce, for example in his graduation show or his Dante collection. McQueen's world was a Manichean one of checks and balances, where everything – cruelty, beauty, sex, death, money, love – could be weighed, measured, bought, sold and pictured. But the economy of desire was implicit too in the smooth, slick surface of Tom Ford's designs for Gucci during the 1990s. Gucci's sleek consumerism, Prada's innovations and Dolce e Gabbana's

212 (*facing page*)   Olivier Theyskens, Gloomy Trips, 1997 (limited edition). Styling Olivier Theyskens. Photograph Les Cyclopes, courtesy Olivier Theyskens

1   Christine Buci-Glucksmann, *Baroque Reason: The Aesthetics of Modernity*, trans. Patrick Camiller, Sage, London, Thousand Oaks and New Delhi, 1994 [1984]: 166.

2   Abigail Solomon-Godeau, 'The Other Side of Venus: The Visual Economy of Feminine Display', in Victoria de Grazia and Ellen Furlough (eds), *The Sex of Things: Gender and Consumption in Historical Perspective*, University of California Press, Berkeley, Los Angeles, London, 1996: 113.

3   Ibid: 114.

excess constitute a separate strand of fashion that has hardly figured in this book. Neither have the lucrative mass markets that Polo Ralph Lauren, the Gap, Nautica and Tommy Hilfiger tapped into in the 1990s, with their specifically American elaborations on the themes of luxury, race and class.[4] Nor the refined but luxurious minimalism of designers such as Giorgio Armani, Jil Sander, Donna Karan, Martin Margiela in his designs for Hermès, Hussein Chalayan's period designing for Tse, and Nicholas Ghesquière at Balenciaga. Commercial luxury brands like Gucci lived the economy of desire that more experimental designers could only picture on the catwalk; but 'only picturing' can give a designer a critical edge that enables them to make explicit what others can do only reflexively and uncritically. And then, once pictured, designers who wish to, like McQueen, who sold a controlling interest in his business to Gucci in December 2000, may also be able to move on and make the dream real, in the form of expanding their markets into the far bigger ones of America and the Far East.

The economy of desire 'operates in the register of the visual'.[5] In her discussion of the late nineteenth-century *femme fatale* – a figure who, I have argued, was inflected in the 1990s in designs by Versace, Galliano and McQueen – Buci-Glucksmann argues that desire comes into being through vision and is subject to 'the imperialism of sight' and the 'cult of images.'[6] I have used Benjamin's concept of dialectical images to explore how images of the past 'spark' when juxtaposed with those of the present to reveal a new interpretation, for example by putting Galliano's 1990s' designs for Dior next to pictures from the 1900 Paris International Exhibition. Benjamin wrote: 'in order for a piece of the past to be touched by present actuality, there must exist no continuity between them', for the historical object is constituted as dialectical image by being 'blasted out of the continuum of history'.[7]

Benjamin's ideas offer art and design historians a sophisticated model of how visual seduction works, because they are predicated on an understanding of how visual similes function in a mass consumer society. In 1938 Adorno criticised the way in which Benjamin created 'a realm where history and magic oscillate', focusing his critique specifically on Benjamin's description of the ragpicker.[8] The same criticism could be levelled today against a ragpicking text that asserts the material base of fashion while largely avoiding its detailed investigation; that is macro rather than micro in its focus; and that predominantly investigates fashion as a semiotic rather than material object of study. Yet to understand the commodity as poetic object in 'a realm where history and magic oscillate' is also to understand its fascination, for dreams are the motor that drive a capitalist economy as much as iron, steel and microchips.

For all its high visibility in the media, much of the fashion discussed in this text is economically negligible. Its cultural capital far outweighs its economic force. Why then is it important? Precisely because it is still 'symbolically central' although economically peripheral.[9] Luxury brands like Dior and Chanel used their 'cultural capital' or 'symbolic centrality' to promote their brands. What is their symbolic centrality, if not the mythic reputation of Paris as a centre of fashion? It is this that Galliano's nostalgic designs con-

4 Teri Agins, *The End of Fashion*, Quill/HarperCollins, New York, 2000.

5 Solomon-Godeau, 'Other Side of Venus', 114.

6 Buci-Glucksmann, *Baroque Reason*: 157

7 Walter Benjamin *The Arcades Project*, trans. Howard Eiland and Kevin McLaughlin, Belnap Press of Harvard University Press, Cambridge, Mass., and London, 1999: 470, and 'Theses on the Philosophy of History', Illuminations, trans. Harry Zohn, Fontana/Collins, 1973 [1955]: 263.

8 Letter of 10 November 1938 in Theodor W. Adorno and Walter Benjamin, *Complete Correspondence 1928–1940*, ed. Henri Loritz, trans. Nicholas Walter, Polity Press, Cambridge, 1999: 282.

9 'Symbolically central though socially peripheral', cited in Peter Stallybrass and Allon White, *The Politics and Poetics of Transgression*, Methuen, London, 1986: 5.

tinually recalled, the commercial antecedents of haute couture and the retailing of luxury goods in nineteenth-century Paris. And this is why fashion at all levels of the market, from mass market to haute couture to experimental and conceptual, continues to be inherently conservative, even though it cleverly makes space for revolutionary designers. Although Margiela's aesthetic of dereliction is avant-garde, his experimentation does not take him outside a capitalist paradigm, it simply fixes him more firmly inside it as the antithesis of Galliano.

Since the late 1980s the definition and delineation of a capitalist paradigm has shifted with globalisation, so that the concepts of first and third worlds are disrupted, as are those of core and margins: with the new possibilities offered by virtuality, and the speed of electronic communications, the spectacle has extended beyond the urban spaces it first sprang from and is at once everywhere and nowhere. If we can no longer be sure of its limitations in time and space it follows that we can no longer be unproblematically either fully inside or outside it (which is the limitation of using Debord). Here Viktor & Rolf are key to the 1990s, as was Warhol to the 1960s: cyphers of indecipherability, their inscrutability is the very device that makes them at once critical and complicit in the spectacle. Like Chalayan, they produce critical and questioning work from the commercial heart of the business itself. Yet however much their work seeks a space outside the 'society of the spectacle' it is always, and simultaneously, recuperated by it. Indeed, this is its most potent appeal, and its strongest mark of contemporaneity, that it is both inside and outside this capitalist paradigm.

Benjamin's model of dialectical images from the 1930s, heavily influenced by the Frankfurt School, posited them as thesis and antithesis that would spark to produce a synthesis, albeit a temporary and fleeting one. But dialectical images today might be even more unstable than those imagined by Benjamin in the 1930s, incapable of even momentary synthesis. Buci-Glucksmann nudges Benjamin's concept of dialectical images slightly further to suggest there is no synthesis in this dialectic: she describes 'a constant reversal of images into their opposite, dialectical images with no synthesis'.[10] An example of this might be the way that past and present coalesce in Dai Rees's crystal and glass face mask made from a sheep's skull that can be interpreted simultaneously as both deathly and magically tranforming. Such imagery is often hard to fix, to use a photographic metaphor, in any coherent way. The conditions of post-industrial modernity tend to suggest that synthesis is a chimera (and fashion teaches us this too) and that the condition of modernity is one of flux and instability, as Baudelaire defined it in the nineteenth century.

However, the instability and theatricality of Dai Rees's mask mark it as Baroque, harking back to seventeenth-century visual art and literature, as much as to the nineteenth century. In other respects, too, the sixteenth and seventeenth centuries were evoked in contemporary design. The shows of the London designers Alexander McQueen, Andrew Groves and Tristan Webber evidenced a fascination with Baroque theatricality, artifice and the staging of perversion in the violence and drama of their stagecraft. Even where their themes were contemporary, based for example on the Troubles in Northern Ireland or Ballard's novel

10 Buci-Glucksmann, *Baroque Reason*: 158.

Cocaine Nights, these were tinged with Jacobean cruelty and sexuality. Their dark stage-craft recalled the German mourning plays that Benjamin likened to 'the emblem books of the Baroque as the stock requisites of gloomy spectacle . . . tirelessly transforming, interpreting and deepening it, the *trauerspiel* rings the changes on its images'.[11] The combination of fascination and horror were, Jonathan Sawday has argued, a 'highly visible part of metropolitan culture of the sixteenth and seventeenth centuries'[12] and they continued to be a spectacular part of metropolitan culture in the 1990s. Sawday discusses the closeness of disgust and attraction that Philipe Ariès has described as 'an attraction to certain ill-defined things at the outer limits of life and death, sexuality and pain', an attraction that was clear in McQueen and Groves's early shows.[13]

In her introduction to a collection of Benjamin's writings Susan Sontag argued that 'the nihilistic energies of the modern era make everything a ruin or a fragment . . . a world whose past has become, by definition, obsolete, and whose present churns out instant antiques.'[14] She saw in his writing a similarity between the seventeenth century and the 1930s when Benjamin was writing: 'both the Baroque and Surrealism . . . see reality as things . . . the genius of Surrealism was to generalise with ebullient candour the Baroque cult of ruins';[15] and she saw this trend in the visual culture of the late twentieth century too. But, as I have argued, the design motifs of decay and dereliction in the work of designers like Robert Cary-Williams and Shelley Fox also evoke the eighteenth-century English Romantic cult of ruins.

My 'pick-and-mix' attitude to the past is parallelled by the way many designers think forwards only by thinking backwards, recycling old things to make them new. As Jean-Michel Rabaté argues, modernity is self-reflexive. It connotes a type of self-consciousness and self-scrutiny that means we can never be entirely unselfconscious.

> Modernity . . . is by definition never contemporaneous with itself, since it constantly projects, anticipates, and returns to its mythic origins, but that also teaches us more about 'the present' which it historicises . . . such a modernity resists any attempt to supersede it and any effort to declare it obsolete, even if those efforts come from so-called postmodernity.[16]

Modernity is thus an effect of a future perfect tense, the future anterior: this will have been. We are not fixed in the present but constantly thinking forwards and projecting backwards, demonstrating a kind of consciousness and self-scrutiny that has been identified as intrinsic to modernity by Anthony Giddens and to Western fashion by Gilles Lipovetsky. Whereas designers who merely fetishise technological novelty can think only forwards, others, like Chalayan, take a modernist style and inflect it with historical trauma and complexity – for example, in his rigid resin dresses which bring the past into the present, or his Medea collection which remakes fashion as archaeology.

For Rabaté, modernity and post-modernity are both spectral cultural forms, generating virtual images to haunt the future. The condition of this historical to-ing and fro-ing in consciousness makes it easy for everyone to operate as cultural ragpickers, using a

11   Walter Benjamin, *The Origin of German Tragic Drama*, trans. John Osborne with an intro. by George Steiner, New Left Books, London, 1977: 231.

12   Jonathan Sawday, *The Body Emblazoned: Dissection and the Human Body in Renaissance Culture*, Routledge, London and New York, 1995: 49.

13   Philippe Ariès, *The Hour of Our Death*, trans. Helen Weaver, Allen Lane, London, 1981: 369.

14   Susan Sontag, intro. to Walter Benjamin, *One Way Street and Other Writings*, trans. Edmund Jephcott and Kingsley Shorter, Verso, London, 1985: 16–17.

15   Ibid.

16   Jean-Michel Rabaté, *The Ghosts of Modernity*, University Press of Florida, Gainsville, 1996: 3.

twentieth-century cut-and-mix aesthetic. That is the process, for example, that defines the working methods of designers as various as Margiela, in his use of old clothes, and Westwood and Galliano in the way they recycle historical imagery from the theatrical dressing-up box. It is also the process I have employed to write about them. And if in doing so I have used Benjamin and Marx more than other thinkers, it is because, as Ulf Poschardt writes, they lend themselves particularly well to remixing, for 'a remix can not only adapt to a new context, but also makes an old (and brilliant) idea contemporary.'[17]

There is a price to pay for this continual to-ing and fro-ing, as there is for modernist self-scrutiny. It means we can never live unselfconsciously in the present but are compelled restlessly to oscillate between different times and ideas. Iain Chambers has used Benjamin's ideas to describe the task of the cultural historian as a 'continual return to events': 'This re-telling, re-citing and re-siting of what passes for historical and cultural knowledge depend upon the recalling and re-remembering of earlier fragments and traces that flare up and flash in our present "moment of danger" as they come to live on in new constellations.'[18] This activity condemns us to repeat and oscillate because this is a way we can make sense of things, by checking and cross-checking; this relay in consciousness is the condition of post-industrial modernity. But there is a risk that we are doomed to ricochet endlessly between modernist experimentation and dark despair, and this continual oscillation mimics the structure of trauma itself, a psychic structure rooted in compulsive repetition that serves as a device to block the memory of the traumatic event.

This oscillation also means that we may shunt pathologically between opposites so that they become profoundly connected, the meaning of one enmeshed in that of the other. One of the themes of this book has been the capacity in fashion for things to turn into their opposite: beauty is inflected with horror, luxury with decay, sex with death, and beauty again with mortality. The relationship between these pairs is that of Derridean *différance*; in all of them the first term is the privileged one, the second the supplement. This supplement is everywhere and always at work; it takes the form of rot and dereliction, for example in Margiela, death and sadism in McQueen, the horror of the commodity form in Galliano, and of the deathliness of the woman of fashion in Benjamin's writing. It is what Lynda Nead has referred to as the residue left by modernity. The logic of the supplement is to destabilise the privileged term and that is also the logic of this book. If the book has been a case study of how a certain type of fashion design can destabilise its opposite, the logic of the supplement leads to the conclusion that all fashion – including privileged (in both senses of the word), high-gloss international luxury fashion – turns out to be shot through with alienation and melancholy, which are always threatening to erupt and disturb the smoothness of its surface.

*   *   *

17   Ulf Poschardt, *DJ Culture,* trans. Shaun Whiteside, Quartet Books, London, 1998: 33.
18   Iain Chambers, *Migrancy, Culture, Identity,* Comedia/Routledge, London and New York, 1994: 7.

An Archaeology of the Imaginary of and in History

That much of the newest fashion cites historical imagery from the past is not in itself new, and there are many examples of fashion revivals since the Renaissance.[19] (Indeed, Ulrich Lehmann has argued that this is the defining characteristic of fashion although one should add that each instance can and should be differentiated historically.[20]) One could cite nineteenth-century women's fashions *à la Watteau*, or some of the earliest women's magazines from the late eighteenth century that were even composed of cuttings and pastings from other magazines. When fashion quotes from the past its backwards looks might be simply nostalgic. Writing in 1981, Barbara Burman, while acknowledging the reasons for fashion revivals to be many and varied, saw revivals principally as a search 'for a paradise lost by time or place . . . there are many visions and many paradises, and as many ways of regaining and realising them.'[21] Rather in the spirit of Walter Benjamin, she went on to say that revivals are often actually arrivals, so transformed are they by their interpreters.[22] For the 'arrivals' from the past of the late 1990s looking back at history was, however, not so much a backwards as a forwards glance, and was one of the ways in which designers revealed themselves to be most modern. These historical returns tell us something about the present and also, perhaps, about our fears and hopes for the future. Frank Kermode has noted that we assume our own time to stand in an extraordinary relation to the future: 'we think of our own crises as pre-eminent, more worrying, more interesting than other crises.'[23] As Kermode argues, we make sense of the past and present by projecting our fears, guesses and inferences about the past and present onto the future, and that 'crisis is a way of thinking about one's moment, and not inherent in the moment itself', for 'it is by our imaginary of past, present and future . . . that the character of our apocalypse must be known.'[24]

For all the appearance of nihilism and violence of much of the work surveyed in this book, as Christine Buci-Glucksmann wrote,

> the nihilistic aesthetic carries the idea of progress: it grounds desire on images, scenes, matter; it materialises difference and excess at the very site of a logic of ambivalence; it creates 'language' . . . with all its effects of estrangement . . . [we now require] a different interpretation of the modern, for which Baudelaire and Benjamin have laid the foundation stones.'[25]

Her argument suggests that the idea of the modern can no longer be predicated on early twentieth-century utopian modernist ideas of progress and revolution but that it might be grounded in a darker, more nihilistic aesthetic that requires a return to Baudelaire and Benjamin to map the modern. Those optimistic modernist ideas and ideals about progress and revolution carried with them an implicit denial of the mess and chaos of history. And if the messy complexity of history is swept under the carpet by the notion of a radical rupture with the past (as is proposed by some theorists of post-modernism and was also,

19 Barbara Burman Baines, *Fashion Revivals: From the Elizabethan Age to the Present Day*, Batsford, London, 1981.

20 See intro. to Ulrich Lehmann, *Tigersprung: Fashion in Modernity*, MIT Press, Cambridge, Mass., and London, 2000.

21 Burman Baines, *Fashion Revivals*: 9.

22 Ibid: 13.

23 Frank Kermode, *The Sense of an Ending: Studies in the Theory of Fiction with a New Epilogue*, Oxford University Press, 2000 [1966]: 94–5.

24 Ibid: 101 and 95.

25 Buci-Glucksmann, *Baroque Reason*: 160.

as Rabaté has argued, a modernist tenet) the 'ghosts of modernity' will come back as an unresolved tension, like a psychoanalytic symptom. Hence the 'ghosts of modernity' are creatures that cannot be laid to rest. In 1986 Lyotard, one of the principal theorists of postmodernism, also identified the modernist desire to start afresh as something against which the present age revolts. Like Rabaté, he too argued, using a loosely psychoanalytic formulation, that to deny the past is to repress it, in which case, like a symptom, we are doomed to repeat it compulsively in order not to remember, or process, it:

> The idea of modernity is closely bound up with this principle that it is possible and necessary to break with tradition and to begin a new way of living and thinking. Today we can presume that this 'breaking' is, rather, a manner of forgetting or repressing the past. That's to say of repeating it. Not overcoming it.[26]

Lyotard's text is compatible with the argument that modernist ideals no longer seem plausible in the light of the dark history of the twentieth century. Recently, philosophers and historians have looked back on this history to investigate the domain of memory and trauma.[27] As I have shown, this concern with memory and the cultural artefact as a trace of the past has inflected fashion too, and for designers at the start of the twenty-first century the map of the modern is not to be plotted on clean sheets of new white paper but painted over old landscapes whose surfaces are already traced with earlier palimpsests. Thus the ghosts of modernity that have haunted this text constitute a psychogeography of fashion.[28] Psychogeography gives us a more contemporary way of using Benjamin's pre-war concept of 'dialectical' images and also answers the criticism of the idea of dialectical images that Adorno made in 1935.[29] Margaret Cohen points out that Buci-Glucksmann addresses this criticism when she argues that Benjamin's archaeology of the modern is 'an *archaeology of the imaginary of and in history*', which I take to be a kind of psychogeography, an unravelling notion of revolution itself as dissent rather than as progress.[30] Buci-Glucksmann asserts that 'the logic of dislocation' stages 'a radical uncanny' that can 'explode Marxisms of progress and replace them with a rent (*déchiré*) Marxism, a Marxism of rending'.[31] The metaphor of tearing returns us yet again to rags, a metaphor for history as much as for revolution, and which is predicated on tearing apart rather than progressively putting together, but not necessarily based on nihilism. For it could just as well be based on a bricolage aesthetic that relies on creation out of contingency and loss. Hence the derelict poses of punk, the romantic fragments of Margiela or Cary-Williams, the modernist alienation of Chalayan's aerodynamic dresses or, as Rebecca Arnold has persuasively argued, the idea that dark and violent fashion imagery came to be seen as the most 'real' in the mid-1990s.[32]

Several designers, especially those working at the margins, in terms of either economics or taste, were able to turn their limited circumstances to advantage, such as Shelley Fox or Boudicca. Viktor & Rolf's work, for all its irony, was also shot through with a kind of love and enthusiasm that recalled the way Warhol's work in the 1960s embraced consumer society wholeheartedly. It is a fact, now, that our sense of what it is to be modern is pro-

26 Jean-François Lyotard, 'Defining the Postmodern' in *ICA Documents 4*: 'Postmodernism', ICA, London, 1986: 6.

27 E.g. Edith Wyschogrod, *An Ethics of Remembering*, Chicago University Press, 1998; Nancy Wood, *Vectors of Memory*, Berg, Oxford and New York, 1999; Marius Kwint, Jeremy Ainsley and Christopher Breward (eds), *Material Memories: Design and Evocation*, Berg, Oxford and New York, 1999.

28 Psychogeography was first defined in *Internationale Situationiste*, no. 1, June 1958 [n.p.] as 'the study of the specific effects of the geographical environment, consciously organised or not, on the emotions and behaviour of individuals.' However, its sense has evolved to describe the way in which a place can acquire meaning and resonance through a build-up or sedimentation of previous histories and their traces, as in e.g. Iain Sinclair, *Lights Out for the Territory: Nine Excursions into the Secret History of London*, Granta, London, 1997.

29 Adorno argued that Benjamin attributed too much redemptive potential to the superstructure, that he relied too much on an idea of collective consciousness, which to Adorno suggested the worst excesses of Jung, that this idea was thus infused with bourgeois sensibility and that Benjamin did not make any class differentiation. See Adorno and Benjamin, *Complete Correspondence*: 104–16. Margaret Cohen suggests that Adorno's criticism was that the concept of dialectical images blurred 'the dialectic operative in capitalist society: between alienated individuals and alienating objective conditions': *Profane Illumination: Walter Benjamin and the Paris of Surrealist Revolution*, University of California Press, Berkeley and London, 1993: 26–7. I am grateful to Elizabeth Wilson for bringing this book to my attention.

30 Cohen, *Profane Illumination*: 26–7.

31 Buci-Glucksmann, *Baroque Reason*: 48.

32 Rebecca Arnold, *Fashion, Desire and Anxiety: Image and Morality in the Twentieth Century*, I. B. Tauris, London and New York, 2001: 32 ff.

foundly bound up in the past and the future, they are overlapped in our imaginations. We can no longer just live in the present and the fashion designers I have looked at make this evident. They excavate ideas and sensibilities from our cultural imagination and make them visible as images and solid as objects. Marx's assertion that 'all that is solid melts into air' is inverted in their work – they take air and make it solid. But then it melts again, just as Marx describes it. So they crystallise it for a second only, before it dissolves like a dialectical image whose truth is fleeting and transient. But this very transience is a kind of truth in a moment of technological, social and political change, and it encapsulates the specificity of this current historical moment, and any other historical moment, with its echoes and reverberations in the past.

If modernist ideals of progress no longer seem appropriate with the hindsight of twentieth-century history, we have to find a language that accounts for the way the past is imbricated in our historical imagination today. Two ghosts that have haunted the present text are those of Baudelaire and Warhol. Baudelaire's writing prefigures the way that beauty is inflected with horror in modernity and Warhol's work implied that sex, death and commerce were connected, particularly in the way that death underwrites the displays of celebrity in consumer culture, for example in his tragic heroines Jackie and Marilyn.[33] Similarly, the spectacular fashion shows of the 1990s were like graveyards of modern technology and spectacle; their showpieces were beautiful husks that, once worn, sat afterwards in studios and warehouses like redundant hardware.

Rabaté argues that the ghosts of modernity return because they cannot rest: banished by modernism they come back as a mark of trauma, as what cannot be accommodated. Yet the possibility of return depends on difference. The nineteenth-century Baudelairean modernity that I have argued erupts through the smooth surfaces of late twentieth-century fashion is not the same as the modernity of today, any more than Warhol's necrophilia is the same as Alexander McQueen's. Rather, the present is haunted by a past to which it no longer corresponds, which is not the same and does not quite fit, for all its similarities. The time is out of joint. An earlier period of proliferation of images through new technologies, of rapid developments in retail and advertising, that was never accommodated by utopian modernism, returns to haunt the present in a form which is slightly out of kilter with it. These are two kinds of 'now-time'.[34] I have understood Chalayan's mobilisation of the past in the present as this kind of ghosting via new technologies of the image as a way of explaining how his modernist experiments are infused with melancholy. The increasingly spectral nature of fashion today, compared to that of the nineteenth century, in the way it can be experienced as image as much as embodied practice, is due in large part to rapid changes in communications; and on the catwalk the showpiece itself, worn only by the model, is an avatar of spectral and disembodied fashion. So Chalayan's designs play sophisticated visual games with mirrors or with computer graphics packages to evoke earlier periods of capitalist development that were tied to new technologies of the image, then print and photographic media rather than computing.

33   See Hal Foster, 'Death in America', and Thomas Crow, 'Saturday Disasters: Trace and Reference in early Warhol', in: Annette Mitchelson (ed.) *Andy Warhol*, *October* Files 2, MIT Press, Cambridge, Mass., and London, 2001: 69–88 and 49–66.

34   Benjamin's *jetztzeit*: Benjamin, 'Theses on the Philosophy of History': 263 and 265.

It is in this sense that much of the fashion imagery I have written about is also a speculative map of the future. Benjamin made the same point when describing the up-to-dateness of fashion that can predict the future before it has happened:

> The most interesting thing about fashion is its extraordinary anticipations . . . thanks to the incomparable nose which the feminine collective has for what lies in waiting in the future. Each season brings, in its newest creations, various secrets of things to come. Whoever understands how to read these semaphores would know in advance not only about new currents in the arts but also about new legal codes, wars and revolutions.'[35]

Adorno's grumpy marginal note to this was: 'I would think, counter-revolutions.'[36] Ulrich Lehmann has argued that so-called post-modern borrowing and quotation at the end of the twentieth century had been anticipated much earlier in the designs of Poiret, Schiaparelli and Yves Saint-Laurent, and that literary deconstruction was anticipated in Balenciaga's 1950s semi-fitted suits with their pronounced darts and seams that indicated their underlying construction.[37] Since, however, these characteristics were also anticipated by the collage aesthetics of Picasso and Schwitters, or the proto-Situationist posturings of Dada, to give just two examples, it cannot really be argued that fashion is inherently more pre-scient than any other field of culture. Nor can its 'predictions' seriously be attributed to fem-inine intuition as Benjamin implies. Rather, these turns and returns are part of a modernist aesthetic that demand, as Hal Foster has argued, the co-ordination of both diachronic (or historical) and synchronic (or social) axes in late twentieth-century art and theory. Foster rejects the notion of post-historical pluralism but argues that geneologies in ideas and art can be traced through '*turns* in critical models and *returns* of historical practices', a model that adapts well to fit fashion and culture generally at the end of the century.[38]

Globalisation

From the 1980s and throughout the 1990s developments in electronics and communications had a major effect on everyday life.[39] Sony Walkmans, mobile telephones, texting, e-mailing, the internet and satellite television changed the everyday experience of time and place. CCTV cameras introduced new techniques of surveillance but also brought into the public realm new and terrible images, such as the last moments of victims of crime. The fall of the Berlin Wall in 1989 and the dissolution of the Soviet Union in 1991 resulted in the expansion eastwards of capitalist hegemony as manufacturers moved in to capitalise on new workforces and new markets. As globalisation increased after the demise of the Soviet bloc, America came more and more to be seen as the biggest market in the world, significantly contributing to the idea that there was no alternative economic system to function as a check or balance to an American-led model of capitalist enterprise. In the 1990s both Communism and socialism were seen as failed experiments by many, not only

35 Benjamin, *Arcades Project*: 63–4.
36 Ibid: 959 n. 3.
37 Lehmann, *Tigersprung*: xx.
38 Hal Foster, *The Return of the Real: The Avant Garde at the End of the Century*, MIT Press, Cambridge, Mass., and London, 1996: x and xii.
39 Tiziana Terranova, 'Posthuman Unbounded: Artificial Evolution and High-tech subcultures', in George Robertson *et al* (eds), *FutureNatural: Nature, Science, Culture*, Routledge, London and New York, 1996: 166.

by those on the right. The idea of liberal democracy as both the inevitable and the best social and economic system was given legitimacy in conservative texts like Francis Fukuyama's *The End of History*.[40] The move to a less interventionist way of managing the economy in Europe went hand in hand with the shrinking of the welfare state, the decline of heavy industry, the rise of new service industries and the decline of old certainties such as jobs for life.

These changes of the last thirty years of the twentieth century, many of them in the last twenty, were part of a broader shift to a knowledge economy. The impact of the information and communications revolution was easily as formidable as that of the effects of European industrialisation from the eighteenth century onwards, which is not to say they were the same. Both produced a sense of instability that enables us to read the nineteenth-century experience of disintegration in the present. Today's technological revolution, too, has produced a sense of upheaval and change that can be compared to the indirect effects of industrialisation in nineteenth-century Paris. We can thus move forward a hundred years to another period of accelerated transition where fashion is taking a prominent role where we find quantum leaps and rapid technological developments.

Jonathan Gershuny has argued that as we develop a knowledge economy capital ceases to be fixed, in the form of land and shares, and becomes human.[41] We have to extract the 'rent' from human capital, that is, knowledge, so our wealth-generating assets have shrunk to our bodies. This is commensurate with themes in furniture and urban design including clothing in which the body is a house, an entire living system, a pod or 'flexible membrane'; fashion in this context is not just cladding but a structural constituent of the edifice of the self. These ideas are explored in the work of Lucy Orta and Vexed Generation, as well as various i-wear designers.

Above all, the rise of the information society has produced, for many, a sense of discontinuity in contemporary sensibilities and social practices.[42] The 'intoxicating dream worlds' of the nineteenth century, with its 'constantly changing flow of commodities, images and bodies' was updated in the late twentieth as a rapid flow of signs and images through the new digital technologies.[43] Although the contemporary experience was led by communications and new technology, rather than by industry, both were periods of accelerated transition, which perhaps explains the prominent role of fashion in each. The nineteenth century was also a period in which images proliferated through new technologies. The advent of new visual technologies such as photography and chromolithography, and their reproduction in newspapers, catalogues and fashion magazines, meant that anything could be circulated, anything could become a commodity.[44] An example of this is the nineteenth-century vogue for *cartes de visite*, and the way that people collected albums-full, both of family and friends and of actresses and other public figures unknown personally to the collector. But what seems new in the late twentieth century is the way that in the process of becoming image certain types of fashion have also become spectral, as much as they have also lent themselves to the process of historical haunting. Perhaps this is an indi-

40   Francis Fukuyama, *The End of History and the Last Man*, Hamish Hamilton, London, 1992.

41   Jonathan I. Gershuny, *Changing Times: Work and Leisure in Postindustrial Society*, Oxford University Press, 2000.

42   For a discussion of the effect of new technologies on sensibilities and social practice see Anthony Giddens, *Runaway World: How Globalisation is Reshaping our Lives,* Profile Books, London, 1999.

43   Mike Featherstone, *Consumer Culture and Postmodernism*, Sage, London, Thousand Oaks and New Delhi, 1991: 70.

44   Jonathan Crary, *Techniques of the Observer: On Vision and Modernity in the Nineteenth Century*, MIT Press, Cambridge, Mass., and London, 1990. Jonathan Crary, *Suspensions of Perception: Attention, Spectacle and Modern Culture*, MIT Press, Cambridge, Mass., and London, 2001. Scott McQuire, *Visions of Modernity: Representation, Memory, Time and Space in the Age of the Camera*, Sage, London, Thousand Oaks and New Delhi, 1998.

cation of the way commodity capitalism mutated with the advent of new communications technology, with fashion again as its paradigm.

The ghosting I describe is particularly modern, due to the increase of 'virtuality' and new digital communications. As well as producing the spectral showpiece on the runway, fashion design has proliferated as image and concept as much as object, taking its definition as 'embodied practice' into the arena of the virtual.[45] The nineteenth century was spectral too in the way that the realm of the commodity was extended by its representation in image and text.[46] However, the late twentieth-century body was further removed in the information age, which is perhaps why the Italian anti-capitalist group the Tute Bianche (the White Overalls) proposed the body itself as a site of resistance and struggle. The Tute Bianche took their point of protest from the transition from Fordism to post-Fordism, arguing that the whole of modern life became subject to capitalist sovereignty under it. The symbolism of white referred both to the 'sum of all colours' to represent the multifarious protesters against this new world order, but also because white is 'the colour of ghosts, a symbol for invisibility' of the disenfranchised under this order.[47] The metaphor can be extended to the way that labour itself becomes invisible in a period of globalisation (or 'multi-national capital' as Jameson terms it[48]) so that the term I have used, 'post-industrial modernity', to differentiate today from an earlier period of 'industrial modernity' is both 'horribly wrong and horribly right'.[49] Wrong because we consume as much as ever before and in that sense our society is nowhere near 'post-industrial', just regulated by 'multi-national capital'. Right because the current trend of removing all dirty industrial production from our clean, information-based Western societies to free-trade zones the other side of the world is the ultimate fetishisation of labour and is, perhaps, only correctly expressed in the ideal of the 'post-industrial' – but this means that it must always be in inverted commas. It is, however, in this sense, and with some irony, that I have adhered to the notion of 'post-industrial modernity' to describe the conditions of fashion today, rather than 'post-modernism'. This is a point I will return to later.

And the new technologies which we see are digital, such as computers where, for most of us, 'the machines involved are not substitutes for mechanical operations but for certain mental and/or linguistic operations . . . these machines presuppose a high level of analysis, not only of the mind, but also of matter.'[50] In other ways too globalisation is spectral. Giddens has argued that the effects of a new global electronic economy driven by financial and entrepreneurial risk at the turn of the century were revolutionary.[51] The flows of electronic money were bigger than those of any previous money market, and much bigger than they had been in the 1980s; more than a trillion dollars was turned over each day on global currency markets at the click of a mouse, with the ability to destabilise previously rock-solid economies. So although I have argued that earlier moments of capitalist transformation have erupted in the present, it is important to stress how very different that present is from any previous moment that can be used to illuminate it.

The immense changes of the last few years are philosophical, as well as economic; and, since philosophical concerns are grounded in the economics and materiality of their time,

45 Elsewhere I have argued that the nature of the commodity has changed in post-modernism: 'Now the fashioned garment circulates in a contemporary economy as part of a network of signs, operating simultaneously in many registers. Whereas it used to exist as, for example, a dress, which preceded its single representation in the form of an advertisement or a fashion photograph, it is now frequently disembodied and deterritorialised. As such, it can proliferate in many more forms, within a larger network of relations: as image, as cultural capital, as consumer goods, as fetish, art exhibition, item of breakfast television, show invitation, or collectable magazine . . . Thus in the technological and information revolution of the late twentieth century, the role of image in fashion shifted. No longer mere representation, the image frequently became the commodity itself, in the form of exclusive fashion shows, Internet websites, television programmes and a new kind of fashion magazine.' Caroline Evans, 'Yesterday's Emblems and Tomorrow's Commodities: The Return of the Repressed in Fashion Imagery Today', in Stella Bruzzi and Pamela Church Gibson (eds), *Fashion Cultures: Theories, Explorations and Analysis*, Routlege, London and New York, 2000: 96–7.

46 I am grateful to Alison Matthews David for her discussion of the way the tailor's dummy developed in the nineteenth century as a substitute for the body, reifying and fetishising a body which was increasingly absent. This effect was augmented by the increase of newspapers, catalogues and journals that use new image technologies further to regulate, define and abstract the body through representation. Alison Matthews David, 'Cutting a Figure: Tailoring, Technology and Social Identity in Nineteenth Century Paris', PhD diss. Stanford University, 2002.

47 The Tute Bianche activists Chiara Cassurino and Federico Martelloni interviewed by Dario Azzellini, 'Tute Bianche', *032c*, 3rd issue, 'What's Next?' (Berlin), Winter 2001/02: 20.

48 Frederic Jameson, *Postmodernism, or the Cultural Logic of Late Capitalism*, Verso, London and New York, 1991.

49 I am grateful to Marketa Uhlirova for this trenchant point which I have left substantially in her words.

50 Lyotard, 'Defining the Postmodern': 10.

51 Giddens, *Runaway World*: 3–9.

it is as well to differentiate nineteenth-century articulations of concepts such as alienation from contemporary ones. To talk about modernist alienation in the present I have drawn, for example, on many modernist concerns in my discussion of Nick Knight's photographs of Aimee Mullins. If the perfection of the fashion model's body is a switching station between life and death, in these images Mullins is configured as a woman who can be simultaneously both active and passive, subject and object, vivacious and deathly. They suggest that the cultural formations of post-industrial modernity differ from those of industrial modernity and that, in the moment of transition from one to another, the relation between object and subject is being re-articulated. Freud's essay on the uncanny, which I relied on heavily in my discussion of the motif of dolls in 1990s fashion, was written immediately after the First World War and is characterised by the sense of alienation and loss which informs much modernist writing of that period. Before Freud, Marx's analysis, and its subsequent glosses and interpretations, suggested that industrialisation inevitably produced a traumatised, alienated or split subject, which was made into an object by the process of commodity fetishism. For Marx, Lukács and Benjamin alienation was the consequence of modern industrial processes. In commodity fetishism 'people and things traded semblances: social relations take on the character of object relations and commodities assume the active agency of people.'[52] But in the movement from an industrial to a post-industrial society, an information-based society, we could perhaps rethink the relationship of subject and object in relation to identity as something more fluid, something not contained or limited by the organic body. We may be at a moment which constitutes a paradigm shift in subjectivities, one in which the objectification on which my arguments have been premised may be challenged by new, and still evolving, ideas of the subject which will cause us to redefine the object too.[53]

Modernity and Post-modernism

I have by and large resisted the term post-modernism in this text, but I would assert, with Lyotard and Habermas, that post-modernism is to be seen as a continuation of modernity rather than a radical rupture with the past.[54] As I have argued strenuously that the ghosts of industrial modernity haunt post-industrial modernity to disrupt the smooth surfaces of fashion in the present, I have adopted the term 'post-industrial modernity' to describe the present moment even though my usage is almost interchangeable with what is commonly referred to as post-modernism.[55] Like Jameson's, my terminology presupposes the cultural manifestations of post-modernity as symptoms of underlying socio-economic conditions. Jameson writes of 'multi-national capital' which is an *avant la lettre* term for globalisation. He borrows from Mandel the phrase 'late capitalism' to mark the third of three stages of capitalist development.

The term modernity, however, might no longer apply to fashion in the late twentieth century in the same way as it is used to describe the experiences of industrialisation and

52 Hal Foster, 'The Art of Fetishism', *The Princeton Architectural Journal*, vol. 4 'Fetish', 1992: 7.

53 See e.g. Christine Battersby, 'Her Body/Her Boundaries: Gender and the Metaphysics of Containment', in Andrew Benjamin (ed.), *The Body: Journal of Philosophy and the Visual Arts*, Academy Editions, London, 1993: 36–8.

54 Jean-François Lyotard, *The Postmodern Condition: A Report on Knowledge*, trans. Geoffrey Bennington and Brian Massumi, University of Minnesota Press, Minneapolis, 1984 [1979]. Jürgen Habermas, *The Philosophical Discourse of Modernity*, trans. Frederick Lawrence, Polity Press, Cambridge, 1987 [1985]. Jameson, *Postmodernism*: xv–xvi, discussed ' "returns of the repressed" of historicity' in late twentieth-century culture and cultural theory, and 'the residuality of the modern and its values' in so-called post-modern tropes such as irony. Identifying what he called the 'New Historicism' as an American theoretical avant-garde and scrutinising it for traces of its 'modernity and postmodernity alike', he suggested that if 'there is no pure postmodernism as such, then the residual traces of modernism must be seen in another light'.

55 With thanks to Marketa Uhlirova for this point.

urbanisation in the nineteenth century. Insofar as both moments encapsulate rapid technological change and social instability, parallels can be drawn; yet there are fundamental differences in the type of change and instability between both periods, which also differentiate the effects of one from the other. Both Simmel and Benjamin, in their writing on modernity, implied the idea of rupture with the past, a sense that could also be said to have characterised the last twenty years of the twentieth century. Hal Foster suggests that today Baudelaire's 'shock' has become electronic; he writes that we are '*wired* to spectacular events' and 'psycho-techno thrills'.[56] The question raised in Foster's observation is whether our electronic shock is radically different from Benjamin's electrical metaphor, or whether traces of the past still echo in the present.[57] Whereas Baudelaire, Simmel and Benjamin wrote about the effects of industrialisation on urban populations, the late twentieth century has been characterised by an information revolution which started thirty years ago with the first satellites in space but has escalated in the last five to ten years with the spread of electronic and digital forms of communication.

With regard to the material base of fashion, I am not convinced that it is either modern or post-modern but rather that it is both. In its production, fashion has never been strictly Fordist, in the way that, for example, the automobile industry became in the modernist period.[58] As an industry it is so large and varied that it comprises both Fordist and post-Fordist production methods, embracing craft techniques and the production line, capitalist exploitation and small-scale entrepreneurship. Small experimental designers still work like pre-industrial artisans; haute couturiers preserve the arcane craft skills and protocols of the *atelier*; chains like Asda and Marks & Spencer use automated production lines, while some large multinationals use cheap labour, sometimes that of children, in countries invisible to their consumers, rather than automated production lines closer to home.

Equally, in terms of consumption fashion cannot be aligned along an axis of modernism and post-modernism as discrete and opposite categories. Historically, fashion and artistic modernism were in many ways inimical to each other. Penny Sparke has argued that fashion itself was anathematised by modernists: 'fashion: what an appalling word' wrote Adolf Loos at the turn of the previous century.[59] Sparke notes that Loos even went so far as to draw an analogy between the bourgeois interior and the Terror in his discussion of the stifling oppression of fabrics.[60] Le Corbusier too denigrated fashion and all things feminine in *L'art décoratif d'aujourd'hui* in 1925.[61] In the early years of the twentieth century it was mass culture, by contrast, that became associated with the feminine.[62] As fashion was demonised by modernists, fashion and femininity became modernism's 'other', its dark continent of excess, waste and pointlessness, the 'rotten' of bourgeois culture against which modernist ideologies rallied.[63] By contrast, the Art Nouveau style at the turn of the century had allied eighteenth-century ideals of womanhood, taste and elitist culture with the late nineteenth-century world of mass consumption.[64] Both stood outside the framework of high modernism; both privileged feminine taste and consumption. As the century developed, alongside modernism ran neo-Baroque trends, the decorative (Art Deco for example) and the anti-utilitarian (Surrealism primarily). So if modern fashion loops back to these earlier

56 Foster, *Return of the Real*: 221–2.

57 Featherstone, *Consumer Culture*, argues that post-modernism is a continuation of modernity, and that is why the writings of Simmel and Benjamin still resonate in the present; see ch. 5, 'The Aestheticization of Everyday Life': 65–82.

58 Fordism is predicated on the interchangeability of parts and the division of labour. Fordist production relies on the idea of the production line, with no outworking; since the nineteenth century at least, fashion production in Britain was based on a mixture of piece work, done at home, and sweated labour based at the employers' premises. The increase of fashion production in sweatshops and small factories in Britain in the twentieth century did not eliminate the use of outworkers, so it is debatable whether the fashion industry can ever be said to have been completely Fordist. I am grateful to Joan Farrer for her help on these points.

'Post-Fordism is characterised by the decline of mass production and mass markets; the rise of niche markets; flexibility of plant and labour; the production of small batches; quick response to change. It uses fragmented supply chains, flexible specialism, "just in time" manufacturing, CAD and manufacture, EPOS data'. From Adam Briggs's paper, 'Fashion as the Articulation of Production and Consumption in Apparel Manufacturing and Marketing', at the London College of Fashion, October 2000. 'Post-Fordism' is thus 'the political economy of postmodernism', see the New Times debate in Martin Jacques and Stuart Hall (eds), *New Times: The Changing Face of Politics in the 1990s*, Lawrence & Wishart, London, 1989. Also M. Wark, 'Fashioning the Future: Fashion, Clothing and the Manufacture of Post-Fordist Culture' *Cultural Studies*, vol. 5, no. 1, 1991; and 'Fashion as a Culture Industry' in Andrew Ross (ed.), *No Sweat: Fashion, Free Trade and the Rights of Garment Workers,* Verso, New York and London, 1997. With thanks to Adam Briggs for these references.

Arguably, fashion was always 'post-Fordist'. In business terms it is erratic and past performance is never a guarantee of future success, which is why it is always a high-risk investment; hence fashion companies are largely unsuited to be floated as public companies (see Agins, *End of Fashion*: 210). Indeed, Marx made exactly the same point about the fickleness of fashion as a business in the 1860s, basing much of his argument on the British textile industry and 'the murderous, meaningless caprices of fashion' that were 'linked to the anarchy of production, where demand cannot be predicted, and where gluts lead to starvation'. Karl Marx, *Capital,* vol. 1, trans. Ben Fowkes, Penguin, Harmondsworth, 1976: 609, and see Esther Leslie, *Walter Benjamin:*

Overpowering Conformism, Pluto Press, London and Sterling, Va. 2000: 10.

59 Adolf Loos, *Spoken into the Void: Collected Essays 1897–1900*, MIT Press, Cambridge, Mass., 1982: 7, quoted in Penny Sparke, *As Long As It's Pink: The Sexual Politics of Taste*, Pandora, London, 1995: 105.

60 Ibid: 20.

61 Le Corbusier, *The Decorative Art of Today*, trans. James I. Dunnett, Architectural Press, London, 1987. Thomas Crow has explicitly identified fashion and commerce as the enemies of modernist and avant-garde art: 'Modernism and Mass Culture in the Visual Arts' in *Modern Art in the Common Culture*, Yale University Press, New Haven and London, 1996: 4. Like Le Corbusier and Loos before him and in common with many other art historians, Crow is hostile to fashion. T. J. Clark also writes: 'I persist in thinking that high fashion's cocktail of artiness and classiness (unattainable elegance spiced with avant-garde risk) is deadly, and deeply woman-hating': *Farewell to an Idea: Episodes from a History of Modernism*, Yale University Press, New Haven and London, 1999: 437. The vehemence of this reaction indicates that, as Lisa Tickner writes, ' "avant-garde" and "fashion" are terms between which there has to be a kind of *cordon sanitaire*': *Modern Life and Modern Subjects*, Yale University Press, New Haven and London, 2000: 193. Nevertheless, as Tickner points out, 'the avant-garde was never free of fashion or commerce or economically independent of the bourgeois society whose tastes and values it disdained' and 'to whom', in Clement Greenberg's words, 'it has always remained attached by an umbilical cord of gold': ibid: 188. Greenberg's phrase is from his much cited essay 'Avant Garde and Kitsch'. Tickner rightly points out that fashion and commerce were never really absent from modernism, but she distinguishes modernism from fashion and commerce by arguing that the former is 'uncomplacent' and 'resistant': ibid: 302 n. 28. For a historically specific analysis of the complex interaction of fashion, art and commodity culture in the work of Paul Poiret see Nancy J. Troy, 'Fashion, Art and the Marketing of Modernism' in *Couture Culture: A Study in Modern Art and Fashion*, MIT Press, Cambridge, Mass., and London, 2003: 18–79.

62 Andreas Huyssen, 'Mass Culture as Woman: Modernism's Other' in *After the Great Divide: Modernism, Mass Culture and Postmodernism*, Macmillan, London, 1986. Crow, *Modern Art*: 3–37.

63 Sparke, *As Long As*: 104.

64 Ibid.

65 Rebecca Arnold, 'Luxury and Restraint: Minimalism in 1990s Fashion', in Nicola White and Ian Griffiths (eds), *The Fashion Business*, Berg, Oxford and New York, 2000: 167–81.

66 Buck-Morss, *Dialectics of Seeing*: 293.

67 Benjamin, *Arcades Project*: 459.

68 Benjamin , *Illuminations*: 263 and 265.

discourses of the body perhaps it is because it never really left them. The 1900 Paris Exhibition was a major showcase for the Art Nouveau style, and this was also the period in which fashion shows began to be staged. It is no accident that Galliano harks back to the bohemians and *femmes galantes* of the same period.

I have discussed Galliano as key at various points in this text but he represents only one strand of fashion in the 1990s. The period also saw a return to modernism via the new trends of deconstruction and grunge, the influence of sportswear, a significant vogue for minimalism, and the rise of major American designers of 'classics' such as Donna Karan, Ralph Lauren and Calvin Klein whose work constitutes the sort of 'classical revival' which has often typified American fashion.[65] The type of gothic fashion I have discussed is the ghost, or shadow, of this rational, American and international style in which, as in Benjamin's dialectical fairytale, 'newness repeats itself mythically'.[66] In 'Konvolut N' Benjamin writes: 'To encompass both Breton and Le Corbusier – that would mean drawing the spirit of contemporary France like a bow, with which knowledge shoots the moment in the heart.'[67] To paraphrase Benjamin, I have not encompassed, say, both Martin Margiela and Brooks Brothers – that would mean drawing the spirit of global capitalism like a bow to shoot the moment in the heart – but have, like Benjamin, focused on the first named. Thus my wider assertions about fashion in this chapter must be read with caution; still, I felt I had to map out my intellectual foundations because of the large historical claims implied in my ideas about haunting and the 'ghosts of modernity', my use of the term post-industrial and my reluctance to use the term post-modernism.

It is important to remember that the term fashion is always broad enough to embody contradiction and complexity, looping back simultaneously to differing design ideologies of the past. This is the 'now-time' of fashion,[68] the two points in the labyrinth that touch by jumping back to earlier moments that are not temporally proximate: 'in order for a part of the past to be touched by the present instant there must be no continuity between them.'[69] Fashion undoes those distinctions among modernism, modernity and post-modernism, because they are no longer discrete categories but are held in a creative tension in fashion, not only in its design but also in its techniques of production, marketing and dissemination. Susan Buck-Morss has argued that Benjamin's

> *Passagen-Werk* suggests that it makes no sense to divide the era of capitalism into formalist 'modernism' and historically eclectic 'post-modernism' as these tendencies have been there from the start of industrial culture. The paradoxical dynamics of novelty and repetition simply repeat themselves anew. Modernism and post-modernism are not chronological eras, but political positions in the century-long struggle between art and technology . . . each position thus represents a partial truth; each will recur 'anew', so long as the contradictions of commodity society are not overcome.[70]

Fashion is a paradigm in the way that it can carry a contradiction – this is very modern – the whole thing is a kind of 'dialectical image' or 'critical constellation' not just of past and present but of differing modernities, and its 'now-time' can hold them together in suspension. Against the orthodoxy of heroic modernism runs a counter-strategy of Surrealism and the decorative arts; against the functionalist account of Fordist and post-Fordist production runs a counter-story of piecemeal, fractured and unsystematic production methods. And against the myth of fashion as always striving for the new is a counter-tale of fashion looping back to earlier moments of modernity in the present. The metaphor of the labyrinth enabled me to argue that two such moments touch when a historical detail doubles back to reveal something about the present. All these 'turns and returns' (as Hal Foster calls them) are held in suspension in the formaldehyde of fashion which is why the way it has developed in the modern period offers an important challenge to dominant discourses of art, design and culture in general.[71]

If it makes sense to talk of industrial culture, it is now time to differentiate the present as a moment of transition to post-industrial, a term I use ironically to express the ghosting of industrial production in a globalised economy. And if we accept the ideas of the 'post' that relate to commerce and economics, and that they have a knock-on effect on culture, we must be in some sort of 'post' culturally too; perhaps fashion can help to elucidate the way that, in the 'post', the past is imbricated in the present, and that this type of obsessive self-scrutiny is part of modernity, however it is characterised. Fashion embodies this ambivalence. Between modernity and post-modernism its multifarious forms have never entirely embraced either one or the other but have straddled both to hold them in a creative tension.

Spoiling

'The world is spoiled. So we will be spoiled too!' cry the pretty, young, robotic models Marie 1 and Marie 2 in Vära Chytilova's 1966 film *Daisies*,[72] as they wreak havoc in their flat, pick up unsuspecting businessmen and turn a restaurant banquet orgy into a destructive catwalk show. A variety of designers make spoiled work that reflects a spoiled world. Modernist ideas about stability, progress and building something solid for the future may seem outdated to this generation of designers. Sometimes their engagement with abjection, alienation and decay seems a more honest way to picture the world than with false optimism and shiny gloss. However, when fashion can put its finger on a pulse and make designer roadkill sexy, when alienation is made over as spectacle, it is tempting to pathologise the culture that produces such imagery. Like the staging of Aristotelian tragedy, the over-theatricality and excess of contemporary fashion suggest that some trauma is being enacted publicly and communally, either the staging of the private in the public spheres, as Selzer argues, or the Baroque staging of cruelty and excess by a conservative culture, as Buci-Glucksmann suggests. The conversion of moral values into production values in current fashion spectacle may be part of a broader cultural shift from ethics to aesthetics that Michel Maffesoli has attributed to the breakdown of social cohesion.[73] He goes further,

69   Benjamin, *Arcades Project*: 470.
70   Buck-Morss, *Dialectics of Seeing*: 359.
71   Mark Wigley's *White Walls, Designer Dresses: The Fashioning of Modern Architecture*, MIT Press, Cambridge, Mass., and London, 1995, gives an original and interesting account of fashion and modernist architecture, but is written from the perspective of a historian using fashion to 'regender' modernist architecture, rather than being an investigation of fashion in its own terms and the way in which it might intersect with modernism.
72   Vära Chytilova, *Daisies* [1966], connoisseur video, London, 1993.
73   Michel Maffesoli, *The Time of the Tribes: The Decline of Individualism in Mass Society*, trans. Mark Ritter, Sage, London and Thousand Oaks, New Delhi, 1996.

writing that aesthetics has replaced ethics as the organising principle of our existence, a point exemplified in the theatricalisation of alienation in 1990s fashion photographs.

Frank Kermode pointed out in 1966 that the literature of apocalypse is endemic to modernism, and certainly apocalyptic fashion visions could be located in this tradition too.[74] The shadow of the end 'lies on the crises of our fictions; we may speak of it as immanent.'[75] He argued that apocalypse, a form of historical allegory, is infinitely flexible and resilient; it can be blended or absorbed, for example with myths of empire (as in Galliano's neo-and post-colonial fictions of Edwardian gowns overlaid with Dinka beaded corsets) and of decadence (McQueen's *femme fatales* and Shaun Leane's jewellery). The myth of Transition, as Kermode called it, the sense that we are at such a significant turning point that the present becomes 'a mere transitional point', could even be said to be exemplified by fashion itself, with its restless imperative for change.

The philosophical concerns of the twentieth century were largely pessimistic, those of alienation and nihilism. Many academics identified the late twentieth century as a period of cultural trauma and anxiety, and perhaps their texts too form part of a set of writings on apocalypse. There are many kinds of fiction other than the literary, in art and design as well as in academic writing and critical theory. In literary criticism, for example, Terry Eagleton proposed a new theory of tragedy, arguing that, far from being dead, it lay at the heart of the contemporary as a core feature of twentieth-century modernism.[76] Perhaps the fashion design and photography I have surveyed is a form of catharsis, perhaps a form of mourning. Perhaps it is a coping stratagem, a way of both articulating and containing trauma. Whether these designs illustrate the dark side of a free market economy, the loosening of social controls, the rise of risk and uncertainty as key elements of 'modernity' and 'globalisation', or whether they have a relation to the 'crisis in gender' of the 1990s asserted by some, are all speculations. Certainly the eschatological tenor specific to modern thought relates to profound changes in economics and politics in the second half of the twentieth century.[77] Kermode argued that, as we experience more rapid transitions in technology and changes in social mobility, we relate these changes to apocalypse, and imagine ourselves at the end of one period and on the edge of a new one. 'The the stage of transition becomes, in our minds, an age in itself', so 'the function of transition is our way of registering the conviction that the end is immanent rather than imminent.'[78] 'Apocalypse is a part of the modern Absurd . . . the set of our fear and desire . . . a permanent feature of a permanent literature of crisis.'[79] Debates in the social sciences about globalisation could also be understood as a literature of crisis, one which we can use to understand our fears today. The concept of globalisation might be simply another incarnation of the sublime of Kant and Burke.[80] New digital flows, and the way that virtuality alters space and time to touch human lives across the globe, give new scope for the experiences of awe and horror on a new scale. Some of this awe and *terribilità* can be read off apocalyptic fashion visions of men falling from buildings, burning catwalks and designer roadkill.

The turn to darker imagery in the fashion I have described cannot, however, be related only to the coming of the machine in the form of new technology, but must also be about

74   Kermode, *Sense of an Ending*: 98.

75   Ibid: 6.

76   Terry Eagleton, *Sweet Violence: The Idea of the Tragic,* Blackwell, Oxford, 2002. See also David Trotter, *Paranoid Modernism*, Oxford University Press, 2001.

77   Kermode, *Sense of an Ending*: 95.

78   Ibid: 101.

79   Ibid: 123–4.

80   For a discussion of the post-modern sublime see Andrew Benjamin, *Art, Mimesis and the Avant-Garde: Aspects of a Philosophy of Difference*, Routledge, London and New York, 1991; Andrew Benjamin (ed.), *ICA Documents 10: Thinking Art, Beyond Traditional Aesthetics*, ICA, London, 1991.

the dark side of a free market economy in which there is no social contract. With the loosening of social controls from the 1960s and the loosening of economic controls during the Thatcher period in Britain, the advent of Reaganite economic policies in USA and the demise of the Eastern bloc in the late 1980s, came greater personal freedom but also the harsh side of a free market economy. In the 1970s punk was dark and nihilistic; so too was the fashion photography of Helmut Newton and Guy Bourdin. The absence of the social contract is potentially alienating for modern subjects, just as it was in the nineteenth century when, as Marx wrote, 'all that is solid melts into air, all that is holy is profaned, and man is at last compelled to face with sober senses, his real conditions of life, and his relations with his kind.'[81] And the harsh conditions of a market-driven economy ensure that, again as Marx wrote, 'men make their own history, but they do not make it just as they please; they do not make under circumstances chosen by themselves, but under circumstances directly encountered, given and transmitted from the past'.[82]

Yet if alienation produces deracinated modern subjects it also gives them a certain freedom to reinvent themselves. Alienation can also be pictured as a 'loosening of the self', and perhaps the person who is best at 'doing' fashion is the person who is best at embracing their own alienation, loving it and obsessively reinventing themselves through it. Fashion can also be linked to the binding or healing of wounded narcissism; and narcissism, clearly relevant to fashion, can be located historically too in the context of Baudelairean modernity.[83] If post-industrial modernity has produced us as mobile subjects, we are at least free to make our own fictions, if not our own history, in a world we never made. For fashion designers and photographers this might mean that the only viable way to go forward is by looking back, like Benjamin's angel of history who is blown backwards into the future by the storm of progress, surveying the wreckage behind him. If the dark history of the twentieth century seems finally to have caught up with fashion design, or vice versa, the only way to work now must surely be, as Gramsci put it, with 'pessimism of the intelligence, optimism of the will.'[84]

81   Karl Marx and Frederick Engels, *The Manifesto of the Communist Party*, trans. Samuel Moore, Progress Publishers, Moscow, 1966 [1848]: 45.

82   Karl Marx, *The Eighteenth Brumaire of Louis Bonaparte* [1852], trans. from the German, Progress Publishers, Moscow, 3rd rev. ed. 1954 [2nd rev. ed. 1869]: 10.

83   See Jonathan Friedman, 'Narcissism, Roots and Postmodernity: The Constitution of Selfhood in the Global Crisis', in Scott Lash and Jonathan Friedman (eds), *Modernity and Identity*, Basil Blackwell, Oxford, 1992: 331–6; see too Mike Featherstone, 'Postmodernism and the Aestheticization of Everyday Life', in ibid: 265–90.

84   Antonio Gramsci, *Selections from the Prison Notebooks,* trans. Quintin Hoare and Geoffrey Nowell Smith, Lawrence & Wishart, London, 1971 [1932]: 175.

Bibliography

Books

Abraham, Nicolas, and Maria Torok, *The Wolf Man's Magic Word: A Cryptonomy*, University of Minneapolis Press, Minnesota, 1986.

—, *The Shell and the Kernel*, vol. 1, trans. and intro. by Nicolas T. Rand, University of Chicago Press, Chicago and London, 1994.

Ackroyd, Peter, *Dressing Up: Transvestism and Drag: The History of An Obsession*, Thames & Hudson, London, 1979.

Addressing the Century: 100 Years of Art and Fashion, Hayward Gallery Publishing, London, 1998.

Adorno, Theodor, *In Search of Wagner*, trans. Rodney Livingstone, Verso, London and New York, 1981.

—and Walter Benjamin, *Complete Correspondence 1928–1940*, ed. Henri Loritz, trans. Nicholas Walter, Polity Press, Cambridge, 1999.

Agins, Teri, *The End of Fashion*, Quill/Harper Collins, New York, 2000.

Alison, Jane, and Liz Farelley (eds), *JAM: style + music + media*, Booth Clibborn, London, 1996.

Als, Hilton, *et al*, *Leigh Bowery*, Violette Editions, London, 1998.

Amelunxen, H. V., S. Inglhaut, and F. Rotzer, *Photography after Photography*, Arts Council of Great Britain, London, 1998.

Anderson, Mark M., *Kafka's Clothes: Ornament and Aestheticism in the Hapsburg Fin de Siècle*, Clarendon Press, Oxford, 1992.

Ansell Pearson, Keith, *Viroid Life: Perspectives on Nietzsche and the Transhuman Condition*, Routledge, London, 1997.

Ariès, Philippe, *Western Attitudes to Death,* trans. Patricia M. Ranum, Johns Hopkins University Press, Baltimore and London, 1974.

—, *The Hour of Our Death*, trans. Helen Weaver, Allen Lane, London, 1981.

—, *Images of Man and Death*, trans. Janet Lloyd, Harvard University Press, Cambridge, Mass., and London, 1985.

Arnold, Rebecca, *Fashion, Desire and Anxiety: Image and Morality in the Twentieth Century*, I. B. Tauris, London and New York, 2001.

Bailey, Peter, *Popular Culture and Performance in the Victorian City*, Cambridge University Press, 1998.

Balsamo, Anne, *Technologies of the Gendered Body,* Duke University Press, Durham, N. C. and London, 1997.

Barker, Francis, Peter Hulme, and Margaret Iverson (eds), *Uses of History*, Manchester University Press, 1991.

Barley, Nick (ed.), *Lost and Found: Critical Voices in New British Design,* Birkhäuser/British Council, Basle, Boston and Berlin, 1999.

Barthes, Roland, *Camera Lucida: Reflections on Photography*, trans. Richard Howard, Vintage, London, 1993 [1980].

Bataille, Georges, *Visions of Excess: Selected Writings, 1927–1939*, ed. and trans. Allan Stoekl, University of Minnesota Press, Minneapolis, 1985.

Baudelaire, Charles, *The Painter of Modern Life and Other Essays*, trans. Jonathan Mayne, Phaidon, London, 2nd ed. 1995.

—, *Complete Poems*, trans. Walter Martin, Carcanet, Manchester, 1997.

Baudrillard, Jean, *Simulations*, trans. Paul Foss *et al*, Semiotext(e), New York, 1983.

—, *The Ecstasy of Communication*, trans. Bernard and Caroline Schutze, Semiotext(e) Autonomia, Brooklyn, N.Y., 1988.

—, *Fatal Strategies*, Semiotext(e), New York, 1990.

—, *Seduction*, trans. Brian Singer, Macmillan, London, 1990 [1979].

—, *Symbolic Exchange and Death*, trans. Iain Hamilton Grant, Sage, London and Thousand Oaks, New Delhi, 1993 [1976].

—, *The Illusion of the End*, trans. Chris Turner, Polity Press, Cambridge, 1994.

Beaton, Cecil, *The Glass of Fashion*, Cassell, London, 1954.

Beauvoir, Simone de, *The Second Sex*, trans. Howard Madison Parshley, Penguin, Harmondsworth, 1972 [1949].

Beck, Ulrich, *Risk Society: Towards a New Modernity*, trans. Mark Ritter, Sage, London and Newbury Park, New Delhi, 1992.

Bell, Daniel, *The Cultural Contradictions of Capitalism*, Heinemann, London, 2nd ed. 1979 [1975].

—, 'The Third Technological Revolution and Its Possible Socio-Economic Consequences', University of Salford, Faculty of Social Sciences Annual Lecture, Salford, 1988.

—, *The Coming of Postindustrial Society: A Venture in Social Forecasting*, Heinemann, London, 1994.

Benjamin, Andrew, *Art, Mimesis and the Avant-Garde: Aspects of a Philosophy of Difference*, Routledge, London and New York, 1991.

—(ed.), *ICA Documents 10: Thinking Art, Beyond Traditional Aesthetics*, ICA, London, 1991.

Benjamin, Walter, *Illuminations*, trans. Harry Zohn, Fontana/Collins, London, 1973 [1955].

Benjamin, Walter, *The Origin of German Tragic Drama*, trans. John Osborne with an intro. by George Steiner, New Left Books, London, 1977.

—, *One Way Street and Other Writings,* with an intro. by Susan Sontag, trans. Edmund Jephcott and Kingsley Shorter, Verso, London, 1985.

—, *Charles Baudelaire: A Lyric Poet in the Era of High Capitalism*, trans. Harry Zohn, Verso, London and New York, 1997.

—, *The Arcades Project*, trans. Howard Eiland and Kevin McLaughlin, Belknap Press of Harvard University Press, Cambridge, Mass., and London, 1999.

Benstock, Shari, and Suzanne Ferriss (eds), *On Fashion*, Rutgers University Press, New Brunswick, N.J., 1994.

Berman, Marshall, *All That is Solid Melts into Air: The Experience of Modernity*, Verso, London, 1983.

—, *Adventures in Marxism*, Verso, London and New York, 1999.

Blau, Herbert, *Nothing In Itself: Complexions of Fashion*, Indiana University Press, Bloomington and Indianapolis, 1999.

Bolton, Andrew, *The Supermodern Wardrobe*, Victoria & Albert Museum, London, 2002.

Bordo, Susan, *Unbearable Weight: Feminism, Western Culture and the Body*, University of California Press, Berkeley, 1993.

Braddock, Sarah, and Marie O'Mahony, *Techno Textiles: Revolutionary Fabrics for Fashion and Design*, Thames & Hudson, London, 1998.

—(eds), *Fabric of Fashion*, British Council, London, 2000.

Bradley, Alexandra, and Gavin Fernandez (eds), *Unclasped: Contemporary British Jewellery*, essay by Derren Gilhooley, afterword by Simon Costin, Black Dog, London, 1997.

Brantlinger, P., *Bread and Circuses: Theories of Mass Culture and Social Decay*, Ithaca, N.Y., 1983.

Breward, Christopher, *The Culture of Fashion*, Manchester University Press, 1995.

—, *The Hidden Consumer: Masculinities, Fashion and City Life 1860–1914*, Manchester University Press, 1999.

Bronfen, Elizabeth, *Over Her Dead Body: Death, Femininity and the Aesthetic*, Manchester University Press, 1992.

—, *The Knotted Subject: Hysteria and Its Discontents*, Princeton University Press, 1998.

Buci-Glucksmann, Christine, *Baroque Reason: The Aesthetics of Modernity*, trans. Patrick Camiller, with an intro. by Bryan S. Turner, Sage, London and Thousand Oaks, New Delhi, 1994 [1984].

Buck-Morss, Susan, *The Dialectics of Seeing: Walter Benjamin and the Arcades Project*, MIT Press, Cambridge, Mass., and London, 1991.

Burch, Noël, *Life to Those Shadows*, trans. Ben Brewster, British Film Institute, London, 1990.

Burman Baines, Barbara, *Fashion Revivals: From the Elizabethan Age to the Present Day*, Batsford, London, 1981.

Butler, Judith, *Gender Trouble: Feminism and the Subversion of Identity*, Routledge, New York and London, 1990.

Butler, Judith, *Bodies that Matter: On the Discursive Limits of "Sex"*, Routledge, London and New York, 1993.

Campbell, Colin, *The Romantic Ethic and the Spirit of Modern Consumerism*, Basil Blackwell, Oxford, 1987.

Carter, Angela, *The Sadeian Woman: An Exercise in Cultural History*, Virago, London, 1979.

—, *Nothing Sacred*, Virago, London, 1982.

Caruth, Cathy (ed.), *Trauma: Explorations in Memory*, Johns Hopkins University Press, Baltimore and London, 1995.

Carver, Terrell, *The Postmodern Marx*, Manchester University Press, 1998.

Certeau, Michel de, *Cultural Practices of Everyday Life*, trans. Stephen Rendall, University of California Press, Berkeley, 1984.

—, *Heterologies: Discourse of the Other*, trans. Brian Massumi, University of Manchester Press, 1986.

Chambers, Iain, *Popular Culture: The Metropolitan Experience*, Routledge, London, 1982.

—, *Migrancy, Culture, Identity*, Comedia/Routledge, London and New York, 1994.

Chamisso, Adalbert von, *The Wonderful Story of Peter Schlemihl*, trans. Leopold von Loewenstein-Wertheim, John Calder, London, 1957 [1813].

Charles-Roux, Edmonde, *Chanel and Her World*, trans. Daniel Wheeler, Weidenfeld & Nicolson, London, 1982 [1979].

Cheney, Liana de Girolami (ed.), *The Symbolism of* Vanitas *in the Arts, Literature and Music*, Edwin Mellen Press, Lewiston, Queenston, Lampeter, 1992.

Chermeyeff, Catherine (ed.), *Fashion Photography Now*, Abrams, New York, 2000.

Chic Clicks: Creativity and Commerce in Contemporary Fashion, Hatje Cantz, Ostfilden Ruit, 2002.

Clark, David, *Urban World/Global City*, Routledge, London and New York, 1996.

Clark, T. J., *The Painting of Modern Life: Paris in the Art of Manet and his Followers*, Princeton University Press and Thames & Hudson, London, 1984.

—, *Farewell to an Idea: Episodes from A History of Modernism*, Yale University Press, New Haven and London, 1999.

Cohen, Margaret, *Profane Illumination: Walter Benjamin and the Paris of Surrealist Revolution*, University of California Press, Berkeley and London, 1993.

Confused/Dazed, Booth Clibborn, London, 1999.

Corbin, Alain, *Woman for Hire: Prostitution and Sexuality in France After 1850*, trans. Alan Sheridan, Harvard University Press, Cambridge, Mass., 1990.

Corbusier, le, *The Decorative Art of Today*, trans. James I. Dunnett, Architectural Press, London, 1987.

Cotton, Charlotte, *Imperfect Beauty: The Making of Contemporary Fashion Photographs*, Victoria & Albert Publications, London, 2000.

Coupland, Douglas, *Generation X*, Abacus, London, 1996 [1991].

Crane, Diana, *Fashion and Its Social Agendas*, University of Chicago Press, 2000.

Crary, Jonathan, *Techniques of the Observer: On Vision and Modernity in the Nineteenth Century*, MIT Press, Cambridge, Mass., and London, 1990.

—, *Suspensions of Perception: Attention, Spectacle and Modern Culture*, MIT Press, Cambridge, Mass., and London, 2001.

—and Sanford Kwinter (eds), *Incorporations, Zone 6*, Zone Books, New York, 1992.

Crisp, Quentin, *The Naked Civil Servant*, Fontana, London, 1977.

Crow, Thomas, *Modern Art in the Common Culture*, Yale University Press, New Haven and London, 1996.

David, Alison Matthews, 'Cutting a Figure: Tailoring, technology and Social Identity in Nineteenth-Century Paris', PhD diss., Stanford University, 2002.

Dean, Carolyn, *The Self and Its Pleasures: Bataille, Lacan and the History of the Decentered Subject*, Cornell University Press, Ithaca and London, 1992.

Debord, Guy, *Society of the Spectacle*, trans. Donald Nicholson-Smith, Zone Books, London, 1994 [1967].

Deitch, Jeffrey, *Post Human*, Musée d'Art Contemporain, Pully/Lausanne, 1992.

Derrida, Jacques, *Specters of Marx: The State of Debt, the Work of Mourning, and the New International*, trans. Peggy Kamuf, Routledge, New York and London, 1994.

Derycke, Luc, and Sandra van de Veire (eds), *Belgian Fashion Design*, Ludion, Ghent and Amsterdam, 1999.

Dickens, Charles, *Our Mutual Friend*, ed. with an intro. by Stephen Gill, Penguin, Harmondsworth, 1985 [1864–5].

Dijksra, Bram, *Idols of Perversity: Fantasies of Feminine Evil in Fin-de-Siècle Culture*, Oxford University Press, Oxford & New York, 1986.

Doane, Mary Ann, *Femmes Fatales: Feminism, Film Theory, Psychoanalysis*, Routledge, London and New York, 1991.

Dollimore, Jonathan, *Sexual Dissidence: Augustine to Wilde, Freud to Foucault*, Clarendon Press, Oxford, 1991.

—, *Death, Desire and Loss in Western Culture*, Allen Lane, Penguin, London, 1998.

Douglas, Mary, *Purity and Danger: An Analysis of the Concepts of Pollution and Taboo*, Routledge, London and New York, 1992 [1966].

Duits, Thimo te, *La Maison Margiela: (9/4/1615)*, trans. Ruth Koenig, Boijmans Van Beuningen Museum, Rotterdam, 1997.

—, *Believe: Walter van Beirendonck and Wild & Lethal Trash!*, with photographs by Juergen Teller, Boijmans Van Beuningen Museum, Rotterdam, 1998.

Dunant, Sarah, and Roy Porter (eds), *The Age of Anxiety*, Virago, London, 1996.

Duve, Thierry de, Arielle Pelenc and Boris Groys, *Jeff Wall*, Phaidon, London, 1996.

Eagleton, Terry, *Sweet Violence: The Idea of the Tragic*, Basil Blackwell, Oxford, 2002.

Elias, Norbert, *The Court Society*, Basil Blackwell, Oxford, 1983.

Eliot, T. S., *Selected Poems*, Faber & Faber, London, 1954.

Ellis, Brett Easton, *Glamorama*, Picador, London and Knopf, New York, 1998.

Ewen, Stuart and Elizabeth, *Channels of Desire: Mass Images and the Shaping of America*, University of Minnesota Press, Minneapolis, 1992.

Falk, Pasi, and Colin Campbell (eds), *The Shopping Experience*, Sage, London, Thousand Oaks and New Delhi, 1997.

Farelley, Liz (ed.), *Jam: Tokyo-London*, Booth-Clibborn, London, 2001.

Farrell, Kirkby, *Post-traumatic Culture: Imagery and Interpretation in the 1990s*, Johns Hopkins University Press, Baltimore, 1998.

Fashion Faces Up: Photographs and Words from the World of Fashion, Steidl, Göttingen, 2000.

Fausch, Deborah, *et al* (eds), *Architecture: In Fashion*, Princeton Architectural Press, 1994.

Featherstone, Mike, *Consumer Culture and Postmodernism*, Sage, London, Newbury Park and New Delhi, 1991.

—and Roger Burrows, *Cyberspace/Cyberbodies/Cyberpunk*, Sage, London, Thousand Oaks and New Delhi, 1995.

Finkelstein, Joanne, *After a Fashion*, Melbourne University Press, 1996.

Foster, Hal, *Compulsive Beauty*, MIT Press, Cambridge, Mass., and London, 1993.

—, *The Return of the Real: The Avant Garde at the End of the Century*, MIT Press, Cambridge, Mass., and London, 1996.

Foucault, Michel, *The Order of Things: An Archaeology of the Human Sciences*, trans. A. M. Sheridan-Smith, Vintage, New York, 1973 [1966].

—, *The Archaeology of Knowledge*, trans. A. M. Sheridan-Smith, Tavistock, London, 1974 [1969].

—, *The History of Sexuality, Volume Two: The Uses of Pleasure*, trans. Robert Hurley, New York, Pantheon, 1985 [1984].

—, *The History of Sexuality, Volume Three: The Care of the Self*, trans. Robert Hurley, Pantheon, New York, 1986 [1984].

Frankel, Susannah, *Visionaries: Interviews with Fashion Designers*, Victoria & Albert Publications, London, 2001.

Freidberg, Anne, *Window Shopping: Cinema and the Postmodern*, University of California Press, Berkeley, Los Angeles and London, 1994.

Freud, Sigmund, 'Creative Writers and Day-dreaming' [1908] in *Works: The Standard Edition of the Complete Psychological Works of Sigmund Freud*, under the general editorship of James Strachey, vol. IX, Hogarth Press, London, 1959: 141–53.

—, 'On Transience' [1916] in *Works: The Standard Edition of the Complete Psychological Works of Sigmund Freud*, under the general editorship of James Strachey, vol. XIV, Hogarth Press, London, 1955: 303–7.

—, 'The Uncanny' [1919] in *Works: The Standard Edition of the Complete Psychological Works of Sigmund Freud*, under the general editorship of James Strachey, vol. XVII, Hogarth Press, London, 1955: 217–56.

—, 'Beyond the Pleasure Principle' [1920] in *Works: The Standard Edition of the Complete Psychological Works of Sigmund Freud*, under the general editorship of James Strachey), vol. XVIII, Hogarth Press, London, 1955: 7–64.

—, 'Medusa's Head' [1922] in *Works: The Standard Edition of the Complete Psychological Works of Sigmund Freud*, under the general editorship of James Strachey, vol. XVIII, Hogarth Press, London, 1955: 273–4.

—, with Josef Breuer, *Studies on Hysteria* [1895] in *Works: The Standard Edition of the Complete Psychological Works of Sigmund Freud*, under the general editorship of James Strachey, vol. II, Hogarth Press, London, 1955.

Fukuyama, Francis, *The End of History and the Last Man*, Hamish Hamilton, London, 1992.

Furedi, Frank, *Culture of Fear: Risk-Taking and the Morality of Low Expectation*, Cassell, London, 1997.

Gamman, Lorraine, and Merja Makinen, *Female Fetishism: A New Look*, Lawrence & Wishart, London, 1994.

Gan, Stephen, *Visionaire's Fashion 2000: Designers at the Turn of the Millennium*, Laurence King, London, 1997.

—, *Visionaire's Fashion 2001: Designers of the New Avant-Garde*, ed. Alix Browne, Laurence King, London, 1999.

Garb, Tamar, *Bodies of Modernity: Figure and Flesh in Fin-de-Siècle France*, Thames & Hudson, London, 1998.

Garber, Marjorie, *Shakespeare's Ghost Writers: Literature as Uncanny Causality*, Methuen, London, 1987.

Gershenfeld, Neil, *When Things Start to Think*, Coronet, London, 1999.

Gershuny, Jonathan I., *Changing Times: Work and Leisure in Postindustrial Society*, Oxford University Press, 2000.

Gibson, Robin, and Pam Roberts, *Madame Yevonde: Colour, Fantasy and Myth*, National Portrait Gallery Publications, London, 1990.

Giddens, Anthony, *Modernity and Self-Identity: Self and Society in the Late Modern Age*, Polity Press, Cambridge, 1991.

—, *Runaway World: How Globalisation is Reshaping our Lives*, Profile Books, London, 1999.

Goncourt, Edmond de, *Pages from the Goncourt Journal* [24 September 1870], trans. Robert Baldick, Oxford University Press, 1978.

Gramsci, Antonio, *Selections from the Prison Notebooks*, trans. Quintin Hoare and Geoffrey Nowell Smith, Lawrence & Wishart, London, 1971.

Gray, Chris Hables (ed.), *The Cyborg Handbook*, Routledge, New York and London, 1995.

Grazia, Victoria de and Ellen Furlough (eds), *The Sex of Things: Gender and Consumption in Historical Perspective*, University of California Press, Berkeley, Los Angeles and London, 1996.

Greenblatt, Stephen, *Renaissance Self-Fashioning: From More to Shakespeare*, University of Chicago Press, 1980.

Greenhalgh, Paul, (ed.), *Modernism in Design*, Reaktion Books, London, 1990.

Guerin, Polly, *Creative Fashion Presentations*, Fairchild Publications, New York, 1987.

Habermas, Jürgen, *The Philosophical Discourse of Modernity*, trans. Frederick Lawrence, Polity Press, Cambridge, 1987 [1985].

Hall-Duncan, Nancy, *The History of Fashion Photography*, Alpine Book Company, New York, 1979.

Hamilton, Peter, and Roger Hargreaves, *The Beautiful and the Damned: The Creation of Identity in Nineteeth-Century Photography*, Lund Humphries in association with the National Portrait Gallery, London, 2001.

Haraway, Donna J., *Simians, Cyborgs and Women: The Reinvention of Nature*, Free Association Books, London, 1991.

Hardt, Michael, and Antonio Negri, *Empire*, Harvard University Press, Cambridge, Mass., and London, 2000.

Hobsbawm, Eric, *Age of Extremes: The Short Twentieth Century 1914–1991*, Michael Joseph, London, 1994.

Houellebecq, Michel, *Atomised*, trans. Frank Wynne, Heinemann, London, 2000 [1999].

Huyssen, Andreas, *After the Great Divide: Modernism, Mass Culture and Postmodernism*, Macmillan, London, 1986.

Izima Kaoru, fa projects, London, 2002.

Jacques, Martin, and Stuart Hall (eds), *New Times: The Changing Face of Politics in the 1990s*, Lawrence & Wishart, London, 1989.

Jameson, Fredric, *Postmodernism, or the Cultural Logic of Late Capitalism*, Verso, London and New York, 1991.

Jardine, Lisa, *Worldly Goods*, Macmillan, London, 1996.

Jay, Martin, *Downcast Eyes: The Denigration of Vision in Twentieth-Century French Thought*, University of California Press, Berkeley and Los Angeles, 1993.

Jones, Amelia, *Body Art/Performing the Subject*, University of Minnesota Press, Minneapolis and London, 1998.

Jones, Ann Rosalind, and Peter Stallybrass, *Renaissance Clothing and the Materials of Memory*, Cambridge University Press, 2000.

Jullian, Philippe, *The Triumph of Art Nouveau: The Paris Exhibition of 1900*, Phaidon, London, 1974.

Kaplan, Louise J., *Female Perversions: The Temptations of Madame Bovary*, Pandora, London, 1991.

Kelley, Mike, *The Uncanny*, Gemeentemuseum, Arnhem, 1993.

Kember, Sarah, *Virtual Anxiety: Photography, New Technologies and Subjectivity*, Manchester University Press, 1998.

Kermode, Frank, *The Sense of an Ending: Studies in the Theory of Fiction with a New Epilogue*, Oxford University Press, 2000 [1966].

Koda, Harold, *Extreme Beauty: The Body Transformed*, Yale University Press, New Haven and London, 2002.

Kracauer, Siegfried, *The Mass Ornament: Weimar Essays*, trans. Thomas Y. Levin, Harvard University Press, Cambridge, Mass., and London, 1995.

Krauss, Rosalind, and Jane Livingston, *L'Amour fou: Photography and Surrealism*, Abbeville, New York and Arts Council of Great Britain, London, 1986.

Kries, M., and A. von Vegesack (eds), *A-POC making: Issey Miyake and Dai Fujiwara*, Vitra Design Museum, Weil am Rhein, 2000

Kristeva, Julia, *The Powers of Horror: An Essay on Abjection*, trans. Leon S. Roudier, Columbia University Press, Ithaca and Oxford, 1982 [1980].

Kuhn, Annette, *The Power of Images: Essays on Representation and Sexuality*, Routledge, New York and London, 1985.

Kwint, Marius, Christopher Breward, and Jeremy Ainsley (eds), *Material Memories: Design and Evocation*, Berg, Oxford and New York, 1999.

Lacou-Labarthe, Philippe, and Jean-Luc Nancy, *The Literary Absolute*, trans. Philip Barnard and Cheryl Lester, State University of New York Press, Albany, 1988.

Lajer-Burcharth, Ewa, *Necklines: The Art of Jacques-Louis David after the Terror*, Yale University Press, New Haven and London, 1999.

Lasch, Christopher, *Culture of Narcissism: American Life in an Age of Diminishing Expectations*, Abacus, London, 1980.

Lash, Scott, and Jonathan Friedman (eds), *Modernity and Identity*, Basil Blackwell, Oxford, 1992.

Latham, Rob, *Consuming Youth: Vampires, Cyborgs and the Culture of Consumption*, University of Chicago Press, 2002.

Ledger, Sally, and Scott McCracken (eds), *Cultural Politics at the Fin de Siècle*, Cambridge University Press, 1995.

Lehmann, Ulrich, *Tigersprung: Fashion in Modernity*, MIT Press, Cambridge, Mass., and London, 2000.

Lemire, Beverlie, *Fashion's Favorite: The Cotton Trade and the Consumer in Britain 1660–1800*, Oxford University Press, 1991.

Leopardi, Giacomo, *Operetti Morali*, Rizzoli, Milan, 1951 [1824].

Leslie, Esther, *Walter Benjamin: Overpowering Conformism*, Pluto Press, London and Sterling, Va., 2000.

Li, Patrick (ed.), *Fashion Time: Creative Time in the Anchorage: Exposing Meaning in Fashion Through Presentation*, Creative Time Inc., New York, 1999.

Lipovetsky, Gilles, *The Empire of Fashion: Dressing Modern Democracy*, trans. Catherine Porter, Princeton University Press, 1994 [1987].

Looking at Fashion, Florence Biennale, Skira, Milan, 1996.

Loos, Adolf, *Spoken into the Void: Collected Essays 1897–1900*, MIT Press, Cambridge, Mass., 1982: 7.

Lovatt-Smith, Lisa, and Patrick Remy (eds), *Fashion Images de Mode*, vol. I, Steidl, Göttingen, 1996.

Lovatt-Smith, Lisa (ed.), *Fashion Images de Mode*, vol. II, Steidl, Göttingen, 1997.

—, *Fashion Images de Mode*, vol. III, Steidl, Göttingen, 1998.

—, *Fashion Images de Mode*, vol. IV, intro. by Marion de Beaupré, Steidl, Göttingen, 1999.

—, *Fashion Images de Mode*, vol. V, intro. by Val Williams, Steidl, Göttingen, 2000.

—, *Fashion Images de Mode*, vol. VI, intro. by Rankin, Vision On, London, 2001.

Lukács, Georgy, *History and Class Consciousness: Studies in Marxist Dialectics*, trans. Rodney Livingstone, Merlin Press, London, 1977 [1923].

Lurie, Celia, *Prosthetic Culture: Photography, Memory and Identity*, Routledge, London and New York, 1998.

Lyotard, Jean-François, *The Postmodern Condition: A Report on Knowledge*, trans. Geoffrey Bennington and Brian Massumi, University of Minnesota Press, Minneapolis, 1984 [1979].

Mack, Michael, *Surface: Contemporary Photographic Practice*, Booth Clibborn, London, 1996.

Maffesoli, Michel, *The Time of the Tribes: The Decline of Individualism in Mass Society*, trans. Mark Ritter, Sage, London, Thousand Oaks and New Delhi, 1996.

Maison Martin Margiela, *Street*, Special Edition, vols I and II, Tokyo, 1999.

Malossi, Gianni (ed.), *The Style Engine. Spectacle, Identity, Design and Business: How the Fashion Industry Uses Style to Create Wealth*, Monacelli Press, New York, 1998.

Maravall, José Antonio, *Culture of the Baroque: Analysis of a Historical Structure*, trans. Terry Cochran, University of Minnesota Press and Manchester University Press, Minneapolis and Manchester, 1986.

Maré, Eric de and Gustave Doré, *The London Doré Saw* [1870], Allen Lane, London, 1973.

Martin, Richard, and Harold Koda, *Infra-Apparel*, Metropolitan Museum of Art, New York, 1993.

Marx, Karl, *The Eighteenth Brumaire of Louis Bonaparte* [1852], trans. from the German, Progress Publishers, Moscow, 3rd rev. ed. 1954 [2nd rev. ed. 1869].

—, *Surveys from Exile: Political Writings, Vol. 2*, ed. and intro. by David Fernbach, Penguin in association with New Left Review, Harmondsworth, 1973: 299–300.

—, *Early Writings*, trans. Rodney Livingstone and Gregor Benton, Penguin, Harmondsworth, 1975.

—, *Capital*, vol. I, trans. Ben Fowkes, Penguin, Harmondsworth, 1976.

—and Frederick Engels, *The Manifesto of the Communist Party*, trans. Samuel Moore, Progress Publishers, Moscow, 1966 [1848].

—, *Collected Works*, vol. X, Lawrence & Wishart, London, 1978.

McCracken, Grant, *Culture and Consumption: New Approaches to the Symbolic Character of Consumer Goods and Activities*, Indiana University Press, Bloomington and Indianapolis, 1990.

McDowell, Colin, *Galliano*, Weidenfeld & Nicolson, London, 1997.

McQuire, Scott, *Visions of Modernity: Representation, Memory, Time and Space in the Age of the Camera*, Sage, London, Thousand Oaks and New Delhi, 1998.

Miller, Daniel, *Shopping, Place and Identity*, Routledge, London, 1998.

Mitchelson, Annette (ed.), *Andy Warhol*, October Files 2, MIT Press, Cambridge, Mass., and London, 2001.

Mode et Art 1960–1990, Palais des Beaux-Arts, Brussels, 1995.

Monde selon ses créateurs, le: Gaultier, Gigli, Westwood, Sybilla, Margiela, Musée de la Mode, Paris, 1991.

Morgan, Stuart (ed.), *Rites of Passage: Art at the End of the Century*, Tate Gallery Publications, London, 1995.

Nead, Lynda, *Victorian Babylon: People, Streets and Images in Nineteenth-Century London*, Yale University Press, New Haven and London, 2000.

Nesbitt, Molly, *Atget's Seven Albums*, Yale University Press, New Haven and London, 1992.

Nickerson, Camilla, and Neville Wakefield, *Fashion: Photography of the Nineties*, Scalo, Zurich, Berlin and New York, 2nd ed. 1998 [1st ed. 1996].

Nietzsche, Friedrich, *A Nietzsche Reader*, selected, trans. and with an intro. by R. J. Hollindale, Penguin, Harmondsworth, 1997.

Nochlin, Linda, *The Body in Pieces: The Fragment as a Metaphor of Modernity*, Thames & Hudson, London, 1994.

Now: A New Generation of Fashion Photographers, Färgfabriken, Stockholm, 1999.

Orta, Lucy, *Refuge Wear*, Jean-Michel Place, Paris, 1996.

—, *Process of Transformation*, Jean-Michel Place, Paris, 1998.

Owens, Craig, *Recognition: Representation, Power and Culture*, ed. Scott Bryson *et al*, University of California Press, Berkeley and Los Angeles, 1992.

Pampilion: An Exhibition of the Work of Dai Rees, photographs by Matt Collishaw, catalogue essay by Jennifer Higgie, Judith Clark Costume, London, 1998.

Perrot, Philippe, *Fashioning the Bourgeoisie: A History of Clothing in the Nineteenth Century*, trans. Richard Bienvenu, Princeton University Press, 1994.

Phelan, Peggy, *Mourning Sex: Performing Public Memories*, Routledge, London and New York, 1997.

Philip-Lorca diCorcia, essay by Peter Galassi, Museum of Modern Art, New York, 1995.

Plant, Sadie, *Zeros and Ones: Digital Women and the New Technoculture*, Fourth Estate, London, 1997.

Poschardt, Ulf, *DJ Culture*, trans. Shaun Whiteside, Quartet, London, 1998.

—(ed.), *Archaeology of Elegance 1980–2000: 20 Years of Fashion Photography*, Thames & Hudson, London, 2002.

Quennell, Peter (ed.), *Mayhew's London: Being Selections from 'London Labour and the London Poor'* [1851], Spring Books, London, 1964.

Quinn, Bradley, *Techno Fashion*, Berg, Oxford and New York, 2002.

Rabaté, Jean-Michel, *Joyce upon the Void: The Genesis of Doubt*, Macmillan, London, 1991.

—, *The Ghosts of Modernity*, University Press of Florida, Gainsville, 1996.

Rabinow, Paul (ed.), *The Foucault Reader*, Penguin, Harmondsworth, 1984.

Rappaport, Erica, *Shopping for Pleasure: Women in the Making of London's West End*, Princeton University Press, 2000.

Ribeiro, Aileen, *Fashion in the French Revolution*, Batsford, London, 1988.

Richards, Thomas, *The Commodity Culture of Victorian England: Advertising and Spectacle 1851–1914*, Verso, London and New York, 1991.

Robins, Kevin, *Into the Image: Culture and Politics in the Field of Vision*, Routledge, London and New York, 1996.

Roche, Daniele, *The Culture of Clothing: Dress and Fashion in the Ancien Régime*, trans. Jean Birrell, Cambridge University Press, 1994.

Rose, Cynthia, *Trade Secrets: Young British Talents Talk Business*, Thames & Hudson, London, 1999.

Ross, Andrew (ed.), *No Sweat: Fashion, Free Trade and the Rights of Garment Workers*, Verso, New York and London, 1997.

Rossi, Aldo, *The Architecture of the City*, MIT Press, Cambridge, Mass., and London, 1982.

Rowell, Margit, *Objects of Desire: The Modern Still Life*, Museum of Modern Art, New York, and Hayward Gallery, London, 1997.

Samuel, Raphael, *Theatres of Memory: Past and Present in Contemporary Culture*, Verso, London, 1994.

Sanders, Mark, Phil Poynter, and Robin Derrick (eds), *The Impossible Image: Fashion Photography in the Digital Age*, Phaidon, London, 2000.

Sawday, Jonathan, *The Body Emblazoned: Dissection and the Human Body in Renaissance Culture*, Routledge, London and New York, 1995.

Schama, Simon, *Citizens: A Chronicle of the French Revolution*, Viking, London and New York, 1989.

Schwartz, Hillel, *The Culture of the Copy*, Zone Books, New York, 1996.

Scott, Alan, *The Limits of Globalization*, Routledge, London and New York, 1997.

Seltzer, Mark, *Serial Killers: Death and Life in America's Wound Culture*, Routledge, New York and London, 1998.

Selzer, Richard, *Mortal Lessons*, Touchstone, New York, 1987.

Sennett, Richard, *The Fall of Public Man*, W. W. Norton, New York and London, 1992.

Shields, Rob (ed.), *Lifestyle Shopping: The Subject of Consumption*, Routledge, London, 1992.

Showalter, Elaine, *The Female Malady: Women, Madness and English Culture 1830–1980*, Virago, London, 1985.

—, *Sexual Anarchy: Gender and Culture at the Fin de Siècle*, Bloomsbury, London, 1991.

Simpson, Mark, *Male Impersonators: Performing Masculinity*, Cassell, London, 1994.

Sinclair, Iain, *Lights Out for the Territory: Nine Excursions into the Secret History of London*, Granta, London, 1997.

Sontag, Susan, *On Photography*, Penguin, Harmondsworth, 1979.

Sparke, Penny, *As Long As It's Pink: The Sexual Politics of Taste*, Pandora, London, 1995.

Springer, C., *Electronic Eros: Bodies and Desire in the Post Industrial Age*, Athlone Press, London, 1996.

Stallybrass, Peter, and Allon White, *The Politics and Poetics of Transgression*, Methuen, London, 1986.

Steele, Valerie, *The Corset: A Cultural History*, Yale University Press, New Haven and London, 2001.

Stewart, Susan, *On Longing: Narratives of the Miniature, the Gigantic, the Souvenir, the Collection*, Duke University Press, Durham, N.C., and London, 1993.

Stone, Alluquère Rosanne, *The War of Desire and Technology at the Close of the Mechanical Age*, MIT Press, Cambridge, Mass., and London, 1995.

Thakara, John (ed.), *Design after Modernism: Beyond the Object*, Thames & Hudson, London, 1988.

Tickner, Lisa, *The Spectacle of Women: Imagery of the Suffragette Campaign*, Chatto & Windus, London, 1987.

—, *Modern Lives and Modern Subjects*, Yale University Press, New Haven and London, 2000.

Wolfgang Tillmans, Taschen, Cologne and London, 1995.

Tisdall, Caroline, *Joseph Beuys*, Soloman R. Guggenheim Foundation, New York, 1979.

Tomlinson, Alan (ed.), *Consumption, Identity and Style*, Comedia, London, 1990.

Tosh, John, *The Pursuit of History: Aims, Methods and New Directions in the Study of Modern History*, Pearson, London, 3rd ed. 2000.

Trauma, Hayward Gallery Publishing, London, 2001.

Trotter, David, *Paranoid Modernism*, Oxford University Press, 2001.

Troy, Nancy J., *Couture Culture: A Study in Modern Art and Fashion*, MIT Press, Cambridge, Mass., and London, 2003.

Tseëlon, Efrat, *The Masque of Femininity: The Presentation of Woman in Everyday Life*, Sage, London, Thousand Oaks and New Delhi, 1995.

Tucker, Andrew, *The London Fashion Book*, Thames & Hudson, London, 1998.

Turner, Bryan S. (ed), *Theories of Modernity and Postmodernity*, Sage, London, Newbury Park and New Delhi, 1990.

Veblen, Thorstein, *The Theory of the Leisure Classes*, Mentor, New York, 1953 [1899].

Viktor & Rolf 1993–99, Artino Foundation, Breda, 1999.

Viktor & Rolf Haute Couture Book, texts by Amy Spindler and Didier Grumbach, Groninger Museum, Gröningen, 2000.

Virilio, Paul, *Open Sky*, trans. Julie Rose, Verso, London and New York, 1997.

Vries, Leonard de, *Victorian Inventions*, John Murray, London, 1971.

Webb, Peter, *Hans Bellmer*, Quartet, London, 1985.

Weeks, Jeffrey, *Inventing Moralities: Sexual Values in an Age of Uncertainty*, Columbia University Press, New York, 1995.

White, Nicola, and Ian Griffiths (eds), *The Fashion Business: Theory, Practice, Image*, Berg, Oxford and New York, 2000.

Wigley, Mark, *White Walls, Designer Dresses: The Fashioning of Modern Architecture*, MIT Press, Cambridge, Mass., and London, 1995.

Wilcox, Claire (ed.), *Radical Fashion*, Victoria & Albert Publications, London, 2001.

Williams, Rosalind H., *Dream Worlds: Mass Consumption in Late Nineteenth-Century France*, University of California Press, Berkeley, and Los Angeles, 1982.

Williams, Val (ed.), *Look at Me: Fashion Photography in Britain 1960 to the Present*, British Council, London, 1998.

Williamson, Judith, *Consuming Passions: The Dynamics of Popular Culture*, Marion Boyars, London and New York, 1986.

Wilson, Elizabeth, *The Sphinx in the City: Urban Life, the Control of Disorder, and Women*, Virago, London, 1991.

—, *Bohemians: The Glamorous Outcasts*, I. B. Tauris, London, 2000.

—, *Adorned in Dreams: Fashion and Modernity*, Virago, London, 1985; 2nd ed. I. B. Tauris, 2003.

Windels, Veerle, *Young Fashion Belgian Design*, Ludion, Ghent and Amsterdam, 2001.

Windlin, Cornel (ed.), *Juergen Teller*, Taschen, Cologne and London, 1996.

Wittgenstein, Ludwig, *Tractatus logico-philosophicus*, trans. P. David, Routledge, London, 1991 [1921].

Wolf, Naomi, *The Beauty Myth*, Vintage, New York, 1991.

Wolff, Janet, *Feminine Sentences: Essays on Women and Culture*, Polity Press, Cambridge, 1990.

Wollen, Peter, *Raiding the Ice Box: Reflections on Twentieth Century Culture*, Verso, London and New York, 1993.

Wood, Nancy, *Vectors of Memory*, Berg, Oxford and New York, 1999.

Wosk, Julie, *Breaking Frame: Technology and the Visual Arts in the Nineteenth Century*, Rutgers University Press, New Brunswick, N.J. 1992.

Wyschogrod, Edith, *Spirit in Ashes: Hegel, Heidegger and Man-Made Death*, Yale University Press, New Haven and London, 1985.

—, *An Ethics of Remembering*. Chicago University Press, 1998.

Zenderland, Leila (ed.) *Recycling the Past: Popular Uses of American History*, University of Pennsylvania Press, Philadelphia, 1978.

Zizek, Slavoj, *The Plague of Fantasies*, Verso, London, 1997.

Zola, Emile, *The Ladies' Paradise*, trans. with an intro. by Brian Nelson, Oxford University Press, Oxford and New York, 1995.

Journal and Book Articles

Anderson, Fiona, 'Exhibition Review: Hussein Chalayan', *Fashion Theory*, vol. 4, issue 2, June 2000: 229–33.

Apter, Emily, 'Masquerade', in Elizabeth Wright, *Feminism and Psychoanalysis: A Critical Dictionary*, Basil Blackwell, Oxford and Cambridge, Mass., 1992: 242–4.

Arnold, Rebecca, 'Heroin Chic', *Fashion Theory*, vol. 3 issue 3, September 1999: 279–95.

—, 'The Brutalized Body, *Fashion Theory*, vol. 3 issue 4, December 1999: 487–501.

—, 'Luxury and Restraint: Minimalism in 1990s Fashion', in Nicola White and Ian Griffiths, *The Fashion Business: Theory, Practice, Image*, Berg, Oxford and New York, 2000: 167–81.

—, 'Vivienne Westwood's Anglomania', in Christopher Breward, Becky Conekin and Caroline Cox (eds), *The Englishness of English Dress*, Berg, Oxford and New York, 2012: 161–72.

—, 'Looking American: Louise Dahl-Wolfe's Fashion Photographs of the 1930s and 1940s', *Fashion Theory*, vol. 6, issue 1, March 2002: 45–60.

Azzellini, Dario, 'Tute Bianche', *032c*, 3rd issue, 'What's Next?' (Berlin), Winter 2001/02: 20–1.

Bailey, Peter, 'Parasexuality and Glamour: The Victorian Barmaid as Cultural Prototype', *Gender and History*, vol. 2, no. 2, 1990: 148–72.

Ballard, J. G., 'Project for a Glossary of the Twentieth Century', in Jonathan Crary and Sanford Kwinter (eds), *Incorporations, Zone 6*, Zone Books, New York, 1992: 268–79.

Bartlett, Djurdja, 'Issey Miyake: Making Things', *Fashion Theory*, vol. 4, issue 4, June 2000: 223–7.

Battersby, Christine, 'Her Body/Her Boundaries: Gender and the Metaphysics of Containment', in Andrew Benjamin (ed.), *The Body: Journal of Philosophy and the Visual Arts*, Academy Editions, London, 1993: 36–8.

Benjamin, Walter, 'Central Park', *New German Critique*, 34, winter 1985 [1972]: 32–58.

Boodroo, Michael, 'Art and Fashion', *Artnews*, September 1990: 120–7.

Bryson, Norman, 'Too Near, Too Far', *Parkett*, 49, 1997: 85–89.

Buckley, Réka C. V., and Stephen Gundle, 'Fashion and Glamour', in Nicola White and Ian Griffiths (eds), *The Fashion Business: Theory, Practice, Image*, Berg, Oxford and New York, 2000: 37–54.

—, 'Flash Trash: Gianni Versace and the Theory and Practice of Glamour', in Stella Bruzzi and Pamela Church Gibson (eds), *Fashion Cultures: Theories, Explanations and Analysis*, Routledge, London and New York, 2000: 331–48.

Buck-Morss, Susan, 'The Flaneur, the Sandwichman and the Whore: The Politics of Loitering', *New German Critique*, 39, fall 1986: 99–140.

Castle, Terry, 'Phantasmagoria', *Critical Enquiry*, vol. 15, no. 1, 1988: 26–61.

Chambers, Iain, 'Maps for the Metropolis: A Possible Guide to the Present', *Cultural Studies*, vol. 1, no. 1, January 1987: 1–22.

Clark, Judith, 'A Note: Getting the Invitation', *Fashion Theory*, vol. 5, issue 3, September 2001: 343–53.

Duggan, Ginger Gregg (ed.), 'Fashion and Performance', special ed., *Fashion Theory*, vol. 5, issue 3, September 2001: 243–70.

Evans, Caroline, 'Martin Margiela: The Golden Dustman', *Fashion Theory*, vol. 2, issue 1, March 1998: 73–94.

—, 'Masks, Mirrors and Mannequins: Elsa Schiaparelli and the Decentered Subject', *Fashion Theory*, vol. 3, issue 1, March 1999: 3–31.

—, 'Living Dolls: Mannequins, Models and Modernity', in Julian Stair (ed.), *The Body Politic*, Crafts Council, London, 2000: 103–16.

—, 'Yesterday's Emblems and Tomorrow's Commodities: The Return of the Repressed in Fashion Imagery Today', in Stella Bruzzi and Pamela

Church Gibson (eds), *Fashion Cultures: Theories, Explorations and Analysis*, Routlege, London and New York, 2000: 93–113.

—, 'Galliano: Spectacle and Modernity', in Nicola White and Ian Griffiths (eds), *The Fashion Business: Theory, Practice, Image*, Berg, Oxford and New York, 2001: 143–66.

—, '"Dress Becomes Body Becomes Dress": Are you an object or a subject? Comme des Garcons and self-fashioning', *032c*, 4th issue, 'Instability', Berlin, October 2002: 82–7.

Foster, Hal, 'The Art of Fetishism', *The Princeton Architectural Journal*, vol. 4, 'Fetish', 1992: 6–19.

—, 'Prosthetic Gods', *Modernism/Modernity*, vol. 4, no. 2, April 1997: 5–38.

—, 'Trauma Studies and the Interdisciplinary: An Interview', in Alex Coles and Alexia Defert (eds), *The Anxiety of Interdisciplinarity*, BACKless Books and Black Dog, London, 1998: 155–68.

Fouser, R., 'Mariko Mori: Avatar of a Feminine God', *Art Text*, nos 60–2, 1998: 36.

Friedman, Jonathan, 'Narcissism, Roots and Postmodernity: The Constitution of Selfhood in the Global Crisis', in Scott Lash and Jonathan Friedman (eds), *Modernity and Identity*, Basil Blackwell, Oxford, 1992: 331–6.

Gill, Alison, 'Deconstruction Fashion: The Making of Unfinished, Decomposing and Re-assembled Clothes', *Fashion Theory*, vol. 2, issue 1, March 1998: 25–49.

Ginsburg, Carlo, 'Morelli, Freud and Sherlock Holmes: Clues and Scientific Method', *History Workshop Journal*, vol. 9, spring 1980: 5–36.

Ginsburg, Madeleine, 'Rags to Riches: The Second-Hand Clothes Trade 1700–1978', *Costume: Journal of the Costume Society of Great Britain*, 14, 1980: 121–35.

Hershberg, Sorrel, and Gareth Williams, 'Friendly Membranes and Multi-Taskers: The Body and Contemporary Furniture', in Julian Stair (ed.), *The Body Politic*, Crafts Council, London, 2000: 58–70.

Internationale Situationiste, no. 1, June 1958, n.p.

Jameson, Fredric, 'Postmodernism, or the Cultural Logic of Late Capitalism', *New Left Review*, vol. 146, 1984: 53–93.

Jobling, Paul, 'Alex Eats: A Case Study in Abjection and Identity in Contemporary Fashion Photography', *Fashion Theory*, vol. 2, issue 3, September 1998: 209–24.

—, 'On the Turn: Millennial Bodies and the Meaning of Time in Andrea Giacobbe's Fashion Photography', *Fashion Theory*, vol. 6, issue 1, March 2002: 3–24.

Kim, Sung Bok, 'Is Fashion Art?', *Fashion Theory*, vol. 2, issue 1, March 1998: 51–71.

Koda, Harold, 'Rei Kawakubo and the Aesthetic of Poverty', *Costume: Journal of the Costume Society of America*, no. 11, 1985: 5–10.

Lehmann, Ulrich, '*Tigersprung*: Fashioning History', *Fashion Theory*, vol. 3, issue 3, September 1999: 297–322.

Leslie, Esther, 'Souvenirs and Forgetting: Walter Benjamin's Memory-work', in Marius Kwint Christopher Breward, and Jeremy Aynsley, J., (eds) *Material Memories: Design and Evocation*, Berg, Oxford and New York, 1999: 107–22.

Loschek, Ingrid, 'The Deconstructionists', in Gerda Buxbaum (ed.), *Icons of Fashion: The Twentieth Century*, Prestel, Munich, London and New York, 1999: 146–7.

Lyotard, Jean-François, 'Defining the Postmodern', in *ICA Documents 4*: 'Postmodernism', ICA, London, 1986: 6–7.

Martin, Richard, 'Destitution and Deconstruction: The Riches of Poverty in the Fashion of the 1990s', *Textile & Text*, 15, no. 2, 1992: 3–8.

—, 'Yeohlee: Energetics: Clothes and Enclosures', *Fashion Theory*, vol. 2, issue 3, September 1998: 287–93.

—, 'A Note: Art & Fashion, Viktor & Rolf', *Fashion Theory*, vol. 3, issue 1, March 1999: 109–20.

McLeod, Mary, 'Undressing Architecture: Fashion, Gender and Modernity', in Deborah Fausch *et al* (eds), *Architecture: In Fashion*, Princeton Architectural Press, 1994: 35–123.

McPhearson, Heather, 'Sarah Bernhardt: Portrait of the Actress as Spectacle', *Nineteenth-Century Contexts: An Interdisciplinary Journal*, special issue 'Sexing French Art', vol. 20, no. 4, 1999: 409–54.

Montague, Ken, 'The Aesthetics of Hygiene: Aesthetic Dress, Modernity and the Body as Sign', *Journal of Design History*, vol. 7, no. 2, 1994: 91–112.

Nava, Mica, 'Modernity's Disavowal: Women, the City and the Department Store', in Pasi Falk and Colin Campbell (eds), *The Shopping Experience*, Sage, London, Thousand Oaks and New Delhi, 1997: 56–91.

O'Neill, Alistair, 'Imagining Fashion: Helmut Lang and Maison Martin Margiela', in Claire Wilcox (ed.), *Radical Fashion*, Victoria & Albert Museum, London, 2001: 38–45.

Osborne, Peter, 'Modernity is a Qualitative, Not a Chronological Category' *New Left Review*, 92, 1992: 65–84.

Owens, Craig, 'The Allegorical Impulse: Towards a Theory of Postmodernism', in Scott Bryson *et al* (eds), *Beyond Recognition: Representation, Power and Culture*, University of California Press, Berkeley, Los Angeles and Oxford, 1992: 52–69.

Poster, Mark, 'Postmodern Virtualities', in Mike Featherstone and Roger Burrows (eds), *Cyberspace/Cyberbodies/Cyberpunk: Cultures of Technological Embodiment*, Sage, London, Thousand Oaks and New Delhi, 1995: 79–95.

Radford, Robert, 'Dangerous Liaisons: Art, Fashion and Individualism', *Fashion Theory*, vol. 2, issue 2, June 1998: 151–63.

Rajchman, John, 'Lacan and the Ethics of Modernity', *Representations*, 15, summer 1986:, 42–56.

Rivière, Joan, 'Womanliness as a Masquerade' [1929], repr. in V. Burgin, J. Donald and C. Kaplan (eds), *Formations of Fantasy*, Routledge, London, 1986: 35–44.

Seltzer, Mark, 'Wound Culture: Trauma in the Pathological Public Sphere', *October*, 80, spring 1997: 3–26.

Shottenkirk, Dena, 'Fashion Fictions: Absence and the Fast Heartbeat', *ZG*, 'Breakdown Issue', 9, 1983: n.p.

Simmel, Georg, 'Fashion' [1904], and 'The Metropolis and Mental Life' [1903], in *On Individuality and Social Forms*, ed. and with an intro. by

Donald N. Levine, University of Chicago Press, 1971: 294–323 and 324–339.

Smedley, Elliott, 'Escaping to Reality: Fashion Photography in the 1990s', in Stella Bruzzi and Pamela Church Gibson (eds), *Fashion Cultures: Theories, Explorations and Analyses*, Routledge, London and New York, 2000: 143–56.

Sobchak, V., 'Postfuturism', in G. Kirkup *et al* (eds), *The Gendered Cyborg: A Reader*, Routledge in association with the Open University, London, 2000: 136–47.

Solomon-Godeau, Abigail, 'The Other Side of Venus: The Visual Economy of Feminine Display', in Victoria de Grazia and Ellen Furlough (eds), *The Sex of Things: Gender and Consumption in Historical Perspective*, University of California Press, Berkeley, Los Angeles and London, 1996: 113–50.

Stallybrass, Peter, 'Marx's Coat', in Patricia Spyer (ed.), *Border Fetishisms: Material Objects in Unstable Spaces*, Routledge, New York, 1998: 183–207.

Terranova, Tiziana, 'Posthuman Unbounded: Artificial Evolution and High-tech Subcultures', in George Robertson *et al* (eds), *Future Natural: Nature, Science, Culture*, Routledge, London and New York, 1996: 165–80.

Townsend, Chris, 'Dead for Having Been Seen', *Izima Kaoru*, fa projects, London, 2002, n.p.

Valverde, Mariana, 'The Love of Finery: Fashion and the Fallen Woman in Nineteenth-Century Social Discourse', *Victorian Studies*, vol. 32, no. 2, winter 1989: 169–88.

Vinken, Barbara, 'Eternity: A Frill on the Dress', *Fashion Theory*, vol. 1, issue 1, March 1997: 59–67.

Wallerstein, Katherine, 'Thinness and Other Refusals in Contemporary Fashion Advertisements', *Fashion Theory*, vol. 2 issue 2, June 1998: 129–50.

Wark, McKenzie, 'Fashioning the Future: Fashion, Clothing and the Manufacture of Post-Fordist Culture', *Cultural Studies*, vol. 5, no. 1, 1991: 61–76.

Wilson, Elizabeth, 'The Invisible Flâneur', *New Left Review*, 191, 1992: 90–110.

—, 'The Rhetoric of Urban Space', *New Left Review*, 209, 1995: 146–60.

Wohlfarth, Irving, 'Et cetera? The Historian as Chiffonnier', *New German Critique*, no. 39, fall 1986: 142–68.

Zahm, Olivier, 'Before and After Fashion: A Project by Martin Margiela', *Artforum*, March 1995: 74–77.

Zukin, Sharon, 'The Postmodern Debate over Urban Form', *Theory, Culture and Society*, vol. 5, nos 2–3, June 1988: 431–46.

Press

Alexander, Hilary, *The Daily Telegraph*, 19 September 2000.

Als, Hilton, 'Gear: Postcard from London', *The New Yorker*, 17 March 1997: 90–5.

Armstrong, Lisa, 'Versace Seizes her Moment', *The Times*, 26 February 2000.

—, 'Frock'n'roll Hall of Fame', *The Times*, 24 July 2000.

Ashworth, Jon, interview with Hussein Chalayan, *The Times*, London, 2 March 1996.

Ballard, J. G., 'Diary', *New Statesman*, 20 December 1999–3 January 2000: 9.

Beard, Steve, 'With Serious Intent', *i-D*, no. 185, April 1999: 141.

Billingham, Richard, 'Untititled I, II and III', *Independent Fashion Magazine*, spring 1998: 10–14.

Blanchard, Tamsin, 'Haute New Things', *The Independent Magazine*, 1 August 1998: 20–2.

—, 'Mind Over Material', *The Observer Magazine*, 24 September 2000: 38–43.

Brown, Heath, 'Donatella's Dynasty', *The Times Magazine*, 15 July 2000: 61–7.

Davis, Louise, 'Frock Tactics', *The Observer Magazine*, 18 February 2001: 36–9.

Dazed & Confused, Alexander McQueen guest editor issue, 'Fashion Able?', no. 46, September 1998: 'ACCESS-ABLE', 68–83.

Flett, Katherine, 'Altered Images', *The Observer Magazine*, 28 May 2000: 20.

Frankel, Susannah, 'Galliano Steams Ahead with Any Old Irony', *The Guardian*, 21 July 1998.

—, 'Galliano', *The Independent Magazine*, 20 February 1999: 12.

—, 'We want to be', *The Independent Magazine*, 8 May 1999: 30.

—, 'Art and Commerce', *The Independent on Sunday*, review section, 10 March 2002: 28–32.

Heath, Ashley, 'Bad Boys Inc', *The Face*, vol. 2. no. 79, April 1995: 102.

Hoare, Sarajane, 'God Save McQueen', *Harpers Bazaar* (USA), June 1996: 30 and 148.

Hume, Marion, 'McQueen's Theatre of Cruelty', *The Independent*, 21 October 1993.

—, 'Scissorhands', *Harpers & Queen*, August 1996: 82.

Lorna V., 'All Hail McQueen', *Time Out*, 24 September–1 October 1997: 26.

Marcus, Tony, 'I am the Resurrection', *i-D*, no. 179, September 1998: 148.

Menkes, Suzy, 'The Macabre and the Poetic', *The International Herald Tribune*, 5 March 1996.

Mower, Sarah, 'Politics of Vanity', *The Fashion*, no. 2, Spring–Summer 2001: 162.

Muir, Robin, 'What Katie Did', *Independent Magazine*, 22 February 1997: 14.

Murphy, Dominic, 'Would You Wear a Coat that Talks Back?' *The Guardian*, Weekend, 21 October 2000: 34.

Picardie, Ruth, 'Clothes by Design, Scars by Accident', *The Independent*, tabloid, 2 May 1997: 8.

Raymond, Martin, 'Clothes with Meaning', *Blueprint*, no. 154, October 1998: 28.

Rickey, Melanie, 'England's Glory', *The Independent*, tabloid, 28 February 1997: 4.

Rumbold, Judy, 'Alexander the Great', *Vogue* (UK), July 1996, catwalk report supplement.

Saner, Emine, 'Designed in London: The £1 m Dress', *The Sunday Times*, 24 September 2000.

Scruby, Jennifer, 'The Eccentric Englishman', *Elle American*, July 1996: 151–4.

Spindler, Amy, 'Critic's Notebook: Tracing the Look of Alienation', *The New York Times*, 24 March 1998.

Starker, Melissa, 'Chalayan UNDRESSED', Columbus Alive, 25 April 2002.

Stungo, Naomi, 'Boudicca', *Blueprint*, no. 154, October 1998: 34–5.

Todd, Stephen, 'The Importance of Being English', *Blueprint*, no. 137, March 1997: 42.

de Villiers, Jonathan, 'Never Mind the Bollocks', *Blueprint*, no. 154, October 1998: 28.

Winwood, Lou, interview with Robert Cary-Williams, *Sleazenation*, vol. 2, issue 11, December 1998: 22.

—, 'It's Snowtime!', *The Guardian*, 3 March 1999.

Women's Wear Daily, 14 March 1995.

—, 16 October 1997.

—, 6 March 2000.

Wood, Gaby, 'Dolly Mixture', *The Observer Magazine*, 27 February 2000: 36–41.

Index